SELLING &
SALES MANAGEMENT

Pearson
Education

We work with leading authors to develop the
strongest educational materials in business and
marketing, bringing cutting-edge thinking and
best learning practice to a global market.

Under a range of well-known imprints, including
Financial Times Prentice Hall, we craft high quality
print and electronic publications which help
readers to understand and apply their content,
whether studying or at work.

To find out more about the complete range of our
publishing please visit us on the World Wide Web at:
www.pearsoneduc.com

SELLING &
SALES MANAGEMENT

Fifth Edition

David Jobber
BA(Econ), MSc, PhD
Professor of Marketing,
University of Bradford Management Centre

Geoff Lancaster
MSc, DMS, FCIM, FLCC, MIMgt, MCIPS
Professor of Marketing,
Macquarie University, Sydney,
University of North London
and Chairman, Durham Associates Ltd

FINANCIAL TIMES
Prentice Hall

An imprint of Pearson Education
Harlow, England · London · New York · Reading, Massachusetts · San Fransisco · Toronto · Don Mills, Ontario · Sydney
Tokyo · Singapore · Hong Kong · Seoul · Taipei · Cape Town · Madrid · Mexico City · Amsterdam · Munich · Paris · Milan

Pearson Education Limited
Edinburgh Gate
Harlow
Essex CM20 2JE
England

and Associated Companies throughout the world

Visit us on the World Wide Web at:
http://www.pearsoneduc.com

First published by Macdonald & Evans Ltd in 1985 under
the title of *Sales Technique and Management*
Second edition published by Pitman Publishing in 1990
Fifth edition 2000

ISBN 0 273 64210 3

British Library Cataloguing-in-Publication Data
A catalogue record for this book is available from the British Library.

Library of Congress Cataloging-in-Publication-Data
A catalog record for this book is available from the Library of Congress

10 9 8 7 6 5 4 3 2
04 03 02 01 00

Typeset by 37.
Printed and bound in Great Britain by T. J. International, Padstow, Cornwall, UK.

CONTENTS

Part Four SALES MANAGEMENT

LIST OF ILLUSTRATIONS

LIST OF TABLES

FOREWORD

The selling and sales management function has not received the attention it deserves from British universities. One reason for this is the paucity of suitable textbooks for undergraduate and postgraduate teaching. This book blends applied theory with the down-to-earth realities of the selling function, and provides a comprehensive coverage of the topic in a readable way. I believe this textbook will find favour among academics and should also stimulate a more in-depth treatment of the subject on marketing and business studies courses.

At the end of each chapter the authors provide mini-case studies and practical exercises to aid tutors in designing tutorial and seminar material, and students in exploring their understanding of the material to be found in the chapters. Typical examination questions are also included to supplement the case studies.

The practitioner, likewise, cannot fail to learn something from this book. The practicalities and problems of selling and sales management are explored in detail, and methods which have proved successful in the real world are explained lucidly.

Both Geoff Lancaster and David Jobber are experienced teachers of sales and marketing, and it is this training which has enabled them to produce an outstanding book.

PROFESSOR PETER DOYLE
University of Warwick

Note: An instructor's manual, including a CD-Rom containing PowerPoint overhead transparencies of selected figures in this book, is available free of charge to lecturers adopting this book.

PREFACE

The text covers what must still be the most important element of the marketing mix for most students and practitioners. With a move away from the selling function towards more esoteric areas of marketing over the past few years, this vital aspect of marketing has been somewhat neglected. However, in the end it has to be face-to-face contact that eventually wins the order, and this text therefore explains and documents the selling and sales management process from both the theoretical and practical viewpoints.

More precisely, the text is split into five logical parts: Sales Perspective, Sales Technique, Sales Environment, Sales Management and Sales Control. Sales Perspective examines selling in its historical role and then views its place within marketing and a marketing organisation. Different types of buyers are also analysed in order to help us achieve an understanding of their thinking and organise our selling effort accordingly. Sales Technique is essentially practical and covers preparation for selling, the personal selling process and sales responsibilities. Sales Environment looks at the institutions through which sales are made; this covers channels, including industrial, commercial and public authority selling followed by selling for resale. International selling is an increasingly important area in view of the ever increasing 'internationalisation' of business and this merits a separate chapter. Sales Management covers recruitment, selection, motivation and training, in addition to how we must organise and compensate salesmen from a managerial standpoint. Finally, Sales Control covers sales budgets and explains how this is the starting point for business planning. Sales forecasting is also covered in this final section, and a guide is given to the techniques of forecasting and why it is strictly a responsibility of sales management and not finance. Each chapter concludes with a mini-case study and practical exercises, together with formal practice questions typical of those the student will encounter in the examination room.

This fifth edition includes a new chapter, 'Direct Marketing and Information Technology Application in Sales'. This reflects the new methods of selling to customers (e.g. direct mail, telemarketing, the Internet) and the impact technology is having on salesforce productivity and modes of doing business. This new edition also contains many new and updated cases to support the effective teaching of selling and sales management. The use of 'Selling and Sales Management in Action' case histories has been expanded to show how principles can be applied in practice. Also a new introduction to the 'Sales Settings' chapter illustrates how environmental and managerial forces are affecting the sales function. Discussion of key (or major) account management has been expanded to include the KAM relational development model and its implications. Finally, this edition continues to place emphasis on international aspects of selling and sales management to reflect the growing importance of international markets to companies.

The text will be invaluable to those students studying for the examinations of the Chartered Institute of Marketing, the Communication, Advertising and Marketing Education Foundation, the London Chamber of Commerce and Industry higher stage selling and sales management subject, marketing specialisms on Higher National Certificate and Diploma in Business Studies, first degrees with a marketing input, and postgraduate courses like the Diploma in Management Studies and Master of Business Administration that have a marketing input. In addition, the text emphasises the practical as well as the theoretical, and it will be of invaluable assistance to salespersons in the field as well as to sales management.

Finally, the authors would like to thank Gordon Lucas for information upon which 'the diversion' and 'winning and losing orders' are based. We should like to make it clear that in all cases in the text the words 'he' and 'she' or 'him' and 'her' are interchangeable and no discrimination is intended. We should also like to thank Belinda Dewsnap, Mike Starkey and Lynn Parkinson for providing excellent material on the applications of information technology in sales.

DJ
GL

Acknowledgements

The publishers wish to thank the following for permission to reproduce copyright material:

Figure 8.1 'Selling process complexity and face-to-face contact dimensions of sales job types' reprinted with permission from the *Journal of Marketing Research*, Vol 23, May 1985, published by the American Marketing Association (Montcrief, 1986).

Figure 8.2 'Growth of the global on-line population', Financial Times Survey 1999, reprinted with permission from the Financial Times.

Part One

SALES PERSPECTIVE

DEVELOPMENT AND ROLE OF SELLING IN MARKETING

OBJECTIVES

After studying this chapter, you should be able to:

1 Understand the implications of production, sales, and marketing orientation.

2 Appreciate why selling generally has a negative image.

3 Know where selling fits into the marketing mix.

4 Identify the responsibilities of sales management.

KEY CONCEPTS

- break-even analysis
- exclusive distribution
- intensive distribution
- market penetration
- market segmentation
- market skimming

- marketing concept
- marketing mix
- product life-cycle
- sales management
- selling
- targeting

1.1 BACKGROUND

Perhaps no other area of business activity gives rise to as much discussion among and between those directly involved and those who are not involved as the activity known as selling. This is not surprising when one considers that so many people derive their livelihood, either directly or indirectly, from selling. Even those who have no direct involvement in selling come into contact with it in their roles as consumers. Perhaps, because of this familiarity, many people have strong, and often misplaced, views about selling and salespeople. Surprisingly, many of these misconceptions are held by people who have spent their working lives in selling; some of this might be due to the well-known saying of 'familiarity breeds contempt'.

It is important to recognise that **selling** and sales management, although closely related, are not the same and we shall start in this chapter by examining the nature and role of selling and sales management in the contemporary organisation and exploring some of the more common myths and misconceptions.

We shall also look at the developing role of selling, because, like other business functions, it is required to adapt and change. Perhaps one of the most important and far reaching of these business changes has been the adoption of the concept and practice of marketing, due to changes in the business environment. Because of the importance of this development to the sales function, we shall examine the place of marketing within the firm and the place of selling within marketing.

The importance of the sales function is now reflected in professional practice as there are now two bodies in the UK that represent the profession – the Institute of Sales and Marketing Management and the Institute of Professional Sales.

1.2　THE NATURE AND ROLE OF SELLING

The simplest way to think of the nature and role of selling (or salesmanship as it is sometimes termed) is that its function is to make a sale. This seemingly obvious statement disguises what is often a very complex process, involving the use of a whole set of principles, techniques and substantial personal skills, and covering a wide range of different types of selling task. Later in the chapter we will establish a more precise meaning for the term selling, but first we will examine the reasons for the intense interest in this area of business activity.

The literature of selling abounds with texts, ranging from the more conceptual approaches to the simplistic 'how it is done' approach. Companies also spend large sums of money training their sales personnel in the art of selling. The reason for all this attention to personal selling is simple: in most companies sales personnel are the single most important link with the customer. The best designed and planned set of marketing efforts may fail because the salesforce is ineffective. This front line role of the salesperson means that for many customers the salesperson *is* the company. Allied with the often substantial costs associated with recruiting, training and maintaining the salesforce, there are powerful reasons for stressing the importance of the selling task and for justifying attempts to improve effectiveness in this area. Part Two of this text is addressed to this important area of sales techniques.

It should be remembered that the term selling encompasses a whole variety of sales situations and activities. For example, there are those sales positions where the sales representative is required primarily to deliver the product to the customer on a regular or periodic basis. The emphasis in this type of sales activity is very different to the sales position where the sales representative is dealing with sales of capital equipment to industrial purchasers. In addition, some sales representatives deal only in export markets whilst others sell direct to the customers in their homes. One of the most striking aspects of the term selling is thus the wide diversity of selling roles.

Irrespective of this diversity of roles, one trend common to all selling tasks is the increasing emphasis on professionalism in selling. This trend, together with its implications for the nature and role of selling, can be best explained if we examine some of the myths and realities which surround the image of selling.

1.3 TYPES OF SELLING

The diverse nature of the buying situation inevitably means that there are many types of selling job: selling varies according to the nature of the selling task. Figure 1.1 shows that there is a fundamental distinction between order-takers, order-creators, and order-getters. Order-takers respond to already committed customers; order-creators do not directly receive orders themselves since they talk to specifiers rather than buyers; whereas order-getters attempt to persuade customers to place an order directly.

There are three types of order-takers: inside order-takers, delivery sales people, and outside order-takers. Order-creators are termed missionary salespeople. Finally, order-getters are either front-line salespeople consisting of new business, organisational or consumer salespeople, or sales support salespeople who can be either technical support salespeople or merchandisers. Both types of order-getters operate in situations where a direct sale can be made. Each type of selling job will now be discussed in more detail.

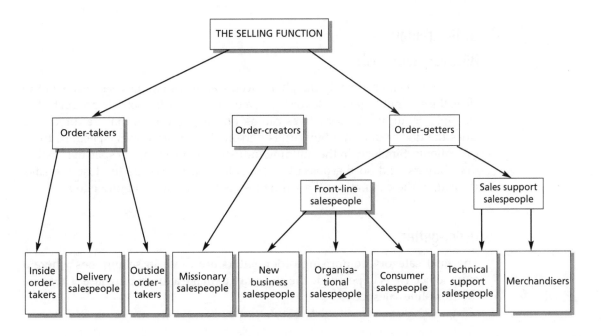

Figure 1.1 Types of selling

Order-takers

Inside order-takers

The typical inside order-taker is the retail sales assistant. The customer has full freedom to choose products without the presence of a salesperson. The sales assistant's task is purely transactional – receiving payment and passing over the goods. Another form of inside order-taker is the telemarketing sales team who support field sales by taking customers' orders over the telephone.

Delivery salespeople

The 'salesperson's' task is primarily concerned with delivering the product. In the UK milk, newspapers and magazines are delivered to the door. There is no attempt to persuade the household to increase the milk order or number of newspapers taken: changes in order-size are customer-driven. Winning and losing orders will be heavily dependent on the reliability of delivery.

Outside order-takers

Unlike inside order-takers, these salespeople visit the customer but their primary function is to respond to customer requests rather than actively seek to persuade. Unlike delivery salespeople, outside order-takers do not deliver. Outside order-takers are a dying breed, being replaced by the more cost-efficient telemarketing teams.

Order-creators

Missionary salespeople

In some industries, notably the pharmaceutical industry, the sales task is not to close the sale but to persuade the 'customer' to specify the seller's products. For example, medical representatives calling on doctors cannot make a direct sale since the doctor does not buy drugs personally but prescribes (specifies) them for patients. Similarly in the building industry, architects act as specifiers rather than buyers, and so the objective of a sales call cannot be to close the sale. Instead, in these situations the selling task is to educate and build goodwill.

Order-getters

The final category comprising order-getters are those in selling jobs where a major objective is to persuade the customer to make a direct purchase. These are the front-line salespeople.

New business salespeople

The selling tasks are to win new business by identifying and selling to prospects (people or organisations who have not previously bought from the salesperson's company).

Organisational salespeople

These salespeople have the job of maintaining close long-term relationships with organisational customers. The selling job may involve team selling where mainstream salespeople are supported by product and financial specialists.

Consumer salespeople

This type of selling task involves selling physical products and services such as double glazing, encyclopaedias, cars, insurance and personal pension plans to individuals.

The second group of order-getters provide sales support to front-line salespeople:

Technical support salespeople

Where a product is highly technical and negotiations are complex, a salesperson may be supported by product and financial specialists who can provide the detailed technical information required by customers. This may be on going as part of a key account team or on a temporary basis with the specialists being called into the selling situation as and when required.

Merchandisers

These provide sales support in retail and wholesale selling situations. Orders may be negotiated nationally at head office, but sales to individual outlets are supported by merchandisers who give advice on display, implement sales promotions, check stock levels, and maintain contact with store managers.

1.4 IMAGE OF SELLING

Ask any group of people not involved in selling what springs to mind on the mention of the word 'selling' and it will prompt a variety of responses. It will evoke a high proportion of negative, even hostile, responses, including 'immoral', 'dishonest', 'unsavoury', 'degrading', 'wasteful', etc. Is such an unfavourable view justified? We suggest not. In fact the underlying attitudes to selling derive from widely held misconceptions about selling, some of which are outlined below.

1 *Selling is not a worthwhile career.* This notion is held by many, the common attitude being that if one has talent then it will be wasted in sales. Unfortunately this attitude is often held by those who are in a position to advise and influence young people in their choice of careers. In some academic circles it is fashionable to denigrate careers in selling, and the consequence is that many of our brighter graduates are not attracted to a career in selling.

2 *Good products will sell themselves and thus the selling process adds unnecessarily to costs.* This view of selling assumes that if you produce a superior product then there will always be buyers. This may be all right if a firm can produce a technologically superior product, but then it is likely that additional costs will accrue in terms of research and development, and there will be continued research and development costs involved in keeping ahead. In addition, as is developed later in the text, the role of selling is not solely to sell; it can be used to feed back information from customers to the firm – particularly product performance information – and this is of direct use to research and development!

3 *There is something immoral about selling, and one should be suspicious about those who earn their living from this activity.* The origins and reasons for this, the most pervasive and damaging of the misconceptions about selling, are unclear, but it perhaps stems from the 'foot in the door' image that has been perpetuated. Such attitudes can make life difficult for the salesperson who has first to overcome the barriers which such mistrust erects in the customer / salesperson relationship.

It has been suggested that some of the more critical responses towards selling derive from a number of misconceptions, but the question still remains as to how and why these misconceptions have arisen and why they still persist. Perhaps, more importantly, those who are concerned to improve the image of selling must be more vociferous, yet objective, in presenting the case for selling. In presenting this case, the first thing to recognise is that misconceptions invariably have some basis of fact. There are always unscrupulous individuals and companies ready to trade on the ignorance and gullibility of the unsuspecting customer. These individuals are not salespeople: at best they are misguided traders and at worst they are crooks. At some times in our lives we inevitably feel that we have purchased something that we did not really want or on terms that we could not really afford, because we were subjected to high-pressure sales techniques.

Selling then is not entirely blameless, but salespeople are becoming more professional in their approach to customers. Some of the worst excesses in selling have been curbed, some legally, but increasingly voluntarily. To overcome some of the misconceptions, selling needs to sell itself, and the following facts about selling should be more universally aired.

1 There is nothing inherently immoral or unscrupulous about selling or about those involved in this activity. Selling provides a mechanism for exchange, and through this process customers' needs and wants are satisfied. Furthermore, most people, at some stage in their lives, are involved in selling – even if it is only selling their skills and personality in an attempt to obtain a job.

2 Selling is now a worthwhile career. Many of those who have spent a lifetime in selling have found it to be a challenging, responsible and rewarding occupation. Inevitably a career in selling means meeting people and working with them, and a selling job often offers substantial discretion in being able to plan one's own work schedule.

3 Good products do not sell themselves. An excellent product may pass unnoticed unless its benefits and features are explained to the customer. What may appear to be a superior product may be totally unsuited to a particular customer. Selling is unique in that it deals with the special needs of each individual customer, and the salesperson, with specialist product knowledge, is in a position to assess these circumstances and advise each customer accordingly.

1.5 THE NATURE AND ROLE OF SALES MANAGEMENT

In the same way that selling has become more professional, so too has the nature and role of **sales management**. The emphasis is now on the word 'management'. Increasingly, those involved in management are being called upon to exercise in a professional way the key duties of all managers, namely, planning, organising and controlling. The emphasis has changed from the idea that to be a good sales manager you had to have the right personality and that the main feature of the job was ensuring that the salesforce were out selling sufficient volume. Although such qualities may be admirable, the duties of the sales manager in the modern company have both broadened and changed in emphasis.

Nowadays the sales manager is expected to play a much more strategic role in the company. The sales manager is required to make a key input into the formulation of company plans, this theme being developed in Chapters 3 and 14. There is thus a need to be familiar with the techniques associated with planning, including sales forecasting and budgeting, and these are dealt with in Chapters 15 and 16. The sales manager also needs to be familiar with the concept of marketing to ensure that sales and marketing activities are integrated – a theme expanded in this chapter. In many companies the emphasis is now less on sales volume and more on profits. The sales manager needs to be able to analyse and direct the activities of the salesforce towards more profitable business. In dealing with a salesforce, the sales manager must be aware of modern developments in human resource management.

Looked at in the manner just outlined, the role of the sales manager may seem to be formidable. He or she must be an accountant, a planner, a personnel manager and a marketer at the same time. However, the prime responsibility is to ensure that the sales function makes the most effective contribution to the achievement of company objectives and goals. In order to fulfil this role, sales managers will undertake the following specific duties and responsibilities:

● The determination of salesforce objectives and goals.
● Stemming from the above, forecasting and budgeting.
● Salesforce organisation, salesforce size, territory design and planning.
● Salesforce selection, recruitment and training.
● Motivating the salesforce.
● Salesforce evaluation and control.

Because these areas encompass the key duties of the sales manager, they are discussed in detail in Parts Four and Five of the text.

Perhaps one of the most significant developments affecting selling and sales management in recent years has been the evolution of the marketing concept. Because of its importance to selling, we will now turn our attention to the nature of this evolution and its effect upon sales activities.

1.6 THE MARKETING CONCEPT

In tracing the development of the **marketing concept** it is customary to chart three successive stages in the evolution of modern business practice:

1 production orientation
2 sales orientation
3 marketing orientation.

Production orientation

This era was characterised by the focus of company efforts on producing a good or service. More specifically, management efforts were devoted to achieving high production efficiency, often through the large-scale production of standardised items. In such a business other functions such as sales, finance and personnel were secondary to the main function of the business, which was to produce. More importantly, the underlying philosophy towards customers was that they would purchase the products, provided that they were available in sufficiently large quantities at a suitably low price.

One of the best known examples of such a philosophy was the Model T factory of Henry Ford. His idea was that if he could produce a standard model vehicle in large quantities using mass production techniques, then he could supply a potential demand for relatively cheap private transport. At the time (in the 1920s in the USA) Ford was correct; there was such a demand and his products proved successful. A production orientation to business was thus suited to an economic climate where potential demand outstripped supply, as was the case in the 1920s prior to the wide-scale introduction of mass production techniques. However, times change, and such a philosophy is not conducive to doing business in today's economic climate, where potential supply usually outstrips demand.

Sales orientation

With the large-scale introduction of mass production techniques in the 1920s and 1930s, particularly in the USA and Western Europe, and the rapid worldwide increase in competition which accompanied this, many firms adopted a sales orientation.

The sales-orientated company is one where the focus of company effort switches to the sales function. The main issue here is not how to produce but, having products, how to ensure that this production is sold. The underlying philosophy towards customers in a sales-orientated business is that, if left to their own devices, customers will be slow or reluctant to buy. In any case, even those customers who are seeking to purchase the type of product or service which the company produces will have a wide range of potential suppliers. This situation is exacerbated when, in addition to sufficient capacity on the supply side, demand is depressed. Such was the case in many of the developed economies in the 1930s, and it was in this period that many of the so-called 'hard sell' techniques were developed. There is no doubt that many of the techniques developed were dubious, not to say dishonest, and much of the tainted image accompanying selling discussed earlier derives from their use.

Even today, many companies adopt a sales-orientated approach to doing business, even though customers are better protected against its worst excesses, as will be discussed in Chapter 11.

Marketing orientation

It is unclear exactly when the idea of marketing or customer orientation began to emerge; indeed in some ways the central importance of the customer has perhaps always been recognised in the long history of trading. Not until the 1950s, however, did the ideas associated with the so-called marketing concept begin to emerge and take shape. The marketing concept – initially an American phenomenon – arose partly as a result of a dissatisfaction with the previously described production and sales orientations, partly as a result of a changing environment, and partly as a result of fundamental business sense.

The marketing concept holds that the key to successful and profitable business rests with identifying the needs and wants of customers and providing products and services to satisfy these needs and wants. On the surface such a concept does not appear to be a far reaching and fundamentally different philosophy of business, but in fact the marketing concept requires a revolution in how a company thinks about, and practises, its business activities as compared with production or sales orientation. Central to this revolution in business thinking is the emphasis given to the needs and wants of the customer. The contrast between this approach and, for example, that of a sales-orientated company is shown in Figure 1.2.

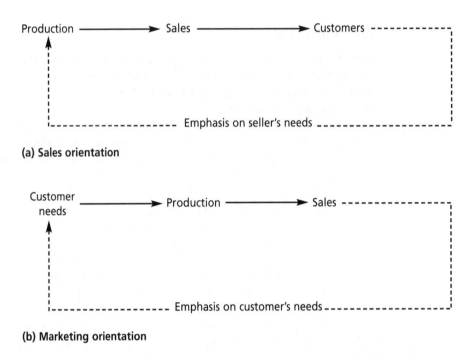

(a) Sales orientation

(b) Marketing orientation

Figure1.2. Sales versus market orientation

Increasingly, companies have come to recognise that this different approach to doing business is essential in today's environment. Consumers are now better educated and more sophisticated than they were. Real incomes have increased steadily over the years and today's consumers now have considerable discretionary spending power to allocate between an increasingly diverse range of products and services. Too many companies have learned the hard way that having what they feel to be a superior product, efficient production and extensive promotion – laudable though these may be – are not sufficient to confer automatic success. In order to stand any chance of success, customer needs must be placed at the very centre of business planning. In part, this stress on understanding the consumer explains the development of those concepts and techniques aimed at understanding buyer behaviour. In Chapter 2 we develop a framework within which consumer and organisational buying behaviour may be analysed.

1.7 IMPLEMENTING THE MARKETING CONCEPT

Subscribing to a philosophy of marketing, even though an important first step, is not the same as putting that philosophy into practice. Implementing the marketing concept requires more than paying lip service to the ideas inherent in the concept. For a company to be marketing orientated requires that a number of changes take place in organisation, in practices and in attitudes. Furthermore, to become operational and of real value to a company requires that the discipline of marketing contributes what might be termed a technology of marketing. By this we mean that management requires the development of a set of tools (techniques and concepts) in order to implement the marketing concept. We have already mentioned that the behavioural sciences can lead to an understanding of buyer behaviour; another example is the development of quantitative and qualitative techniques of marketing research for analysing and appraising markets. Some of the more important and useful concepts in marketing are now discussed.

Market segmentation and targeting

Because marketing focuses on customer needs and wants, this requires that companies identify these needs and wants and then develop marketing programmes to satisfy them as a route to achieving company objectives. The diversity of customer needs and wants, and the multiplicity of ways in which these may be satisfied, mean that few, if any, companies are in a position to serve effectively all the customers in a market. **Market segmentation** is the process of identifying those clusters, or segments, of customers in a market which share similar needs and wants and will respond in a similar and unique way to a given marketing effort. Having identified the various segments in a market, a company can then decide which of these segments are most attractive and to which it can market most effectively. Company marketing efforts can then be tailored specifically to the needs of these segments on which the company has decided to target its marketing.

Market segmentation and **targeting** are two of the most useful concepts in marketing, and a whole set of techniques have been developed to aid companies in their application. Among some of the more important benefits of effective segmentation and targeting are the following:

1 A clearer identification of market opportunities and particularly the analysis of gaps in a market.
2 The design of product and market appeals, which are more finely tuned to the needs of the market.
3 The focusing of marketing and sales efforts on those segments with the greatest potential.

There are a number of bases for segmenting markets, which may be used singly or in combination. For example, a manufacturer of toothpaste may decide that the market segments best on the basis of age, i.e. the seller discovers that the different age groups in the market for the product have different wants and needs and vary in what they require from the product. The seller will find that the various segments will respond more favourably, in terms of sales, if the products and marketing programmes are more closely tailored to the needs of each segment. Alternatively, the seller may find that the market for toothpaste segments on the basis of income – the different income groups in the market vary in their product requirements. Finally, the seller may find that the market segments on the basis of a combination of both income and age characteristics. Among some of the more frequently used bases for segmentation are the following:

1 *Consumer products/markets*
- age
- sex
- income
- social class
- geographical location
- type of residence (A Classification of Residential Neighbourhoods – ACORN)
- personality
- benefits sought
- usage rate, e.g. heavy users versus light users.

2 *Industrial products/markets*
- end-use market/type of industry/product application
- benefits sought
- company size
- geographical location
- usage rate.

Whatever the base(s) chosen to segment a market, there is no doubt that the application of the concepts of segmentation and targeting is a major step towards becoming marketing orientated.

The marketing mix

In discussing the notion of market segmentation, we have frequently alluded to the company marketing programme. By far the most important decisions within this marketing programme, and indeed the essence of the marketing manager's task within a company, are decisions on the controllable marketing variables: decisions on prices, products, promotion and distribution. Taken together, these four variables comprise what is termed the **marketing mix** – a concept which, like segmentation and targeting, is central to modern marketing practice. Some writers now take a broader view of the marketing mix and include segmentation and targeting in its definition.

Generally speaking, company management has a number of variables, or ingredients, which it can control. For example, the management of a company has discretion over the range of products to be produced, their features, quality levels, etc. The task of marketing management is to blend these ingredients together into a successful recipe. The term marketing mix is appropriate, for there are many marketing mix ingredients and even more ways of combining them. In order to simplify the classification problem which this causes, the major ingredients of the mix are often referred to as 'the four Ps' – product, price and promotion, with distribution being referred to as place. (The term 'four Ps' used to describe the marketing mix was first used by E. Jerome McCarthy (1960).) In turn, each of the four Ps elements requires that a number of decisions be made, for example, about the following:

- *Price*. Price levels; credit terms; price changes; discounts.
- *Product*. Features; packaging; quality; range.
- *Promotion*. Advertising; publicity; sales promotion; personal selling.
- *Place*. Inventory; channels of distribution; number of intermediaries.

It will be seen that personal selling is considered to be one component of the promotional decision area of the marketing mix. We shall return to the place of selling in the mix later in this chapter, whilst the notion of a promotional mix is considered in more detail in Chapter 3. At this stage we will consider in greater detail the other elements of the mix.

Product

Many believe that product decisions represent the most important ingredient of the marketing mix. Decisions in this area, they argue, have the most direct and long-lasting influence on the degree of success which a company enjoys. At first glance this may seem to constitute evidence of a production as opposed to marketing orientated stance. However, it does not. There is no doubt that product decisions are the most important of the marketing decisions which a company makes. It is true that unless there is a potential demand – a true market need – for a product then no matter how good it is, it will not succeed. This is not to say that decisions about products should be made in isolation. It is also true that there are many examples of products which had considerable market potential, but failed because of poor promotional, pricing and distribution decisions. Nevertheless, most salespeople know to their cost the difficulties of selling a poor or inappropriate product, even if that product is heavily advertised and competitively priced. In effect, product decisions determine the upper limit to a company's sales potential. The effectivenss of decisions on the other elements of the mix determine the extent to which this potential is realised.

It should be stressed that the term product covers anything that a company offers to its customers for the purpose of satisfying their needs. In addition to the physical, tangible products offered for sale, there are also services and skills. Non-profit organisations also market their services to potential customers. Increasingly, charities, educational establishments, libraries, museums and even political candidates make use of the techniques of marketing. There are a number of schemes for classifying products, depending upon the basis chosen for classification. For example, a broad distinction can be made between consumer and industrial products, the basis for classification here being the end-use/buyer.

Regardless of how and on what basis a product or service is classified, one of the most important factors to bear in mind about the product is that the customer is purchasing a package of benefits, not product features. This concept of a product is yet another example of a market-orientated approach to doing business. It looks at the product from the point of view of what the customer is actually purchasing, i.e. needs and wants. For example,when people purchase cosmetics they are purchasing attractiveness, etc. Theodore Levitt (1962) provides us with perhaps one of the most graphic examples of this concept of a product when he states: 'Purchasing agents do not buy quarter inch drills; they buy quarter inch holes.' Viewing the product in this way can provide useful insights which can be used in the marketing of a product. In the sales area it can be used to develop the sales presentation by stressing the ways in which the product or service provides a solution to the customer's problems.

The product life-cycle

One of the most useful concepts in marketing derives from the idea that most products tend to follow a particular pattern over time in terms of sales and profits. This pattern is shown in Figure 1.3 and is known as the product life-cycle curve.

The product life-cycle is analogous to the life-cycle pattern of humans, and

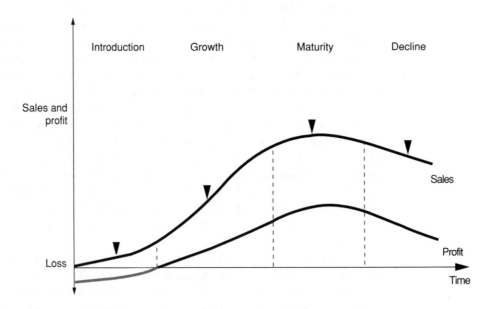

Figure 1.3 The product life-cycle curve

16

has four distinct stages – introduction (birth), growth, maturity and eventually decline. Its shape can be best explained by outlining briefly the nature of each of the stages.

1 *Introduction*. In this stage of the product life-cycle, sales growth is relatively slow. Dealers must be persuaded to stock and promote the product; consumers must be made aware of its existence, persuaded to be interested, and convinced that it is a worthwhile purchase. They may even have to be educated in how to use the product and their existing purchasing and life-style habits changed. There are no profits at this stage, and heavy launch costs can often mean a large financial deficit.

2 *Growth*. After the initial slow acceptance, sales begin to escalate at a relatively rapid pace. There is a snowball effect as word-of-mouth communication and advertising begin to take effect. Dealers may request to stock the product. Small profits begin to be made.

3 *Maturity*. The growth of sales begins to slow as the market begins to become saturated. Few new buyers are attracted to the product and there is a high proportion of repeat sales. Attracted by the high profit and sales figures, competitors have now entered the market. Partly because of this increased competition, profits, having peaked, then begin to decline during this stage.

4 *Decline*. Sales begin to fall and already slim profit margins are depressed even further. Customers have begun to become bored with the product and are attracted by newer, improved products. Dealers begin to de-stock the product in anticipation of reduced sales.

Implications of the product life-cycle

Not all products exhibit such a typical cycle of sales and profits. Some products have hardly any life-cycle at all (a large proportion of new products are unsuccessful in the marketplace). Similarly, sales may be reduced abruptly even in a period of rapid sales growth as a result of, say, the introduction of a new and better competitive product. Products vary too in the length of time which they take to pass through the life-cycle. Unlike the human life span, there is no such thing as an average life expectation for products. Nevertheless, the fact that a great number of products do tend to follow the generalised life-cycle pattern has a number of implications for marketing and sales strategies. Some of these are considered in more detail in Chapter 3. Two of the more important implications of the product life-cycle concept are considered now.

The first, and perhaps most obvious, implication of the concept is that even the most successful products have a finite life. Further, there is some evidence that suggests that intensifying competition and rapid technological change are leading to a shortening of product life-cycles. This explains the importance and emphasis now attached to the continued development of new products. The salesforce have an important role to play in this process. Because of their often daily contact with customers, they are usually the first to detect signs that products are about to embark upon the period of decline. Their often detailed knowledge of customers, competitors and market requirements makes them potentially a very valuable source of new product ideas.

A second implication of the life-cycle concept is that different marketing and sales strategies may be appropriate to each stage. Again this is covered in greater detail in Chapter 3, but clearly sales tactics – indeed the very nature of the selling task – is likely to vary according to the stage of the life-cycle. For example, in the introductory stage the emphasis may be on locating potential prospects. In the growth stage, the salesforce may find themselves having to deal with the delicate issue of rationing their customers as demand increases more rapidly than capacity. In the maturity and decline stages, the salesforce will increasingly have to rely on competitive pricing and special offers in order to combat increasing competition and falling sales.

Product adoption and diffusion processes

This theory was first put forward by Everett Rogers in 1962 and it is closely related to the product life-cycle process. It describes innovative behaviour and it holds that the characteristics of a new product can affect its rate of adoption. Figure 1.4 describes its characteristics.

Consumers are placed into one of five 'adopter' categories, each of which has different behavioural characteristics. These adopter categories contain the percentages of first-time buyers (i.e. not repeat buyers) that fall into each

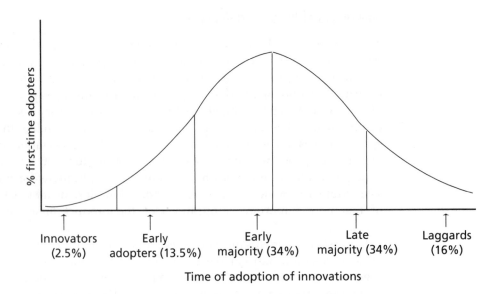

Figure 1.4 The adoption of innovations

category. What will attract first-time buyers to a product or service, and the length of time it will take for the diffusion process to be completed, will depend upon the nature of the product or service.

If we consider a new range of female fashions, then the time taken for the diffusion process to be completed might be less than one year. Here, the innovators (i.e. the first 2½ per cent) are likely to be fashion-conscious rich people. However, if we consider a new type of computer software then innovators are more likely to be technically minded computer 'experts' and the time for diffusion will be over a longer period. Similarly, although microwave ovens were developed over 20 years ago they have not yet fully diffused through the marketplace. Having said this, many potential consumers will never adopt for a variety of reasons (e.g. some people refuse to have a television because it destroys the art of conversation).

A number of factors can determine the rate at which the innovation is taken up:

- its *relative advantage* over other products or services in the marketplace;
- the extent to which it is *compatible* with the potential needs of customers;
- its *complexity* in terms of how it can be used and understood;
- its *divisibility* in terms of how it can be tried beforehand on some kind of test basis before a commitment is made to purchase;
- its *communicability*, which is the degree to which the innovation can be described or demonstrated prior to purchase.

Pricing

As with the product element of the mix, pricing decisions encompass a whole variety of decision areas. Pricing objectives must be determined, price levels set, decisions must be made as to credit and discount policies, and a procedure established for making price changes. Here we will consider some of the more important inputs to pricing decisions, in particular from the point of view of how they affect selling and sales management.

Inputs to pricing decisions

In the determination of price levels, a number of factors must be considered. The main factors include the following:

1 *Company objectives.* In making pricing decisions, a company must first determine what objectives it wishes its pricing to achieve within the context of overall company financial and marketing objectives. For example, company objectives may specify a target rate of return on capital employed. Pricing levels for individual products should reflect this objective. Alternatively, or additionally, a company may couch its financial objectives in terms of early cash recovery or a specified payback period for the investment.

2 *Marketing objectives.* These may shape the pricing decision. For example, a company may determine that the most appropriate marketing strategy for a new product which it has developed is to aim for a substantial market share as quickly as possible. Such a strategy is termed a **market penetration** strategy. It

is based on stimulating and capturing demand backed by low prices and heavy promotion. At the other extreme, the company might determine that a **market skimming** strategy is appropriate. Here, high initial prices are set – again often backed by high levels of promotional spending – and the cream of the profits is taken before eventually lowering the price. When the price is lowered an additional, more price-sensitive band of purchasers then enters the market. Whatever the financial and marketing objective set, these determine the framework within which pricing decisions are made. Such objectives should be communicated to sales management and to individual members of the sales team.

3 *Demand considerations.* In most markets the upper limit to the prices which a company is able to charge for its products and services is determined by demand. Put simply, one is able to charge only what the market will bear. This tends to over-simplify the complexities of demand analysis and its relationship to pricing decisions. These complexities should not, however, deter the pricing decision-maker from considering demand in his or her deliberations. One of the most straightforward notions about the relationship between demand and price is the concept of a demand curve for a product, as shown in Figure 1.5. Although it is a simple concept, the demand curve contains much useful information for the decision-maker. It shows that at lower prices, higher quantities are normally demanded. It is also possible to read off the curve the quantity demanded at any given price. Finally, it is possible to assess how sensitive demand is to changes in price. In other words, we can calculate the percentage change in quantity demanded for any given percentage price increase or decrease. Such information is extremely useful for making pricing decisions, but obtaining information about the relationship between the price and demand is not easy. Factors other than price have an important effect on demand. Despite this, pricing decisions must reflect demand considerations and some estimate should be made of

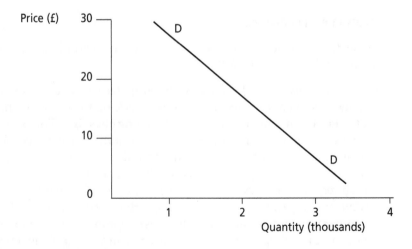

Figure 1.5 The demand curve

the likely relationship between demand levels and price. Here again, the salesforce can play a key role in the provision of such information and many companies make full use of this resource when pricing their products. A final point to be considered is the slope of the demand curve. The one shown in Figure 1.5 is a 'conventional' one, in that it slopes downwards to the right; it means that at lower prices, higher quantities are demanded. It is, however, dangerous to assume that this is always the case. In some circumstances it is possible to charge too low a price for a product or service; far from increasing demand, such low prices actually reduce it. This can be the case for products that are bought because they *are* highly priced, i.e. where there is some prestige attached to having purchased what everyone knows is an expensive product. Similarly, low prices may cause the customer to suspect the quality of a product.

4 *Cost considerations*. If demand determines the upper threshold for price, then costs determine the lower one. In the profit-making organisation, in the long run, prices charged need to cover the total costs of production and marketing, with some satisfactory residue for profit. In fact companies often begin the process of making decisions on price by considering their costs. Some techniques of pricing go further, prices being determined solely on the basis of costs; for example, total costs per unit are calculated, a percentage added for profit, and a final price is computed. Such cost-plus approaches to pricing, although straightforward, have a tendency to neglect some of the more subtle and important aspects of the cost input. As with demand, cost considerations can be quite complex. One of the important distinctions which a cost-plus approach often neglects is the distinction between the fixed and variable costs of producing a product. Fixed costs are those which do not vary – up to the limit of plant capacity – regardless of the level of output, e.g. rent and rates. Variable costs do differ with the level of output – as it increases, so too do total variable costs, and vice versa as production is decreased, e.g. direct labour costs, raw materials, etc. This apparently simple distinction is very useful for making pricing decisions and gives rise to the technique of **break-even analysis**. Figure 1.6 illustrates this concept. Fixed, variable and total costs are plotted on the chart, together with a sales revenue curve. Where the revenue curve cuts the total cost curve is the break-even point. At this point the company is making neither profit nor loss. From the break-even chart it is possible to calculate the effect on the break-even point of charging different prices and, when this is combined with information on demand, break-even analysis is quite a powerful aid to decision-making. Sales managers should know something of the different costing concepts and procedures and, whilst they do not need detailed accounting knowledge, they should be familiar with the procedures that go into the costing of the products they are responsible for selling.

5 *Competitor considerations*. Few companies are in the position of being able to make pricing decisions without considering the possible actions of competitors. Pricing decisions, particularly short-term tactical price changes, are often made as a direct response to the actions of competitors. Care should

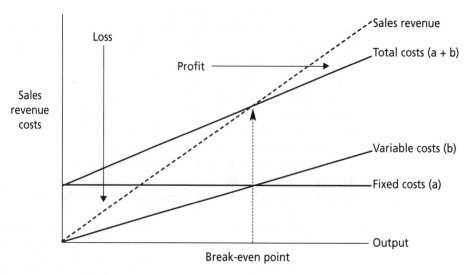

Figure 1.6 A simple break-even chart

be taken in using this tactic, particularly when the movement of price is downwards. Once lowered, price can be very difficult to raise, and where possible a company should consider responses other than price reduction to combat competition.

Distribution

The distribution (or place) element of the marketing mix, particularly the management of physical distribution, has long been felt to be one of the areas in business where substantial improvements and cost savings can be made. Representing, as it often does, a substantial portion of total costs in a company, the distribution area has in recent years attracted considerable attention in terms of new concepts and techniques designed to manage better this important function. The management of distribution has now been recognised as being a key part of the strategic management of a company, and in larger organisations it is often the responsibility of a specialist. Because of this we can do no more here than to give a non-specialist overview of some of the more important aspects of this element of the mix.

In its broadest sense distribution is concerned with all those activities required to move goods and materials into the factory, through the factory and to the final consumer. Examples of the type of decision areas encompassed in the distribution element of the marketing mix are as follows:

1 *The selection of distribution channels.* This involves determining in what manner, and through which distribution outlets, goods and services are to be made available to the final consumer. Marketing channels may be very short, e.g. where goods and services are sold direct to the customer such as via mail

order. Alternatively, the channel may include a whole set of intermediaries, including brokers, wholesalers and retailers. In addition to selecting the route through which products will reach consumers, decisions must also be made as to the extent of distribution coverage. For example, some companies have a policy of **exclusive distribution** where only a small number of selected intermediaries are used to distribute company products. In other cases, a company may decide that it requires as wide a distribution cover as possible (**intensive distribution**), and will seek a large number of distribution outlets.

2 *Determining the level of customer service.* In addition to selecting channels of distribution, decisions must also be made as to factors such as delivery periods and methods of transportation. Reduced delivery times can, of course, be a significant advantage to a company in marketing its products. On the other hand, such reductions are often accompanied by a necessity to increase inventory levels, thereby increasing costs. A policy decision must therefore be made as to the appropriate level of customer service, after consideration of the relative benefits and costs involved.

3 *The terms and conditions of distribution.* Included under this heading would be conditions of sale on the part of distributors, minimum order/stocking quantities and the determination of credit, payment and discount terms for distributors.

There are other areas to be considered in the distribution element of the marketing mix, and in Chapter 9 we explore channel management in greater detail.

At this point we should note that distribution decisions have a significant impact on sales activities, e.g. the extent of distribution directly influences territory design and route planning (dealt with in detail in Chapter 14). Terms and conditions of distribution influence the framework within which sales are negotiated. The management of physical distribution influences the all-important delivery terms which the salesforce are able to offer their customers. Probably no other area of the marketing mix has such a far ranging influence on the sales process.

Promotion

This final element of the marketing mix has the most direct influence on sales because personal selling itself is considered as one element of the total promotional mix of a company. Other elements of this promotional sub-mix include advertising, sales promotion and publicity.

All of these sub-elements are covered throughout the text in a variety of contexts and their relationships with selling are fully examined.

1.8   THE RELATIONSHIP BETWEEN SALES AND MARKETING

Throughout this chapter we have examined the nature and roles of selling and sales management and have discussed a general move towards marketing orientation. In addition, we have seen that sales efforts influence, and are influenced by, decisions taken on the ingredients of a company's marketing mix, which in turn affect its overall marketing efforts. It is essential, therefore, that sales and marketing be fully integrated. The adoption of the marketing concept has, in many companies, been accompanied by changes in organisational structure, together with changes in the view of what constitutes the nature of selling.

Examples of the possible organisational implications of adopting the marketing concept are shown in Figure 1.7 which shows the organisation charts of a sales orientated and a marketing orientated company.

Perhaps the most notable difference between the pre- and post-marketing orientated company is the fact that sales are later seen to be a part of the activity of the marketing function. In fact, in the marketing orientated company the marketing function takes on a much wider controlling and co-ordinating role across the range of company activities. This facet of marketing orientation is often misunderstood by those in sales, and a great deal of resentment is often engendered between sales and marketing. Such resentment is often due to insensitive and undiplomatic management when making the changes often necessary to reorientate a company. Selling is only a part of the total marketing programme of a company, and this total effort should be co-ordinated by the marketing function. The marketing concept, however, does not imply that sales activities are any less important, nor that marketing executives should hold the most senior positions in a company.

In addition to changes in organisational structure, the influence of the marketing function and the increased professional approach taken to sales, described earlier in this chapter, has meant that the nature and role of this activity has changed. Selling and sales management are now concerned with the analysis of customers' needs and wants and, through the company's total marketing efforts, with the provision of benefits to satisfy these needs and wants.

Figure 1.8 gives an overview of the relationship between marketing and personal selling and outlines the key areas of sales management.

As with all parts of the marketing mix, the personal selling function is not a stand-alone element but one that must be considered in the light of overall marketing strategy. At the product level, two major marketing considerations are the choice of target market and the creation of a differential advantage. Both of these decisions have an impact on personal selling.

Target market choice

The definition of a target market has clear implications for sales management because of its relationship with **target accounts**. Once the target market has been

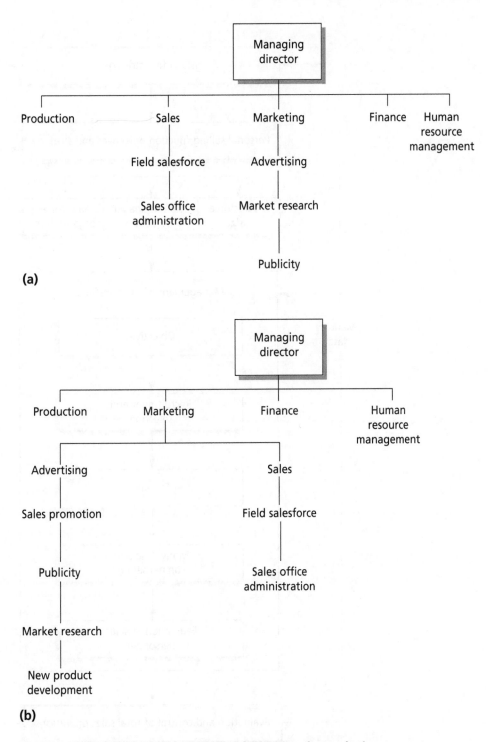

**Figure 1.7 Organisational implications of adopting the marketing concept:
(a) company organisation chart, sales-orientated company;
(b) company organisation chart, market-orientated company**

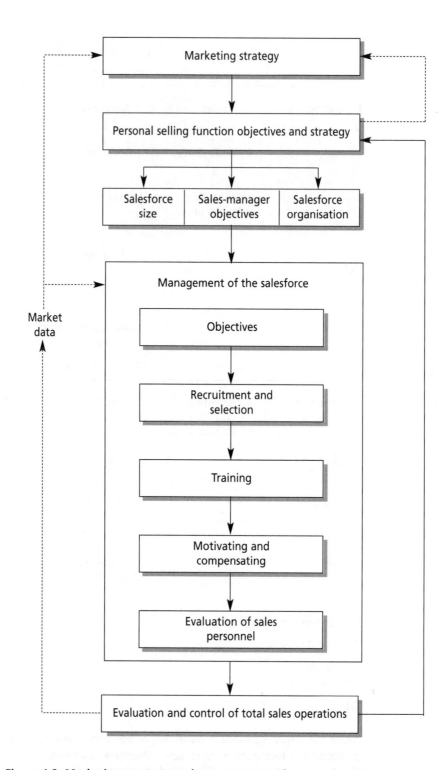

Figure 1.8 Marketing strategy and management of personal selling

defined (e.g. organisations in a particular industry over a certain size) sales management can translate that specification into individual accounts to target. Salesforce resources can, therefore, be deployed to maximum effect.

Differential advantage

The creation of a differential advantage is the starting point of successful marketing strategy but this needs to be communicated to the salesforce and embedded in a sales plan which ensures that they are able to articulate it convincingly to customers. Two common dangers are:

● the salesforce undermine the differential advantage by repeatedly giving in to customer demands for price concessions;
● the features that underlie the differential advantage are communicated but the customer benefits are neglected. Customer benefits need to be communicated in terms which are meaningful to customers. This means, for example, that advantages such as higher productivity may require translation into cash savings or higher revenue for financially-minded customers.

The second way in which marketing strategy affects the personal selling function is through strategic objectives. Each objective – build, hold, harvest and divest – has implications for sales objectives and strategy, and these are outlined in Table 1.1. Linking business or product area strategic objectives with functional area strategies is essential for the efficient allocation of resources, and effective implementation in the marketplace.

As we have seen, selling objectives and strategies are derived from marketing strategy decisions, and should be consistent with other elements of the marketing mix. Indeed marketing strategy will determine if there is a need for a salesforce at all, or whether the selling role can be better accomplished using some other medium such as direct mail. Objectives define what the selling function is expected to achieve. Objectives are typically defined in terms of the following:

● sales volume (e.g. 5 per cent growth in sales volume)
● market share (e.g. 1 per cent increase in market share)
● profitability (e.g. maintenance of gross profit margin)
● service levels (e.g. 20 per cent increase in number of customers regarding salesperson assistance as 'good or better' in annual customer survey)
● salesforce costs (e.g. 5 per cent reduction in expenses)

Salesforce strategy defines how those objectives will be achieved. The following may be considered:

● call rates
● percentage of calls on existing versus potential accounts
● discount policy (the extent to which reductions from list prices is allowed)
● percentage of resources
  – targeted at new versus existing products
  – targeted at selling versus providing after-sales service

Table 1.1 Marketing strategy and sales management

Strategic marketing objective	Sales objective	Sales strategy
Build	• Build sales volume • Increase distribution • Provide high service levels	• High call rates on existing accounts • High focus during call • Call on new accounts (prospecting)
Hold	• Maintain sales volume • Maintain distribution • Maintain service levels	• Continue present call rates on current accounts • Medium focus during call • Call on new outlets when they appear
Harvest	• Reduce selling costs • Target profitable accounts • Reduce service costs and inventories	• Call only on profitable accounts • Consider telemarketing or dropping the rest • No prospecting
Divest	• Clear inventory quickly	• Quantity discounts to targeted accounts

(Adapted from Strakle *et al.*, 1986)

- targeted at field selling versus telemarketing
- targeted at different types of customer (e.g. high versus low potential)
● improving customer and market feedback from the salesforce
● improving customer relationships

1.9 CONCLUSIONS

The nature and role of selling and sales management have been outlined and discussed, and some of the more widely held misconceptions about these activities have been explored. It has been suggested that selling and sales management are becoming more professional, and those individuals involved in these activities must now be highly trained and skilled in a range of managerial techniques.

One of the most significant developments in modern business thinking and practice has been the development of the marketing concept. Companies have moved from being production orientated, through being sales orientated to marketing orientation.

Some of the key concepts in marketing were outlined, including market segmentation and targeting, the product life-cycle and the marketing mix. The implications of marketing orientation for sales activities and the role of selling in the marketing programme have been demonstrated.

Because of the emphasis given in marketing to the needs and wants of the customer, the next chapter is concerned with exploring further the nature of consumer and organisational buying behaviour.

PRACTICAL EXERCISE
Mephisto Products Ltd

'Yet another poor year', reflected the senior executive of Mephisto Products. 'Profits down by 15 per cent, sales and turnover static in a market which was reckoned to be growing at a rate of some 20 per cent per annum. It cannot go on.' These were the thoughts of Jim Bullins, and he contended that the company would be out of business if the next year turned out to be as bad.

Jim Bullins had been senior executive at Mephisto for the past three years. In each of these years he had witnessed a decline in sales and profits. The company produced a range of technically sophisticated electromechanical control devices for industry. The major customers of Mephisto were in the chemical processing industry. The products were fitted to the customer's processing plant in order to provide safety and cut-out mechanisms, should anything untoward happen in the manufacturing process.

The products were sold through a UK salesforce of some twelve people. Each represented a different area of the country and all were technically qualified mechanical or electrical engineers. Although some 95 per cent of Mephisto's sales were to the chemical industry, there were many more applications for electromechanical control devices in a wide variety of industries.

The reason that sales were concentrated in just the one industry was historical, in that the firm's founder, James Watkinson, had some 30 years earlier married the daughter of the owner of a major detergent manufacturer. As an engineer, Watkinson had seen the potential for such devices in this type of manufacture and, with the aid of a small loan from his father-in-law, had commenced manufacture of such devices, initially for his father-in-law's company and later for wider application in the chemical industry. Watkinson had long since resigned from active participation in Mephisto Products, although he still held a financial interest. However the philosophy which Watkinson had brought to the business was one which still pervaded business thinking at Mephisto.

The essence of this philosophy was centred on product and production excellence, backed by strong technical sales support. Watkinson had believed that if the product was right, i.e. well designed and manufactured to the highest level of quality, there would be a market. Needless to say, such a product then needed selling (because customers were not necessarily aware that they had a need for such safety mechanisms) and salespeople were encouraged to use what may be described as high-pressure salesmanship, pointing out the consequences of not having such mechanisms in a manufacturing plant. They therefore tended to emphasise the negative aspects (of not having such devices) rather than the positive aspects (of how good they were, time saving in the case of plant breakdown, etc.). Needless to say, in Watkinson's day, such products then needed selling and, even though sales were to industrial purchasers, it was felt that such selling techniques were justified. This philosophy still pertained, and new salespeople were urged to remember that, unless they were pressed, most customers would not consider updating their control equipment.

Little advertising and sales promotion was carried out by the company, although from time to time, when there was a little spare cash, the company did purchase advertising space in *The Chemical Processors' Quarterly*. Pricing was done on a cost-plus basis, with total costs being calculated and a fixed percentage added to account for profits. Prices were thus fixed by the accounts department, and sales had no say in how they were established. This led to much dissent among the salespeople, who constantly argued that prices were not competitive and that if they were cut, sales could be increased substantially.

Delivery times were slow compared with the average in the industry, and there were few discounts for large-order quantities, with the salesperson first having to clear such discounts with accounts before agreeing to such an arrangement. Again, Watkinson's old philosophy still prevailed: 'If they want the product badly enough, they will wait for it', and 'Why offer discounts for large quantities – if they did not want that many they would not order them.'

During the previous five years, from being a relatively successful company, market share for Mephisto Products dropped substantially. The market became much more competitive with many new entrants, particularly from EU countries coming into the UK market, which had traditionally been supplied by UK manufacturers. Many of these new entrants had introduced new and updated products to the market, with such products drawing upon recent advances in electronics. These new products were seen by the market as being technically innovative, but the view taken by Mephisto management was that they were faddish and once the electronics novelty had worn off, customers would come back to their superior products.

Unlike many of his colleagues, Jim Bullins was worried by developments over the past five years, and felt that there was a need for many changes. He was aware that the more successful new entrants to the industry had introduced a marketing philosophy into their operations. Compared with ten years ago, it was now common practice for companies to appoint marketing managers. Furthermore, he knew from talking to other people in the industry that such companies considered sales to be an integral part of marketing. At a recent meeting with his senior staff, he mentioned to the sales manager the possibility of appointing a marketing director. The sales manager, who was shortly expecting to be made sales director, was scathing about the idea. His view was that marketing was suitable for a baked beans manufacturer but not for a company engaged in the manufacture and sale of sophisticated control devices for the chemicals industry. He argued that Mephisto's customers would not be swayed by superficial advertising and marketing ploys.

Although Jim Bullins always took heed of advice from his senior managers, recent sales figures had convinced him that the time had now come to make some changes. He would start, he decided, by appointing a marketing manager in the first instance. This person would have marketing experience and would come, most probably, from the chemical industry. The person appointed would have equal status to the sales manager, and ultimately either the new appointee or the existing sales manager would be promoted to the board of directors.

DISCUSSION QUESTIONS

1 What do you think is wrong with Mephisto Products' approach to sales and marketing?

2 Comment upon the following as they exist now at Mephisto Products:
   (a)   marketing orientation;
   (b)   the marketing mix;
   (c)   the product life-cycle.

3 What problems can you anticipate if Jim Bullins goes ahead and appoints a marketing manager?

4 If appointed, what problems can you foresee for the new marketing manager?

5 What general advice can you give to the company to make it more marketing orientated?

EXAMINATION QUESTIONS

1 Discuss the place of selling in the marketing mix.

2 How does the role of selling tend to differ between
   (a)   industrial products and
   (b)   consumer products?

3 Differentiate between production, sales and marketing orientation.

4 Give reasons as to why the shape of the curve of the product live-cycle is similar to that of the adoption of innovations curve.

chapter 2

CONSUMER AND ORGANISATIONAL BUYER BEHAVIOUR

OBJECTIVES

After studying this chapter, you should be able to:

1 Understand the different motivations of consumer and organisational buyers.

2 Formulate strategies for approaching consumer and organisational buyers.

3 Recognise the importance of relationship management.

KEY CONCEPTS

- buy phase
- consumer decision-making process
- decision-making unit (DMU)
- just-in-time purchasing
- organisational buying behaviour
- relationship management
- reverse marketing
- total quality management

2.1 DIFFERENCES BETWEEN CONSUMER AND ORGANISATIONAL BUYING

There are a number of important differences in emphasis between consumer and organisational buying which have important implications for the marketing of goods and services in general and the personal selling function in particular.

Fewer organisational buyers

Generally, a company marketing industrial products will have fewer potential buyers than one marketing in consumer markets. Often 80 per cent of output, in the former case, will be sold to perhaps 10–15 organisations. This means that the importance of one customer to the industrial marketer is far in excess of that to the consumer marketing company. However, this situation is complicated in some consumer markets where the importance of trade intermediaries, e.g. supermarkets, is so great that, although the products have an ultimate market of many millions of people, the companies' immediate customers rank alongside those of important industrial buyers.

Close, long-term relationships between organisational buyers and sellers

Because of the importance of large customers, it makes sense for suppliers to invest in long-term relationships with them. This is reflected in the growth of key account selling where dedicated sales and marketing teams are employed to service major customers. Customers, too, see the advantages of establishing close relationships with suppliers. Ford, for example, has reduced its number of suppliers from 30,000 to 3,000 and many now have single-supplier status. The nature of relationships in many consumer markets is different: customers and manufacturers rarely meet, and for many supermarket products brand switching is common.

Organisational buyers are more rational

Although organisational buyers, being people, are affected by emotional factors, e.g. like or dislike of a salesperson, the colour of office equipment, etc., it is probably true that, on the whole, organisational buying is more rational. Often decisions will be made on economic criteria. This is because industrial buyers have to justify their decisions to other members of their organisation. Caterpillar tractor salespeople based their sales presentation on the fact that, although the initial purchase price of their tractors was higher than the competition, over the life of the tractor costs were significantly lower. This rational, economic appeal proved very successful for many years. Customers are increasingly using life-cycle cost and value-in-use analysis to evaluate products. Rail companies, for example, calculate the life-cycle costs including purchase price, running and maintenance costs when ordering a new locomotive.

Organisational buying may be to specific requirements

It is not uncommon in industrial marketing for buyers to determine product specifications and for sellers to tailor their product offerings to meet them. This is feasible because of the large potential revenue of such products, e.g. railway engines. This is much less a feature of consumer marketing, where a product offering may be developed to meet a need of a market segment but, beyond that, meeting individual needs would prove uneconomic.

Reciprocal buying may be important in organisational buying

Because an industrial buyer may be in a powerful negotiating position with a seller, it may be possible to demand concessions in return for placing the order. In some situations the buyer may demand that the seller buys some of the buyer's products in return for securing the order. A buyer of tyres for a car manufacturer may demand that, in return for the contract, the tyre producer buys its company cars from the car manufacturer.

Organisational selling/buying may be more risky

Industrial markets are sometimes characterised by a contract being agreed before the product is made. Further, the product itself may be highly technical and the seller may be faced with unforeseen problems once work has started. For example Scott-Lithgow won an order to build an oil rig for British Petroleum, but the price proved uneconomic given the nature of the problems associated with its construction. GEC won the contract to develop the Nimrod surveillance system for the Ministry of Defence but technical problems caused the project to be terminated with much adverse publicity. Another example was British Rail which encountered technical problems with the commissioning of the Class 60 diesel locomotive built by Brush Traction, although, happily, these were eventually resolved.

Organisational buying is more complex

Many industrial purchases, notably those which involve large sums of money and which are new to the company, involve many people at different levels of the organisation. The managing director, product engineers, production managers, purchasing manager and operatives may influence the decision of which expensive machine to purchase. The sales task may be to influence as many of these people as possible and may involve multi-level selling by means of a sales team, rather than an individual salesperson (Corey, 1991).

Negotiation is often important in organisational buying

Negotiation is often important in organisational buying because of the presence of professional buyers and sellers, and the size and complexity of organisational buying. The supplier's list price may be regarded as the starting point for negotiation, but the price actually paid will depend on the negotiation skills and power bases of buyers and sellers.

2.2 CONSUMER BUYER BEHAVIOUR

Consumers are individuals who buy products and services for personal consumption. Sometimes it is difficult to classify a product as being a consumer or organisational good. Cars, for example, sell to consumers for personal consumption and to organisations for use in carrying out their activities (e.g. to provide transport for a sales executive). For both types of buyer, an understanding of customers can only be obtained by answering the following questions:

- *Who* is important in the buying decision?
- *How* do they buy?
- *What* are their choice criteria?
- *Where* do they buy?
- *When* do they buy?

This chapter addresses the first three of these questions since they are often the most difficult to answer.

Who buys?

Many consumer purchases are individual. When purchasing a Mars bar a person may make an impulse purchase upon seeing an array of confectionery at a newsagent's counter. However, decision-making can also be made by a group such as a household. In such a situation a number of individuals may interact to influence the purchase decision. Each person may assume a role in the decision-making process. Engel *et al.* (1993) describe five roles. Each may be taken by husband, wife, children or other members of the *buying centre*:

1 *Initiator* – the person who begins the process of considering a purchase. Information may be gathered by this person to help the decision.
2 *Influencer* – the person who attempts to persuade others in the group concerning the outcome of the decision. Influencers typically gather information and attempt to impose their choice criteria on the decision.
3 *Decider* – the individual with the power and/or financial authority to make the ultimate choice regarding which product to buy.
4 *Buyer* – the person who conducts the transaction: who calls the supplier, visits the store, makes the payment and effects delivery.
5 *User* – the actual consumer/user of the product.

One person may assume multiple roles in the buying group. In a toy purchase, for example, a girl may be the *initiator* and attempt to *influence* her parents who are the *deciders*. The girl may be *influenced* by her sister to buy a different brand. The *buyer* may be one of the parents who visits the store to purchase the toy and bring it back to the home. Finally both children may be *users* of the toy. Although the purchase was for one person, marketers have four opportunities – two children and two parents – to affect the outcome of the purchase decision.

The marketing implications of understanding who buys lies within the areas of marketing communications and segmentation. An identification of the roles played within the buying centre is a prerequisite for targeting persuasive communications. As the previous discussion has demonstrated, the person who actually uses or consumes the product may not be the most influential member of the buying centre, nor may they be the decision-maker. Even when they do play the predominant role, communication to other members of the buying centre can make sense when their knowledge and opinions may act as persuasive forces during the decision-making process. The second implication is that the changing role and influences within the family buying centre are providing new opportunities to creatively segment hitherto stable markets (e.g. cars).

The consumer decision-making process – how they buy

Behavioural scientists regard the **consumer decision-making process** as a problem-solving or need-satisfaction process. Thus, an electronic calculator may be bought in order to solve a problem – inaccuracy or slowness in arithmetic – which itself defines the need – fast and accurate calculations. In order to define which calculator to buy a consumer may pass through a series of steps (Engel *et al.*, 1993) as illustrated in Figure 2.1.

Needs

In the case of the calculator, the needs (stimulated by problem identification) are essentially *functional*. In this situation the salesperson would be advised, after identifying the buyer's needs, to demonstrate the speed and accuracy of the

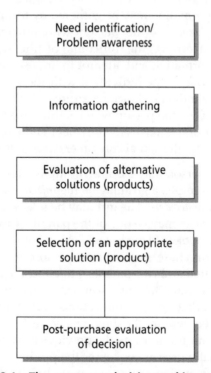

Figure 2.1   The consumer decision-making process
(Adapted from Engel *et al.*, 1993)

calculators he/she is selling. Successful selling may involve identifying needs in more detail – for example, are special features required or does the buyer only have to perform a standard, basic set of calculations, implying a less elaborate and cheaper calculator? However, for other products need-satisfaction may be in terms of more *emotional* or *psychological* needs. For example, a Sheaffer pen is bought largely for its status rather than any marginal functional superiority over other pens. An accurate assessment of the kinds of needs which a product is satisfying will enable a salesperson to plan the sales presentation correctly, presenting the product as a means of satisfying the buyer's needs or solving the buyer's problems.

How do needs arise? They may occur as a natural process of life; for example, the birth of children in a family may mean that a larger car is required. They may, also, arise because of stimulation. An advertisement for video-recorders or a salesperson's talk may create the need for extra in-house entertainment and, at the same time, provide a means of satisfying that need.

Information gathering

Many needs can only be satisfied after a period of information search. Thus a prospective car purchaser who requires a small, economical car may carry out a considerable search before deciding on the model which best satisfies these needs. This search may involve visiting car showrooms, watching car programmes on television, reading car magazines and *Which?* reports and talking to friends. Clearly, many sources of information are sought besides that provided by the salesperson in the showroom. Indeed, in some situations the search may omit the salesperson until the end of this process. The buyer may reduce the number of alternatives to a manageable few and contact the salesperson only to determine the kind of deal offered on the competing models.

Evaluation of alternatives and selection of the best solution

Evaluation may be thought of as a system as depicted in Figure 2.2.

1 *Evaluative (choice) criteria*. These are the dimensions used by consumers to compare or evaluate products or brands. In the car example the relevant evaluative criteria may be fuel economy, purchase price and reliability.
2 *Beliefs*. These are the degrees to which, in the consumer's mind, a product possesses various characteristics, e.g. roominess.
3 *Attitudes*. These are the degrees of liking or disliking a product, and are in turn dependent on the evaluative criteria used to judge the products and the beliefs about the product measured by those criteria. Thus beliefs imply knowledge, e.g. model X does 36 miles per gallon at a steady 56 miles per hour, whereas attitudes imply liking or disliking, e.g. model X is poor with regard to fuel economy.
4 *Intentions*. These measure the probability that attitudes will be acted upon. The assumption is that favourable attitudes will increase purchase intentions, i.e. the probability that the consumer will buy.

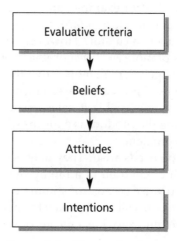

Figure 2.2   The evaluation system

Given this system, it makes sense for a salesperson to find out from a prospect the evaluative criteria being used to judge alternative products. For example, a stereo system salesperson will attempt to find out whether a potential buyer is evaluating alternative stereo units primarily in terms of external design or sound quality. Further, it can be effective to try to change evaluative criteria. For example, if the stereo system salesperson believes that the competitive advantage of the product range lies in its sound quality but the buyer's criterion is primarily external design, the salesperson can emphasise the sound quality of the product and minimise the importance of external design. Alternatively, if the primary consideration of the buyer is sound quality but a competitor's system is preferred, the sales task is to change attitudes in favour of their own system. Tools at their disposal include the use of performance comparisons from hi-fi magazines, and in-shop demonstrations.

Post-purchase evaluation of decision

The art of effective marketing is to create customer satisfaction. Most businesses rely on repeat purchasing, which implies that customers must gain satisfaction from their purchases (otherwise this will not occur). Festinger (1957) introduced the notion of 'cognitive dissonance' partly to explain the anxiety felt by many buyers of expensive items shortly after purchase. The classic case of this are the car buyers who assiduously read car advertisements after having bought the car in an effort to dispel the anxiety caused by not being sure that they have made the correct purchase.

Salespeople often try to reassure buyers, after the order has been placed, that they have made the right decision, but the outcome of the post-purchase evaluation is dependent on many factors besides the salesperson's reassurance. The quality of the product and the level of after-sales service play an obvious part in creating customer goodwill, and it is the salesperson who can help buyers in ensuring that the product they buy best matches their needs in the first place. This implies that it may not be in the salesperson's long-term interest to pressure buyers into buying higher-priced items which possess features not really wanted – although this may increase short-term profit margins (and commission) it may lead to a long-term fall in sales as consumers go elsewhere to replace the item.

Choice criteria

Choice criteria are the various features (and benefits) a customer uses when evaluating products and services. They provide the grounds for deciding to purchase one brand or another. Different members of the buying centre may use different choice criteria. For example, a child may use the criterion of self-image when choosing shoes whereas a parent may use price. The same criterion may be used differently. For example, a child may want the most expensive video-game while the parent may want a less expensive alternative. Choice criteria can change over time due to changes in income through the family life-cycle. As disposable income rises so price may no longer be a key choice criterion but is replaced by considerations of status or social belonging.

Choice criteria can be economic, social or personal. *Economic criteria* include performance, reliability and price. *Social criteria* include status and the need for social belonging. For example, Nike, Reebok and Adidas trainers need 'street cred' to be acceptable to large numbers of the youth market. Social norms such as convention and fashion can also be important choice criteria, with some brands being rejected as too unconventional (e.g. fluorescent spectacles) or out of fashion (Mackeson stout).

Personal criteria concern how the product or service relates to the individual psychologically. An important issue here is self-image which is the personal view we hold of ourselves. For example, one person might view herself as a young, upwardly mobile, successful executive and wish to buy products that reflect that image. Audi tried to appeal to such a person when they ran an advertising campaign that suggested Audi drivers 'arrived' more quickly than other drivers. Many purchase decisions are 'experimental' in that they evoke feelings of fun, pride, pleasure, boredom or sadness. Such feelings need to be taken into account when marketing products or services. For example, in retail marketing, stores such as Next, Principles, and Marks & Spencer recognise the importance of creating the right atmosphere through the correct choice of in-store colour and design.

Salespeople and marketing managers need to understand the choice criteria being used by consumers when they evaluate their products or services. Such knowledge allows the salesperson to tailor the correct appeal to each customer he or she talks to, and provides marketing managers with the basis for product or service design, and the correct messages to use in advertising.

2.3 FACTORS AFFECTING THE CONSUMER DECISION-MAKING PROCESS

There are a number of factors which affect the consumer decision-making process and the outcome of that process. These can be classified under three headings:

1 the buying situation;
2 personal influences;
3 social influences.

The buying situation

Howard and Sheth (1969) identified three types of buying situation:

1 Extensive problem-solving.
2 Limited problem-solving.
3 Automatic response.

When a problem or need is new, the means of solving that problem are expensive and uncertainty is high, a consumer is likely to conduct extensive problem-solving. This will involve a high degree of information search and close examination of alternative solutions. Faced with this kind of buyer the salesperson can create immense goodwill by providing information and assessing alternatives from the product range in terms of how well their benefits conform to the buyer's needs. The goodwill generated with this type of buyer in such a buying situation may be rewarded by a repeat purchase when the buying situation changes to one of limited problem-solving. Thus successful car salespeople often find themselves with a group of highly loyal buyers who purchase from them, even if the dealership changes, because of the trust built up during this stage.

Limited problem-solving occurs when the consumer has some experience with the product in question and may be inclined to stay loyal to the brand previously purchased. However, a certain amount of information search and evaluation of a few alternatives occurs as a rudimentary check that the right decision is being made. This process provides a limited opportunity for salespeople of competing products to persuade consumers that they should switch model or brand by providing relevant comparative information and, perhaps, by providing risk-reducing guarantees, e.g. free replacement of any defective parts.

Companies who have built up a large brand franchise will wish to move their customers to the state of automatic response. Advertising may be effective in keeping the brand in the forefront of the consumer's mind and in reinforcing already favourable attitudes towards the brand. In this situation, personal selling to the ultimate consumer may be superfluous. Companies selling consumer durables may offer generous trade-in terms for their old models: Black and Decker have used this technique whereby an old, unusable lawnmower could be traded-in as part payment on a new model.

A key influence on whether a consumer conducts extensive or limited problem-solving or automatic response is his or her level of **involvement** with the purchase. High involvement is associated with important purchases that are of high personal relevance. When a purchase affects one's self-image, has a high degree of perceived risk, has social (e.g. status) implications, and has the capacity to give a lot of pleasure, it is likely to be high involvement. When the opposite is the case, the consumer is likely to experience low involvement with the purchase. Figure 2.3 shows the relationship between involvement and the buying situation.

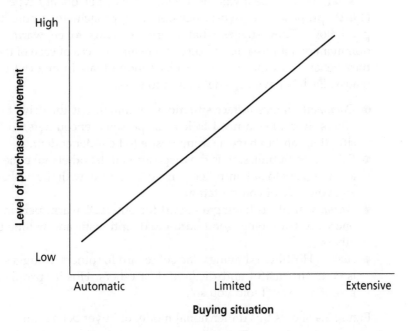

Figure 2.3   Level of purchase involvement and the buying situation

In high-involvement situations (e.g. car or house purchase), the customer is looking for lots of information upon which to make a decision. A salesperson must be able to provide that information and be able to answer in-depth queries. In low-involvement situations, the customer is not likely to be an active searcher for information. Repetitive advertising is often used for these kinds of purchases.

Personal influences

A second group of factors which influences the consumer decision-making process concerns the psychology of the individuals concerned. Relevant concepts include personality, motivation, perception and learning.

Although personality may explain differences in consumer purchasing, it is extremely difficult for salespeople to judge accurately how extrovert or introvert, conventional or unconventional, a customer is, for example. Indeed, reliable personality measurement has proved difficult, even for qualified psychologists. Brand personality is the characterisation of brands as perceived by consumers. Brands may be characterised as 'for young people' (Levis), 'brash' (Castlemaine XXXX) or 'intelligent' (Guinness). This is a dimension over and above the physical (e.g. colour) or functional (e.g. task) attributes of a brand. By creating a brand personality a marketer may create appeal to people who value that characterisation. Research by Ackoff and Emsott (1975) into brand personalities of beers showed that most consumers preferred the brand of beer that matched their own personality.

Sellers need to be aware of different buyer personality types. Buzzotta *et al.* (1982) proposed a two-dimensional approach to understanding buyer psychology. They suggest that everyone tends to be warm or hostile, and dominant or submissive. Although there are degrees of each of these behaviours, they believe it is meaningful to place individuals in one cell of a two-by-two matrix. Each behaviour is defined as follows:

- *Dominant.* In face-to-face situations, dominance is the drive to take control of others. It implies a need to lead in personal encounters, to have control of situations and to have a strong desire to be independent.
- *Submissive.* Submission is the disposition to let others take the lead. It implies a willingness to be controlled, a need to comply with the wishes of others, and an avoidance of confrontation.
- *Warm.* Warmth is having a regard for others. A warm person is described as one who is outgoing, good humoured, optimistic and willing to place trust in others.
- *Hostile.* Hostility is having a lack of regard for others. It suggests a person who is cold, distrustful and disdainful of others. Hostile people like to be in a position to say 'I told you so'.

Figure 2.4 shows this dimensional model of buyer behaviour.

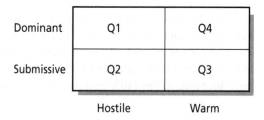

Figure 2.4   Dimensional model of buyer behaviour

Buzzotta *et al.* (1982) claim that, although there are as many distinctions as people, in general each person primarily falls into one of the four groups. To help identify each type, the salesperson must look for their hallmarks:

Q1: *Dominant-hostile.* They are loud, talkative, demanding and forceful in their actions. They are hard-nosed, aggressive and assertive. They are usually difficult to get along with and can be offensive. They tend to distrust salespeople.

Q2: *Submissive-hostile*. These people are cold, aloof and uncommunicative. They tend to be loners and work in jobs that demand concentration rather than socialisation, e.g. research, accountancy and computer programming. When responding to questions, they tend to be short and terse, e.g. 'maybe', 'all right', 'possibly'. Q2s prefer to avoid sales interviews, but if they cannot avoid them they take on a passive, almost detached role.

Q3: *Submissive-warm*. They are extrovert, friendly, understanding, talkative and positive-minded people who are not natural leaders. They prefer to buy from someone they like and view a sales interview as a social occasion. Generally they accept most of what the salesperson tells them but, if they feel any doubt, will postpone the decision to buy – possibly to seek advice from friends.

Q4: *Dominant-warm*. These people are adaptable and open-minded but are not afraid to express their ideas and opinions. They tend to want proof of sales arguments and become impatient of woolly answers. They are not hesitant to buy from anyone who can prove to their satisfaction that there is a benefit to be gained. They like to negotiate in a business-like manner, and can be demanding and challenging in a sales interview.

What are the implications for selling? Decormier and Jobber (1993) argue that salespeople should modify their behaviour accordingly:

Q1. To win the respect of dominant-hostile people, the appropriate salesperson behaviour is to adjust their dominance level upward to meet that of the buyer. This would involve sitting upright, maintaining eye contact, listening respectfully (but passively) and answering directly. Once Q1 buyers realise that the salesperson is their psychological equal, a meaningful discussion can take place.

Q2. When first meeting with a submissive-hostile Q2 buyer, a salesperson should not attempt to dominate, but gradually try to gain his or her trust. The salesperson should match the buyer's dominance level and ask open-ended questions in a slow, soft manner. The salesperson should lower his or her stature, keeping eyes and head at the same level as the buyer.

Q3. Submissive-warm people like and trust people. The salesperson should satisfy their social needs by being warm and friendly. He or she should not attempt to dominate, but should instead share the social experience. Once liking and trust have been established, the salesperson should guide the interview towards the goal of decision-making.

Q4. Dominant-warm people consider respect more important than being liked. To gain respect, the salesperson should match the Q4's dominance level while maintaining a warm (empathetic) manner. Sales arguments need to be backed up whenever possible by evidence.

Sellers also need to probe for the motivations of the buyer. The true reason or motive for purchase may be obscure. However, by careful probing a salesperson is likely to find out some of the real motives for purchase some of the time.

Motivation is clearly linked to needs; the more strongly a need is perceived by a consumer, the more likely he or she is to be moved towards its satisfaction. Thus, a salesperson can increase buyer motivation by stimulating need recognition, by showing the ways in which needs can be fulfilled and by attempting to understand the various motives which may be at work in the decision-making process. These may be functional, e.g. time saved by a convenience food, or psychological, e.g. the status imparted by the ownership of a Jaguar or BMW car.

Not everyone with the same motivations will buy the same products, however. One of the reasons for this is that how someone decides to act depends upon his or her *perception* of the situation. One buyer may perceive a salesperson as being honest and truthful while another may not. Three selective processes may be at work on consumers.

1 *Selective exposure.* Only certain information sources may be sought and read.
2 *Selective perception.* Only certain ideas, messages and information from those sources may be perceived.
3 *Selective retention.* Only some of them may be remembered.

In general, people tend to forget more quickly and to distort or avoid messages that are substantially at variance with existing attitudes.

Learning is also important in consumer decision-making. Learning refers to the changes in a person's behaviour as a result of his or her experiences. A consumer will learn which brand names imply quality and which salespeople to trust.

Life-style

Life-style patterns have attracted much attention from marketing research practitioners. *Life-style* refers to the patterns of living as expressed in a person's activities, interests and opinions. Life-style analysis, or *psychographics*, groups consumers according to their beliefs, activities, values and demographic characteristics such as education and income. For example, Research Bureau Ltd, a UK marketing research agency, investigated life-style patterns among housewives, and found eight distinct groups:

1 *The young sophisticates:* extravagant, experimental, non-traditional; young, ABC1 social class, well educated, affluent, owner-occupiers, full-time employed; interested in new products; sociable with cultural interests.
2 *The home-centred:* conservative, less quality conscious, demographically average, middle class, average income and education; lowest interest in new products; very home-centred; little entertaining.
3 *Traditional working class:* traditional, quality conscious, unexperimental in food, enjoys cooking; middle-aged, DE social group, less education, lower income, council house tenants; sociable; husband and wife share activities, like betting.
4 *Middle-aged sophisticates:* experimental, not traditional; middle aged, ABC1 social class, well-educated, affluent, owner-occupiers, full-time housewives, interested in new products; sociable with cultural interests.

5 *Coronation Street housewives:* quality conscious, conservative, traditional; DE social class, tend to live in Lancashire and Yorkshire TV areas, less educated, lower incomes, part-time employment; low level of interest in new products; not sociable.

6 *The self-confident:* self-confident, quality conscious, not extravagant; young, well educated, owner-occupier, average income.

7 *The homely:* bargain seekers, not self-confident, house-proud, C1C2 social class, tend to live in Tyne Tees and Scottish TV areas; left school at an early age; part-time employed; average level of entertaining.

8 *The penny-pinchers:* self-confident, house-proud, traditional, not quality conscious; 25–34 years, C2DE social class, part-time employment, less education, average income; enjoy betting, enjoy saving, husband and wife share activities, sociable.

Life-style analysis has implications for marketing since life-styles have been found to correlate with purchasing behaviour. A company may choose to target a particular life-style group (e.g. the middle-aged sophisticates) with a product offering, and use advertising which is in line with the values and beliefs of this group. As information on readership/viewing habits of life-style groups becomes more widely known so media selection may be influenced by life-style research.

Social influences

Major social influences on consumer decision-making include social class, reference groups, culture and the family.

The first of these factors, social class, has been regarded as an important determinant of consumer behaviour for many years. Social class in marketing is based upon the occupation of the head of the household or main income earner. The practical importance of social class is reflected in the fact that respondents in market research surveys are usually classified by their social class, and most advertising media give readership figures broken down by social class groupings. These are shown in Table 2.1. However, the use of this variable to explain differences in purchasing has been criticised. It is often the case that people within the same social class may have different consumption patterns. Within the C2 group, i.e. skilled manual workers, it has been found that some people spend a high proportion of their income on buying their own house, furniture, carpets and in-home entertainment, while others prefer to spend their money on more transitory pleasures such as drinking, smoking and playing bingo.

Such findings have led to a new classificatory system called ACORN (A Classification of Residential Neighbourhoods) which classifies people according to the type of area they live in. This has proved to be a powerful discriminator between different lifestyles, purchasing patterns and media exposure (Baker *et al.*, 1979).

Table 2.1 Social class categories

Social grade	All adults 15+ (%)
A	3.1
B	17.7
C1	27.8
C2	22.2
D	17.6
E	11.7

KEY:

Social grade	Social status	Occupation
A	Upper middle class	Higher managerial, administrative or professional
B	Middle class	Intermediate managerial, administrative or professional
C1	Lower middle class	Supervisory or clerical and junior managerial, administrative or professional
C2	Skilled working class	Skilled manual workers
D	Working class	Semi and unskilled manual workers
E	Those at the lowest level of subsistence	State pensioners or widows (no other earner), casual or lowest grade

Source: adapted from National Readership Survey, July 1996–June1997.

The term 'reference group' is used to indicate a group of people that influence a person's attitude or behaviour. Where a product is conspicuous, e.g. clothing or cars, the brand or model chosen may have been strongly influenced by what the buyer perceives as acceptable to his or her reference group, e.g. a group of friends, the family, or work colleagues. Reference group acceptability should not be confused with popularity. The salesperson who attempts to sell a car using the theme 'that it's very popular' may conflict with the buyer's desire to aspire to an 'exclusive' reference group, for which a less popular, more individual, model may be appropriate.

Culture refers to the traditions, taboos, values and basic attitudes of the whole society within which an individual lives. It is of particular relevance to international marketing, since different countries have different cultures, affecting the conduct of business and how products are used. In Arab countries, for example, a salesperson may find themselves conducting a sales presentation in the presence of a competitor's salesperson. In France chocolate is sometimes eaten between slices of bread.

The family is sometimes called a primary reference group and may play a significant part in consumer buyer behaviour; the decision as to which product or brand to purchase may be a group decision, with each family member playing a distinct part. Thus, in the purchase of motor cars, traditionally the husband decided upon the model, while his wife chose the colour (Doyle and Hutchinson, 1973). The purchase of cereals may be strongly influenced by children. The cleaning properties of a carpet fibre may be relatively unimportant to the principal breadwinner but of greater significance to the partner who performs the housework tasks. When a purchase is a group decision, a salesperson will be wise to view the benefits of his or her products in terms of each of the decision-makers or influencers.

2.4 ORGANISATIONAL BUYER BEHAVIOUR

Organisational buyer behaviour has usefully been broken down into three elements by Fisher (1976):

1 *Structure*. The 'who' factor – who participates in the decision-making process, and their particular roles.
2 *Process*. The 'how' factor – the pattern of information getting, analysis, evaluation and decision-making which takes place as the purchasing organisation moves towards a decision.
3 *Content*. The 'what' factor – the choice criteria used at different stages of the process and by different members of the decision-making unit.

Structure

An essential point to understand in organisational buying is that the buyer or purchasing officer is often not the only person who influences the decision, or who actually has the authority to make the ultimate decision. Rather, the decision is in the hands of a **decision-making unit (DMU)**, or buying centre as it is sometimes called. This is not necessarily a fixed entity. The people in the DMU may change as the decision-making process continues. Thus a managing director may be involved in the decision that new equipment should be purchased, but not in the decision as to which manufacturer to buy it from.

Webster (1995) and Bonoma (1982) have identified six roles in the structure of the DMU:

1 *Initiators*. Those who begin the purchase process.
2 *Users*. Those who actually use the product.
3 *Deciders*. Those who have the authority to select the supplier/model.
4 *Influencers*. Those who provide information and add decision criteria throughout the process.
5 *Buyers*. Those who have authority to execute the contractual arrangements.
6 *Gatekeepers*. Those who control the flow of information, e.g. secretaries who may allow or prevent access to a DMU member, or a buyer whose agreement must be sought before a supplier can contact other members of the DMU.

The factors which influence the nature of the DMU will be examined later. Obviously, for different types of purchase the exact formation will vary. For very important decisions the structure of the DMU will be complex, involving numerous people within the buying organisation. The salesperson's task is to identify and reach the key members in order to convince them of his or her product's worth. Often, talking only to the purchasing officer will be insufficient, since this may be only a minor influence on which supplier is chosen.

Salespeople need to avoid two deadly sins:

1 Working within their 'comfort zone'. This is where they spend too much time

with people they like and feel comfortable with, but who are unimportant with regard to which product to buy or which supplier to use.

2 Spending too much time with 'nay sayers'. These are people who can say 'no' (the power of veto) but who do not have the authority to say 'yes'. It is the latter group to whom most communicational effort should be channelled, i.e. the decision-makers.

When the problem to be solved is highly technical, suppliers may work with engineers in the buying organisation in order to solve problems and secure the order. An example where this approach was highly successful involved a small US company that secured a large order from a major car company owing to its ability to work with the company in solving the technical problems associated with the development of an exhaust gas recirculation valve (Cline and Shapiro, 1978). In this case, its policy was to work with company engineers and to keep the purchasing department out of the decision until the last possible moment, by which time only it was qualified to supply the part.

Where DMU members are inaccessible to salespeople, advertising may be used as an alternative. Also, where users are an important influence and the product is relatively inexpensive and consumable, free samples given by the salespeople may be effective in generating preference.

Process

Figure 2.5 describes the **decision-making process** for an industrial product (Robinson *et al.*, 1967). The exact nature of the process will depend on the buying situation. In some situations some stages will be omitted; for example, in a routine re-buy situation the purchasing officer is unlikely to pass through stages 3, 4 and 5 (search for suppliers and an analysis and evaluation of their proposals). These stages will be bypassed, as the buyer, recognising a need – perhaps shortage of stationery – routinely reorders from the existing supplier.

In general, the more complex the decision and the more expensive the item, the more likely it is that each stage will be passed through and that the process will take more time.

1 *Need or problem of recognition*. Needs and problems may be recognised through either internal or external factors. An example of an internal factor would be the realisation of undercapacity leading to the decision to purchase plant or equipment. Thus, internal recognition leads to active behaviour (*internal/active*). Some problems which are recognised internally may not be acted upon. This condition may be termed *internal/passive*. A production manager may realise that there is a problem with a machine but, given more presing problems, decides to live with it. Other potential problems may not be recognised internally, and only become problems because of *external cues*. A production manager may be quite satisfied with the production process until being made aware of another more efficient method. Clearly these different problems have important implications for the salesperson. The

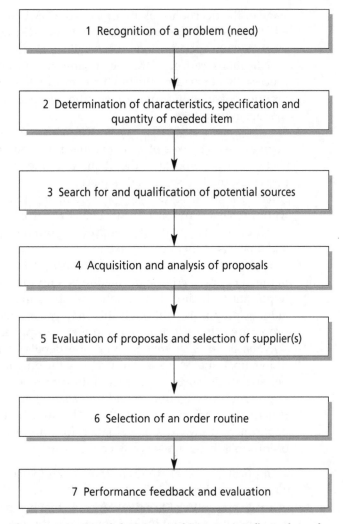

Figure 2.5   The organisational decision-making process (buy phases)

internal/passive condition implies that there is an opportunity for the salesperson, having identified the condition, to highlight the problem by careful analysis of cost inefficiencies and other symptoms, so that the problem is perceived to be more pressing and in need of solution (internal/active). The internal/active situation requires salespeople to demonstrate a differential advantage of one of their products over the competition. In this situation problem stimulation is unnecessary, but where internal recognition is absent, the salesperson can provide the necessary external cues. A fork-lift truck sales representative might stimulate problem recognition by showing how their trucks can save the customer money, due to lower maintenance costs, and lead to more efficient use of warehouse space through higher lifting capabilities.

2 *Determination of characteristics, specification and quantity of needed item.* At this

stage of the decision-making process the DMU will draw up a description of what is required. For example, it might decide that five lathes are required to meet certain specifications. The ability of a salesperson to influence the specifications can give their company an advantage at later stages of the process. By persuading the buying company to specify features that only their product possesses (*lockout criteria*), the salesperson may virtually have closed the sale at this stage.

3 *Search for and qualification of potential sources*. A great deal of variation in the degree of search takes place in organisational buying. Generally speaking, the cheaper, less important the item, and the more information the buyer possesses, the less search takes place.

4 *Acquisition and analysis of proposals*. Having found a number of companies who, perhaps through their technical expertise and general reputation, are considered to be qualified to supply the product, proposals will be called for and analysis of them undertaken.

5 *Evaluation of proposals and selection of suppliers*. Each proposal will be evaluated in the light of the criteria deemed to be important to each DMU member. It is important to realise that various members may use different criteria when judging proposals. Although this may cause problems, the outcome of this procedure is the selection of a supplier or suppliers.

6 *Selection of an order routine*. Next the details of payment and delivery are drawn up. Usually this is conducted by the purchasing officer. In some buying decisions this stage is merged into stages 4 and 5 when delivery is an important consideration in selecting a supplier.

7 *Performance feedback and evaluation*. This may be formal, where a purchasing department draws up an evaluation form for user departments to complete, or informal through everyday conversation.

The implications of all this are that a salesperson can affect a sale through influencing need recognition, through the design of product specifications and by clearly presenting the advantages of his/her product over competition in terms which are relevant to DMU members. By early involvement, a salesperson can benefit through the process of **creeping commitment**, whereby the buying organisation becomes increasingly committed to one supplier through its involvement in the process and the technical assistance it provides.

Content

This aspect of organisational buyer behaviour refers to the **choice criteria** used by members of the DMU to evaluate supplier proposals. These criteria are likely to be determined by the performance criteria used to evaluate the members themselves. Thus a purchasing manager who is judged by the extent to which he or she reduces purchase expenditure is likely to be more cost conscious than a production engineer who is evaluated in terms of the technical efficiency of the production processes he or she designs.

Table 2.2   Choice criteria

Economic	Emotional
● price	● prestige
● delivery	● personal risk reduction
● productivity – cost versus revenues	● office politics
● life-cycle costs	● quiet life
● reliability	● pleasure
● durability	● reciprocity
● upgradability	● confidence
● technical assistance	● convenience
● commercial assistance	
● safety	

As with consumers, organisational buying is characterised by both functional (economic) and psychological (emotive) criteria (see Table 2.2). Key functional considerations may be, for plant and equipment, return on investment, while for materials and component parts they might be cost savings, together with delivery reliability, quality and technical assistance. Because of the high costs associated with production down-time, a key concern of many purchasing departments is the long-run development of the organisation's supply system. Psychological factors may also be important, particularly when suppliers' product offerings are essentially similar. In this situation the final decision may rest upon the relative liking for the suppliers' salesperson. A number of important criteria are examined below.

1 Quality

The emergence of **total quality management** as a key aspect of organisational life reflects the importance of quality in evaluating a supplier's products and services. Many buying organisations are unwilling to trade quality for price. In particular, buyers are looking for consistency of product or service quality so that end-products (e.g. motor cars) are reliable, inspection costs are reduced and production processes run smoothly. They are installing just-in-time delivery systems which rely upon incoming supplies being quality guaranteed. Jaguar cars under Sir John Egan moved from a price-orientated purchasing system to one where quality was central and purchasing departments were instructed to pay more provided the price could be justified in terms of improved quality of components.

2 Price and life-cycle costs

For materials and components of similar specification and quality, price becomes a key consideration. For standard items such as ball-bearings price may be critical to making a sale given that a number of suppliers can meet delivery and specification requirements. However, it should not be forgotten that price is only one component of cost for many buying organisations. Increasingly buyers take into account **life-cycle costs** which may include productivity savings, maintenance costs and residual values, as well as initial purchase price, when evaluating products. Marketers can use life-cycle costs analysis to break into an account. By calculating life-cycle costs with a buyer, new perceptions of value may be achieved.

3 Continuity of supply

Another major cost to a company is a disruption of a production run. Delays of this kind can mean costly machine down-time and even lost sales. Continuity of supply is, therefore, a prime consideration in many purchase situations. Companies which perform badly on this criterion lose out even if the price is competitive because a small percentage price edge does not compare with the costs of unreliable delivery. Supplier companies who can guarantee deliveries and realise their promises can achieve a significant differential advantage in the marketplace. Organisational customers are demanding close relationships with 'accredited suppliers' who can guarantee reliable supply, perhaps on a just-in-time basis.

4 Perceived risk

Perceived risk can come in two forms: functional risk such as the uncertainty with respect to product or supplier performance; and psychological risk such as criticism from work colleagues. This latter risk – fear of upsetting the boss, losing status, being ridiculed by others in the department, or, indeed losing one's job – can play a determining role in purchase decisions. Buyers often reduce uncertainty by gathering information about competing suppliers, checking the opinions of important others in the buying company, only buying from familiar and/or reputable suppliers and by spreading risk through multiple sourcing.

5 Office politics

Political factions within the buying company may also influence the outcome of a purchase decision. Interdepartmental conflict may manifest itself in the formation of competing 'camps' over the purchase of a product or service. Because department X favours supplier 1, department Y automatically favours supplier 2. The outcome does not only have purchasing implications but political implications for the departments and individuals concerned.

6 Personal liking/disliking

A buyer may personally like one salesperson more than another and this may influence supplier choice, particularly when competing products are very similar. Even when supplier selection is on the basis of competitive bidding it is known for purchasers to help salespeople they like to 'be competitive'. Obviously perception is important in all organisational purchases, as how someone behaves depends upon the perception of the situation. One buyer may perceive a salesperson as being honest, truthful and likeable while another may not. As with consumer behaviour, three selective processes may be at work on buyers:

● *Selective exposure.* Only certain information sources may be sought.
● *Selective perception.* Only certain information may be perceived.
● *Selective retention.* Only some information may be remembered.

The implications of understanding the content of the decision are that, first, a salesperson may need to change their sales presentation when talking to different DMU members. Discussion with a production engineer may centre on the technical superiority of the product offering, while much more emphasis on cost factors may prove beneficial when talking to the purchasing officer. Second, the choice criteria used by buying organisations change over time as circumstances change. Price may be relatively unimportant to a company when trying to solve a highly visible technical problem, and the order will be placed with the supplier who provides the necessary technical assistance. Later, after the problem has been solved and other suppliers become qualified, price may be of crucial significance.

2.5 FACTORS AFFECTING ORGANISATIONAL BUYER BEHAVIOUR

Cardozo (1980) identified three factors which influence the composition of the DMU, the nature of the decision-making process and the criteria used to evaluate product offerings. These factors are as follows:

● the buy class
● the product type
● the importance of the purchase to the buying organisation.

These are illustrated in Figure 2.6.

The buy class

Industrial purchasing decisions were studied by Robinson *et al.* (1967), who concluded that buyer behaviour was influenced by the nature of the buy class. They distinguished between a new task, a modified re-buy and a straight re-buy.

A *new task* occurs when the need for the product has not arisen previously so that there is little or no relevant experience in the company, and a great deal of information is required. A *straight re-buy*, on the other hand, occurs where an organisation buys previously purchased items from suppliers already judged acceptable. Routine purchasing procedures are set up to facilitate straight re-

Figure 2.6   Influences on organisational purchasing behaviour

buys. The *modified re-buy* lies between the two extremes. A regular requirement for the type of product exists, and the buying alternatives are known, but sufficient change has occurred to require some alteration of the normal supply procedure.

The buy classes affect organisational buying in the following ways. First, the structure of the DMU changes. For a straight re-buy possibly only the purchasing officer is involved, whereas for a new buy senior management, engineers, production managers and purchasing officers are likely to be involved. Modified re-buys often involve engineers, production managers and purchasing officers, but senior management, except when the purchase is critical to the company, is unlikely to be involved. Second, the decision-making process is likely to be much longer as the buy class changes from a straight re-buy to a modified re-buy and, then, a new task. Third, in terms of influencing DMU members, they are likely to be much more receptive for new task and modified re-buy situations than straight re-buys. In the latter case the purchasing manager has already solved the purchasing problems and has other problems to deal with. So why make it a problem again?

The first implication of this buy class analysis is that there are big gains to be made if the salesperson can enter the new task at the start of the decision-making process. By providing information and helping with any technical problems which can arise, the salesperson may be able to create goodwill and creeping commitment which secures the order when the final decision is made. The second implication is that since the decision process is likely to be long, and many people are involved in the new task, supplier companies need to invest heavily in sales human resources for a considerable period of time. Some firms employ missionary sales teams, comprising their best salespeople, to help secure big new-task orders.

Salespeople in straight re-buy situations must ensure that no change occurs when they are in the position of the supplier. Regular contact to ensure that the customer has no complaints may be necessary, and the buyer may be encouraged to use automatic recording systems. For the non-supplier the salesperson has a difficult task unless poor service or some other factor has caused the buyer to become dissatisfied with the present supplier. The obvious objective of the salesperson in this situation is to change the buy class from a straight re-buy to a modified re-buy. Price alone may not be enough since changing supplier represents a large personal risk to the purchasing officer. The new supplier's products might be less reliable, and delivery might be unpredictable. In order to reduce this risk, the salesperson may offer delivery guarantees with penalty clauses and be very willing to accept a small (perhaps uneconomic) order at first in order to gain a foothold. Supplier acquisition of a total quality management standard such as BS5750 may also have the effect of reducing perceived buyer risk. Or it may be necessary to agree to undertake a buyer's Supplier Quality Assurance programme. Many straight re-buys are organised on a contract basis, and buyers may be more receptive to listening to non-supplier salespeople prior to contract renewal.

Value analysis and life-cycle cost calculations are other methods of moving purchases from a straight re-buy to a modified re-buy situation. *Value analysis,* which can be conducted by either supplier or buyer, is a method of cost reduction in which components are examined to see if they can be made more cheaply. The items are studied to identify unnecessary costs that do not add to the reliability or functionality of the product. By redesigning, standardising or manufacturing by less expensive means, a supplier may be able to offer a product of comparable quality at lower cost. Simple redesigns like changing a curved edge to a straight one may have dramatic cost implications. *Life-cycle cost analysis* seeks to move the cost focus from the initial purchase price to the total cost of owning and using a product. There are three types of life-cycle costs: (1) purchase price; (2) start-up costs and (3) post-purchase costs. Start-up costs would include installation, lost production and training costs. Post-purchase costs include operating (e.g. fuel, operator wages), maintenance, repair and inventory costs. Against these costs would be placed residual values (e.g. trade-in values of cars). Life-cycle cost appeals can be powerful motivators. For example, if the out-supplier can convince the customer organisation that its product has significantly lower post-purchase costs than the in-supplier despite a slightly higher purchase price, it may win the order. This is because it will be delivering a higher *economic value to the customer*. This can be a powerful competitive advantage and, at the same time, justify the premium price.

The product type

Products can be classified according to four types: materials, components, plant and equipment, and MROs.

1. Materials to be used in the production process, e.g. steel.
2. Components to be incorporated in the finished product, e.g. alternator.

         } Product constituents

3. Plant and equipment.
4. Products and services for maintenance, repair and operation (MROs), e.g. spanners, welding equipment and lubricants.

         } Production facilities

This classification is based upon a customer's perspective – how the product is used – and may be used to identify differences in organisational buyer behaviour. First, the people who take part in the decision-making process tend to change according to product type. For example, it has been found that senior management tend to get involved in the purchase of plant and equipment or, occasionally, when new materials are purchased if the change is of fundamental importance to company operations, e.g. if a move from aluminium to plastic is being contemplated. Rarely do they involve themselves in component or MRO supply. Similarly, design engineers tend to be involved in buying components and materials but not normally MRO and plant and equipment. Second, the decision-making process tends to be slower and more complex as product type moves from:

MRO → Components → Materials → Plant and equipment

For MRO items, 'blanket contracts' rather than periodic purchase orders are increasingly being used. The supplier agrees to resupply the buyer on agreed price terms over a period of time. Stock is held by the seller and orders are automatically printed out by the buyer's computer when stock falls below a minimum level. This has the advantage to the supplying company of effectively blocking the efforts of the competitors' salesforces for long periods of time.

Classification of suppliers' offerings by product type gives the salesforce clues as to who is likely to be influential in the purchase decision. The sales task is then to confirm this in particular situations and attempt to reach those people involved. A salesperson selling MROs is likely to be wasting effort attempting to talk to design engineers, whereas attempts to reach operating management are likely to prove fruitful.

Importance of purchase to buying organisation

A purchase is likely to be perceived as being important to the buying organisation when it involves large sums of money, when the cost of making the wrong decision, e.g. in lost production, is high and when there is considerable uncertainty about the outcome of alternative offerings. In such situations, many people at different organisational levels are likely to be involved in the decision and the process is likely to be long, with extensive search and analysis of information. Thus extensive marketing effort is likely to be required, but great opportunities present themselves to sales teams who work with buying organisations to convince them that their offering has the best payoff; this may involve acceptance trials, e.g. private diesel manufacturers supplying rail companies with prototypes for testing, engineering support and testimonials from other users. Additionally, guarantees of delivery dates and after-sales service may be necessary when buyer uncertainty regarding these factors is high.

2.6 DEVELOPMENTS IN PURCHASING PRACTICE

A number of trends have taken place within the purchasing function which have marketing implications for supplier firms. The advent of just-in-time purchasing and the increased tendency towards central purchasing, reverse marketing and leasing have all changed the nature of purchasing and altered the way in which suppliers compete.

1 Just-in-time purchasing

The **just-in-time** (JIT) concept aims to minimise stocks by organising a supply system which provides materials and components as they are required. As such, stockholding costs are significantly reduced or eliminated and thus profits are increased. Furthermore, since the holding of stocks is a hedge against machine breakdowns, faulty parts and human error, they may be seen as a cushion which acts as a disincentive to management to eliminate such inefficiencies.

A number of just-in-time practices are also associated with improved quality. Suppliers are evaluated on their ability to provide high-quality products. The effect of this is that suppliers may place more emphasis on product quality. Buyers are encouraged to specify only essential product characteristics which means that suppliers have more discretion in product design and manufacturing methods. Also, the emphasis is on the supplier certifying quality which means that quality inspection at the buyer company is reduced and overall costs are minimised since quality control at source is more effective than further down the supply chain.

The total effects of just-in-time can be enormous. Purchasing inventory and inspection costs can be reduced, product design can be improved, delivery streamlined, production down-time reduced, and the quality of the finished item enhanced.

However, the implementation of JIT requires integration into both purchasing and production operations. Since the system requires the delivery of the exact amount of materials or components to the production line as they are required, delivery schedules must be very reliable and suppliers must be prepared to make deliveries on a regular basis – perhaps even daily. Lead times for ordering must be short and the number of defects very low. An attraction for suppliers is that it is usual for long-term purchasing agreements to be drawn up. The marketing implications of the JIT concept is that to be competitive in many industrial markets, e.g. motor cars, suppliers must be able to meet the requirements of this fast-growing system.

An example of a company that employs JIT is the Nissan car assembly plant at Sunderland in the UK. The importance of JIT to its operations has meant that the number of component suppliers in the north-east of England has increased from three when Nissan arrived in 1986 to 27 in 1992. Nissan adopt what they term 'synchronous supply' – parts are delivered only minutes before they are needed. For example, carpets are delivered by Sommer Allibert, a French supplier, from its nearby facility to the Nissan assembly line in sequence for fitting to the correct model. Only 42 minutes elapse between the carpet being ordered and fitted to the car. The stockholding of carpets for the Nissan Micra is now only 10 minutes! Just-in-time practices do carry risks, however, if labour stability cannot be guaranteed. Renault discovered this to their cost when a strike at its engine and gearbox plant caused its entire French and Belgian car production lines to close in only ten days.

2 Centralised purchasing

Where several operating units within a company have common requirements and where there is an opportunity to strengthen a negotiating position by bulk buying, **centralised purchasing** is an attractive option. Centralisation encourages purchasing specialists to concentrate their energies on a small group of products, thus enabling them to develop an extensive knowledge of cost factors and the operation of suppliers. The move from local to centralised buying has important marketing implications. Localised buying tends to focus on short-term cost and profit considerations whereas centralised purchasing places more emphasis on long-term supply relationships. Outside influences, e.g. engineers, play a greater role in supplier choice in local purchasing organisations since less specialised buyers often lack the expertise and status to question the recommendations of technical people. The type of purchasing organisation can therefore give clues to suppliers regarding the important people in the decision-making unit and their respective power positions.

3 Reverse marketing

The traditional view of marketing is that supplier firms will actively seek the requirements of customers and attempt to meet those needs better than the competition. This model places the initiative with the supplier. Purchasers could assume a passive dimension relying on their suppliers' sensitivity to their needs, and technological capabilities to provide them with solutions to their problems. However, this trusting relationship is at odds with a new corporate purchasing situation that developed during the 1980s and is gaining momentum. Purchasing is taking on a more proactive, aggressive stance in acquiring the products and services needed to compete. This process whereby the buyer attempts to persuade the supplier to provide exactly what the organisation wants is called **reverse marketing** (Blenkhorn and Banting, 1991). Figure 2.7 shows the difference between the traditional model and this new concept.

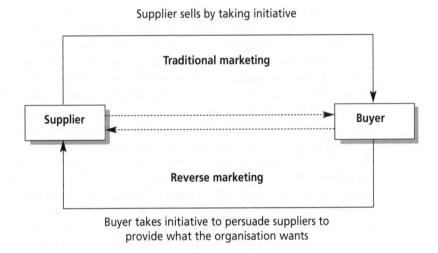

Figure 2.7   Reverse marketing

The essence of reverse marketing is that the purchaser takes the initiative in approaching new or existing suppliers and persuading them to meet their supply requirements. The implications of reverse marketing are that it may pose serious threats to uncooperative in-suppliers but major opportunities to responsive in- and out-suppliers. The growth of reverse marketing presents two key benefits to suppliers who are willing to listen to the buyer's proposition and carefully consider its merits. First, it provides the opportunity to develop a stronger and longer-lasting relationship with the customer, and second, it could be a source of new product opportunities that may be developed to a broader customer base later on.

4 Leasing

A *lease* is a contract by which the owner of an asset (e.g. a car) grants the right to use the asset for a period of time to another party in exchange for payment of rent. The benefits to the customer are that a leasing arrangement avoids the need to pay the cash purchase price of the product or service, is a hedge against fast product obsolescence, may have tax advantages, avoids the problem of equipment disposal and, with certain types of leasing contracts, avoids some maintenance costs. These benefits need to be weighed against the costs of leasing which may be higher than outright buying.

There are two main types of lease: financial (or full payment) leases and operating leases (sometimes called rental agreements). A **financial lease** is a longer-term arrangement that is fully amortised over the term of the contract. Lease payments, in total, usually exceed the purchase price of the item. The terms and conditions of the lease vary according to convention and competitive conditions. Sometimes the supplier will agree to pay maintenance costs over the leasing period. This is common when leasing photocopiers, for example. The lessee may also be given the option of buying the equipment at the end of the period. An **operating lease** is for a shorter period of time, is cancellable, and is not completely amortised. Operating lease rates are usually higher than financial lease rates since they are shorter term. When equipment is required intermittently this form of acquisition can be attractive since it avoids the need to let plant lie idle. Many types of equipment such as diggers, bulldozers and skips may be available on short-term hire as may storage facilities.

Leasing may be advantageous to suppliers because it provides customer benefits that may differentiate product and service offerings. As such it may attract customers who otherwise may find the product unaffordable or uneconomic. The importance of leasing in such industries as cars, photocopying and data processing has led an increasing number of companies to employ leasing consultants to work with customers on leasing arrangements and benefits. A crucial marketing decision is the setting of leasing rates. These should be set with the following in mind:

1 the desired relative attractiveness of leasing versus buying (the supplier may wish to promote/discourage buying compared with leasing);
2 the net present value of lease payments versus outright purchase;
3 the tax advantages of leasing versus buying to the customer;
4 the rates being charged by competition;
5 the perceived advantages of spreading payments to customers; and
6 any other perceived customer benefits, e.g. maintenance and insurance costs being assumed by the supplier.

2.7 RELATIONSHIP MANAGEMENT

The discussion of reverse marketing in section 2.6 gave examples of buyers adopting a proactive stance in their dealings with suppliers, and introduced the importance of buyer–seller relationships in marketing between organisations. The Industrial Marketing and Purchasing Group (Turnbull and Cunningham, 1981) developed the **interaction approach** to explain the complexity of buyer–seller relationships. This approach views these relationships as taking place between two active parties. Thus reverse marketing is one manifestation of the interaction perspective. Both parties may be involved in adaptations to their own process or product technologies to accommodate each other, and changes in the activities of one party are unlikely without consideration of, or consulation with, the other party. In such circumstances a key objective of industrial markets will be to manage customer relationships. Not only should formal organisational arrangements such as the use of distributors, salespeople and sales subsidiaries be considered but also the informal network consisting of the personal contacts and relationships between supplier and customer staff. Marks & Spencer's senior directors meet the boards of each of its major suppliers twice a year for frank discussions. When Marks & Spencer personnel visit a supplier it is referred to as a 'royal visit'. Factories may be repainted, new uniforms issued and machinery cleaned. This reflects the exacting standards that the company demands from its suppliers and the power it wields in its relationship with them.

The reality of organisational marketing is that many suppliers and buying organisations have been conducting business between themselves for many years. For example, Lucas has been supplying components to Rover (and its antecedents) for over 50 years. Marks & Spencer has trading relationships with suppliers that stretch back almost 100 years. Such long-term relationships can have significant advantages to both buyer and seller. Risk is reduced for buyers since they get to know people in the supplier organisation and know who to contact when problems arise. Communication is thus improved and joint problem-solving and design management can take place. Sellers gain through closer knowledge of buyer requirements, and by gaining the trust of the buyer an effective barrier to entry for competing firms may be established. New product development can benefit from such close relationships. The development of machine-washable lambswool fabrics, and easy-to-iron cotton shirts came about because of Marks & Spencer's close relationships with UK manufacturers.

Close relationships in organisational markets are inevitable as changing technology, shorter product life-cycles and increased foreign competition place marketing and purchasing departments in key strategic roles. Buyers are increasingly treating trusted suppliers as **strategic partners**, sharing information and drawing on their expertise when developing cost-efficient, quality-based new products. The marketing implication is that successful organisational marketing is more than the traditional manipulation of the four Ps – product, place, promotion and price. Its foundation rests upon the skilful handling of customer relationships. This had led some companies to appoint customer relationship managers to oversee the partnership and act in a communicational and co-ordinated role to ensure customer satisfaction. Still more companies have reorganised their salesforces to reflect the importance of managing key customer relationships effectively. This process is called 'key' or major account management.

2.8 CONCLUSIONS

Understanding buyer behaviour has important implications for salespeople and sales management. Recognition that buyers purchase products in order to overcome problems and satisfy needs implies that an effective sales approach will involve the discovery of these needs on the part of the salesperson. Only then can he or she sell the offering from the range of products marketed by the company which best meets these needs.

When the decision-making unit is complex, as in many organisational buying situations, the salesperson must attempt to identify and reach key members of the DMU in order to persuade them of his/her product's benefits. He/she must also realise that different members may use different criteria to evaluate the product and, thus, may need to modify his/her sales presentation accordingly.

The next chapter is concerned with the development of sales strategies which reflect the buyer behaviour patterns of the marketplace.

PRACTICAL EXERCISE

The Lost Computer Sale

Jim Appleton, managing director of Industrial Cleaning Services, had decided that a personal computer could help solve his cash flow problems. What he wanted was a machine which would store his receipts and outgoings so that at a touch of a button he could see the cash flow at any point in time. A year ago he got into serious cash flow difficulties simply because he didn't realise that, for various reasons, his short-term outflow greatly exceeded his receipts.

He decided to visit a newly opened personal computer outlet in town on Saturday afternoon. His wife, Mary, was with him. They approached a salesperson seated behind a desk.

Jim	Good afternoon. I'm interested in buying a personal computer for my business. Can you help me?
Salesperson	Yes, indeed, sir. This is the fastest growing network of personal computer centres in the country. I have to see a colleague for a moment but I shall be back in a few minutes. Would you like to have a look at this brochure and at the models we have in the showroom?

Salesperson gives them the brochures, and leaves them in the showroom.

Mary	I don't understand computers. Why are some bigger than others?
Jim	I don't know. What baffles me are all these buttons you have to press. I wonder if you have to do a typing course to use one?

Jim and Mary look round the showroom asking each other questions and getting a little confused. The salesperson arrives after five minutes.

Salesperson   Sorry to take so long but at least it's given you a chance to see what we have in stock. You tell me you want a computer for work. I think I have just the one for you.

Salesperson takes Jim and Mary to a model.

Salesperson   This could be just up your street. Not only will this model act as a word processor, it will do your accounts, financial plans and stock control as well. It has full graphic facilities so that you can see trend lines on the screen at the touch of the button.

Mary   It looks very expensive. How much will it cost?

Salesperson   A lot less than you think. This one costs £2,000, which is quite cheap.

Mary   I've seen advertisements in newspapers for computers which are a lot less expensive.

Salesperson   Yes, but do they have 32 bit local bus graphic facilities and do they have 4 megabytes of RAM?

Mary   I don't know, but they looked quite good to me.

Jim   It looks very complicated to use.

Salesperson   No more complicated than any of the other models. The computer comes with a full set of instructions. My twelve-year-old son could operate it.

Jim   What's this button for?

Salesperson   That moves the cursor. It allows you to delete or amend any character you wish.

Jim   I see.

Salesperson   I've left the best till last. Included in the price are three software programs which allow the machine to be used for spreadsheet analysis, stock control and word processing. I'm sure your business will benefit from this computer.

Jim   My business is very small. I only employ five people. I'm not sure it's ready for a computer yet. Still, thank you for your time.

DISCUSSION QUESTIONS

1 What choice criteria did Jim and Mary use when deciding whether to buy a computer and which model to buy?

2 Did the salesperson understand the motives behind the purchase? If not, why not? Did he/she make any other mistakes?

3 Imagine that you were the salesperson. How would you have conducted the sales interview?

EXAMINATION QUESTIONS

1 Compare and contrast the ways in which consumers and organisations buy products and services.

2 Of what practical importance is the study of organisational buyer behaviour to the personal selling function?

CHAPTER 3

SALES STRATEGIES

OBJECTIVES   After studying this chapter, you should be able to:

1 Understand and appreciate the differences between sales and marketing strategies.

2 Appreciate where the key marketing concepts fit into the planning process.

3 Identify component parts of the promotional mix.

4 Differentiate between objectives, strategies and tactics.

KEY CONCEPTS
- branding
- budget
- promotional mix
- push and pull strategies

- sales forecast
- sales planning process
- SWOT analysis

3.1   SALES AND MARKETING PLANNING

It is important to recognise the fact that, to be effective, sales activities need to take place within the context of an overall strategic marketing plan. Only in this way are we likely to ensure that our sales efforts complement, rather than compete with, the rest of our marketing activities. Sales strategies and tactics may only be arrived at, implemented and assessed against a framework of company-wide objectives and strategic planning processes. As a prelude to discussing sales strategies and tactics later in this chapter, the nature and purpose of strategic market plans and the place of selling in these plans is outlined and discussed.

3.2   THE PLANNING PROCESS

The nature of the **sales planning process** is outlined in Figure 3.1. This deceptively simple process can be likened to that of operating a domestic central heating system. One first determines the temperature required, timing, etc. (setting objectives), and the procedures which must be followed in order to make sure that this is achieved (determining operations). Next one has to organise oneself to implement appropriate procedures, including making sure that all the necessary resources are available (organisation). At this stage one can go ahead and commence operation of the system (implementation). Finally, one needs to check how the system is operating, in particular the temperature level which is being achieved (measuring results). Any deviations in required temperature are then reported and corrected through the thermostatic system (re-evaluation and control).

This planning process is also described through the acronym 'MOST' which is meant to describe the process from the general to the specific as : mission; objective; strategy; tactics.

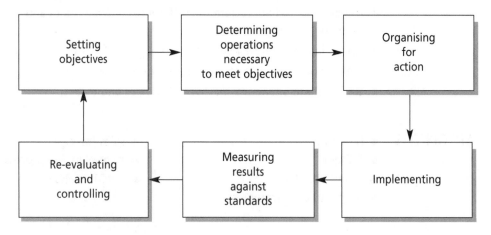

Figure 3.1 The planning process

3.3 ESTABLISHING MARKETING PLANS

In fact there is no universal way of establishing an ideal marketing plan; neither is the process simple in actual practice because every planning situation is unique. Conceptually, however, the process is comparatively simple, comprising a series of logical steps.

Business definition

As a prerequisite to the determination of marketing plans, careful consideration should be given to defining (or redefining) the overall role or mission of the business. This issue is perhaps best addressed by senior management asking and answering the question 'What business are we in?' Always, the definition of the role of a business should be couched in terms of what customer needs are being served by a business rather than in terms of what products or services are being produced. For example, the manufacturer of microcomputers might define the company as being in the business of rapid problem-solving. In the automobile industry, companies might define their business as being the provision of transport, status, etc., rather than the manufacture of cars.

This process of business definition is extremely important. Not only does it ensure that a company thinks in terms of its customers' wants and needs but, in terms of the planning process, it forms a focusing mechanism for much of what follows.

Analysis of current marketing situation

Business definition is followed by analysis of the current marketing situation. The precise content of this step in the preparation of the marketing plan will vary from company to company, but normally the analysis will encompass the following factors:

Market analysis

Examples of the data and analysis required under this heading would include the following:

1 Current and recent size and growth of market. In the multi-product company this analysis needs to be made in total, by product/market and by geographical segment.
2 The analysis of customer needs, attitudes and trends in purchasing behaviour.
3 Current marketing mix.
4 Competitor analysis, including an appraisal of the following:
   ● current strategy
   ● current performance, including market share analysis
   ● their strengths and weaknesses
   ● expectations as to their future actions.
   In addition to analysing existing competition, the much more difficult task of appraising potential new entrants should be carried out at this stage.
5 The analysis of broad macro-environment trends – economic, demographic, technological, political and cultural – which might influence the future of the company's products.

Analysis of strengths/weaknesses, opportunities and threats

Here management must make a realistic and objective appraisal of company strengths and weaknesses in the context of potential opportunities and threats (**SWOT analysis**). Opportunities and threats to the future of a business stem primarily from factors outside the direct control of a company and in particular from trends and changes in those factors which were referred to earlier as the macro-environment – namely economic, political, technological and cultural factors. It is important to recognise that the determination of what constitutes an opportunity/threat, and indeed the appraisal of strengths and weaknesses, must be carried out concurrently. An 'apparent' strength, for example a reputation for quality, becomes a real strength only when it can be capitalised on in the marketplace.

Statement of objectives

On the basis of the preceding steps the company must now determine specific objectives and goals which it wishes to achieve. These objectives, in turn, form the basis for the selection of marketing strategies and tactics.

Companies often have objectives in a number of areas – financial objectives, technological objectives and so on. Needless to say, here we are concerned primarily with marketing objectives, although these must be supportive of and consistent with objectives in other areas. In addition to this element of consistency, objectives should be expressed unambiguously, preferably quantitatively, and with an indication of the time span within which the objectives are planned to be achieved. This time span of planned activities often gives rise to some confusion in the planning literature. Marketing plans are often categorised as being short range, intermediate range and long range; the confusion arises from the fact that there is no accepted definition of what constitutes the appropriate time horizon for each of these categories. What is felt to comprise long-term planning in one company (say 5–10 years) may be considered intermediate in another. It is suggested that the different planning categories are identical in concept although clearly they differ in detail. Furthermore the different planning categories are ultimately related to each other – achieving long-term objectives requires first that intermediate and short-term objectives be met.

One of the most important documents in a company, however, and one which the sales manager will play a key part in preparing, is the annual marketing plan. The remainder of this chapter discusses planning in the context of the preparation of this annual document.

Determining market and sales potential – forecasting sales

A crucial step in the development of marketing plans is the assessment of market and sales potential followed by the preparation of a detailed **sales forecast**. Market potential is the maximum possible sales that are available for an entire industry during a stated period of time. Sales potential is the maximum possible portion of that market which a company could reasonably hope to achieve under the most favourable conditions. Finally, the sales forecast is the portion of the sales potential that the company estimates that it will achieve. The sales forecast is in fact a very important step in the preparation of company plans. Not only are the marketing and sales functions directly affected in their planning considerations by this forecast, but other departments, including production, purchasing and personnel, will use the sales forecast in their planning activities. Sales forecasting, therefore, is a prerequisite to successful planning and is considered in detail in Chapter 15.

Generating and selecting strategies

Once marketing objectives have been defined and market potential assessed, consideration may be given to the generation and selection of strategies. Broadly, strategies encompass the set of approaches which the company will use to achieve its objectives.

This step in the process is complicated by the fact that there are often many alternative ways in which each objective can be achieved. For example, an increase in sales revenue of 10 per cent can be achieved by increasing prices, increasing sales volume at the company level (increasing market share) or increasing industry sales. At this stage it is advisable, if time consuming, to generate as many alternative strategies as possible. In turn, each of these strategies can be further evaluated in terms of their detailed implications for resources and in the light of the market opportunities identified earlier. Finally, each strategy should be examined against the possibility of counter-strategies on the part of competitors.

From this list of alternative strategies a choice must be made with regard to the broad marketing approach which the company considers will be the most effective in achieving objectives. This must then be translated into a strategy statement which must be communicated to and agreed with all those managers who will influence its likely degree of success or failure. Once again, the specific contents of such a strategy statement will vary between companies, but as an example a strategy statement might encompass the following areas:

1 A clear statement of marketing objectives.
2 A description of the choice of strategies for achieving these objectives.
3 An outline of the broad implications of the selected strategies with respect to the following key areas in marketing:
   ● target market
   ● positioning
   ● marketing mix
   ● marketing research.

At this stage the strategy statement should give a clear and concise indication of where the major marketing efforts of the company will be focused. Once this has been discussed and agreed we can progress to the next step of preparing a detailed plan of action.

Preparing the marketing programme

The strategy statement prepared in the previous step provides the input for the determination of the detailed programme required to implement these strategies. The first step in the preparation of this programme is the determination of the marketing mix. Detailed decisions must be made with respect to product policy, pricing, promotion and distribution. Further, care needs to be taken to ensure that the various elements of the marketing mix are integrated, i.e. that they work together to achieve company objectives in the most effective manner.

At this stage what has previously been an outline plan for guiding decision-making becomes a detailed operating plan. It is on the basis of this part of the plan that the day-to-day marketing activities and tactics of the company will be organised, implemented and assessed.

Allocating necessary resources – budgeting

Having made detailed decisions with respect to the elements of the marketing mix, the next step is to assemble a **budget** for each of these elements. In most companies limited resources ensure that managers from the different functional areas have to compete for these scarce resources. At this stage it is likely that much discussion will take place between those responsible for each element of the marketing mix. In addition it may be found that initial marketing objectives, strategies and detailed plans for the marketing programme to achieve the forecast level of sales may, in the light of financial and other resource constraints, be unrealistic. In this event modifications to the original plan may have to be made.

It should be noted that at this stage an estimate can be made of both costs and revenues and a forecast profit and loss statement prepared.

Implementation and control

The procedure so far should have resulted in the preparation of a detailed document setting out what is to be done, when it will be done, who is responsible and estimated costs and revenues. Once approved, details of the marketing plan should be communicated to everyone involved. This communication is an essential, and often neglected, aspect of marketing planning. It is surprising how many companies have elaborate marketing plans which are not implemented because key people have not been informed or have not agreed the proposed plan.

Finally, the plan should include an outline of the control mechanisms that will be applied to the plan. This should include details of major objectives and key parameters in the measurement of the degree of success in achieving the objectives. This part of the marketing plan should specify what is to be measured, how it is to be measured and what data are required for measurement. It may also include details of what action is to be taken in the light of deviations from the plan. This so-called contingency planning is a key feature of any planning process, recognising as it does that plans need to be flexible in order to accommodate possible unforeseen or unpredictable changes in the market.

The overall marketing planning process is summarised in Figure 3.2.

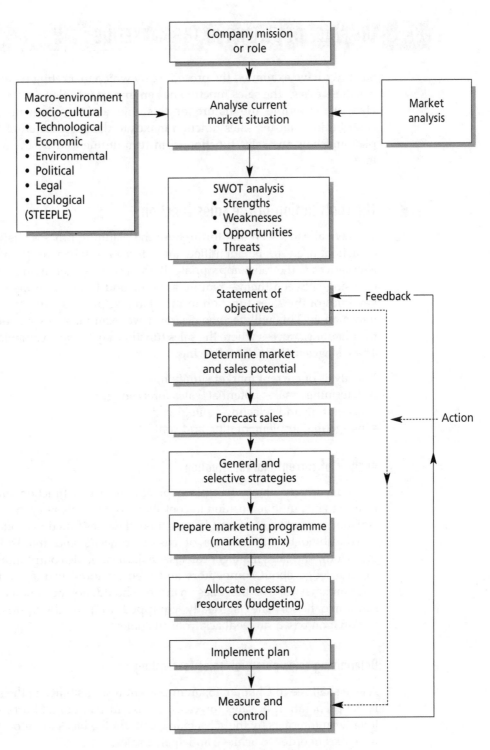

Figure 3.2   An overview of the marketing planning process

3.4 THE PLACE OF SELLING IN THE MARKETING PLAN

So far we have examined the procedure by which marketing plans are prepared. Needless to say, the sales function has an important role to play in this process. Here we examine the nature of this role and, in particular, look at the contribution that the sales function makes to the preparation of the marketing plan and how the sales function is, in turn, influenced by the marketing plan itself.

The contribution of the sales function

We have already seen that throughout the planning process alternative courses of action need to be identified and decisions taken as to which of these alternatives is the most appropriate. Both of these – identifying alternatives and choosing between them – require accurate and timely information. One of the key roles of the sales function in the planning process is the provision of such information. This will become clearer if we examine just some of the stages in the planning process where the sales function can make a valuable contribution. These stages include the following:

1 analysis of current market situation;
2 determining sales potential/sales forecasting;
3 generating and selecting strategies;
4 budgeting, implementation and control.

Analysis of current market situation

Its proximity to the marketplace places the sales function and its human resources in a unique position to contribute to the analysis of the current market situation facing the company. In particular, the sales function is often well placed to contribute to the analysis of customer needs and trends in purchasing behaviour. The sales manager can also make a valuable contribution with respect to knowledge about competitors and their standing in the marketplace. This informational role of the sales manager should not be ignored; through the salesforce he or she is ideally equipped to provide up-to-date accurate information based on feedback from customers.

Determining sales potential/sales forecasting

As we shall see in Chapter 15, an important responsibility of the sales manager is the preparation of sales forecasts for use in planning. Short-, medium- and long-term forecasts by the sales manager form the basis for allocating company resources in order to achieve anticipated sales.

Generating and selecting strategies

Although the final decision about the appropriate marketing strategies to adopt in the marketplace rests with marketing management, the sales manager must be prepared, and encouraged, to make an input to this decision. Once again, the sales function is ideally placed to comment on the appropriateness of any suggested strategies.

A point worth mentioning here is that the sales manager should actively encourage the sales staff to comment upon the appropriateness of company marketing strategies. Often the field salesforce can assess accurately how existing target markets will respond to company marketing initiatives.

Budgeting, implementation and control

The preparation of the sales forecast is a necessary prerequisite to the preparation of detailed plans. The sales forecast is also used in the preparation of the sales budget.

On the basis of the sales forecast, the sales manager must determine what level of expenditure will be required to achieve the forecasted level of sales. The important thing to remember about this budget is that it is the cornerstone of the whole budgeting procedure in a company. Not only the activities of the sales department, but also production, personnel, finance, and research and development will be affected by this budget. Because of this importance, sales budgets are considered in more detail in Chapter 16. At this stage it is sufficient to note that in preparing the sales budget the sales manager must prepare an outline of the essential sales activities required to meet the sales forecast, together with an estimate of their costs. The precise contents of the annual sales budget will vary between companies, but will normally include details of salaries, direct selling expenses, administrative costs and commissions and bonuses.

Having agreed the sales budget for the department, the sales manager must assume responsibility for its implementation and control. In preparing future plans, an important input is information on past performance against budget and, in particular, any differences between actual and budgeted results. Such 'budget variances', both favourable and unfavourable, should be analysed and interpreted by the sales manager as an input to the planning process. The reasons for budget variances should be reported, together with details of any remedial actions which were taken and their effects.

The influence of the marketing plan on sales activities: sales strategies and tactics

Any planning process is effective only to the extent that it influences action. An effective marketing planning system therefore influences activities, both strategic and tactical, throughout the company. Perhaps this influence is most clearly seen through decisions relating to the marketing programme or marketing mix.

Sales strategies are most directly influenced by planning decisions on the promotional element of the marketing mix. Here we will consider briefly the notion of a 'mix' of promotional tools, outlining the considerations in the choice of an appropriate mix and the implications for sales strategies. In particular, the important and often misunderstood relationship between advertising and selling is explained and discussed. We will conclude this section by examining briefly the nature of sales tactics.

The promotional mix

Earlier in this chapter we suggested that an important facet of marketing planning is the preparation of a marketing programme, the most important step in this preparation being the determination of the marketing mix – product, price, distribution and promotion. As selling is in fact only one element in the promotion part of this mix, it is therefore customary to refer to the **promotional mix** of a company.

This promotional mix (or, more correctly, the communications mix) is made up of four major elements:

1 advertising;
2 sales promotion;
3 publicity; and
4 personal selling.

In most companies all four can contribute to company sales, but a decision has to be made as to where to place the emphasis. This decision is made at the planning stage. In addition, it is important that the elements of the promotional mix work together to achieve company objectives, and an important planning task of management is the co-ordination of promotional activities.

Several factors influence the planning decision as to where to place the emphasis within the promotional mix. In some firms the emphasis is placed on the salesforce with most, if not all, of the promotional budget being devoted to this element of the mix. In others, advertising or sales promotion are seen as being much more efficient and productive than personal selling. Perhaps the most striking aspect of the various promotional tools is the extent to which they can be substituted, one for another. Companies within the same industry differ markedly in where they place the promotional emphasis. This makes it dangerous to be specific about developing the promotional mix within a particular company. As a guide, however, some of the more important factors influencing this decision are outlined below.

1 *Type of market*. In general, advertising and sales promotion play a more important role in the marketing of consumer products, whereas personal selling plays the major role in industrial marketing. The reasons for this stem from the differences between industrial and consumer marketing, which were outlined in Chapter 2, and are most obvious where we contrast the marketing

of fast-moving consumer goods (fmcg) with the marketing of often highly technical, expensive capital goods to industry. Despite this, it is a mistake to conclude – as is often done – that advertising does not have a role to play in the marketing of industrial products. Indeed, the potential contribution of advertising is often mistakenly undervalued by the sales personnel and discounted as a waste of valuable company resources. The relationship between advertising and sales is considered later in this chapter.

2 *Stage in the buying process.* In Chapter 2 it was suggested that for both industrial and consumer products it is useful to consider the stages which the prospective purchaser passes through en route to making a purchase decision. Although there are a number of ways in which this process may be conceptualised, essentially it consists of the potential purchaser moving from a position of being unaware of a company and/or its products, through to being convinced that the products or services of this company are the most appropriate to the buyer's needs. The sequential nature of this process is shown in Figure 3.3.

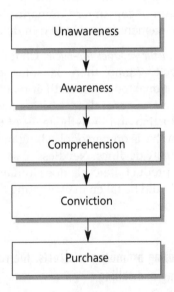

Figure 3.3   Stages in the buying process

Evidence suggests that, for a given outlay, advertising and publicity are more effective in the earlier stages of moving potential purchasers through from unawareness to comprehension. Personal selling, on the other hand, is more cost-effective than other forms of promotional activity at the conviction and purchase stages. This is not to suggest that 'cold calling' is not an important area of sales activity; however, as we shall see later, such cold calling is rendered much more effective if the customer is already aware of your company and its products.

3 *Push versus pull strategies.* One of the most important determinants in the choice of promotional mix is the extent to which a company decides to concentrate its efforts in terms of its channels of distribution. This can perhaps be best illustrated if we contrast a push strategy with that of a pull strategy.

- A **push strategy** is where the focus of marketing effort is aimed at pushing the product through the channel of distribution. The emphasis is on ensuring that wholesalers and retailers stock the product in question. The notion is that if channel members can be induced to stock a product they, in turn, will be active in ensuring that your product is brought to the attention of the final customer. In general a push strategy entails a much greater emphasis on personal selling and trade promotion in the promotional mix.
- A **pull strategy** relies much more heavily on advertising to promote the product to the final consumer. The essence of this approach is based on the notion that if sufficient consumer demand can be generated for a product this will result in final consumers asking retailers for the product. Retailers will then ask their wholesalers for the product, who will in turn contact the producer. In this way the product is 'pulled' through the channel by creating consumer demand via aggressive advertising. (Channel management is considered in detail in Chapter 9.)

4 *Stage in the product life-cycle.* Chapter 1 introduced the notion of the product life-cycle. Again there is some evidence to suggest that the different promotional tools vary in their relative effectiveness over the various stages of this cycle. In general, advertising and sales promotion are most effective in the introduction and growth stages of the life-cycle, whereas it is suggested that the emphasis on personal selling needs to increase as the market matures and eventually declines. Needless to say, although there is no doubt that the stage of the product life-cycle does influence the choice of marketing strategy, great care should be taken in evaluating the consequences of this influence for sales strategies.

Co-ordinating promotional efforts: the relationship between advertising and selling

In discussing the factors affecting the choice of promotional tools, it may have appeared that to some extent these tools are mutually exclusive – for example, one chooses to concentrate either on advertising or personal selling. This is not the case; the relationship between the various promotional tools, including personal selling, should be complementary and co-ordinated. Perhaps this rather obvious point would not need to be stressed were it not for the fact that often this complementary relationship is misunderstood. Nowhere is this misunderstanding more evident than in the relationship between advertising and selling.

It is an unfortunate fact that many sales managers and their salesforces believe that expenditure on advertising is a waste of company resources. Very rarely, they argue, does a customer ever purchase simply because a product is advertised, particularly where that customer is an industrial purchaser. Because of this, the argument continues, the money 'wasted' on advertising would be better spent where it will have a direct and immediate effect – on the salesforce. Increasingly, the evidence suggests that this notion that advertising money is wasted in industrial markets is misplaced. Among the functions that advertising can perform in such markets are the following:

1 Corporate advertising can help to build the reputation of a company and its products.
2 Advertising is particularly effective in creating awareness among prospective clients. The sales representative facing a prospect who is unaware of the company or product faces a much more difficult selling task than the representative who can build on an initial awareness.
3 Advertising can aid the sales representative in the marketing of new products by shouldering some of the burden of explaining new product features and building comprehension.
4 Advertising using return coupons may be used to open up new leads for the salesforce.

Overall, by far the greatest benefit of advertising in industrial markets is seen, not through a direct effect on sales revenue, but in the reduction of overall selling costs. Evidence suggests that, given adequate frequency, this reduction in selling costs to customers exposed to advertising may be as high as 30 per cent. Conversely, the non-advertiser may find itself at a serious disadvantage. The cost of selling to customers exposed to competitors' advertising may be increased by as much as 40 per cent.

In marketing consumer goods, **branding** and brand image are very important and advertising is generally thought to be the most effective promotion tool. However, personal selling and a well-trained salesforce can contribute significantly to increased market penetration by influencing stockists to allocate more shelf space to company products and persuading new dealers to stock them.

At all times, sales and advertising should be co-ordinated to achieve company objectives. It is important for sales personnel to be informed about company advertising campaigns. This advertising should be utilised in selling, the advertising theme being reinforced in the sales presentation.

From sales strategies to tactics

We have seen that a number of factors influence the setting for sales strategies. It was suggested that this influence is most direct in determining the relative emphasis to be given to sales activities in overall company and promotional strategy. Sales strategies are of course also influenced by the marketing and sales objectives specified in the marketing planning document. As an illustration, a marketing objective of increased market share may mean that the sales manager has to ensure that sales in the forthcoming year increase by 10 per cent. Further, the planning document should specify the route or strategy by which this objective will be accomplished, e.g. 'Additional sales effort is to be targeted on the opening of new accounts.' Sales objectives and strategies, therefore, also stem directly from the planning process, after consulation and agreement with relevant personnel.

Having agreed these strategic guidelines, a more detailed set of activities must be built into the planning process. The sales manager must determine the specific actions required to achieve sales goals, i.e. tactics.

Tactics encompass the day-to-day activities of the sales function in the achievement of marketing and sales objectives. Tactics also include actions which require to be taken in response to unexpected short-term events in the marketplace, for example a special promotional effort by a competitor. The relationship between objectives, strategies and tactics is shown in Figure 3.4.

Figure 3.4 The relationship between objectives, strategies and tactics

Tactical decisions represent what might be termed a 'fine tuning' of sales activities and encompass many of the decision areas covered in greater detail elsewhere in this text; for example, the deployment of sales personnel – territory design and planning (Chapter 14) – can be considered a tactical aspect of sales. Similarly, the design of incentive systems (Chapter 13) should form part of a tactical plan, designed to accomplish sales goals within the framework of sales strategies.

The importance of sound tactics should not be underestimated; even the best-formed strategies often fail for want of proper tactics. As an example of the use and importance of tactics in selling, we will consider briefly an aspect of purchasing which is of vital interest to many companies, namely brand/supplier loyalty.

Brand/supplier loyalty

If we examine the purchase of products and services over time, we find that often the purchasing sequence of individuals indicates that they repeatedly buy the same brand of a product, or, if the product is an industrial one, that they consistently buy from a particular supplier. For such individuals, if we imagine that the brand or supplier in question is called X, the purchasing sequence would be as shown below:

Purchase occasion	1	2	3	4	5	6
Brand purchased/supplier	X	X	X	X	X	X

There is no doubt that brand/supplier loyalty does exist. Moreover, the cultivation of such loyalty among customers often accounts for a significant part of tactical marketing and sales effort, representing, as it does, a substantial market asset to a company.

Before considering the part that sales tactics can play in this process of cultivating brand loyalty, it is important to explain precisely what is meant by brand loyalty. This apparently simple notion in fact gives rise to some misunderstanding.

Let us return to our purchasing sequence shown above. Although we have suggested that such a sequence is associated with a brand-loyal customer, the existence of such an array of purchases for a customer does not, of itself, constitute evidence that this customer *is* brand loyal. There are in fact a number of possible explanations for this purchasing behaviour. One such explanation might be the fact this customer concentrates much of his or her purchasing in one particular retail outlet and it so happens that this particular retail outlet only stocks brand X of this product, i.e. the customer exhibits loyalty, but to the store, rather than the brand. Another possible explanation is that this customer in fact pays little regard to the particular brand or supplier; he or she is not consciously brand loyal at all, but rather has simply slipped into the habit of purchasing this brand and cannot be bothered to switch. In this second example it is of course true to say that at least the customer must be reasonably satisfied with the brand being purchased consistently; presumably if this were not the case, or the customer became dissatisfied for any reason, he or she would then make the decision to switch. Nevertheless, this is not true brand loyalty.

True brand or supplier loyalty exists when customers make a conscious decision to concentrate their purchases on a particular brand, because they consider that supplier or brand superior to others. There may be a number of reasons/bases for such perceived superiority, e.g. superior quality, better delivery and after-sales services, the availability of credit, or some combination of these or other factors. In fact, in discussing the possible reasons for brand/supplier loyalty, we enter the realms of motives, perceptions, attitudes, etc. – complex behavioural areas discussed in the previous chapter.

The concept of brand/supplier loyalty therefore is a difficult one and care should be taken in interpreting the often conflicting evidence for its causes. Nevertheless, there are some indications that the salesperson can play a key role in helping to establish brand/supplier loyalty amongst a firm's customers. One of the reasons for this is that learning theory suggests that we have a tendency to repeat experiences that give us pleasure and to avoid those that do not.

Among the most powerful and lasting impressions that serve as a source of pleasure or displeasure in purchasing activities are the experiences in the face-to-face encounters with sales staff. Favourable attitudes and behaviour of sales personnel in dealing with their customers can contribute significantly to the creation of brand/supplier loyalty.

3.5 CONCLUSIONS

The framework for sales strategies and tactics has been established. We have seen that these are developed and operated within the framework of marketing planning. The sales function makes a valuable contribution to the establishment of marketing plans, providing, as it does, key data on customers, markets, competitors, sales forecasts and budgets. In turn, selling activities are directly influenced by decisions taken at the marketing planning stage.

We have looked at planning decisions for the marketing programme or marketing mix and, specifically, at the promotional mix in a company. Factors such as type of product market, steps in the buying process, push versus pull strategies and stage in the product life-cycle have all been shown to influence promotional and therefore sales strategies.

Finally, we looked at sales tactics, the relationship between advertising and selling, and the important area of brand/supplier loyalty. It was shown that advertising plays a key role in aiding the sales effort, reducing selling costs and easing the sales task. Brand/supplier-loyal customers are a valuable asset to any company and the salesforce is central to the establishment and maintenance of such customer loyalty.

PRACTICAL EXERCISE

Auckland Engineering plc

Jim Withey, sales manager for Auckland Engineering plc, a well-established engineering company based in the Midlands, had been contemplating the memo he had received two days earlier from his newly appointed marketing director:

Memo
To: J Withey, sales manager
From: D C Duncan, marketing director
Date: 16 January 2000
Subject: Preparation of annual marketing plan

You will recall that, at our series of preliminary meetings to discuss future marketing plans for the company, I suggested that I was unhappy with the seemingly haphazard approach to planning. Accordingly, you will recall it was agreed between departmental heads that each would undertake to prepare a formal input to next month's planning meeting.

At this stage I am not seeking detailed plans for each product market, rather I am concerned that you give some thought to how your department can contribute to the planning process. Being new to the company and its product/markets, I am not entirely up to date on what has been happening to the market for our products, although as we all know our market share at 35 per cent is down on last year. I would particularly like to know what information your department could contribute to the analysis of the situation.

To help you in your own analysis I have summarised below what I feel came out of our first planning meetings.

● *Business definition* It was agreed that the business needs redefining in customer terms. An appropriate definition for our company would be as follows: 'Solutions to engine component design and manufacturing problems.'

● *Strengths, weaknesses, opportunities and threats*, i.e. SWOT analysis.
The main *strengths* of our company are as follows:
– We have excellent customer awareness and an image of reliability and quality.
– Our salesforce is technically well qualified.
– Our manufacturing flexibility is second to none. We can respond quickly and effectively to individual customer needs.
Our main *weaknesses* are as follows:
– Our prices are approximately 10 per cent above the industry average.
– We are spending a far higher proportion of our turnover on advertising than some of our main competitors.
– Our salesforce is not skilled in generating new leads.
Major *opportunities* are as follows:
– Some of our major competitors are having difficulty keeping their customers because of quality and delivery problems. Buyers in the industry seem particularly prone to switching their suppliers.
– Recent legislation in the industry means that our research and development programme on the new TDIX component, with its emphasis on lower exhaust emission levels, should prove advantageous.
– Recent and forecast trends in the exchange rate should help our export marketing efforts.
Major *threats* are shown below:
– Our largest customer is threatening to switch to another supplier because of our higher average prices.
– Apart from the TDIX programme, we have not been keeping pace with the rapid technological change in the industry.
– Some of our major export markets are threatened by the possibility of import restrictions.

- *Objectives.*
  Financial.
  – To increase our return on capital employed by 5 per cent after taxes.
  – Our net profit in the forthcoming year to be £3.0 million.
  Marketing.
  – Sales revenue to be increased to £24 million in the forthcoming year.

- *Marketing strategy.*
  Target markets.
  – Major manufacturers of diesel engines world-wide.
  Positioning.
  – Highest engineering quality and after-sales service in the supply of specialist low-volume diesel engine components.

I would of course welcome your comments on my analysis of the situation, together with your views on the appropriateness of the objectives I have set.

In addition, for the next meeting I suggest that as sales manager you give some thought as to where the relative emphasis should be placed in our promotional effort. As I have already mentioned in my summary of our preliminary meetings, we seem to be spending an excessive amount on advertising compared with our competitors. Perhaps you could appraise me of your thoughts on this, as I understand that you were instrumental in raising our advertising budget from 3 per cent to 5 per cent of our turnover last year. As you are well aware, from a limited budget we must decide where to place the relative emphasis in our promotional mix. Perhaps you would indicate what you feel are the major considerations in this decision.

DISCUSSION QUESTIONS

1 Give a brief outline of the ways in which you as sales manager can contribute to the marketing planning process at Auckland Engineering.

2 Looking at Mr Duncan's analysis of your previous meetings, what issues/problems do you see which are of particular relevance to the activities of the sales-force?

3 How would you respond to Mr Duncan's comments on the promotional mix and, in particular, to his comments about the level of advertising expenditure?

4 What is the point in conducting a SWOT analysis?

EXAMINATION QUESTIONS

1 Explain the differences between marketing strategies and sales strategies.

2 What is the relationship between objectives, strategies and tactics?

3 Discuss the component parts of the communications mix.

Part Two

SALES TECHNIQUE

SALES RESPONSIBILITIES AND PREPARATION

OBJECTIVES   After studying this chapter, you should be able to:

1 Itemise sales responsibilities.
2 Evaluate sources of sales prospects.
3 Take a systematic approach to keeping customer records.
4 Understand the importance of self-management in selling.
5 Assess what preparation is needed prior to selling.
6 Understand the art of negotiation.
7 Plan individual sales interviews.

KEY CONCEPTS
- complaint handling
- preparation
- presentation planning
- prospecting
- sales cycle
- sales negotiation

4.1   SALES RESPONSIBILITIES

The *primary* responsibility of a salesperson is to conclude a sale successfully. This task will involve the identification of customer needs, presentation and demonstration, negotiation, handling objections and closing the sale. These skills are discussed in detail in Chapter 5. In order to generate sales successfully, a number of *secondary* functions are also carried out by most salespeople. Although termed secondary, they are vital to long-term sales success. These are

- prospecting
- maintaining customer records and information feedback
- self-management
- handling complaints
- providing service.

Salespeople are also responsible for implementing sales and marketing strategies. This issue will be considered later in this chapter.

Prospecting

Prospecting is the searching for and calling upon customers who, hitherto, have not purchased from the company. This activity is not of uniform importance across all branches of selling. It is obviously far more important in industrial selling than retail selling; for example, a salesperson of office equipment may call upon many new potential customers, whereas a furniture salesperson is unlikely to search out new prospects – they come to him/her as a result of advertising and, perhaps, high street location.

A problem sometimes associated with salespeople who have worked for the same company for many years is that they rely on established customers to provide repeat orders rather than actively seeking new business. Certainly, it is usually more comfortable for the salesperson to call upon old contacts, but the nature of much industrial selling is that, because product life is long, sustained sales growth depends upon searching out and selling to new customers.

Sources of prospects

1 *Existing customers.* This is a highly effective method of generating prospects and yet tends to be under-used by many. A wealth of new prospects can be obtained simply by asking satisfied customers if they know of anyone who may have a need for the kinds of products or services being sold. This technique has been used successfully in life insurance and industrial selling but has applications in many other areas also.

  Having obtained the names of potential customers, the salesperson, if appropriate, can ask the customer if he/she may use the customer's name as a reference. The use of reference selling in industrial marketing can be highly successful since it reduces the perceived risk for a potential buyer.

2 *Trade directories.* A reliable trade directory such as *Kompass* or *Dunn and Bradstreet* can prove useful in identifying potential industrial buyers. The *Kompass* directory, for example, is organised by industry and location and provides such potentially useful information as

- name, address and telephone number of companies;
- names of board members;
- size of firm, by turnover and number of employees;
- type of products manufactured or distributed.

  For trade selling, the *Retail Directory* provides information regarding potential customers, organised by various types of retail outlet. Thus a salesperson selling a product suitable for confectioners and newsagents could use the listing of such retailers under the CTN heading (confectioners, tobacconists and newsagents) to obtain relevant names, addresses, telephone numbers and, also, an indication of size through the information given regarding number of branches.

3 *Inquiries.* Inquiries may arise as a natural consequence of conducting business. Satisfied customers may by word of mouth create inquiries from 'warm'

prospects. Many companies stimulate inquiries, however, by advertising (many industrial advertisements use coupon return to stimulate leads), direct mail and exhibitions. This source of prospects is an important one and the salesperson should respond promptly. The inquirer may have an urgent need seeking a solution and may turn to the competition if faced with a delay. Even if the customer's problem is not so urgent, slow response may foster unfavourable attitudes towards the salesperson and his/her company's products.

The next priority is to screen out those inquiries which are unlikely to result in a sale. A telephone call has the advantage of giving a personalised response, and yet is relatively inexpensive and not time-consuming. It can be used to check how serious the inquiry is and to arrange a personal visit should the inquiry prove to have potential. This process of checking leads to establish their potential is known as *qualifying*.

4 *The press*. Perhaps under-used as a source of prospects, the press is nevertheless important. Advertisements and articles can give clues to potential new sources of business. Articles may reveal diversification plans which may mean a company suddenly becomes a potential customer; advertisements for personnel may reveal plans for expansion, again suggesting potential new business.

5 *Cold canvassing*. This method involves calling on every prospect who might have a need for the salesperson's product. A brush salesperson, for example, may attempt to call upon every house in a village. A variant of this method is the 'cool canvass', where only certain groups of people are canvassed, i.e. those who are more likely to buy since they possess some qualifying feature; for example, only companies over a certain size may be judged viable prospects. Calling cold on big company buyers is unlikely to be successful, however. A more effective approach is to send a letter in advance explaining the business the company is in, followed by a call to make an appointment (Lee, 1984).

Customer records and information feedback

A systematic approach to customer record-keeping is to be recommended to all repeat-call salespeople. An industrial salesperson should record the following information:

1 Name and address of company
2 Name and position of contact(s)
3 Nature of business
4 Date and time of interview
5 Assessment of potential
6 Buyer needs, problems and buying habits
7 Past sales with dates
8 Problems/opportunities encountered
9 Future actions on the part of salesperson (and buyer).

Record cards should be provided by management and salespeople encouraged to use them as part of the sales plan before each visit.

Salespeople should also be encouraged to send back to head office information which is relevant to the marketing of company products. Test market activity by competition, news of imminent product launches, rumours of policy changes on the part of trade and industrial customers and competitors, and feedback on company achievement regarding product performance, delivery and after-sales service are just some of the kinds of information that may be useful to management.

Self-management

This aspect of the sales job is of particular importance since a salesperson is often working alone with the minimum of personal supervision. A salesperson may have to organise his or her own call plan. This involves dividing territory into sections to be covered day by day and deciding the best route to follow between calls. Often it makes sense to divide a territory into segments radiating outwards, from the salesperson's home at the centre. Each segment is designed to be small enough to be covered by the salesperson during one day's work.

Many salespeople believe that the most efficient routing plan involves driving out to the furthest customer and, then zig-zagging back to home base. However it can be shown that adopting a round-trip approach will usually result in lower mileage. Such considerations are important with respect to efficiency, as an alarming amount of time can be spent on the road as opposed to face-to-face with buyers. A survey conducted on behalf of the Institute of Marketing into selling practice in the UK (PA Consultants, 1979) found that, on average, only 20–30 per cent of a salesperson's normal working day is spent face-to-face with customers. Although this study was conducted over 20 years ago, matters have not improved since then. In fact, this figure is now nearer 20 per cent rather than 30 because salespeople are increasingly called upon to carry out ancillary work such as customer surveys, service work and merchandising. Some companies take this responsibility out of the salesperson's hands and produce daily worksheets showing who is to be called on and in what order.

Another factor which may be the responsibility of the salesperson is deciding on call frequency. It is sensible to grade customers according to potential. For example, consumer durable salesmen may categorise the retail outlets they are selling to into A, B and C grades. A grade outlets may be visited every fortnight, B grade every month and C grade once every three months. The principle applies to all kinds of selling, however, and may be left to the salesperson's discretion or organised centrally as part of the sales management function. The danger of delegating responsibility to salespeople is that the criteria used to decide frequency of visit are 'friendliness with the buyer' or 'ease of sale' rather than sales potential. On the other hand, it can be argued that a reponsible salesperson is in the best position to decide how much time needs to be spent with each customer.

Handling complaints

Dealing with complaints may seem, at first, to be a time-consuming activity which diverts a salesperson from the primary task of generating sales. A marketing orientation for a salesforce, however, dictates that the goal of an organisation is to create customer satisfaction in order to generate profit. When dissatisfaction identifies itself in the form of a complaint, this necessary condition for long-term survival is clearly not being met.

Complaints vary in their degree of seriousness and in the authority which the salesperson holds in order to deal with them. No matter how trivial the complaint may seem, the complainant should be treated with respect and the matter dealt with seriously. In a sense, dealing with complaints is one of the after-the-sale services provided by suppliers. It is therefore part of the mix of benefits a company offers its customers, although it differs in essence since the initial objective is to minimise its necessity. Nevertheless, the ability of the salesperson to empathise with the customer and his or her problem and to react sympathetically can create considerable goodwill and help foster long-term relationships.

With this in mind, many companies give the customer the benefit of the doubt when this does not involve high cost, even though they suspect that the fault may be caused by inappropriate use of the product on the part of the customer; for example, garden fork manufacturers may replace prematurely broken forks, even though the break may have been caused by work for which the fork was not designed.

When the salesperson does not have the authority to deal with the complaint immediately, his or her job is to submit the relevant information in written form to head office so that the matter can be taken further.

Providing service

Salespeople are in an excellent position to provide a 'consultancy' service to their customers. Since they meet many customers each year, they become familiar with solutions to common problems. Thus an industrial salesperson may be able to advise customers on improving productivity or cutting costs. Indeed, the service element of industrial selling is often incorporated into the selling process itself, e.g. computer salespeople may offer to conduct an analysis of customer requirements and produce a written report in order to complete a sale. The salesperson who learns solutions to common problems and provides useful advice to his or her customers builds an effective barrier to competitive attacks and strengthens buyer–seller relationships.

Another area where salespeople provide service is in trade selling. They may be called upon to set up in-store displays and other promotions for wholesalers and retailers. Some companies employ people to do this on a full-time basis. These people are called merchandisers and their activities provide support to traditional salespeople, who can thus spend more time selling.

Customer service in retailing

At Richer Sounds, the UK-based audio chain, customer service begins when potential customers enter the door. Salespeople are trained to acknowledge customers by asking casually 'Are you OK there?' or 'Are you happy browsing, sir/madam?' The purpose is not to sell them anything but to let customers know that the salesperson is aware of their presence and that they can contact him/her when they are ready. A sign over the door says 'browsers welcome' and they mean it – without the fear of being hassled by salespeople.

Customers should not be pre-judged. The same quality of service must be provided to customers who are shabbily dressed, pompous, flashy, aggressive, rude or boring. The whole selling operation should be transparent. There should be no pressure, no trying to disguise a poor product and no catches. Salespeople should be honest and if they do not have the right information should reply, 'I'm sorry I don't know but I shall try to find out'.

Sometimes it is not possible to make a sale because the product in question is not stocked. The salesperson should still provide a service by advising the customer where they might get it. Argos and Tandy catalogues are held for this purpose. Quite often customers will stop and think before they walk out to see if they can buy something as a mark of appreciation.

Richer Sounds advocate the policy of 'under-promise, over-deliver'. Overpromising can ruin long-term relationships so their salespeople never promise customers 'the moon' just to make a sale.

Even though Richer Sounds tries hard to give 100 per cent customer service, complaints are bound to happen. They even encourage them. They recognise that every disgruntled customer on average tells 20 people about it. By receiving complaints they have the chance to put things right and learn from their mistakes. A short, tear-off questionnaire is included with receipts. The questionnaire covers eight points including the customer's assessment of the quality of the service they have received, and there is space for comments. An after-sales service questionnaire which asks only four questions is also used to monitor service and invite complaints.

Salespeople should not change their customer focus once the sale is made: the service should be followed through until the customer is out of the shop. Salespeople should thank them for their custom, give them their name to contact if there are any problems, and perhaps help them to the car. If the customer is uncertain about their purchase they will be told that the salesperson will call them after a few days to check that they are happy with the product.

Based on Richer, J. (1995) 'The Richer Way', EMAP Business Communications.

Retail salespeople also provide customer service. Selling audio equipment, for example, is an opportunity to help the customer to make the correct choice for a given budget. Richer Sounds is a UK-based chain of audio stores that prides itself on good customer service. The accompanying case history on p. 90 illustrates some of the techniques of providing exceptional customer service.

Salespeople may also be called upon to provide after-sales service to customers. Sales engineers may be required to give advice on the operation of a newly acquired machine or provide assistance in the event of a breakdown. Sometimes they may be able to solve the problem themselves, while in other cases they will call in technical specialists to deal with the problem.

Implementing sales and marketing strategies

The salesforce is also charged with the responsibility of implementing sales and marketing strategies designed by management. Misunderstandings regarding strategy can have grave implications. For example, the credibility of a premium price and high quality position in the marketplace can be seriously undermined by a salesforce too eager to give large price discounts. The solution might be to decide discount structure at managerial level (both sales and marketing management will have an input to this decision) based upon the price sensitivity of various market segments. The salesforce would then be told the degree to which price could be discounted for each class of customer. In this way the product's positioning strategy would remain intact while allowing the salesforce some discretion to discount when required.

Successful implementation can mean the difference between winning or losing new accounts. An effective method of gaining an account in the face of entrenched competition is the **diversion**. The aim is to distract a rival into concentrating its efforts on defending one account (and therefore neglecting another). The following Selling and Sales Management case history provides a true account of how a salesperson for a computer company diverted a well-entrenched rival to defend an account (The Bank) in order to win another (The Insurance Company).

In this example, the stakes and costs were high. The management at A believed that the cost of loaning a £1 million computer to The Bank was justified (*a*) by a strategically important penetration of a major market, and (*b*) by the potential profit to be gained by selling to The Insurance Company. This was a managerial decision and was obviously dependent on judgement, but the example shows the principle of using 'diversion' as a method of winning major accounts.

4.2 PREPARATION

The ability to think on one's feet is of great benefit to salespeople, since they will be required to modify their sales presentation to suit the particular needs and problems of their various customers and to respond quickly to unusual objections and awkward questions. However, there will be much to be gained by careful **preparation** of the selling task. Some customers will have similar problems; some questions and objections will be raised repeatedly. A

The Diversion

In 1993, a computer company (A) was seeking its first high-profile installation in a major European city. A successful breakthrough sale was believed to be strategically important. It was considering two prospective customers: 'The Bank' and 'The Insurance Company'.

At The Bank, a rival computer company (B) was entrenched. Using a network of contacts, A's salesperson did a thorough reconnaissance. He discovered that B's salesperson at The Bank was deeply entrenched through good service and effective relationship building. The conclusion was that the situation for A was hopeless. However, The Bank's information technology manager opined that if A offered them a free computer (£1 million) The Bank would 'have to consider their offer'.

The Insurance Company was a customer of a third computer company (C) and company B. A's sales manager had senior contacts at The Insurance Company and found them dissatisfied with C, approaching a capacity shortage which would force the purchase of a large computer (likely to be over £10 million). The problem was that B was well respected by The Insurance Company. Also the same salesperson from B serviced both The Bank and The Insurance Company accounts. Fortunately, B's salesperson had not called upon The Insurance Company recently. The task: to perpetuate B's absence. To accomplish it, the 'diversion strategy' was used.

A called at The Bank and offered a computer 'free for a year' and made an occasional follow-up call, while selling diligently (but quietly) at The Insurance Company. The ensuing flap at The Bank was quite spectacular. The switching costs associated with A's complete replacement of B would have been significant, and so The Bank began to ask a lot of questions about switch-over plans and arrangements. (It was rumoured that B's salesperson was staying awake at night composing new questions that The Bank might ask of A!) In the face of these questions A's salesperson responded deliberately (after all, he was spending most of his time selling at The Insurance Company). The struggle at The Bank raged on with A's credibility relentlessly eroded by B's clever and determined defence.

In due course, B's sales team was successful in their defence of The Bank account. However, their gratification was dimmed by the news that A had won a larger order (£10 million) at The Insurance Company.

sales-person can therefore usefully spend time considering how best to respond to these recurring situations.

Within this section attention will be given to preparation not only for the selling task, in which there is little or no scope for the salesperson to bargain with the buyer, but also for where selling may involve a degree of negotiation between buyer and seller. In many selling situations, buyers and sellers may negotiate price, timing of delivery, product extras, payment and credit terms, and trade-in values. These will be termed *sales negotiations*. In others, the salesperson may have no scope for such discussions; in essence the product is offered on a take-it-or-leave-it basis. Thus, the salesperson of bicycles to dealers may have a set price list and delivery schedule with no authority to deviate from them. This will be termed *pure selling*.

Preparation for pure selling and sales negotiations

A number of factors can be examined in order to improve the chances of sales success in both sales negotiations and pure selling.

Product knowledge and benefits

Knowledge of product features is insufficient for sales success. Because people buy products for the benefits they confer, successful salespeople relate product features to consumer benefits; product features are the means by which benefits are derived. The way to do this is to look at products from the customer's point of view. Table 4.1 shows a few examples.

Table 4.1   Product features and customer benefits

Product feature	Customer benefit
Retractable nib on ballpoint pen	Reduces chances of damage
High rev. speed on spin dryer	Clothes are dried more thoroughly
High reach on forklift truck	Greater use of warehouse space
Stream-feeding (photocopiers)	Faster copying
Automatic washing machine	More time to spend on doing other less mundane activities

By analysing the products they are selling in this way, salespeople will communicate in terms which are meaningful to buyers and therefore be more convincing. In industrial selling, the salesperson may be called upon to be an adviser or consultant who is required to provide solutions to problems. In some cases this may involve a fairly deep understanding of the nature of the customer's business, in order to be able to appreciate the problems fully and to suggest the most appropriate solution. Thus the salesperson must not only know his or her products' benefits but the types of situation in which each would be appropriate. In computer selling, for example, successful selling requires an appreciation of which system is most appropriate given customer needs and resources. This may necessitate a careful examination of customer needs through a survey conducted by the seller. Sometimes the costs of the survey will be paid for by the prospective customer, later to be subtracted from the cost of the equipment should an order result.

Preparation of sales benefits should not result in an inflexible sales approach. Different customers have different needs which implies they seek different benefits from products they buy. One high-earning salesperson of office equipment attributed his success to the preparation he conducted before every sales visit; this involved knowing his product's capabilities, understanding his client's needs, and matching these together by getting his wife to test him every evening and at the weekend (Kennedy *et al.*, 1980).

Knowledge of competitors' products and their benefits

Knowledge of competitive products offers several advantages:

● It allows a salesperson to offset the strengths of competitors' products, which may be mentioned by potential buyers, against their weaknesses. For example, a buyer might say 'Competitor X's product offers cheaper maintenance costs,' to which a salesperson might reply 'Yes, but these cost savings are small compared to the fuel savings you get with our machine.'
● In industrial selling sales engineers may work with a buying organisation in order to solve a technical problem. This may result in a product specification being drawn up in which the sales engineers may have an influence. It is obviously to their benefit that the specification reflects the strengths and capabilities of their products rather than the competition. Thus knowledge of competitive strengths and weaknesses will be an advantage in this situation.

Competitive information can be gleaned from magazines, e.g. *Which?*, sales catalogues and price lists, from talking to buyers and from direct observation, e.g. of prices in supermarkets. It makes sense to keep such information on file for quick reference. Vauxhall gives its salespeople a brief with a résumé of the strengths and weaknesses of its car range, along with those of its competitors.

Sales presentation planning

Although versatility, flexibility and the ability to 'think on one's feet' are desirable attributes, there are considerable advantages to **presentational planning**:

1 The salesperson is less likely to forget important consumer benefits associated with each product within the range he or she is selling.
2 The use of visual aids and demonstrations can be planned into the presentation at the most appropriate time to reinforce the benefit the salesperson is communicating.
3 It builds confidence in the salesperson, particularly the newer, less-experienced, that he/she is well equipped to do the job efficiently and professionally.
4 Possible objections and questions can be anticipated and persuasive counter-arguments prepared. Many salespeople who, to an outsider, seem naturally quick-witted have developed this skill through careful preparation beforehand, imagining themselves as buyers and thinking of objections that they might raise if they were in such a position. For example, many price objections can be countered by reference to higher product quality, greater durability, high productivity and lower offsetting life-cycle costs, e.g. lower maintenance, fuel or human resources costs.

Setting sales objectives

The essential skill in setting call objectives is to phrase them in terms of what the salesperson wants the customer to do rather than what the salesperson will do. The type of objective set may depend upon the **sales cycle** of the product and the stage reached in that cycle with a prospective customer.

The sales cycle refers to the time that can reasonably be expected to pass before an order is concluded. With many retail sales this is short; often, unless a sale is concluded during the first visit, the customer will buy elsewhere. In this situation it is reasonable to set a sales close objective. With capital goods, like aeroplanes, gas turbines and oil rigs, the sales cycle is very long, perhaps running into years. Clearly, to set a sales objective in terms of closing the sale is inappropriate. For producers with longer sales cycles, sensible objectives may be:

- for the customer to define clearly what his or her requirements are;
- to have the customer visit the production site;
- to have the customer try the product, e.g. fly on an aircraft;
- to have the customer compare the product versus competitive products in terms of measurable performance criteria, e.g. for pile driving equipment this might be the number of metres driven per hour.

The temptation, when setting objectives, is to determine them in terms of what the salesperson will do. An adhesive salesperson may decide that the objective of the visit to a buyer is to demonstrate the ease of application and adhesive properties of a new product. While this demonstration may be a valuable and necessary part of the sales presentation, it is not the ultimate goal of the visit. This may be to have the customer test the product over a four-week period, or to order a quantity for immediate use.

Understanding buyer behaviour

The point was made in Chapter 2 that many organisational buying decisions are complex, involving many people whose evaluative criteria may differ, and that the purchasing officer may play a minor role in deciding which supplier to choose, particularly with very expensive items.

The practical implication of these facts is that careful preparation may be necessary for industrial salespeople, either when selling to new companies or when selling to existing customers where the nature of the product is different. In both situations, time taken trying to establish who the key influencers and decision-makers are will be well rewarded. In different companies there may be different key people, e.g. secretaries (office stationery), production engineers (lathes), design engineers (components), managing directors (computers), so the salesperson needs to be aware of the real need to treat each organisation individually.

Other practical information which a salesperson can usefully collect includes the name and position of each key influencer and decision-maker, the times most suitable for interview, the types of competitive products previously purchased by the buying organisation, and any threats to a successful sale or special opportunities afforded by the situation. Examples in the last category would include personal prejudices held by key people against the salesperson, his company, or its products, while positive factors might include common interests which could form the basis of a rapport with the buyer, or favourable experiences with other types of products sold by the salesperson's company.

Preparation for sales negotiations

In addition to the factors outlined in the previous section, a sales negotiator will benefit by paying attention to the following additional factors during preparation.

Assessment of the balance of power

In the **sales negotiation**, seller and buyer will each be expecting to conclude a deal which is favourable to themselves. The extent to which each is successful will depend upon their negotiating skills and the balance of power between the parties. This balance will be determined by four key factors:

1 *The number of options available to each party*. If a buyer has only one option – to buy from the seller in question – then that seller is in a powerful position. If the seller, in turn, is not dependent on the buyer, but has many attractive potential customers for the products, then again he or she is in a strong position. Conversely, when a buyer has many potential sources of supply, and a seller has few potential customers, the buyer should be able to extract a good deal. Many buyers will deliberately contact a number of potential suppliers to strengthen their bargaining position.

2 *The quantity and the quality of information held by each party*. ('Knowledge is power' – Machiavelli.) If a buyer has access to a seller's cost structure then he or she is in a powerful position to negotiate a cheaper price, or at least avoid paying too high a price. If a seller knows how much a buyer is willing to pay, then their power position is improved.

3 *Need recognition and satisfaction*. The greater the salesperson's understanding of the needs of the buyer and the more capable he or she is of satisfying those needs, the stronger will be the bargaining position. In some industrial marketing situations, suppliers work with buying organisations to solve technical problems in the knowledge that to do so will place them in a very strong negotiating position. The more the buyer believes that his or her needs can be satisfied by only one company, the weaker is the buyer's negotiating stance. In effect, the seller has reduced the buyer's number of options by uniquely satisfying these needs.

4 *The pressures on the parties*. Where a technical problem is of great importance to a buying organisation, its visibility high and its solution difficult, any

supplier who can solve it will gain immense bargaining power. If, on the other hand, there are pressures on the salesperson, perhaps because of low sales returns, then a buyer should be able to extract extremely favourable terms during negotiations in return for purchasing from him or her.

The implications of these determinants of the balance of power are that before negotiations (and, indeed, during them) salespeople will benefit by assessing the relative strength of their power base. This implies that they need information. If the seller knows the number of companies who are competing for the order, their likely stances, the criteria used by the buying organisation when deciding between them, the degree of pressure on key members of the decision-making unit, and any formula they might use for assessing price acceptability, an accurate assessment of the power balance should be possible.

This process should lessen the chances of pricing too low or of needlessly giving away other concessions like favourable payment terms. Judicious negotiators will at this stage look to the future to assess likely changes in the balance of power. Perhaps power lies with the supplier now, but overpowering or 'negotiating too sweet a deal' might provoke retribution later when the buyer has more suppliers from which to choose.

Determination of negotiating objectives

It is prudent for negotiators to set objectives during the preparation stage. This reduces the likelihood of being swayed by the heat of the negotiating battle and of accepting a deal which, with hindsight, should have been rejected. This process is analogous to a buyer at an auction paying more than he or she can afford because they allow themselves to be swept along by the bidding. Additionally, when negotiation is conducted by a team, discussion of objectives helps co-ordination and unity.

It is useful to consider two types of objectives (Kennedy *et al.*, 1980):

1 *'Must have' objectives*. The 'must have' objectives define a bargainer's minimum requirements; for example, the minimum price at which a seller is willing to trade. This determines the negotiating breakpoint.
2 *'Would like' objectives*. These are the maximum a negotiator can reasonably expect to get; for example, the highest price a seller feels he or she can realistically obtain. This determines the opening positions of buyers and sellers.

When considering 'must have' objectives it is useful to consider one's BATNA – Best Alternative to a Negotiated Agreement' (Fisher and Ury, 1991). This involves the identification of one's alternative if agreement cannot be reached. It sets a standard against which any offer can be assessed, and guards against accepting unfavourable terms when pressured by a more powerful buyer.

Figure 4.2 describes a negotiating scenario where a deal is possible since there is overlap between the highest price the buyer is willing to pay (buyer's 'must have' objective) and the lowest price the seller is willing to accept (seller's 'must

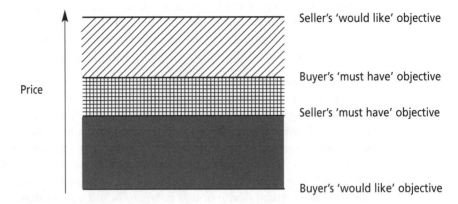

Figure 4.1 A negotiating scenario
(Adapted from Winkler, 1996)

have' objective). The price actually agreed will depend upon the balance of power between the two parties and their respective negotiating skills.

Concession analysis

Since negotiation implies movement in order to achieve agreement, it is likely that concessions will be made by at least one party during the bargaining process. Preparation can aid negotiators by analysing the kinds of concession which might be offered to the other side. The key to this concession analysis is to value concessions the seller might be prepared to make through the eyes of the buyer. By doing this it may be possible to identify concessions which cost the seller very little and yet be highly valued by the buyer. For example, to offer much quicker delivery than is usual may cost a seller very little because of spare capacity, but if this is highly valued by the buyer the seller may be able to trade it in return for a prompt payment agreement.

Below are listed the kinds of issue that may be examined during concession analysis:

● Price.
● Timing of delivery.
● The product – its specification, optional extras.
● The price – ex works price, price at the buyer's factory gate, installation price, in-service price.
● Payment – on despatch, on receipt, in working order, credit terms.
● Trade-in terms, e.g. cars.

The aim of concession analysis is to ensure that nothing which has value to the buyer is given away freely during negotiations. A skilful negotiator will attempt to trade concession for concession so that ultimately an agreement which satisfies both parties is reached.

Proposal analysis

A further sensible activity during the preparation stage is to estimate the proposals and demands the buyer is likely to make during the course of negotiation, and the seller's reaction to them. This is analogous to the anticipation of objections in pure selling – it helps when quick decisions have to be made in the heat of the negotiation.

It is also linked to concession analysis, for when a buyer makes a proposal, e.g. favourable credit terms, he or she is really asking the seller to grant a concession. The skilful salesperson will ask for a concession in return – perhaps a less onerous delivery schedule. By anticipating the kinds of proposals the buyer is likely to make, the seller can plan the kinds of counter-proposals he or she wishes to make. In some situations, the appropriate response may be the 'concession close' (see Chapter 5).

4.3 CONCLUSIONS

This chapter has examined the responsibilities of salespeople, i.e. to gain sales, to prospect for new customers, to maintain customer records and provide information feedback, to manage their work, to handle complaints, and to provide service.

An important element in managing their work is preparation, this being examined in detail. A distinction is made between sales negotiations, where a certain amount of bargaining may take place, and pure selling, where the salesperson is given no freedom to bargain. The following are important in preparation:

1 product knowledge and customer benefits;
2 knowledge of competitors' products and their benefits;
3 sales presentation planning;
4 setting sales and negotiation objectives;
5 understanding buyer behaviour;
6 assessing the power balance;
7 concession analysis;
8 proposal analysis.

The next chapter, on personal selling skills, considers how to use this preparation in the actual selling situation.

PRACTICAL EXERCISE

The O'Brien Company

The O'Brien Company manufactures and markets a wide range of luggage including suitcases, handbags and briefcases. The company is organised into two divisions – consumer and industrial. The consumer division sells mainly through retail outlets whereas the industrial division markets direct to companies, who buy luggage (especially briefcases) for use by their executives.

You have recently been appointed as a salesperson for the industrial division and have been asked to visit a new potential client with a view to selling him briefcases. The potential customer is Brian Forbes, the managing director (and owner) of a medium-sized engineering company in the Midlands with subsidiaries in Manchester, Leeds and Bristol. They employ a salesforce of twenty men selling copper piping. In addition, it is estimated that the company employs around forty marketing, personnel, production and accountancy executives.

The O'Brien Company markets two ranges of executive briefcase. One is made from good quality plastic, with imitation hide lining. It is available in black only and is priced at £25 for the lockable version and £22 for the non-lockable type. The other de-luxe range is manufactured from leather and real hide and is priced at £95. Colours available are black, brown, dark blue and claret. Additional features are a number-coded locking device, a variable depth feature which allows the briefcase to be expanded from its usual 87.5 mm to 137.5 mm, individual gilt initialling on each briefcase, an ink-resistant interior compartment for pens, and three pockets inside the lid to take different sized papers/documents. The plastic version has only the last of these features and is 75 mm in depth.

Quantity discounts for both ranges are as follows:

Quantity	Reduction
10–19	2%
20–39	3%
40–79	4%
80 or more	6%

Very little is known about Brian Forbes or his company apart from the information already given. However, by chance, an acquaintance of yours who works as a salesperson for a machine tool company visited Mr Forbes earlier in the year.

DISCUSSION QUESTIONS

1 What are your sales objectives? What extra information would be useful?

2 Prepare a sales presentation for the briefcases.

3 Prepare a list of possible objections and your responses to them.

EXAMINATION QUESTIONS

1 What considerations should be taken into account when deciding on the amount of prospecting a salesperson should do?

2 Discuss the contribution of preparation to the selling process.

CHAPTER 5

PERSONAL SELLING SKILLS

OBJECTIVES   After studying this chapter, you should be able to:

1 Distinguish the various phases of the selling process.

2 Apply different questions to different selling situations.

3 Understand what is involved in the presentation and the demonstration.

4 Know how to deal with buyers' objections.

5 Understand and apply the art of negotiation.

6 Close a sale.

KEY CONCEPTS
- buying signals
- closing the sale
- demonstrations
- needs analysis
- negotiation

- objections
- personal selling skills
- reference selling
- sales presentation
- trial close

The basic philosophy underlying the approach to personal selling adopted in this book is that selling should be an extension of the marketing concept. This implies that, for long-term survival, it is in the best interests of the salesperson and his or her company to identify customer needs and aid customer decision-making by selecting from the product range those products which best fit the customer's requirements. This philosophy of selling is in line with Weitz (1981) and the contingency framework. This suggests that the sales interview gives an unparalleled opportunity to match behaviour to the specific customer interaction that is encountered. This is not to deny the importance of personal persuasion. In the real world, it is unlikely that a product has clear advantages over its competition on all points, and it is clearly part of the selling function for the salesperson to emphasise those superior features and benefits which the product possesses. However, the model for personal selling advocated here is that of a salesperson acting as a need identifier and problem-solver. The view of the salesperson as being a slick fast-talking confidence trickster is unrealistic in a world where most sellers depend upon repeat business and where a high proportion of selling is conducted with professional buyers.

The inappropriate use of high pressure selling techniques can lead to customer annoyance and antagonism. This can lead to marketing opportunities for more enlightened companies as discussed in the following case history.

A new way to sell cars: the case of Daewoo

Marketing research has shown that many people dread the thought of buying a new car. Traditionally cars have been sold through dealers employing salespeople paid in part through commission and trained in the art of negotiation. From the customer's point of view, this could lead to high pressure sales techniques and endless haggling about price. Rarely was the list price of the car the lowest price that the salesperson would accept.

Based upon this customer dissatisfaction, Daewoo, a Korean car manufacturer, redefined the way cars are sold. Instead of salespeople, they employ non-commission customer advisors whose job it is to help customers choose the car which best meets their needs. Customers can enter Daewoo showrooms (they sell direct) without fear of being descended upon by pushy salespeople; their customer advisors will only approach customers when asked to do so.

Daewoo prices are fixed with no hidden extras. Delivery and number plates are free. The price displayed on the car is the price the customer pays. This frees the customer from the burden of bargaining. The result is a more pleasant buying experience and a competitive advantage based on an innovative selling and distribution approach.

Research studies, summarised by Schuster and Danes (1986), have shown that successful selling is associated with the following:

1 asking questions;
2 providing product information, making comparisons, and offering evidence to support claims;
3 acknowledging the viewpoint of the customer;
4 agreeing with the customer's perceptions;
5 supporting the customer;
6 releasing tension.

These important findings should be borne in mind by salespeople when in a sales interview.

As with the development of all skills, the theoretical approach described in this chapter needs to be supplemented by practical experience. Many companies use role playing as a method of providing new salespeople with the opportunity to develop their skills in a situation where sales trainees can observe and correct behaviour. An example of such an exercise, where students and salespeople can apply some of the techniques outlined in this chapter, is given at the end of Chapter 13.

In order to develop personal selling skills it is useful to distinguish six phases of the selling process. These are shown in Figure 5.1. These phases need not occur in the order shown; objections may be raised during presentation or during negotiation, or a trial close may be attempted at any point during the presentation if buyer interest is high. Furthermore, negotiation may or may not take place and may occur during any of the stages.

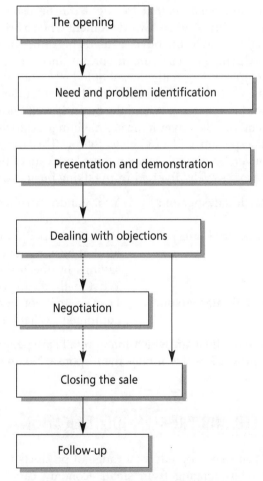

Figure 5.1 The personal selling process

5.1 THE OPENING

Initial impressions can cloud later perceptions, and so it is important to consider the ways in which a favourable initial response can be achieved.

Buyers expect salespeople to be business-like in their personal appearance and behaviour. Untidy hair and a sloppy manner of dress can create a lack of confidence. Further, the salesperson who does not respect the fact that the buyer is likely to be a busy person, with many demands on his or her time, may cause irritation on the part of the buyer.

Salespeople should open with a smile, a handshake and, in situations where they are not well known to the buyer, introduce themselves and the company they represent. Common courtesies should be followed. For example, they should wait for the buyer to indicate that they can sit down or, at least, ask the buyer if they may sit down. Attention to detail, like holding one's briefcase in the left hand so that the right can be used for the handshake, removes the possibility of an awkward moment when a briefcase is clumsily transferred from right to left as the buyer extends his or her hand in greeting.

Opening remarks are important since they set the tone for the rest of the sales interview. Normally they should be business-related since this is the purpose of the visit; they should show the buyer that the salesperson is not about to waste the buyer's time. Where the buyer is well known and where, by his or her own remarks, the buyer indicates a willingness to talk about a more social matter, the salesperson will obviously follow. This can generate close rapport with the buyer, but the salesperson must be aware of the reason for being there, and not be excessively diverted from talking business. Opening remarks might be:

Trade salesperson: Your window display looks attractive. Has it attracted more custom?

Industrial salesperson: We have helped a number of companies in the same kind of business as you are in to achieve considerable savings by the use of our stock control procedures. What methods do you use at present to control stock?

Retail salesperson: I can see that you appear to be interested in our stereo equipment. What kind of system had you in mind?

The cardinal sin which many retail salespeople commit is to open with 'Can I help you?' which invites the response 'No, thank you, I'm just looking.'

5.2 NEED AND PROBLEM IDENTIFICATION

Most salespeople have a range of products to sell. A car salesperson has many models ranging from small economy cars to super luxury top-of-the-range models. The computer salesperson will have a number of systems to suit the needs and resources of different customers. A bicycle retailer will have models from many different manufacturers to offer customers. A pharmaceutical salesperson will be able to offer doctors a range of drugs to combat various illnesses. In each case, the seller's first objective will be to discover the problems and needs of the customer. Before a car salesperson can sell a car, he or she needs to understand the customer's circumstances. What size of car is required?

Is the customer looking for high fuel economy or performance? Is a boot or a hatchback preferred? What kind of price range is being considered? Having obtained this information the salesperson is in a position to sell the model which best suits the needs of the buyer. A computer salesperson may carry out a survey of customer requirements prior to suggesting an appropriate computer system. A bicycle retailer should ask who the bicycle is for, what type is preferred, e.g. mountain or racing bicycle, and the colour preference, before making sensible suggestions as to which model is most suitable. A pharmaceutical salesperson will discuss with doctors the problems which have arisen with patient treatment; perhaps an ointment has been ineffective or a harmful side-effect has been discovered. This gives the salesperson the opportunity to offer a solution to such problems by means of one of his or her company's products.

This '**needs analysis**' approach suggests that early in the sales process the salesperson should adopt a question-and-listen posture. In order to encourage the buyer to discuss his or her problems and needs, salespeople tend to use 'open' rather than 'closed' questions. An open question is one which requires more than a one-word or one-phrase answer:

- 'Why do you believe that a computer system is inappropriate for your business?'
- 'What were the main reasons for buying the XYZ photocopier?'
- 'In what ways did the ABC ointment fail to meet your expectations?'

A closed question, on the other hand, invites a one-word or one-phrase answer. These can be used to obtain purely factual information, but excessive use can hinder rapport and lead to an abrupt type of conversation which lacks flow. Examples of closed questions are

- 'Would you tell me the name of the equipment you currently use?'
- 'Does your company manufacture 1000 cc marine engines?'
- 'What is the name of your chief mechanical engineer?'

In practice, a wide variety of questions may be used during a sales interview (DeCormier and Jobber, 1993). Thirteen types of question and their objectives, together with examples, are given in Table 5.1.

Salespeople should avoid the temptation of making a **sales presentation** without finding out the needs of their customers. It is all too easy to start a sales presentation in the same rigid way, perhaps by highlighting the current bargain of the week, without first questioning the customer as to his or her needs.

At the end of this process, the salesperson may find it useful to summarise the points that have been raised to confirm an understanding with the buyer. For example:

'Fine, Mr and Mrs Jones. I think I have a good idea of the kind of property you are looking for. You would like a four-bedroom house within fifteen minutes' drive of Mr Jones' company. You are not bothered whether the house is detached or semi-detached, but you do not want to live on an estate. The price range you are considering is between £120,000 and £150,000. Does this sum up the kind of house you want, or have I missed something?'

Table 5.1 Types of question used in personal selling

Type of question	Objective	Example
Tie down question	Used for confirmation or to commit a prospect to a position	You want the program to work, don't you?
Leading question	Direct or guide a prospect's thinking?	How does that coat feel on you?
Alternative question	Used to elicit an answer by forcing selection from two or more alternatives	Would you prefer the red or blue model?
Statement/Question	A statement is followed by a question which forces the prospect to reflect upon the statement	This machine can spin at 5000 rpm and process 3 units per minute. What do you think of that productivity?
Sharp angle question	Used to commit a prospect to a position	If we can get it in blue, is that the way you would want it?
Information-gathering questions	Used to gather facts	How many people are you currently employing?
Opinion-gathering questions	Used to gather opinions or feelings	What are your feelings concerning the high price of energy?
Confirmation questions	Used to elicit either agreement or disagreement about a particular topic	Do my recommendations make sense?
Clarification questions	Reduce ambiguities, generalities and non-committal words to specifics	When you say … exactly what do you mean?
Inclusion questions	Present an issue for the prospect's consideration in a low-risk way	I don't suppose you'd be interested in a convertible hard-top, would you?
Counterbiasing	To attain sensitive information by making a potentially embarrassing situation appear acceptable	Research shows that most drivers exceed the speed limit. Do you ever do so?
Transitioning	Used to link the end of one phase to the next phase of the sales process	In addition to that, is there anything else that you want to know? (No) What I'd like to do now is talk about …
Reversing	Used to pass the responsibility of continuing the conversation back to the prospect by answering a question with a question	(When can I expect delivery?) When do you want delivery?

Source: DeCormier and Jobber, 1993

5.3 THE PRESENTATION AND DEMONSTRATION

Once the problems and needs of the buyer have been identified, the presentation follows as a natural consequence.

The first question to be addressed is presentation of what? The preceding section has enabled the salesperson to choose the most appropriate product(s) from his or her range to meet customer requirements. Second, having fully discussed what the customer wants, the salesperson knows which product benefits to stress. A given product may have a range of potential features which confer benefits to customers, but different customers place different priorities on them. In short, having identified the needs and problems of the buyer, the presentation provides the opportunity for the salesperson to convince the buyer that they can supply the solution.

The key to this task is to recognise that buyers purchase benefits and are only interested in product features in as much as they provide the benefits that the customer is looking for. Examples of the relationship between certain product features and benefits are given in Chapter 4. Training programmes and personal preparation of salespeople should pay particular attention to deriving the customer benefits their products bestow.

Benefits should be analysed at two levels: those benefits which can be obtained by purchase of a particular type of product, and those that can be obtained by purchasing that product from a particular supplier. For example, automatic washing machine salespeople need to consider the benefits of an automatic washing machine compared with a twin-tub, as well as the benefits that their company's automatic washing machines have over competitors' models. This proffers maximum flexibility for the salesperson in meeting various sales situations.

The danger of selling features rather than benefits is particularly acute in industrial selling because of the highly technical nature of many industrial products, and the tendency to employ sales engineers rather than salespeople. Perkins Diesels found this to be a problem with their sales team after commissioning market research to identify strengths and weaknesses of their sales and marketing operation (Reed, 1983), but it is by no means confined to this sector. Hi-fi salespeople who confuse and infuriate customers with tedious descriptions of the electronic wizardry behind the products they sell are no less guilty of this sin.

A simple method of relating features and benefits in a sales presentation is to link them by using the following phrases:

- 'which means that'
- 'which results in'
- 'which enables you to'.

For example, an estate agent might say, 'The house is situated four miles from the company where you work (product feature) which means that you can easily be at work within fifteen minutes of leaving home' (customer benefit). Or an office salesperson might say, 'The XYZ photocopier allows streamfeeding (product feature) which results in quicker photocopying' (customer benefit). Finally, a car salesperson may claim that 'This model is equipped with overdrive (product feature) which enables you to reduce petrol consumption on motorways' (customer benefit).

The term 'presentation' should not mislead the salesperson into believing that they alone should do all the talking. The importance of asking questions is not confined to the needs and problem identification stage. Asking questions as part of the presentation serves two functions. First, it checks that the salesperson has understood the kinds of benefits the buyer is looking for. After explaining a benefit it is sound practice to ask the buyer, 'Is this the kind of thing you are looking for?' Second, asking questions establishes whether the buyer has understood what the salesperson has said. A major obstacle to understanding is the use of technical jargon which is unintelligible to the buyer. Where a presentation is necessarily complicated and lengthy, the salesperson would be well advised to pause at varous points and simply ask if there are any questions. This gives the buyer the opportunity to query anything that is not entirely clear. This questioning procedure allows the salesperson to tailor the speed and content of his presentation to the circumstances which face him. Buyers have different backgrounds, technical expertise and intelligence levels. Questioning allows the salesperson to communicate more effectively because it provides the information necessary for the seller to know how to vary the presentation to different buyers.

Many sales situations involve risk to the buyer. No matter what benefits the salesperson discusses, the buyer may be reluctant to change from the present supplier or change the present model because to do so may give rise to unforeseen problems – delivery may be unpredictable or the new model may be unreliable. Assurances from the salesperson are, of themselves, unlikely to be totally convincing – after all, they would say that, wouldn't they! Risk is the hidden reason behind many failures to sell. The salesperson accurately identifies customer needs and relates product benefits to those needs; the buyer does not offer much resistance, but somehow does not buy. A likely reason is that the buyer plays safe, sticking to the present supplier or model in order to lessen the risk of aggravation should problems occur.

How, then, can a salesperson reduce risk? There are four major ways:

● reference selling
● demonstrations
● guarantees
● trial orders.

Reference selling

Reference selling involves the use of satisfied customers in order to convince the buyer of the effectiveness of the salesperson's product. During the preparation stage a list of satisfied customers, arranged by product type, should be drawn up. Letters from satisfied customers should also be kept and used in the sales presentation in order to build confidence. This technique can be highly effective in selling, moving a buyer from being merely interested in the product to being convinced that it is the solution to his or her problem.

Demonstrations

Chinese proverb: 'Tell me and I'll forget; show me and I may remember; involve me and I'll understand.'

Demonstrations also reduce risk because they prove the benefits of the product. A major producer of sales training films organises regional demonstrations of a selection of them in order to prove their quality to training managers. Industrial goods manufacturers will arrange demonstrations to show their products' capabilities in use. Car salespeople will allow customers to test drive cars.

For all but the most simple of products it is advisable to divide the demonstration into two stages. The first stage involves a brief description of the features and benefits of the product and an explanation of how it works. The second stage entails the actual demonstration itself. This should be conducted by the salesperson. The reason behind this two-stage approach is that it is often very difficult for the viewers of the demonstration to understand the principles of how a product works while at the same time watching it work. This is because the viewers are receiving competing stimuli. The salesperson's voice may be competing for the buyers' attention with the flashing lights and noise of the equipment.

Once the equipment works, the buyers can be encouraged to use it themselves under the salesperson's supervision. If the correct equipment, to suit the buyers' needs, has been chosen for demonstration, and it performs reliably, the demonstration can move the buyers very much closer to purchase.

There now follows more practical advice upon what must be regarded as an extremely important part of the personal selling process, for without a demonstration the salesperson is devoid of one of his or her principal selling tools.

Pre-demonstration

1 Make the process as brief as possible, but not so brief as not to be able to fulfil the sales objective of obtaining an order, or of opening the way for further negotiations. It is basically a question of 'balance', in that the salesperson must judge the individual circumstances and 'tailor' the demonstration accordingly. Some potential buyers will require lengthier or more technical demonstrations than others.

2 Make the process as simple as possible, bearing in mind that some potential purchasers will be less technically minded than others. Never 'over-pitch' such technicality, because potential buyers will generally pretend that they understand, and will not want to admit that they do not because of 'loss of face'. They will see the demonstration through, and probably make some excuse at the end to delay the purchase decision. The likelihood is that they will not purchase (or at least not purchase from you). This point is deliberately emphasised, because it is a fact that many potential sales are lost through demonstrations that are too technical.

3 Rehearse the approach to likely objections with colleagues (e.g. with one acting as an 'awkward' buyer). Work out how such objections can be addressed and overcome through the demonstration. The use of interactive video is useful here, as you can witness your mistakes and rehearse a better demonstration and presentation.

4 Know the product's selling points and be prepared to advance these during the course of the demonstration. Such selling points must, however, be presented in terms of benefits to the customer. Buyer behaviour must, therefore, be ascertained beforehand. By so doing, it will be possible to maximise what is euphemistically called the 'you' or 'u' benefits.

5 The demonstration should not go wrong if it has been adequately rehearsed beforehand. However, machines do break down and power supplies sometimes fail. Be prepared for such eventualities (e.g. rehearse an appropriate verbal 'routine', and have a back-up successful demonstration available on video). The main point is not to be caught out unexpectedly and to be prepared to launch into a contingency routine as smoothly as possible.

Conducting the demonstration

1 Commence with a concise statement of what is to be done or proved.
2 Show how potential purchasers can participate in the demonstration process.
3 Make the demonstration as interesting and as satisfying as possible.
4 Show the potential purchaser how the product's features can fulfil his or her needs or solve his or her problems.
5 Attempt to translate such needs into a desire to purchase.
6 Do not leave the purchaser until he or she is completely satisfied with the demonstration. Such satisfaction will help to justify ultimate expenditure and will also reduce the severity and incidence of any complaints that might arise after purchasing.
7 Summarise the main points by re-emphasising the purchasing benefits that have been put forward during the demonstration. Note that we state purchasing benefits and *not* sales benefits because purchasing benefits relate to individual buying behaviour.
8 The objectives of a demonstration should be: (*a*) to enable the salesperson to obtain a sale immediately (e.g. a car demonstration drive given to a member of the public); or (*b*) to pave the way for future negotiations (e.g. a car demonstration drive given to a car fleet buyer).
9 Depending upon the objective above, in the case of (*a*) ask for the order now, or in the case of (*b*) arrange for further communication in the form of a meeting, a telephone call, a letter, an additional demonstration to other members of the decision-making unit, etc.

Advantages of demonstrations

1 Demonstrations are a useful ancillary in the selling process. They add realism

to the sales routine in that they utilise more human senses than mere verbal descriptions or visual presentation.

2 When a potential customer is participating in a demonstration it is easier for the salesperson to ask questions in order to ascertain buying behaviour. This means that the salesperson will not need to emphasise inappropriate purchasing motives later in the selling process.

3 Such demonstrations enable the salesperson to maximise the 'u' benefits to potential purchasers. In other words, the salesperson can relate product benefits to match the potential buyer's buying behaviour and adopt a more creative approach, rather than concentrating upon a pre-prepared sales routine.

4 Customer objections can be more easily overcome if they can be persuaded to take part in the demonstration process. In fact, many potential objections may never even be aired, because the demonstration process will make them invalid. It is a fact that a sale is more likely to ensue if fewer objections can be advanced initially, even if such objections can be satisfactorily overcome.

5 There are advantages to customers in that it is easier for them to ask questions in a more realistic way in order to ascertain the product's utility more clearly and quickly.

6 Purchasing inhibitions are more quickly overcome and buyers declare their purchasing interest sooner than in face-to-face selling/buying situations. This makes the demonstration a very efficient sales tool.

7 Once a customer has participated in a demonstration there is less likelihood of 'customer remorse' (i.e. the doubt that value for money is not good value after all). By taking part in the demonstration and tacitly accepting its results, the purchaser has *bought* the product and not been *sold* it.

Guarantees

Guarantees of product reliability, after-sales service, and delivery supported by penalty clauses can build confidence towards the salesperson's claims and lessen the costs to the buyer should something go wrong. Their establishment is a matter for company policy rather than the salesperson's discretion but, where offered, the salesperson should not underestimate their importance in the sales presentation.

Trial orders

The final strategy for risk reduction is for salespeople to encourage trial orders, even though they may be uneconomic in company terms and in terms of salespeople's time in the short term, when faced with a straight re-buy (*see* Chapter 2). Buyers who habitually purchase supplies from one supplier may recognise that change involves unwarranted risk. It may be that the only way for a new supplier to break through this impasse is to secure a small order which, in effect, permits the demonstration of the company's capability to provide consistently high-quality products promptly. The confidence, thus built, may lead to a higher percentage of the customer's business in the longer term.

5.4 DEALING WITH OBJECTIONS

Objections should not always be viewed with dismay by salespeople. Many objections are simply expressions of interest by the buyer. What the buyer is asking for is further information because he or she is interested in what the salesperson is saying. The problem is that the buyer is not, as yet, convinced. Objections highlight the issues which are important to the buyer. For example, Ford, when training salespeople, make the point that a customer's objection is a signpost to what is really on their mind.

An example will illustrate these points. Suppose an industrial salesperson working for an adhesives manufacturer is faced with the following objection: 'Why should I buy your new adhesive gun when my present method of applying adhesive – direct from the tube – is perfectly satisfactory?' This type of objection is clearly an expression of a desire for additional information. The salesperson's task is to provide it in a manner which does not antagonise the buyer and yet is convincing. It is a fact of human personality that the argument which is supported by the greater weight of evidence does not always win the day; people do not like to be proved wrong. The very act of changing a supplier may be resisted because it may imply criticism of a past decision on the part of the buyer. For a salesperson to disregard the emotional aspects of dealing with objections is to court disaster. The situation to be avoided is where the buyer digs in his or her heels on principle, because of the attitude of the salesperson.

So, the effective approach for dealing with objections involves two areas: the preparation of convincing answers, and the development of a range of techniques for answering objections in a manner which permits the acceptance of these answers without loss of face on the part of the buyer. The first area has been covered in the previous chapter. A number of techniques will now be reviewed to illustrate how the second objective may be accomplished. These are shown in Figure 5.2.

Listen and do not interrupt

Experienced salespeople know that the impression given to buyers by the salesperson who interrupts the buyer in midstream is that the salesperson believes that:

● the objection is obviously wrong;
● it is trivial;
● it is not worth the salesperson's time to let the buyer finish.

Interruption denies the buyer the kind of respect he/she is entitled to receive

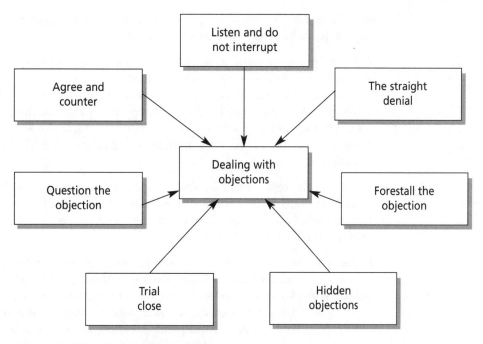

Figure 5.2 Dealing with objections

and may lead to a misunderstanding of the real substance behind the objection. The correct approach is to listen carefully, attentively and respectfully. The buyer will appreciate the fact that the salesperson is taking the problem seriously and the salesperson will gain through having a clear and full understanding of what the problem really is.

Agree and counter

This approach maintains the respect the salesperson shows to the buyer. The salesperson first agrees that what the buyer is saying is sensible and reasonable, before then putting forward an alternative point of view. It therefore takes the edge off the objection and creates a climate of agreement rather than conflict. For example:

Buyer: The problem with your tractor is that it costs more than your competition.

Salesperson: Yes, the initial cost of the tractor is a little higher than competitors' models, but I should like to show you how, over the life-time of the machine, ours works out to be far more economical.

This example shows why the method is sometimes called the 'yes … but' technique. The 'yes' precedes the agree statement, while the 'but' prefaces the counter-argument. There is no necessity to use these words, however. In fact, in some sales situations the buyer may be so used to having salespeople use them that the technique loses some of its effectiveness. Fortunately there are other approaches which are less blatant. For example:

1 'I can appreciate your concern that the machine is more expensive than the competition. However, I should like to show you ...'
2 'Customer XYZ made the same comment a year ago. I can assure you that he is highly delighted with his decision to purchase because the cost savings over the life-time of the machine more than offset the initial cost difference.'
3 'That's absolutely right – The initial cost is a little higher. That's why I want to show you ...'

The use of the reference selling technique can be combined with the agree and counter method to provide a powerful counter to an objection. For example, salespeople of media space in newspapers that are given away free to the public often encounter the following objection:

Buyer (e.g. car dealer): Your newspaper is given away free. Most of the people who receive it throw it away without even reading it.

Salesperson: I can understand your concern that a newspaper which is free may not be read. However, a great many people do read it to find out what second-hand cars are on the market. Mr Giles of Grimethorpe Motors has been advertising with us for two years and he is delighted with the results.

The straight denial

This method has to be handled with a great deal of care since the danger is that it will result in exactly the kind of antagonism which the salesperson is wishing to avoid. However, it can be used when the buyer is clearly seeking factual information. For example:

Buyer: I expect that this upholstery will be difficult to clean.
Salesperson: No, Mr Buyer, absolutely not. This material is made from a newly developed synthetic fibre which resists stains and allows marks to be removed simply by using soap, water and a clean cloth.

Question the objection

Sometimes an objection is raised which is so general as to be difficult to counter. For example, a customer might say he or she does not like the appearance of the product, or that the product is not good quality. In this situation the salesperson should question the nature of the objection in order to clarify the specific problem at hand. Sometimes this results in a major objection being reduced to one which can easily be dealt with.

Buyer: I'm sorry but I don't like the look of that car.
Salesperson: Could you tell me exactly what it is that you don't like the look of?

Buyer: I don't like the pattern on the seats.

Salesperson: Well in fact this model can be supplied in a number of different upholstery designs. Shall we have a look at the catalogue to see if there is a pattern to your liking?

Another benefit of questioning objections is that, in trying to explain the exact nature of objections, buyers may themselves realise these are really quite trivial.

Forestall the objection

With this method, the salesperson not only anticipates an objection and plans its counter, but actually raises the objection as part of his or her sales presentation.

There are two advantages of doing this. First, the timing of the objection is controlled by the salesperson. Consequently, it can be planned so that it is raised at the most appropriate time for it to be dealt with effectively. Second, since it is raised by the salesperson, the buyer is not placed in a position where, having raised a problem, he or she feels that it must be defended.

The danger with using this method, however, is that the salesperson may highlight a problem the buyer had not thought of. It is most often used where a salesperson is faced with the same objection being raised time after time. Perhaps buyers are continually raising the problem that the salesperson is working for one of the smallest companies in the industry. The salesperson may pre-empt the objection in the following manner: 'My company is smaller than most in the industry which means that we respond quicker to our customers' needs and try that bit harder to make sure our customers are happy.'

Turn the objection into a trial close

A *trial close* is where a salesperson attempts to conclude the sale without prejudicing the chances of continuing the selling process with the buyer should they refuse to commit themself.

The ability of a salesperson to turn the objection into a trial close is dependent upon perfect timing and considerable judgement. Usually it will be attempted after the selling process is well under way, and the salesperson judges that only one objection remains. Under these conditions he or she might say the following: 'If I can satisfy you that the fuel consumption of this car is no greater than that of the Vauxhall Vectra, would you buy it?'

When dealing with objections, the salesperson should remember that heated arguments are unlikely to win sales – buyers buy from their friends, not their enemies.

Hidden objections

Not all prospects state their objections. They may prefer to say nothing because to raise an objection may cause offence or may prolong the sales interaction. Such people may believe that staying on friendly terms with the salesperson and at the end of the interview stating that they will think over the proposal is the best tactic in a no-buy situation. The correct salesperson response to hidden objections is to ask questions in an attempt to uncover their nature. If a salesperson believes that a buyer is unwilling to reveal their true objections, he or she should ask such questions as:

● 'Is there anything so far which you are unsure about?'
● 'Is there anything on your mind?'
● 'What would it take to convince you?'

Uncovering hidden objections is crucial to successful selling because to convince someone it is necessary to know what he or she needs to be convinced of. However, with uncommunicative buyers this may be difficult. As a last resort the salesperson may need to 'second guess' the reluctant buyer and suggest an issue which they believe is causing the problem and ask a question such as: 'I don't think you're totally convinced about the better performance of our product, are you?'

5.5 NEGOTIATION

In some selling situations, the salesperson or sales team have a degree of discretion with regard to the terms of the sale. **Negotiation** may therefore enter into the sales process. Sellers may negotiate price, credit terms, delivery times, trade-in values and other aspects of the commercial transaction. The deal that is arrived at will be dependent upon the balance of power (*see* Chapter 4) and the negotiating skills of the respective parties.

The importance of preparation has already been mentioned in the previous chapter. The buyer's needs, the competition which the supplier faces and knowledge about the buyer's business and the pressures upon him or her should be estimated. However, there are a number of other guidelines to aid the salespeople actually engaged in the negotiation process.

Start high but be realistic

There are several good reasons for making the opening stance high. First, the buyer might agree to it. Second, it provides room for negotiation. A buyer may come to expect concessions from a seller in return for purchasing. This situation is prevalent in the car market. It is unusual for a car salesperson not to reduce the advertised price of a car to a cash purchaser. When considering how high to go, the limiting factor must be to keep within the buyer's realistic expectations, otherwise they may not be willing to talk to the seller in the first place.

Attempt to trade concession for concession

Sometimes it may be necessary to give a concession simply to secure the sale. A buyer might say that he or she is willing to buy if the seller drops the price by £100. If the seller has left themselves negotiating room, then this may be perfectly acceptable. However, in other circumstances, especially when the seller has a degree of power through being able to meet buyer requirements better than competition, the seller may be able to trade concessions from the buyer. A simple way of achieving this is by means of the 'if … then' technique (Kennedy *et al.*, 1980).

1 'If you are prepared to arrange collection of these goods at our premises, then I am prepared to knock £10 off the purchase price.'
2 'If you are prepared to make payment within twenty-eight days, then I am willing to offer a 2½ per cent discount.'

This is a valuable tool at the disposal of the negotiator since it promotes movement towards agreement and yet ensures that proposals to give the buyer something are matched by proposals for a concession in return.

It is sensible, at the preparation stage, to evaluate possible concessions in the light of their costs and values, not only to the seller but also to the buyer. In (1) above, the costs of delivery to the seller might be much higher than the costs of collection to the buyer. The net effect of the proposal, therefore, is that the salesperson is offering a benefit to the buyer at very little cost to the seller.

Buyers' negotiating techniques

Buyers also have a number of techniques which they use in negotiations. Sellers should be aware of their existence, for sometimes their effect can be devastating. Kennedy *et al.* (1980) describe a number of techniques designed to weaken the position of the unsuspecting sales negotiator.

First, the shotgun approach involves the buyer saying 'Unless you agree immediately to a price reduction of 20 per cent we'll have to look elsewhere for a supplier.' In a sense, this is the 'if … then' technique played on the seller, but in this setting the consequences are more serious. The correct response depends upon the outcome of the assessment of the balance of power conducted during preparation. If the buyer does have a number of options, all of which offer the same kind of benefits the seller's product offers, then the seller may have to concede. If the seller's product offers clear advantages over competition, then the salesperson may be able to resist the challenge.

A second ploy used by buyers is the 'sell cheap, the future looks bright' technique: 'We cannot pretend that our offer meets you on price, but the real payoff for you will come in terms of future sales.' This may be a genuine statement – in fact the seller's own objective may have been to gain a foothold in the buyer's business. At other times it is a gambit to extract the maximum price concession from the seller. If the seller's position is reasonably strong he or she should ask for specific details and firm commitments.

A final technique is known as 'Noah's Ark' – because it's been around that long! The buyer says, tapping a file with one finger, 'You'll have to do much better in terms of price. I have quotations from your competitors which are much lower.' The salesperson's response depends upon his or her level of confidence. The salesperson can call the buyer's bluff and ask to see the quotations; or take the initiative by stating that they assume the buyer is wishing for them to justify the price; or, if flushed with the confidence of past success, can say 'Then I advise you to accept one of them.'

5.6 CLOSING THE SALE

The skills and techniques discussed so far are not, in themselves, sufficient for consistent sales success. A final ingredient is necessary to complete the mix – the ability to **close the sale**.

Some salespeople believe that an effective presentation should lead the buyer to ask for the product without the seller needing to close the sale themself. This sometimes happens, but more usually it will be necessary for the salesperson to take the initiative. This is because no matter how well the salesperson identifies buyer needs, matches product benefits to them and overcomes objections, there is likely to be some doubt still present in the mind of the buyer. This doubt may manifest itself in the wish to delay the decision. Would it not be better to think things over? Would it not be sensible to see what competitor XYZ has to offer? The plain truth, however, is that if the buyer does put off buying until another day it is as likely that he or she will buy from the competition. While the seller is there, the seller is at an advantage over the competition; thus part of the salesperson's job is to try to close the sale.

Why, then, are some salespeople reluctant to close a sale? The problem lies in the fact that most people fear rejection. Closing the sale asks the buyer to say yes or no. Sometimes it will be no and the salesperson will have been rejected. Avoiding closing the sale does not result in more sales, but rejection is less blatant. The most important point to grasp, then, is not to be afraid to close. Accept the fact that some buyers will inevitably respond negatively, but be confident that more will buy than if no close had been used.

A major consideration is timing. A general rule is to attempt to close the sale when the buyer displays heightened interest or a clear intention to purchase the product. Salespeople should therefore look out for such **buying signals** and respond accordingly. Purchase intentions are unlikely to grow continuously throughout the sales presentation; they are more likely to rise and fall as the presentation progresses (*see* Figure 5.3). The true situation is reflected by a series of peaks and troughs. An example will explain why this should be so. When a

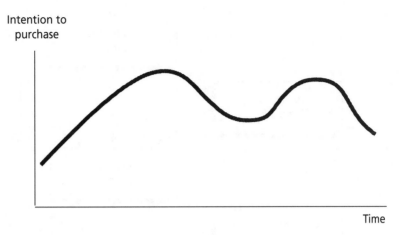

Figure 5.3 **The level of buyer's purchase intentions throughout a sales presentation**

salesperson talks about a key benefit which exactly matches the buyer's needs, purchase intentions are likely to rise sharply. However, the buyer then perhaps raises a problem, which decreases the level, or perhaps doubts arise in the buyer's mind as to whether the claims made for the product are completely justified. This causes purchase intentions to fall, only to be followed by an increase as the salesperson overcomes the objection or substantiates the claim.

In theory the salesperson should attempt to close at a peak. In practice, judging when to close is difficult. The buyer may be feigning disinterest, and throughout a sales interview several peaks may be expected to occur. Which peak should be chosen for the close? Part of the answer lies in experience. Experienced salespeople know intuitively if intentions are sufficiently favourable for a close to be worthwhile. Also, if need and problem identification have been conducted properly, the salesperson knows that a rough guide as to when to close is after they match all product benefits to customer needs; theoretically, intentions should be at a peak then.

Not all buyers conform to this theoretical plan, however, and the salesperson should be prepared to close even if the planned sales presentation is incomplete. The method to use is the **trial close**. This technique involves asking for the order in such a way that if the timing is premature the presentation can continue with the minimum of interruption. Perhaps early in the presentation the customer might say 'Yes, that's just what I'm looking for', to which the salesperson replies 'Good, when do you think you would like delivery.' Even if the buyer says they have not made up their mind yet, the salesperson can continue with the presentation or ask the customer a question, depending on which is most appropriate to the situation.

A time will come during the sales interview when the salesperson has discussed all the product benefits and answered all the customer's questions. It is, clearly, decision time; the buyer is enthusiastic but is hesitating. There are a number of closing techniques which the salesperson can use (see Figure 5.4).

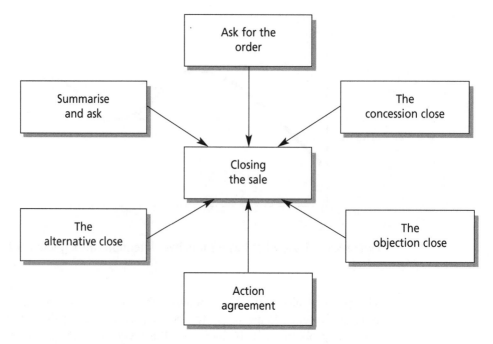

Figure 5.4   Closing the sale

Simply ask for the order

The simplest technique involves asking directly for the order:

- 'Shall I reserve you one?'
- 'Would you like to buy it?'
- 'Do you want it?'

The key to using this technique is to keep silent after you have asked for the order. The salesperson has asked a closed question implying a yes or no answer. To break the silence effectively lets the buyer off the hook. The buyer will forget the first question and reply to the salesperson's later comment.

Summarise and then ask for the order

This technique allows the salesperson to remind the buyer of the main points in the sales argument in a manner which implies that the moment for decision has come and that buying is the natural extension of the proceedings.

> Well, Mr Smith, we have agreed that the ZDXL4 model meets your requirements of low noise, high productivity and driver comfort at a cost which you can afford. May I go ahead and place an order for this model?

The concession close

This involves keeping one concession in reserve to use as the final push towards agreement: 'If you are willing to place an order now, I'm willing to offer an extra 2½ per cent discount.'

The alternative close

This closing technique assumes that the buyer is willing to purchase but moves the decision to whether the colour should be red or blue, the delivery should be Tuesday or Friday, the payment in cash or credit, etc. In such circumstances the salesperson suggests two alternatives, the agreement to either thus closing the sale.

- 'Would you like the red one or the blue one?'
- 'Would you like it delivered on Tuesday or Friday?'

This technique has been used by salespeople for many years and consequently should be used with care, especially with professional buyers who are likely to have experienced its use many times and know exactly what the salesperson is doing.

The objection close

This closing technique has been mentioned briefly earlier in this chapter. It involves the use of an objection as a stimulus to buy. If the salesperson is convinced that the objection is the major stumbling block to the sale, they can gain commitment from the buyer by saying: 'If I can convince you that this model is the most economical in its class, will you buy it?' A positive response from the buyer and reference to an objective statistical comparison by the seller effectively seals the sale.

Action agreement

In some situations it is inappropriate to attempt to close the sale. For many industrial goods the sales cycle is long and a salesperson who attempts to close the sale at early meetings may cause annoyance. In selling pharmaceutical products, for example, salespeople do not try to close a sale but instead attempt to achieve 'action agreement' whereby either the salesperson or the doctor agree to do something before their next meeting. This technique has the effect of helping the doctor–salesperson relationship to develop and continue.

A useful characteristic for salespeople is persistence. Making a decision to spend large quantities of money is not easy. In most sales situations, no one product is better than its competitors on all evaluative criteria. This means that the salespeople for all of these products stand some chance of success. The final decision may go to the one who is the most persistent in their attempts to persuade the customer that the product meets the buyer's needs. Children learn very quickly that if they are initially refused what they want, asking a second or third time may be successful. The key is knowing where to draw the line before persistence leads to annoyance.

Once the sale is agreed, the salesperson should follow two rules. First, they should never display emotions. No matter how important the sale is, and how delighted the salesperson feels, he or she should remain calm and professional. There will be plenty of opportunity later to be euphoric. Second, leave as quickly as is courteously possible. The longer he or she stays around, the greater the chance the buyer will change their mind, and cancel the order.

5.7 FOLLOW-UP

This final stage in the sales process is necessary to ensure that the customer is satisfied with the purchase and that no problems with such factors as delivery, installation, product use and training have arisen. Salespeople may put off the follow-up call because it does not result in an immediate order. However, for most companies repeat business is the hallmark of success and the follow-up call can play a major role by showing that the salesperson really cares about the customer rather than only being interested in making sales.

The follow-up call can also be used to provide reassurance that the purchase was the right one. As we have already seen, many customers suffer from cognitive dissonance, i.e. being anxious that they have made the right choice.

This chapter has stressed the importance of changing the sales approach according to the differing needs and circumstances of customers. The following case discussion continues this theme by showing how different British and German customers can be.

SELLING
AND SALES
MANAGEMENT
IN ACTION

Selling in Germany

Salespeople have to be aware of the need to adapt their approach to differing customers and different ways of doing business. Major differences in the ways British and German companies do business were described by two German employees of British computer company Psion:

"With German firms there is much greater emphasis on bureaucracy and proper procedure. With British firms things are done in a much more off-the-cuff way which means that they can react more flexibly and it is possible to act on a client's requirements very rapidly. In Germany, particularly with big German companies, you have to go through a very long bureaucratic procedure.

I think the Germans are very precise. Their attitude is 'I want this thing by 10.15 a.m. not at 10.16 a.m.' If you order something in the UK, you ask 'When will it arrive?' You will be told 'You'll have it next month'."

The office hierarchy is very important in Germany. For example, office subordinates may not be willing to take even the smallest decision while their boss is away. Salespeople can waste a lot of valuable time under such circumstances by attempting to sell to persons not authorised to take the decision of whether to buy the product or not.

The Germans place great emphasis on personal contact and usually expect to meet business partners face-to-face. However, one-to-one meetings are rare, with senior executives normally bringing along at least one colleague. Sometimes they appear confident, almost arrogant. The correct response is to be polite and correct. Germans are not impressed by covering up uncertainty with humour, particularly not at first meetings.

German business people should be addressed by their title and surname: Herr Schmidt or Frau Strauss. Dress is sober. Lunch is an important element in German business negotiations, although it may well be in the company canteen since business guests are rarely invited out for lavish meals.

Often suppliers' salesforces are expected to negotiate with purchasing departments which may have considerable organisational power. Attempts to bypass the purchasing department may cause annoyance. Face-to-face contact at trade fairs, and advertising campaigns are often used to communicate with engineers and other technical people.

Based on BBC2 Television (1993) 'Germany Means Business: The Frankfurt Contenders', January 5; Forden, J. (1988) 'Doing business with the Germans', Director, July, pp. 102–4; Welford, R. and Prescott, K. (1992) 'European Business', London; Pitman Publishing, p. 208; and Wolfe, A. (1991) 'The Eurobuyer: how European businesses buy', Marketing Intelligence and Planning, 9(5), pp. 9–15.

5.8 CONCLUSIONS

The skills involved in personal selling have been explored in this chapter. The necessary skills have been examined under the following headings:

1 The opening.
2 Need and problem identification.
3 Presentation and demonstration.
4 Dealing with objections.
5 Negotiation.
6 Closing the sale.
7 The follow-up.

The emphasis in this chapter has been on identifying the needs and problems of the potential buyer and presenting a product or service as a means of fulfilling that need or solving that problem.

Having identified the skills necessary for successful selling, we will examine later, in Part Three, the types of environment in which selling takes place.

PRACTICAL EXERCISE

The Mordex Photocopier Company

You have an appointment to see George Kirby, sales office manager of Plastic Foods Ltd, with regard to the hire of a Mordex photocopier. You are bristling with anticipation as you know the present contract which Plastic Foods has with Clearprint, your closest competitor, is up for renewal. You have not met Mr Kirby before.

As you enter Mr Kirby's office you notice that Mr Kirby appears a little under pressure.

After introducing yourself, you say, 'I'd like to talk with you about how we can improve the efficiency of your photocopying operation. I see that you use the Clearprint ZXR photocopier at the moment. What kinds of documents do you photocopy in the sales office?'

The discussion continues, with you attempting to assess his staff's requirements with regard to photocopying facilities and his attitude towards the Clearprint machine.

One need is the ability of the photocopier to collate automatically, since some of the documents which are photocopied are quite lengthy. Another requirement is for the photocopy to be of the highest quality since it is usual for photocopies of standard letters to be sent to clients. The Clearprint photocopier does *not* have a collating facility, and the quality, while passable, is not totally satisfactory. Further, there are sometimes delays in repairing the machine when it breaks down, although generally it is quite reliable.

At the end of the discussion you summarise the points that have been raised: staff time is being wasted collating lengthy documents, the quality of photostat is not totally satisfactory, repairs are not always carried out promptly. Mr Kirby agrees that this is a fair summary.

DISCUSSION QUESTIONS

During the sales interview the following objections were raised. How would you deal with them?

1 'I'm sorry, I have an urgent meeting in ten minutes time. Can we make it quick?'

2 'We haven't had any major problems with the Clearprint so far.'

3 'Doesn't your firm have a bad reputation?'

4 'Aren't your hiring charges much higher than Clearprint's?'

5 'How do I know your service will be any better than Clearprint's?'

6 'My staff have got used to using the Clearprint. I'll have to spend time showing them how to use your machine.'

7 'Let me think about it. The Clearprint rep is coming next week. I should like to discuss the points you've raised with him.'

EXAMINATION QUESTIONS

1 If the product is right and the sales presentation is right, there is no need to close the sale. Discuss.

2 Discuss the ways in which a salesperson can attempt to identify buyer needs.

CHAPTER 6

SELLING TO AND MANAGING KEY ACCOUNTS

OBJECTIVES

After studying this chapter, you should be able to:

1 Understand what a key account is and the advantages and disadvantages of key account management.

2 Decide whether key account management is suitable in a given situation.

3 Appreciate the tasks and skills of key account management.

4 Understand the special skills and techniques necessary to sell to key accounts.

5 Recognise the ways in which relationships with key accounts can be built.

6 Identify the key components of a key account information and planning system.

KEY CONCEPTS

- key account management
- relational development model
- implied and explicit needs
- situation, problem, implication and need-pay off questions
- relationship building
- key account information and planning system

Important changes are taking place in the personal selling function. Companies are reducing the size of their salesforce in response to increasing buyer concentration, the trend towards centralised buying, and in recognition of the high costs of maintaining a field salesforce. This latter factor has fuelled a move towards telemarketing. Perhaps the most significant change, however, has been the rise in importance of selling to, and managing key accounts resulting from the growing concentration of buying power into fewer hands. These days companies often find over 70 per cent of sales coming from a few key customers. These key customers require special treatment since the loss of even one of them would significantly affect a supplier's sales and profits.

In this chapter we shall discuss what a key account is, the advantages and drawbacks to key account management, the factors which influence the move to key account management, the skills required and how to select, and sell to, key accounts. Since the objective of key account management is to develop relationships over time, we shall also examine how to build account relationships. Finally, we shall consider key account planning and evaluation.

6.1 WHAT IS KEY ACCOUNT MANAGEMENT?

Key account management is a strategy used by suppliers to target and serve high potential customers with complex needs by providing them with special treatment in the areas of marketing, administration and service. In order to receive key account status, a customer must have high sales potential. A second characteristic is that of complex buying behaviour, e.g. large decision-making units with many choice criteria often found in dispersed geographical locations. The decision-making unit may be located in different functional areas and varying operating units. Third, key account status is more likely to be given to customers willing to enter into a long-term alliance or partnership. Such relationships offer buyers many benefits including reliability of supply, risk reduction, easier problem solving, better communications and high levels of service. Key accounts that are geographically spread are often called national accounts.

Key account handling requires a special kind of attention from the seller that may be beyond the capacity of the regular field salesforce. Some of the key responsibilities of key account managers are planning and developing relationships with a wide range of people in the customer firms, mobilising personnel and other resources in their own firms to assist the account, and co-ordinating and motivating the efforts and communications of their company's field salespeople in their calls on the various departments, divisions and geographical locations of the key account (Wotruba and Castleberry, 1993).

According to Hise and Reid (1994), the six most critical conditions that are needed to ensure the success of key account management are as follows:

- integration of the key account programme into the company's overall sales effort;
- senior management's understanding of, and support for, the key account unit's role;
- clear and practical lines of communication between outlying sales and service units;
- establishment of objectives and missions;
- compatible working relationships between sales management and field salespeople;
- clear definition and identification of customers to be designated for key account status.

Some important distinctions between transactional selling and key account management are shown in Table 6.1.

Table 6.1 Distinctions between transactional selling and key account management

	Transactional selling	Key account management
Overall objective	Sales	Preferred supplier status
Sales skills	Asking questions, handling objections, closing	Building trust, providing excellent service
Nature of relationship	Short, intermittent	Long, more intense interaction
Salesperson goal	Closed sale	Relationship management
Nature of salesforce	One or two salespeople per customer	Many salespeople often involving multifunctional teams.

6.2 ADVANTAGES AND DANGERS OF KEY ACCOUNT MANAGEMENT

A number of advantages to the supplier have been identified with key account management:

1 Close working relationships with the customer – the salesperson knows who makes what decisions and who influences the various players involved in the decision-making process. Technical specialists from the selling organisation can call on technical people (e.g. engineers) in the buying organisation, and salespeople can call upon administrators, buyers and financial people armed with the commercial arguments for buying.

2 Improved communication and co-ordination – the customer knows that a dedicated salesperson or sales team exists and they know who to contact when a problem arises.

3 Better follow-up on sales and service – the extra resources devoted to the key account means there is more time to follow up and provide service after a key sale has been concluded.

4 More in-depth penetration of the DMU – there is more time to cultivate relationships within the key account. Salespeople can 'pull' the buying decision through the organisation from the users, deciders and influencers to the buyer, rather than face the more difficult task of 'pushing' it through the buyer into the organisation, as is done with more traditional sales approaches.

5 Higher sales – most companies who have adopted key account selling techniques claim that sales have risen as a result.

6 The provision of an opportunity for advancement for career salespeople – a

tiered salesforce system with key account selling at the top provides promotional opportunities for salespeople who wish to advance within the salesforce rather than to enter a traditional sales management position.

7 Lower costs through joint agreement of optimum production and delivery schedules, and demand forecasting.

8 Co-operation on research and development for new products and joint promotions (e.g. within the fast-moving consumer goods/retail sector).

However, Burnett (1992) points out that key account management is not without its potential dangers. For example:

1 When resources are channelled towards a limited number of companies, the supplier runs the risk of increased dependence on, and vulnerability to, relatively few customers.

2 The risk of pressure on profit margins if a customer chooses to abuse its key account status.

3 The possible danger of a customer applying ever-increasing demands for higher levels of service and attention once they know that they have preferred customer status.

4 Focusing resources on a few key accounts may lead to neglect of smaller accounts, some of which may have high long-term potential.

5 The team approach required by key account management may be at odds with the career aspirations of certain high achievers who prefer a more individualistic approach and object to the dilution of praise which has to be shared with other people when a big order is won. Thus care is required when recruiting key account salespeople.

6.3 DECIDING WHETHER TO USE KEY ACCOUNT MANAGEMENT

An important question is the suitability of key account management to suppliers. Clearly it is only one form of salesforce organisation (others are discussed in Chapter 14 which covers organisation and compensation) and care is needed in deciding whether the extra resources and costs associated with its implementation can be justified. The greater the extent to which the following circumstances exist, the more likely a company is to move towards setting up key accounts (Burnett, 1992).

1 A small number of customers account for a high proportion of the supplier's sales.

2 There is potential for differentiation of the product and/or service provided by the supplier in a way that is highly valued by the customer.

3 Customers exhibit complex buying behaviour with large decision-making units applying varied choice criteria often in multiple locations meaning that a geographical organisational structure is inappropriate.

4 Multifunction contacts between supplier and customer are required.

5 Significant cost savings are possible through dealing selectively with a small number of large customers, and joint agreements of production and delivery schedules.

6 There is a danger of different salespeople from the supplier's salesforce calling upon the same customer to sell different products or offer conflicting solutions to problems.

7 The establishment of in-depth communications and strong relationships with customers may lead to the opportunity of tailoring products and services to specific customer needs.

8 Customers are centralising their operations.

9 Competition is improving its account handling by moving to key account management.

6.4 THE TASKS AND SKILLS OF KEY ACCOUNT MANAGEMENT

A study by the Bureau of Business Practice (1986) reported that choosing the best person to manage and co-ordinate key account programmes is second only in importance to obtaining support from top management. Selecting the best person requires a full understanding of the tasks and skills required of the job. Simply choosing the company's top salesperson to handle the management of a key account is not recommended because the jobs are so different (Maher, 1984) with the latter requiring a higher level of managerial ability (e.g. leadership, co-ordination, development of account strategies and communication).

Wotruba and Castleberry (1993) surveyed key account salespeople to identify the tasks performed and skills required of the job. The top ten of each are listed in Table 6.2. This list can be used to choose criteria for the recruitment, selection and evaluation of key account managers. It is not surprising that relationship building skills are paramount, and this topic will be explored later in this chapter. Next, though, we consider the special selling skills required to sell to key accounts.

6.5 KEY ACCOUNT MANAGEMENT RELATIONAL DEVELOPMENT MODEL

The development and management of a key account can be understood as a process between buyers and sellers. The KAM relational development model plots the typical progression of a buyer–seller relationship based upon the nature of the customer relationship (transactional or collaborative) and the level of involvement with customers (simple or complex). It shows five of the six stages identified by Millman and Wilson (1995): pre-KAM, early-KAM, mid-KAM, partnership-KAM and synergistic-KAM (see Figure 6.1). A sixth stage (uncoupling-KAM) represents the breakdown of the relationship which can happen at any point during the process.

Table 6.2   Tasks performed and skills required by key account management

Tasks	Skills
1 Develop long-term relationships	Relationship building
2 Engage in direct contact with key customers	Co-ordination
3 Maintain key account records and background information	Negotiation
4 Identify selling opportunities and sales potential of existing key accounts	Human relations
5 Monitor competitive developments affecting key accounts	Focus on specific objectives
6 Report results to upper management	Diagnosing customer problems
7 Monitor and/or control key account contracts	Presentation skills
8 Make high level presentations to key accounts	Generating visibility, reputation
9 Co-ordinate and expedite service to key accounts	Communication
10 Co-ordinate communications among company units servicing key accounts.	Working in a team.

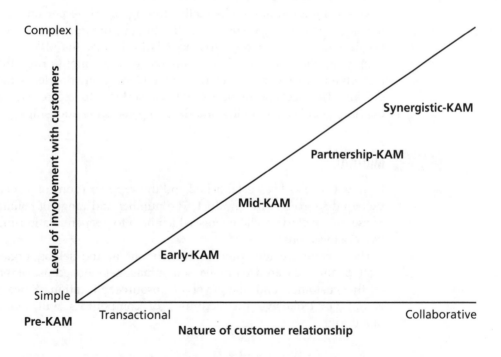

Figure 6.1   Key account relational development model

Pre-KAM

Pre-KAM describes preparation for KAM or 'prospecting'. The task is to identify those accounts with the potential for moving towards key account status and to avoid wasting investment on those accounts that lack the potential. Pre-KAM selling strategies involve making products and services available while attempting to gather information about customers so that their key account potential can be assessed. Where an account is thought to have potential but breaking into the account is proving difficult, patience and persistence is required. A breakthrough may result from the 'in' supplier doing something wrong, e.g. refusing to quote for a low-profit order or failing to repair equipment promptly.

Early-KAM

Early-KAM involves the exploration of opportunities for closer collaboration by identifying the motives, culture and concerns of the customer. The selling company needs to convince the customer of the benefits of being a 'preferred customer'. It will seek to understand the customer's decision-making unit and processes, and the problems and opportunities that relate to the value adding processes. Product and service adaptations may be made to fit customer needs better. An objective of the sales effort will be to build trust based on consistent performance and open communications.

Most communication is channelled through one salesperson (the key account manager) and a single contact at the buying organisation. This makes for a fragile relationship, particularly as it is likely that the seller is one of many supplying the account. The customer will be monitoring the supplier's performance to assess competence and to identify any problems that might arise quickly. The account manager will be seeking to create a more attractive offering, establish credibility and deepen personal relationships.

Mid-KAM

By now trust has been established and the supplier is one of a small number of preferred sources of the product. The number and range of contacts increases. These may include social events which help to deepen relationships across the two organisations.

The account review process carried out at the selling organisation will tend to move upwards to involve senior management because of the importance of the customer and the level of resource allocation. Since the account is not yet exclusive the activities of competitors will require constant monitoring.

Partnership KAM

This is the stage where the buying organisation regards the supplier as an important strategic resource. The level of trust will be sufficient for both parties to be willing to share sensitive information. The focus of activities moves to joint problem-solving, collaborative product development and mutual training of the other firm's staff.

The buying company is now channelling nearly all of its business in the relevant product group(s) to the one supplier. The arrangement is formalised in a partnership agreement of at least three years duration. Performance will be monitored and contacts between departments of the two organisations extensive. The buying organisation will expect guaranteed continuity of supply, excellent service, and top quality products. A key task of the account manager is to reinforce the high levels of trust to exclude potential competitors.

Synergistic-KAM

Synergistic-KAM is the ultimate stage of the relational development model. Buyer and seller see one another not as two separate organisations, but as part of a larger entity. Top management commitment manifests itself in joint board meetings, and joint business planning, research and development, and market research take place. Costing systems become transparent, unnecessary costs are removed, and process improvements are mutually achieved. For example, a logistics company together with one of its retail key accounts has six cross-boundary teams working on process improvements at any one time (McDonald and Rogers, 1998).

Uncoupling-KAM

This is where transactions and interactions cease. The causes of uncoupling need to be understood so that it can be avoided. Breakdowns are more often attributable to changes in key personnel and relationship problems than price conflicts. The danger of uncoupling is particularly acute in early-KAM when the single point of contact prevails. If, for example, the key account manager leaves to be replaced by someone who in the buyer's eyes is less skilled, or there is a personality clash, the relationship may end.

A second cause of uncoupling is a breach of trust. For example, the breaking of a promise over a delivery deadline, product improvement or equipment repair can weaken or kill a business relationship. The key to handling such problems is to reduce the impact of surprise. The supplier should let the buying organisation know immediately a problem becomes apparent. It should also show humility when discussing the problem with the customer.

Companies also uncouple through neglect. Long-term relationships can foster complacency and customers can perceive themselves as being taken for granted. Cultural mismatches can occur, for example, when the customer stresses price whereas the supplier focuses on life-cycle costs. Difficulties can also occur between bureaucratic and entrepreneurial styles of management.

Product or service quality problems can also provoke uncoupling. Any kind of performance problem, or perceptions that rivals now offer superior performance, can trigger a breakdown in relations. 'In' suppliers must build entry barriers by ensuring that product and service quality is constantly improved and that any problems are dealt with speedily and professionally.

Not all uncoupling is instigated by the buying company. A key account may be derated or terminated because of loss of market share or the onset of financial problems that impair the attractiveness of the account.

6.6 SELLING TO KEY ACCOUNTS

The skills and techniques discussed in Chapter 5 have provided a firm foundation for understanding the basics of selling. However, there are special characteristics of key accounts which mean that additional considerations are needed to sell successfully to these larger customers. Let us compare the characteristics of low value sales and key sales as summarised in Table 6.3.

The differences between a low value sale (e.g. the purchase of a single telephone answering machine by a company) and a key sale (e.g. the purchase of a new computing system for the whole company) shown in Table 6.3 have implications for the selling process. First, since key sales require multiple calls and the decision (involving many people) is often made when the seller is not present, the use of closing techniques is severely limited. Indeed their use may cause customer annoyance and antagonism since the time and situation will almost certainly be inappropriate.

Second, since the key sale usually results in an ongoing relationship (e.g. after-sales support would be vital with the sale of a new computing system), the people making the sale may become inseparable from the product itself in the customer's mind. Finally, since key sales involve large amounts of money and are highly visible, they incur high risk for those involved in the decision.

Table 6.3 Characteristics of low value and key sales

Low value sale	Key sale
Sale often made in one call	Multiple calls required
Decision usually made when seller is present	Decision often made when seller is not present (e.g. in committee)
Decision made by one or few people	Decision involves many people
May be a one-off event	Usually an ongoing relationship
Low expenditure	High expenditure
Low risk	High risk

Consequently, a key task of selling is to convince the customer that the value of the purchase outweighs the expenditure and risks involved.

Effective selling to key accounts has been the subject of research conducted by the Huthwaite Research Group, culminating in a book that presented their findings and described an approach to achieving key sales (Rackham, 1987). The following discussion describes the sales approach advocated by this research team. The sales process is given in Figure 6.2. It comprises a four-stage model:

1 a preliminary stage designed to open the call;
2 an investigation stage where facts about, and the needs of, the customer are discovered;
3 a demonstration of capability stage, where the salesperson shows how he or she can help the customer;
4 the final stage is to obtain a commitment from the customer to continue to the next phase of the sale. This recognises that key sales require multiple calls, and that the call objective will not be to close the sale but to end with some kind of commitment (e.g. to attend a product demonstration) on the part of the customer.

Each of these stages will now be described.

Preliminaries

The preliminary stage is given much less attention than the other stages by the Huthwaite Research Group, simply because they did not find significant

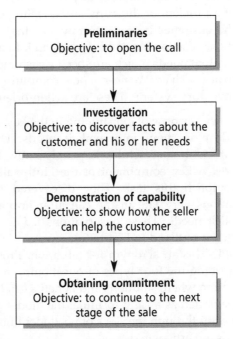

Figure 6.2 Stages in a sales call to key accounts

differences in the effectiveness of various approaches. They found that successful salespeople used a wide variety of openings whereas less successful salespeople were more rigid, relying on one preferred way to open the call. However, a common thread linking successful preliminaries for first-time visits was that they established the following:

● *who* the seller was (name, company, line of business)
● *why* the seller was there (topic(s) to discuss)
● the right of the seller to ask questions (this was referred to in Chapter 5 as *permissioning*, and might involve asking the question, 'Would you mind if I asked you a few questions about …?'

A key aspect of opening the call is not to spend too much time on preliminaries; it is more productive to devote time to the next two stages of investigation and demonstrating capabilities.

Investigation

This is a crucial stage in selling to key accounts. According to Rackham (1987), sales success is more dependent on implementation of investigating skills than any other factor. Questions are used to discover facts about the customer and to identify needs. He identifies two types of needs:

1 **Implied needs** which were expressed by customers as problems, difficulties or dissatisfactions such as 'our existing computing process is too slow' or 'I'm unhappy with the flexibility of our inventory system'. However, recognition of a problem or difficulty and a feeling of dissatisfaction does not mean that the customer is ready to buy. For that to happen, the problem/difficulty/ dissatisfaction has to be developed into an explicit need.
2 **Explicit needs** which are specific customer expressions of wants, or intentions to act, such as 'We need a new computing system' or 'I intend to install a new inventory system'. These are action-orientated needs that trigger purchase.

A key purpose of questioning in the key sale is to discover implied needs and to develop them into explicit needs. Uncovering implied needs alone is insufficient: successful salespeople know how to translate them into explicit needs. A key component of the Huthwaite Research Group's approach is to accomplish this task. They discovered that successful salespeople offered solutions very late in the call after implied needs had been developed into explicit needs. These observations led to the creation of the SPIN® strategy which is outlined in Figure 6.3.

SPIN® is an acronym for Situation, Problem, Implication and Need-payoff, describing the four types of questioning required to move the customer to the situation where solutions and benefits can be examined. Although it should not be regarded as a rigid formula, the model provides a set of guidelines taking a sales call through the steps of need identification and development until explicit needs are articulated.

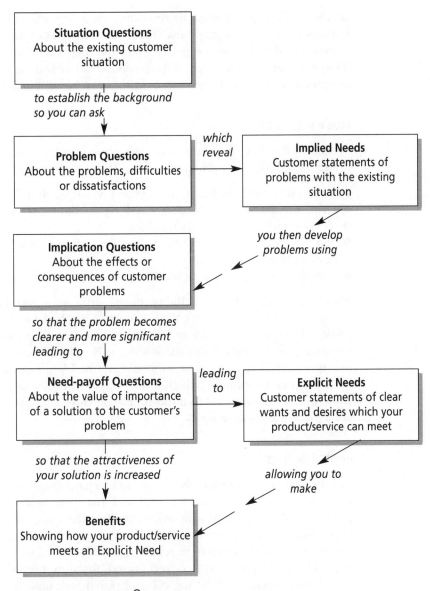

Figure 6.3   The SPIN® model
Reproduced with permission of the Huthwaite Research Group Ltd, Rotherham, UK.
(SPIN® is a registered trademark of Huthwaite Research Group)

Situation questions

These are used to identify facts about the customer (e.g. their position, responsibilities and role in the buying decision), their business (e.g. type, sales volume, rate of growth, number of employees) and specific information relevant to the product field (e.g. current products and/or services used, when purchased). These questions establish the background to the customer's existing situation. They are crucial to first-time visits but also on repeat calls since changes in situations may need to be identified. The problem with situation questions is that they are often boring for the customer who may grow impatient if too many are asked. Successful salespeople do their homework as part of their call preparation so that situation questions can be kept to a minimum.

Problem questions

Instead of dwelling on unnecessary situation questions, successful salespeople spend more time on problem questions. Typical examples are as follows:

- 'Are you completely happy with your present machine?'
- 'What are the disadvantages of handling the data manually?'
- 'Is your equipment entirely reliable?'
- 'Isn't it difficult to get a service person out quickly to repair your photocopier?'
- 'Are there any quality problems?'

These are designed to reveal the problems, difficulties and dissatisfactions with the current situation so that the customer's implied needs can be identified. Although important in selling, the Huthwaite Research found their use to be more strongly linked to sales success in smaller rather than larger sales. The key in larger sales is not to follow immediately the identification of implied needs with suggested solutions (which often happens); rather the salesperson should use implication questions to build up the perceived seriousness of the problem before offering a solution.

Implication questions

Two important distinctions between smaller and larger sales are the levels of expenditure involved and the personal risk associated with each type of purchase. Making a key sale often involves the purchaser sanctioning large expenditure and accepting a high level of personal risk of a mistake being made. These are the costs of purchase. Customers need to be convinced that the implications of the problems recognised through problem questioning are sufficiently severe to offset the costs of purchase. Some customers are able to see the implications clearly for themselves, but in many cases the true seriousness of the problem will only be perceived through the salesperson using implication questions.

Implication questions are designed to encourage customers to state the consequences, effects or implications of their problems. They magnify the size of the implied needs (problems, difficulties, dissatisfactions) in the current situation. For example, a problem question may have revealed that a machine is unreliable; an implication question would ask for the consequences of this unreliability, e.g. loss of output, greater personal inconvenience and aggravation, higher costs because of the need for more overtime payments.

Typical implication questions are:

- 'What effect does unreliability have on output?'
- 'Could unreliability lead to increased costs?'
- 'Does the difficulty of using the computer lead to higher training costs?'
- 'How does the late delivery of parts affect your customers?'
- 'What are the implications of your supplier's slow repair service?'

Implication questions are central to success in selling to key accounts because they build up the customer's perception of the severity of the problem. Rackham termed these 'sad questions' because they focused on problems such as increased costs, lower output and slow delivery. The next step is to use need-payoff questions to build up the customer's perception of the value or usefulness of a solution.

Need-payoff questions

Need-payoff questions transfer the focus of attention from problems, difficulties and dissatisfactions to a more positive solution-centred discussion. For example, problem questions may have revealed that a machine is unreliable; implication questions may have discovered that the implications are higher costs and lower output; need-payoff questions can now focus on the value of a solution.

Seller	'… so your main problem is machine unreliability leading to higher costs and lower output. (*need-payoff question*) So, from what you've said, you'd be interested in a machine that would be more reliable?'
Customer	'Yes, we need to sort out this problem.'
Seller	(*need-payoff question*) 'If your machine only had a down-time of two hours for maintenance every six months, how would that affect costs?'
Customer	'It would drastically reduce overtime payments; it might save up to £50,000 a year.'
Seller	(*need-payoff question*) 'And how would output be affected?'
Customer	'Output might go up 5 per cent producing an extra £100,000 worth of components.'

Need-payoff questions were termed 'happy' questions by Rackham because they focus on the usefulness or value of solving a problem. They produce responses from customers that are pleasing.

Typical examples of need-payoff questions are:

- 'How would reducing down-time help you?'
- 'Why would reducing preparation time be important to you?'
- 'What benefits would you see in a faster machine?'
- 'Why would you like to see a reduction in inventory levels?'
- 'Would eliminating the need to train staff save you money?'

Such questions focus on the value of solving the problems the customer is facing, and they create a positive helpful atmosphere in which to do business.

Furthermore, they ask the customer to tell the salesperson the benefits rather than the other way around. Thus customers convince themselves of the value of solving the problems. Crucially, the process provides the opportunity for the customer as a member of the decision-making unit to rehearse describing those benefits to other people in the DMU. The importance of this is explained in the following case history.

SELLING
AND SALES
MANAGEMENT
IN ACTION

Selling to a key account

A highly successful salesperson in the process control industry was once asked how he had sold a multi-million pound system to a major oil company. He replied that the key was to remember that the salesperson only plays a small part in the selling process. The real selling takes place when the salesperson is not there, when the people to whom he/she sold go back and try to convince the others. His success came about because he made sure the people he talked to knew how to sell on his behalf.

He was like a director of a play. His work was during rehearsals but he did not take part in the performance. Too many salespeople want to be great actors, but even if they are great performers, they won't be on stage for more than a tiny fraction of the selling time. The successful salesperson needs to rehearse the rest of the cast to ensure the show will not be a 'flop'.

Adapted from Rackham, N. (1987) *'Making Major Sales'*, Gower, p. 63.

Providing customers with the chance to explain the usefulness of the solution to the salesperson gives them valuable practice for when they need to present a convincing explanation to other people in their company. This aids the internal selling that is so often necessary in key account sales.

The combination of implication and need-payoff questions, then, has moved the customer from describing implied needs (e.g. a problem with machine unreliability, or difficulty with using a computer) to developing explicit needs ('I need a more reliable machine', or 'I would like a computer that is easier to use'). The dual effect of building up the seriousness of the problem (through implication questions) and recognition of the value of the solution (through need-payoff questions) is to convince the customer of the need to find a solution through a purchase.

Usually need-payoff questions will follow problem and implication questions as suggested by the SPIN® acronym. Indeed Rackham found that top sales-people built up the perception of problems before asking need-payoff questions. However, there are exceptions to this sequence, depending on the sales situation.

For example, if the customer volunteers an explicit need (e.g. 'we must buy a more reliable machine') at an early stage in the call, then it would be sensible to move directly to need-payoff questions to build up the perceived value of a new machine. There are also circumstances when need-payoff questions should not be used. If, for example, a customer suggests an explicit need, (e.g. 'I need a photocopier that can copy colour slides') a need-payoff question like 'Why do you need copies of colour slides?' would be appropriate if the saleperson was able to supply a copier that met this need since it would encourage the customer to consider and build up the importance of that need. However, if the salesperson could not meet that need, asking a need-payoff question would be unwise for the very same reason.

Demonstration of capability

The natural next step after developing explicit needs through implication and need-payoff questions is to demonstrate the seller's capability to meet those needs. To do this, product benefits which relate directly to expressed needs should be used, for example:

Buyer   (*expressed need*) 'I want a system that has an error rate of less than 1 in 200,000.'
Seller   (*benefit*) 'I'm pleased to say that our system can give you that. It has an error rate of less than 1 in 500,000.'

The key is to wait until an explicit need has been stated; then the salesperson knows the benefit (a statement which shows how an expressed need can be satisfied) is important to the customer. Presenting potential solutions too soon is a common mistake in selling to key accounts. The problem is that the customer is often not convinced of a need and therefore raises objections. For example, when trying to sell a word processor:

Buyer   (*implied need*) 'We do have a problem with the use of different fonts on our current system.'
Seller   (*potential solution*) 'Yes, I've heard reports about that problem with the type of system you have. Our software has been developed without the bugs that cause the problems you have been experiencing.'
Buyer   (*objection*) 'That's fine but you won't find me paying £3,500 just to sort out a few problems with fonts.'

Since the salesperson has failed to build up the problem and the value of the solution in the buyer's mind by means of implication and need-payoff questions, the buyer understandably raises an objection concerning cost.

Obtaining commitment

Rather than trying to close the sale, most sales calls to key accounts attempt to accomplish a commitment which moves the sale forwards towards a decision, such as

● obtaining the customer's agreement to attend a product demonstration
● getting the customer to test a new material

● persuading the customer to grant access to a higher level of decision-maker.

Attempts to close the sale using inappropriate and badly timed closing techniques may cause customer annoyance when dealing with sophisticated buyers who realise what is going on. Such practices spoil the personal relationships that are so vital in key account selling. Instead a three-step process is proposed by Rackham (1987), in which the salesperson should:

1 Check that key concerns have been covered

The complexity of key account buying means that the customer may still have doubts, points of confusion or concerns as the end of the sales call approaches. Effective salespeople ask their customers if they have any points or concerns that need to be addressed. For example:

Seller 'OK, that seems to have covered the key issues. Is there anything else you would like me to tell you about? '

2 Summarise the benefits

To give a clear picture of the key points of discussion, and to avoid any misunderstanding, successful salespeople summarise the key issues before proposing a commitment. For example:

Seller 'Fine, we have discussed how the new system will reduce costs by around £50,000 a year through faster operation and its simple controls. Also we have seen how the system uses tried-and-tested components which means that the reliability problems you have been having are a thing of the past.'

3 Propose a commitment

The natural next step is to propose a commitment (or action agreement). This should both advance the sale, and be realistic given the stage of the decision-making process reached and the degree of interest being shown by the customer. An example of a commitment proposal might be:

Seller 'I'm glad you like what we have been talking about. Could I suggest that the next step would be for you and your quality control manager to visit a local company to see our system in action.'

This section of the chapter has examined a four-stage model for selling into key accounts. Next we shall explore the key aspects of key account management, beginning with relationship building.

6.7 BUILDING RELATIONSHIPS WITH KEY ACCOUNTS

The importance of relationship building with customers is reflected in Chapter 7 of this book, entitled 'Relationship Selling'. However, there are certain ways in which suppliers can build relationships with key accounts. Five ways of building strong customer relationships will now be described.

1 Personal trust

The objective is to build confidence and reassurance.
Methods:

- ensure promises are kept
- reply swiftly to queries, problems and complaints
- establish high (but not intrusive) frequency of contact with key account
- arrange factory/site visits
- engage in social activities with customer
- give advance warning of problems.

2 Technical support

The objective is to provide know-how and improve the productivity of the key account.
Methods:

- research and development co-operation
- before- and after-sales service
- provide training
- dual selling (supplier helps key account to sell).

3 Resource support

The objective is to reduce the key account's financial burden.
Methods:

- provide credit facilities
- create low interest loans
- engage in co-operative promotions to share costs
- engage in counter-trade (accept payment by means of goods or services rather than cash).

4 Service levels

The objective is to improve the quality of service provision.

Methods:

- reliable delivery
- fast/just-in-time delivery
- install computerised re-order systems
- give fast accurate quotes
- defect reduction (right first time).

5 Risk reduction

The objective is to lower uncertainty in the customer's mind regarding the supplier, and the products/services provided.
Methods:

- free demonstrations
- free/low-cost trial period
- product guarantees
- delivery guarantees
- preventative maintenance contracts
- proactive follow-ups
- reference selling.

Suppliers should consult the above checklist to evaluate the cost/benefit of using each of the methods of building strong relationships with each account. A judgement needs to be made regarding the value each key account places on each method and the cost (including executive and management time) of providing the item.

Managing relationships involves taking care in day-to-day meetings with customers. Table 6.4 gives a list of some key dos and don'ts of key account management.

6.8 KEY ACCOUNT INFORMATION AND PLANNING SYSTEM

The importance of key accounts means that suppliers need to consider the information that needs to be collected and stored for each account, and the objectives, strategies and control systems that are required to manage the accounts. This can be accomplished by a key account information and planning system. The benefits of planning systems include the following:

Consistency

The plan provides a focal point for decisions and action leading to better consistency and co-ordination between managers.

Table 6.4   Handling relationships with key accounts

Key account do's

Work with the account to agree an actionable account plan.
Understand key account decision making:
● key choice criteria
● roles of decision making unit
● how decisions are made.
Only ever agree to what can be delivered.
Resolve issues quickly.
Confirm agreements in writing.
Communicate internally to identify unresolved problems (e.g. late delivery).
Treat customers as 'experts' to encourage them to reveal information.
View issues from the customer's (as well as your own) perspective.
Ask questions: knowledge is power.

Key account don'ts

Don't let a small issue spoil a relationship.
Don't expect to win everything, giving a concession may improve the relationship.
Don't divulge confidential information from other accounts.
Don't view negotiations as win-lose scenarios. Try to create win-win situations.
Don't be afraid to say 'No' when the circumstances demand it.
Don't deceive: if you do not know the answer, say so.

Monitoring of change

The planning process forces managers to review the impact of change on the account, and to consider the actions required to meet the new challenges.

Resource allocation

The planning process asks fundamental questions about resource allocation. Some of the questions that require addressing are, should the account receive more, the same or less resources; how should those resources be deployed; and how should resources be allocated between accounts?

Competitive advantage

Planning promotes the search for better ways of servicing the account in order to keep out competing firms.

The building block for the planning system is the account audit which is based on the creation of an information system that collects, stores and disseminates essential account data. Table 6.5 shows the kind of data that may form such a system. Hard data record the facts and figures of the account such as the products sold and markets served, and the sales volume (units), revenue and profits generated by the customer. Such general data provide the fundamental background information to the account.

Table 6.5   A key account information system

	Type of data	
	Hard	*Soft*
General	Addresses, telephone facsimile and telex numbers, e-mail addresses	Decision-making unit members
	Customer products sold and markets served (size and growth rates)	Choice criteria
		Perceptions and attitudes
		Buying processes
	Sales volume and revenue	Assessment of relationships
	Profits	Problems and threats
	Capital employed	Opportunities
	Operating ratios (e.g. return on capital employed, profit margin)	Suppliers' strengths and weaknesses
		Competitors' strengths and weaknesses
		Environmental changes affecting account now and in the future
Specific	Supplier's sales to account by product	
	Supplier's price levels and profitability by product	
	Details of discounts and allowances	
	Competitors' products, price levels and sales	
	Contract expiry dates	

Specific hard data cover issues that focus on the transactions between seller and customer such as the seller's sales and profits by product, supplier and competitor's price levels, competitor's products sold to the customer, their volume and revenue, details of discounts and contract expiry dates. Absolute levels, trends and variations from targets will be recorded.

Soft data complement hard data by providing qualitative (and sometimes more subjective) assessments of the account situation. A key requirement is the holding of buyer behaviour data such as the names, positions and roles of decision-making unit members, their choice criteria/perceptions/attitudes and buying processes. An assessment of the ongoing relationships should be made, and any problems, threats and opportunities defined. The suppliers' and competitors' strengths and weaknesses should be analysed in both absolute and relative terms. Finally, external changes (such as declining markets, changes in technology and potential new competition) should be monitored as they may affect future business with the account.

The outcome of this account audit can be summarised in a strengths, weaknesses, opportunities and threats (SWOT) analysis (see Figure 6.4). The internal strengths and weaknesses of the supplier are summarised as they relate to the opportunities and threats relevant to the account. SWOT analysis provides a convenient framework for making decisions to improve the effectiveness of key account management and provides insights to develop the account plan. For example, action can be taken to exploit opportunities by building on strengths, and to minimise the impact of threats.

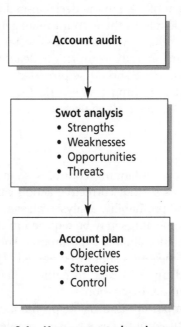

Figure 6.4 Key account planning system

An account plan comprises objectives, strategies and control procedures:

Objectives

The account plan should set out clear objectives for the planning period. Typically objectives will be stated in terms of sales and profit-by-product for each account for the planning period. Pricing objectives will state target price changes for the period. Where more than one supplier services the account, share-of-business objectives may be set. For example, the SWOT analysis may identify an opportunity resulting from service problems associated with a competitor. This may encourage the development of an objective to raise the share of business from 40 to 55 per cent.

A long sales cycle is characteristic of many key account sales. It is, therefore, often sensible to couch objectives in terms of gaining customer commitment rather than of achieving a sales close, particularly if the account planning period is relatively short. Such objectives must be set in terms of customer responses, not seller actions. For example, suitable objectives may be to persuade the customer to visit the seller's site, agree to a product demonstration, or give the seller's new product an extended trial.

Strategies

Strategies are the means by which objectives are achieved. For example, the objective of persuading the customer to visit the seller's site would require a statement of who in the decision-making unit should be targeted, the identities of the people in the account management team responsible for reaching these people, what action they need to take to persuade the customer to make the visit, and activity completion deadlines. Obviously not every detail can be planned: scope should be provided for individual initiative and enterprise, but without a guiding framework, the activities may become unco-ordinated or, worse still, the task neglected.

Control

An account planning control system checks progress on the achievement of objectives so that corrective action can be taken when needed. Computerised sales and profitability analysis can evaluate actual performance against objectives. Review meetings may be required to compare both quantitative and qualitative performance against expectations. The frequency, coverage and composition of review meetings should be agreed. The agenda for these meetings should be decided upon in time to gather, analyse and present information relevant to topics under discussion.

An important issue is the profitability of each key account. A check should be made on account costs as well as sales revenue. Account costs may be broken down as follows:

(i) Sales staff costs
These would include the costs of all sales staff working on the account, e.g. the account manager, account executives and any field salesforce activity related to the account. For example, for a multiple retailer account, the account manager would reach an agreement with the field salesforce manager to provide a certain level of support (perhaps two visits per store per week). The costs of these visits would be included in the calculation of sales staff costs.

(ii) Support staff costs
In a technical environment such as telecommunications or information technology, this would comprise people such as systems engineers who might undertake pre-bid analysis and planning, and also any dedicated maintenance people.

(iii) Other sales and marketing costs

These might include account specific promotions, special packaging and special payment terms such as discounts. Special distribution arrangements, e.g. to individual stores rather than one central warehouse, would also fall into this category of account costs.

The above is an example of how a company may break down account costs, but organisations have the choice of how best to categorise account costs given their own circumstances and requirements. By itemising costs, results can be compared against budget and areas that require investigation will be revealed.

6.9 CONCLUSIONS

This chapter has examined the crucial task of selling to and managing key accounts. Selling skills tend to differ between low-cost and key sale situations. The additional skills and techniques necessary to sell to key customers have been examined.

An important ingredient in managing key accounts is the ability to manage relationships over a long period of time. We have discussed ways to build trust, provide technical and resource support, improve service levels, and reduce risk for the customer. Additionally this chapter has examined ways of deciding whether a key account system is appropriate and, if it is, how to create a key account information and planning system.

PRACTICAL EXERCISE

Cloverleaf plc

Cloverleaf plc was a UK-based supplier of bottling plant used in production lines to transport and fill bottles. Two years ago it opened an overseas sales office targeting Germany, France and the Benelux countries. It estimated that there were over 1000 organisations in those countries that had bottling facilities, and that a key sales push in northern Europe was therefore warranted. Sales so far had been disappointing with only three units having been sold. Expectations had been much higher than this, given the advantages of their product over that produced by their competitors.

Technological breakthroughs at Cloverleaf meant that their bottling lines had a 10 per cent speed advantage over the nearest competition with equal filling accuracy. A key problem with competitor products was unreliability. Down-time due to a line breakdown was extremely costly to bottlers. Tests by Cloverleaf engineers at their research and development establishment in the UK had shown their system to be the most reliable on the market.

Cloverleaf's marketing strategy was based around high quality, high price competitive positioning. They believed that the superior performance of their product justified a 10 per cent price premium over their key competitors who were all priced at around £1 million for a standard production line. Salespeople were told to stress the higher speed and enhanced reliability when talking to customers. The sales organisation in northern Europe consisted of a sales manager with three salespeople assigned to Germany, France and the Benelux countries respectively. A technical specialist was also available when required. When a sales call required specialist technical assistance, a salesperson would contact the sales office to arrange for the technical specialist to visit the prospect, usually together with the salesperson.

Typically, four groups of people inside buying organisations were involved in the purchase of bottling equipment, namely the production manager, the production engineer, the purchasing officer and, where large sums of money were involved (over £½ million), the technical director. Production managers were mainly interested in smooth production flows and cost savings. Production engineers were charged with drawing up specifications for new equipment, and in large firms, they were usually asked to draw up state-of-the-art specifications. The purchasing officers, who were often quite powerful, were interested in the financial aspects of any purchase, and technical directors, while interested in technical issues, also appreciated the prestige associated with having state-of-the-art technology.

John Goodman was the sales executive covering France. While in the sales office in Paris, he received a call from Dr Leblanc, the technical director of Commercial SA, a large Marseille-based bottling company who bottled under licence a number of key soft drink brands. They had a reputation for technical excellence and innovation. Goodman made an appointment to see Dr Leblanc on 7 March. He was looking forward to making his first visit to this company. The following extracts are taken from his record of his sales calls:

March 7
Called on Dr Leblanc who told me that Commercial SA had decided to purchase a new bottling line as a result of expansion, and asked for details of what we could provide. I described our system and gave him our sales literature. He told me that three of our competitors had already discussed their system with him. As I was leaving, he suggested that I might like to talk to M. Artois, their production engineer, to check specifications.

March 8
Visited M. Artois who showed me the specifications that he had drawn up. I was delighted to see that our specifications easily exceeded them but was concerned that his specifications seemed to match those of one of our competitors, Hofstead Gm., almost exactly. I showed M. Artois some of our technical manuals. He did not seem impressed.

March 11
Visited Dr Leblanc who appeared very pleased to see me. He asked me to give

him three reasons why they should buy from us. I told him that our system was more technologically advanced than the competition, was more reliable and had a faster bottling speed. He asked me if I was sure it was the most technologically advanced. I said that there was no doubt about it. He suggested I contact M. Bernard, the purchasing manager. I made an appointment to see him in two days' time.

March 13
Called on M. Bernard. I discussed the technical features of the system with him. He asked me about price. I told him I would get back to him on that.

March 15
Visited Dr Leblanc who said a decision was being made within a month. I repeated our operational advantages and he asked me about price. I told him I would give him a quote as soon as possible.

March 20
Saw M. Bernard. I told him our price was £1.1m. He replied that a key competitor had quoted less than £1m. I replied that the greater reliability and bottling speed meant that our higher price was more than justified. He remained unimpressed.

March 21
Had a meeting with Mike Bull my sales manager to discuss tactics. I told him that there were problems. He suggested that all purchasing managers liked to believe they were saving their company money. He told me to reduce my price by £50,000 to satisfy M. Bernard's ego.

March 25
Told M. Bernard of our new quotation. He said he still did not understand why we could not match the competition on price. I repeated our technical advantages over the competition and told him that our 10 per cent faster speed and higher reliability had been proven by our research and development engineers.

March 30
Visited Dr Leblanc who said a meeting had been arranged for April 13 to make the final decision but that our price of £1.05m was too high for the likes of M. Bernard.

April 4
Hastily arranged a meeting with Mike Bull to discuss the situation. Told him about Dr Leblanc's concern that M. Bernard thought our price was too high. He said that £1m was as low as we could go.

April 5
Took our final offer to M. Bernard. He said he would let me know as soon as a decision was made. He stressed that the decision was not his alone; several other people were involved.

April 16
Received a letter from M. Bernard stating that the order had been placed with Hofstead Gm. He thanked me for the work I had put into the bid made by Cloverleaf plc.

DISCUSSION QUESTION

Analyse the reasons for the failure to secure the order and discuss the lessons to be learnt for key account management.

EXAMINATION QUESTIONS

1 Discuss the differences between the characteristics of low and high value sales.

2 What are the key skills required of a key account manager?

3 Distinguish between implicit and explicit needs. Discuss their importance in selling to key accounts.

CHAPTER 7

RELATIONSHIP SELLING

OBJECTIVES   After studying this chapter, you should be able to:

1 Relate to the ideas put forward by the early quality practitioners.

2 See that quality now embraces the organisation as a whole rather than being the sole concern of manufacturing.

3 Understand how freer world trade is driving companies towards accepting the need for quality in terms of their relationships with their customers and their suppliers.

4 Appreciate the role that is being played by 'just-in-time' manufacturing in bringing about these changes.

5 Understand the notion of reverse marketing and the change it is bringing about in the traditionally accepted roles of the field salesperson.

6 Understand the notion of relationship selling as being the tactical marketing and sales key stemming from the adoption of reverse marketing.

KEY CONCEPTS
- total quality management (TQM)
- customer care
- relationship marketing
- product or project champion
- best practice benchmarking (BPB)
- supply chain integration (SCI)
- opening account
- relationship selling

7.1   FROM TOTAL QUALITY MANAGEMENT TO CUSTOMER CARE

'There is only one valid definition of business: to create customers. It is the customer who determines the nature of the business. Consequently, any business has two basic functions:

- marketing (customer orientation)
- innovation.'

This far-sighted quotation came from Peter Drucker (1973), and it was originally said in 1954.

Another management thinker, who is more often associated with engineering than with management, was W. Edwards Deming who has been credited with guiding the Ford Motor Company (USA) towards a sharp focus on quality, not just in manufacturing, but in all of its operations including selling. He formulated a mature theory of quality in the 1970s based upon his observations of Japanese manufacturing. His theory revolved around 14 points of philosophical thinking, and he is widely regarded as being the modern quality guru. His thinking has changed the way that manufacturing companies operate, as was evidenced from earlier applications in the late 1970s and early 1980s through 'quality circles', or self-motivated works committees assigned to the improvement of quality. This tactical thinking has now been replaced by the more mature and strategic view of **total quality management (TQM)** that dominates present-day thinking, not just in manufacturing, but in all areas of company activity.

Taeger (1992) contends that these early ideas of quality still tend to trigger mental pictures that are more related to manufacturing than to the business of selling. This is because its phraseology and concepts relate back to the origins of the quality philosophy of the manufacturing processes from whence Deming took his inspiration. Taeger goes on to say that the difficulty in measuring the success of the quality process in sales is that, even when the initial phase has passed, there are rarely any positive pointers that can be identified as having been improved as a result of the introduction of TQM as part of the philosophy of selling.

Despite some negative thinking that still exists in relation to the perception of quality, it is a fact that since the 1980s many bigger companies have recognised that the key to success is the need to evolve from a production- and cost-dominant stance, towards one of serving a diverse range of customers through personal contact. A key factor in this transition relates to the process of forming relationships. As the strategic perspective of companies is changing from regional thinking to global thinking, the selling model is changing from a 'transactions' focus to a 'relationships' focus.

Schill and McArthur (1992) contend that this evolution is taking place now, with marketing taking on more of a strategic dimension, and with manufacturing, finance and human resource management being integrated and matched to support a coherent competitive strategy to assist marketing in such matters as cost leadership and product differentiation.

As the world-wide political and regulatory climate continues to be increasingly liberal towards the encouragement of free trade, it becomes more difficult to sustain market leadership based on short-term sales-orientated transactions. Sellers must engage in building and maintaining long-lasting relationships with their customers. Stalk *et al*. (1992) cite the case of Honda's original success in motorcycles resulting from the company's distinctive capability in dealer management, which departed from the traditional relationship between motorcycle manufacturers and dealers. Honda provided operating procedures and policies of merchandising, selling, floor-planning and service management. It trained all its dealers and their staff in these new management systems and supported them with a computerised dealer management information system.

Customer-focused quality is now essential because it involves a change from an operations-centred to a customer-targeted activity. As the move towards a global economy quickens, so customers demand quality in terms of their relationships with sellers, with increased emphasis being placed on reliability, durability, ease of use and after-sales service. This leads to the modern notion of **customer care**. Customer care is a philosophy which ensures that products or services and the after-care associated with serving customers' needs at least meets, and in most cases exceeds, expectations.

In support of this view, it can be argued that customer loyalty can no longer be relied upon because there is greater product and service choice. According to Sasaki (1991) marketing must react to this in a positive way by integrating new customers into a company in an attempt to develop a new relationship between them and the company. These new customers expect products or services to be in harmony with their lifestyles and values, and he contends that a winning product concept is generated when designers and consumers share a contemporary atmosphere and interact with each other, in other words when customers feel more 'involved'. This is central to the notion of customer care. He further proposes that this atmosphere can be created as a result of technological advancements in mature cultures where style, tastes and demand can be better anticipated, and where suitable products can be developed.

This view is evidenced by the approach of Nissan, the Japanese car manufacturer, when they saw that their market share was in decline. They changed their organisational structure and company philosophy to reflect, as its first priority, the concept of customer satisfaction. Development times were cut, leading to quicker lead times, and this, coupled with a greater awareness of what customers wanted, had the effect of turning the fortunes of the company around and placing it in a more stable position in the marketplace. Further, more recent, evidence of the success that close attention to customer needs can create, is provided by the case of the Microsoft Corporation. Microsoft realised that the average person had little training or knowledge of computer software or programming. They replaced technical jargon with easily understandable icons and graphical representations of the tasks to be done. Microsoft is now the largest software company in the world and its founder, Bill Gates, is now one of the richest men in the world.

The idea of total product quality has been explored by Brooks and Wragg (1992), who contend that it is relevant to manufacturing companies adopting a market driven approach to TQM. This infers that market-led quality can ensure that customers perceive that quality is built into both the product and the service component of the total product offering, as illustrated in Figure 7.1.

Market driven TQM and the development of a total product quality for manufacturing companies, are concepts upon which companies should focus. As product parity is reached between different product offerings, so companies can gain a competitive advantage by increasing the total service component of their market offerings. This is more than simply offering an after-sales service, it is a programme of total customer care.

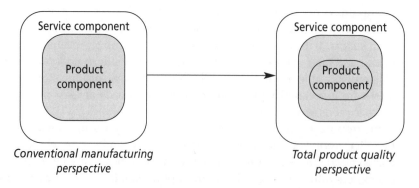

Figure 7.1 Internal to external focus of total quality perspective

7.2 FROM JIT TO RELATIONSHIP MARKETING

Christopher *et al.* (1991) have absorbed the TQM ideas of bringing together quality, marketing and customer service, and have labelled the resulting mixture **relationship marketing**. Relationship marketing means that organisations must be designed to enable them to pick up changes in the marketplace on a continuing basis. This is where the quality chain must be anchored.

This is the essence of what is termed **business process re-engineering**; for example, Toyota based its pioneering **just-in-time (JIT)** management system around the needs of customers. Work was reorganised to accommodate a variety of customer preferences in terms of the fastest possible response time and it is described as a system that delivers input to its production site at the rate and time it is needed. It thus reduces inventories within the firm, and is a mechanism for regulating the flow of products between adjacent firms in the distribution system channel.

The notion of JIT has already been dealt with from a buyer behaviour point-of-view in Chapter 2. In this context it is argued that in a well-synchronised JIT manufacturing system, customer demands can be met and profits maintained or increased through a reduction in stockpiles and inventory levels which do not gain in value as they await the production process. In fact, they cost the organisation money in terms of financing an unproductive resource. In such a system the supplier and manufacturer relationship is critical, and close associations must be developed. This typically means a reduction in the number of suppliers, and more long-term relationships. Rosenberg and Campbell (1985) have said that salespeople spend less time selling and more time liaising between buyer, engineer and their own production management. This leads us to the notion of relationship selling which will be discussed later.

Relationship marketing means that an organisation's marketing effort should be designed around a series of contacts with customers over time, rather than based on single transactions. This means that more non-marketing people are involved in the process, and has led to the notion of what Gummesson (1991) terms the **part-time marketer** as these non-marketing people are increasingly brought into contact with customers at an operational level. He states that TQM has become an integrator between production-orientation and marketing-orientation, and the convergence of these two approaches towards the same goal aims to create customer-perceived quality and customer satisfaction.

This view is further supported by Clark and Fujimoto (1990) who contend that the traditionally held view of marketing is too assumption based, and slow to respond to new customer demands. Traditional company and marketing structures are too hierarchical and rigid, and thus cannot respond to new segments or niches within a market. Clark and Fujimoto further state that in industries ranging from cars and computers to jet engines and industrial controls, new products are the focal point of competition. Developing high-quality products should be at the top of the competitive agenda for senior managers around the world.

Many companies now bring marketing into product development at a much earlier stage in the decision-making process. Temporary task forces are set up as project teams which involve personnel from different departments led by a team leader or project manager to oversee the introduction of new products. Such people are called 'product champions' or 'project champions'. In the automotive industry this normally starts at the design stage of a new vehicle when the product concept is being developed through initial brainstorming, and lasts right through to the product's launch. As a result there is continuity of interest and impetus, and it is not a matter of the project being 'handed over' to the next stage of the development through to launch process.

At a practical level the Department of Trade and Industry (1993) have introduced what they term **best practice benchmarking (BPB)**. This involves an organisation forming a project team comprising people from multifunctional areas, such as marketing, production, quality and purchasing. The team's task is to obtain information about products or companies in their industry which have a higher level of performance or activity, and to identify areas in their own organisation that need improving. The team also needs to be given the facility for research on product development and quality. It is contended that the benefits of shared knowledge in such a multifunctional team mean that companies implementing BPB should find that this drives members of the team to meet new standards, or even to exceed them.

7.3   THE NOTION OF REVERSE MARKETING

At this juncture we re-introduce the notion of **reverse marketing**. The significance of this to the selling function will be seen shortly. Reverse marketing has already been described in Chapter 2 (see Figure 2.7).

Although buyers have the purchasing power to initiate commercial transactions, it is traditionally the case within organisational buying situations that sellers tend to visit buyers, and this indeed forms the focus of this text. This is sometimes termed transactional marketing where the emphasis tends to be upon a single sale, and the time horizon tends to be short-term. Quality is generally seen to be the concern of production, and there tends to be an emphasis on product features and price.

To re-emphasise what was said earlier, the notion of reverse marketing occurs where buyers tend to take the initiative and they source suppliers (sellers). This scenario is particularly applicable in retailing and in JIT manufacturing situations. JIT manufacturing has proved to be so economical and efficient, that it will form an increasing trend in production line manufacturing situations where a relatively standardised product is being produced on a continuous basis. In this situation, buyers seek to source suppliers whom they will retain for a long period. The main criteria being sought from suppliers rest upon the quality of their goods and the reliability of their supplies as and when they are demanded. In JIT situations downtime on the production line resulting from faulty components or late delivery can prove very expensive. This view is supported by Deans and Rajagopal (1991) who say that the cheapest component procured by driving hard bargains with multiple sources is not necessarily the least expensive in the long run. Once the cost of poor quality is factored in – down-time on the production line, rework, scrap, warranty work, legal fees, etc. – the cheapest may well prove to be the most costly.

Leenders and Blenhorn (1988) state that many companies take a minimum of two years to achieve acceptable quality standards from suppliers in the situation just described. To discuss contracts for six months or one year is meaningless. Purchasing development costs must be recovered, and this has to be done over longer periods of time. Suppliers and buyers form a long-term 'co-makership' agreement where both parties derive mutual benefits.

Kearney (1994) conducted a wide-ranging study which concluded that the next wave of business improvement will not be obtained by looking at business in isolation, but by looking at the supply chain as a whole to find new opportunities to improve overall effectiveness. Additional areas of duplication and waste become evident and offer new sources of cost reduction. Service to the end customer can be driven to even higher standards by focusing the whole supply chain towards that goal, rather than diluting the efforts of individual companies through conflicting objectives. This broader vision is termed **supply chain integration (SCI)**.

The report goes on to conclude that closer relationships between suppliers and customers will become a competitive necessity. It does, however, caution that a naive belief in an ill-defined concept of partnership as a universal panacea will be counter-productive. A level of realism is required in SCI to take account of the practical difficulties of integration, the level of sophistication of the participants, and the nature of competitive advantage and power within the supply chain. Each company has a different mix (or portfolio) of supply chain relationships, each operating at different levels and the key is to select the right one for the right supply chain.

It is a fact of life at the current time that the trend towards reverse marketing will gather momentum. Buyers as a group are becoming more professional and indeed such professionalism is needed in JIT purchasing situations. So how does a seller cope with buyer needs once the company is an 'in' supplier and a long-term relationship is anticipated? This brings us back to the notion of relationship marketing. Gronroos (1990) argues that implementing the traditional view of marketing is unsatisfactory. He quotes the limitations of the 'four Ps', and claims that other 'Ps', such as people and planning, have to be added in an attempt to cover new marketing perspectives. He agrees with the concept of a company basing its activities on customer needs and wants in target markets, but argues that this still smacks of production orientation since these ideas stem from the firm and not from the marketplace. His redefinition of marketing perhaps sums up the concept of reverse marketing and the resultant cognition of relationship marketing when he states that:

> Marketing is to establish, maintain and enhance long term customer relationships at a profit so that the objectives of the parties involved are met. This is done by a mutual exchange of promises.

7.4 FROM RELATIONSHIP MARKETING TO RELATIONSHIP SELLING

Cox et al. (1995) put forward a very interesting view from a procurement angle when they contend that substantial additional value could be secured in buyer/supplier relationships by securing a greater focus on the supply chain. From the purchasing point-of-view this involves an integrated approach to value acquisition from suppliers, value addition from manufacturing and value delivery to customers.

Added to this view is the fact that the most important feature of buyer/seller transactional relationships tends to revolve around price; indeed negotiation is one of the key issues in the sales presentation. However, a new view has emerged, based on the notion of **open accounting**. This kind of agreement is only possible when long-term relationships between buyers and sellers have been established in a typical JIT production situation. Here price negotiation does not feature in buyer/seller transactions, because each side sees the other side's price make-up. Buyers will have access to the seller's accounts in terms of the cost build-up for components or materials that are being supplied. These accounts will show the amount of material, labour and expenses plus overheads that have been incorporated into the cost of such products. As the notion 'open accounting' would suggest, complete open access is afforded. Equally, suppliers will have access to the manufacturer's accounts to conduct a similar analysis. A mutually acceptable margin for profit will then be agreed between the buyer and the supplier so, in effect, the pricing element of the marketing mix has now become redundant, which perhaps gives additional credence to the earlier view relating to Gronroos' new definition of marketing.

All of the above suggests that certain tactics are needed to implement relationship marketing. This type of marketing is about the strategic thinking that accompanies the new view of marketing brought about as a result of reverse marketing. It is now contended that relationship selling concerns the tactical features of securing and building up the relationships implicit in relationship marketing.

Barnet *et al.* (1995) observe striking differences between Western and Japanese approaches to the sharing of technological effort. In Europe, an average of 54 per cent of the approximate 6,800 engineering hours needed to produce a new model are contributed by subcontractors. In the USA only about 14 per cent of the 4,200 engineering hours needed are contributed by subcontractors. In Japan, the hours required to produce a new model are lower at 3,900 but about 72 per cent of those are supplied by subcontractors. The subcontractors' ability to participate in product design gives the Japanese customer the advantage of sharing the work load, and reducing the time to market, through what is called **simultaneous engineering**. In such a relationship it is common for the partners to provide access to shared technology.

Thus the role of marketing is changing. Selling is often viewed as a tactical arm of the marketing function and its role is also changing.

In addition to the changes that have been identified so far, the marketing environment is changing in other ways. The penetration of the world-wide market by satellite and cable television means that 'blockbuster' promotional campaigns are becoming increasingly difficult to sustain owing to the fragmentation of viewers' patterns of watching television programmes. Brand loyalty will thus be more difficult to maintain. As the effectiveness of above-the-line media diminishes in general, so it will become a less attractive form of promotion for advertisers. There will be a move towards below-the-line activity as more cost-effective campaigns can now be mounted through precisely targeted direct marketing approaches. This will lead to more effective ways of generating sales leads. 'Push' rather than 'pull' promotional techniques will become increasingly popular and, of course, a 'push' promotional strategy is very much the concern of the sales function. It will also mean a general increase in customer care programmes which will be viewed as very effective means of customer retention. Big companies, who might have viewed the unique selling proposition as being their 'winning card' when dealing with customers in the past, will be compelled to adopt more of a small business philosophy by staying adjacent to their customers in terms of understanding their needs and looking after them post-sale. Gronroos (1994) contends that we are now experiencing, as the result of the growing awareness of the relationship marketing approach, a return to the natural systems-orientated way of managing customer relationships which existed before marketing became a 'clinical' decision-making discipline or an over-organised and isolated function.

Lancaster and Reynolds (1998) suggest some of the activities that are increasingly becoming the responsibility of the sales function when they describe an expanded role for the modern salesperson. Some of the views of this enlarged role have been extended into what can now be regarded as a modern view of the tactics of relationship selling.

7.5   TACTICS OF RELATIONSHIP SELLING

Customer retention constitutes a prime objective of relationship selling, and this can only be achieved in an organisational selling situation by having full regard to customers' needs, and by working to form long and trustworthy relationships. In such situations it can be seen that the length of time individual salespersons stay in particular posts may well increase since buyers generally stay in their positions about twice as long as field salespeople.

Thus it is anticipated that under relationship selling circumstances the time individual salespeople spend in a particular post will move towards that of their purchasing counterparts. Why should this be the case? It can be postulated that buyers, because of the type of role they fulfil, have what may be termed a more 'sedate' occupational lifestyle than that of the traditional salesperson whose lifestyle 'on the road' can be quite hectic. Buyers are thus more 'settled', and stay in post longer. As buyers become more proactive in the marketplace under the system of reverse marketing, so their lifestyle will become more akin to the lifestyle of the field salesperson. Although there is pressure to purchase effectively, this is a different kind of pressure to the pressure to sell in terms of reaching sales targets and quotas in a given period. At the same time, the role of the field salesperson will also experience a different kind of work pressure under reverse marketing. The pressure will focus on the longer-term goal of customer retention rather than sales targets and quotas. In fact, it is even contended that in such circumstances the traditional sales commission system might well disappear to be replaced by a higher basic salary plus bonuses shared by the expanded sales team whose ranks have been swelled by the concept of the part-time marketer. This might include production, quality and finance people, amongst others.

Different qualities will be required of field sales people in relationship selling situations. There will be a move away from the qualities of sales people that are quoted in Figure 12.1. The importance of features like determination, self-motivation, resilience and tenacity, whilst still important when establishing long-term relationships, might well be overtaken by the greater relevance of features like acceptability, attention to detail and the general ability to 'get along' with people on a long-term basis. To a certain extent the 'cut and thrust' that one traditionally associates with field selling positions will be supplanted by a calmer environment of working together as a team that includes members of both the salesperson's own company and the buyer's company. However, caution must be exercised when interpreting selling relationships. Research by Kinniard (1993) has shown that the sales role is attracting empathetic people who are not always successful because they mistake friendliness as meaning that a relationship has been established and naively anticipate that business will flow automatically.

Sales visits to individual customers are likely to be longer in duration, and this will result in less individual sales calls being made. In fact, in some situations, it can even be envisaged that there might well be somebody from the supplier's company permanently in place at the customer's company. This is already being practised by some high technology companies, e.g. those that provide computer software and hardware to large retail organisations.

At a more practical level, the following two activities which currently tend to be regarded as ancillary to the task of selling will become more important:

● **Information gathering** in terms of collecting market information and intelligence is becoming an increasingly important part of the task of selling. Such information gathering feeds into the company's marketing information system as shown in Figure 7.2.

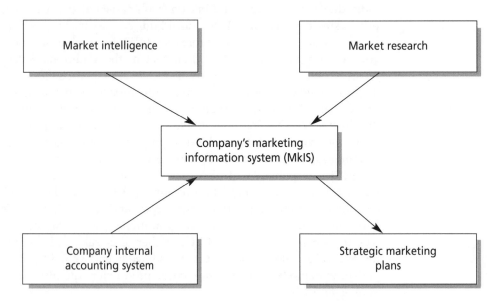

Figure 7.2   Marketing information system

A company's marketing information system (MkIS) has three inputs which are marketing research, market intelligence, and the company's own internal accounting system. These are input into the MkIS which captures the data on a database. Marketing research is provided by the marketing department from their own primary and secondary research, and from commissioned survey data. The company's internal accounting system relates to sales analyses by customer purchases over periods of time by customer group, by geographical area, by size of order, and by any other combination that may be required. Market intelligence relates to information about competitors and the products and services they supply, plus information as to how they generally 'perform' with their customers. It also relates to the company's own customers. Field sales personnel are extremely good collectors of market information and intelligence. The responsibility of salespeople as collectors of such information will expand, and information technology skills will become increasingly important as individual salespersons interact in terms of input to and output from the MkIS as part of their routine activities. There is, of course, an output from the MkIS and this contributes to the strategic marketing planning system. Thinking about business in general is becoming more strategic and long-term, and the MkIS is the principal data input into strategic marketing plans. The role of the individual salesperson will become of more strategic value as the salesperson's regular reports are input to the MkIS which in turn inputs into the organisation's longer-term marketing plans.

● **Servicing** is the second area in which the role of the sales person will become invaluable. This will include a certain amount of first line servicing, so product application will be important as well as product knowledge, but what we refer to here is servicing in the broader sense of serving customers on a highly individualistic basis. The phenomenon of field sales personnel staying longer in such positions will provide them with more time to acquire such skills. However, it is likely that such sales personnel will come from more technical backgrounds such as engineering or chemistry. Servicing will also include the provision of technical advice in relation to such matters as levels of quality, arranging after-sales service, establishing improved customer care programmes, and even offering consultancy services. More practical matters, such as agreeing delivery schedules, expediting individual orders, and occasionally, progressing payment for orders supplied, will also feature in this context. In JIT manufacturing situations the salesperson's company will form part of the supply chain which stretches not only forwards to the end customer, but also backwards towards the sources of prime manufacture, so buyers might need information from the salesperson's suppliers as part of the process of supply chain integration (SCI).

Swenson and Herche (1994) used established scales as measures of salesperson performance and ascertained their ability or motivation to adapt their approach to meet customers' needs. The ability to become customer-orientated as opposed to being sales-orientated, and to determine whether or not the salesperson does actually use motivation to achieve the results that benefit both themselves and the customer, was ascertained. They concluded that the personal values of 'achievement', self-direction', 'self-respect' and 'self-accomplishment' were the key factors for successful salespeople. They further concluded that these social values could enhance the recruitment and selection of salespeople. Does all of this suggest that the salesperson of the future will not need to be versed in any of the skills of selling? In a word, no! Prospecting skills will always be needed from leads that will be increasingly generated from direct marketing approaches rather than from cold calling. Skills of sales presentation will also be required in such circumstances. Negotiation skills too will still be needed. Communication skills have always been an important part of the field salesperson's armoury, but under traditional marketing such skills have been honed in such a way as to win orders through 'telling them what they want (or need) to know'. Under systems of reverse marketing, communications skills will still be essential, but the customer/sales person dyad will be more in terms of equals than of an 'us and them' situation.

7.6 CONCLUSIONS

This chapter has examined current trends in the marketplace, and has looked at these trends in the context of likely future changes within the selling function.

It has traced the development of the movement towards relationship selling from its earliest roots based on quality issues through to the more mature notion of total quality management (TQM). In a more discerning marketplace customers desire, and deserve, the best in terms of quality, and the selling implications of such expectations have been discussed.

Just-in-time manufacturing (JIT) is growing apace as a manufacturing technique, with the result that longer-term selling relationships are becoming the norm. Traditional marketing is thus beginning to be replaced by reverse marketing with buyers becoming more proactive in initiating commercial transactions including long-term strategic relationships.

Relationship selling comprises the raft of sales tactics that actually deliver relationship marketing strategy to the company and to customers.

PRACTICAL EXERCISE

Midlands Switchgear Limited

Midlands Switchgear Limited is a large manufacturing concern based in Wolverhampton. It was founded in 1904 and owed its initial growth to the expansion of tramway services in the early part of the twentieth century.

Today, the company relies largely upon sales to the regional electricity companies, and to National Power and PowerGen, the national generators. Its products are widely used in the electricity distribution network, namely in electricity substations. It manufactures switchgear, but many of the component parts are bought in. Such bought in components include current transformers, relays, switches and the cabinets in which they are housed. The company operates a sourcing policy of two preferred suppliers from a pool of five for each component that is purchased. This is to ensure continuity of supply in an industry that now demands 'instant' response. This is a trend that has become particularly prevalent since the privatisation of the electricity industry in the early 1990s.

The purchasing department is responsible for routine procurement, but inputs to the purchase decision, as to which suppliers to use, come from the following:

● Phil Stonehouse BSc (electrical engineering) who is the Commercial Director. He is responsible for sales and marketing, contracts and transportation.
● Martin Gilbert BSc (electrical engineering) and member of the Institute of Electrical Engineers, who is Director of Engineering. He is responsible for engineering and product design.
● Roy Young BSc (electrical engineering) and PhD (electronics) who is also a

member of the Institute of Electrical Engineers. He is Technical Director and is responsible for product development and acts as a 'trouble shooter' for customers' technical queries.

● Harold Charlesworth who is a qualified member of the Chartered Institute of Management Accountants. He is in overall charge of the financial function, but his specialist input in this context is in the areas of budget-setting and costing.

The domestic UK market for the company's products is not regarded as being particularly price-sensitive. UK manufacturers have traditionally been sheltered from European and other competition by several non-tariff barriers. The principal one has been the ability of switchgear manufacturers to provide service backup at four hours' notice. The physical nature of power distribution in the UK differs from many other countries, including those in the European Union, so although there is no 'official' non-tariff barrier, the technicalities that must be understood, and the infrastructure that must be developed, before non-UK competitors can compete, can be quite daunting.

When purchasing components for switchgear, the following considerations are particularly important:

● customer specifications as to the manufacturer of instrumentation;
● quality of products which usually means purchasing from 'approved' suppliers;
● service and spares availability;
● prompt delivery record;
● price considerations.

DISCUSSION QUESTIONS

1 What are the drawbacks to the decision-making unit at Midlands Switchgear Limited from:
   (a) Midland Switchgear's viewpoint?
   (b) the viewpoint of a prospective company wishing to become an 'approved' supplier?

2 What do you feel are the main commercial threats facing Midlands Switchgear Limited? Having identified these threats, how do you feel the company should best reorganise to overcome these threats?

3 From the viewpoint of a company wishing to sell relays to Midlands Switchgear Limited, draw up an outline sales strategy of how you would approach the company.

EXAMINATION QUESTIONS

1 Discuss the implications of the move towards relationship marketing in organisational buying/selling situations in the context of how this might change the role of selling.

2 Total quality management is a philosophy of management that should permeate every

aspect of the organisation and not simply be the concern of production. What is meant by this statement in terms of how TQM can affect the selling function?

3 Describe the key elements of a customer care programme that would be appropriate in a manufacturing or service environment with which you are familiar.

4 What are the implications for salespersons of the adoption of supply chain integration by larger manufacturers?

CHAPTER 8

DIRECT MARKETING AND INFORMATION TECHNOLOGY APPLICATIONS IN SALES

OBJECTIVES After studying this chapter you should be able to:

1 Understand the meaning of direct marketing.

2 Appreciate the range of direct marketing methods and their applications.

3 Know the uses of the Internet in sales and marketing.

4 Understand the advances made in information technology as they relate to selling and sales management.

5 Know the specific information applications in retailing and trade marketing.

KEY CONCEPTS
- direct marketing
- direct mail
- telemarketing
- direct response advertising
- catalogue marketing
- Internet marketing
- E-commerce

- information technology
- office packages
- computer based training
- electronic point of sale
- category management
- electronic data interchange

Two key changes that are reshaping the face of selling are the growth of direct marketing activity and the use of information technology as an aid to the process of selling and sales management. This chapter explores the major changes that are taking place and their impact on the way companies sell products and use information technology in the sales function. It begins by explaining the nature of direct marketing and the methods used to interact directly with customers. The impact of information technology on such activities as database management, telemarketing and the Internet are explored. The second part of this chapter examines other information technology applications in selling and sales management.

8.1 DIRECT MARKETING

Direct marketing attempts to acquire and retain customers by contacting them without the use of an intermediary. The objective is to achieve a direct response which may take one of the following forms:

- a purchase over the telephone or by post
- a request for a catalogue or sales literature
- an agreement to visit a location/event (e.g. an exhibition)
- participation in some form of action (e.g. joining a political party)
- a request for a demonstration of a product
- a request for a salesperson's visit

Direct marketing, then, is the distribution of products, information and promotional benefits to target consumers through interactive communication in a way which allows response to be measured. It covers a wide array of methods, including the following:

1 direct mail
2 telemarketing (both inbound and outbound)
3 direct response advertising (coupon response or 'phone now')
4 electronic media (Internet, interactive cable TV)
5 catalogue marketing
6 inserts (leaflets in magazines)
7 door-to-door leafleting

Direct marketing activity, including direct mail, telemarketing and telephone banking, is regulated by a European Commission Directive that came into force at the end of 1994. Its main provisions were that suppliers cannot insist upon pre-payments; consumers must be told the identity of the supplier, the price, the quality of the product and any transport charges, the payment and delivery methods, and the period over which the solicitation remains valid; orders must be met within 30 days unless otherwise indicated; a cooling-off period of 30 days is mandatory and cold calling by telephone, fax or electronic mail is restricted unless the receiver has given prior consent.

Like sales promotion, direct marketing has experienced growth in usage. Smith (1993) outlines five factors that have fuelled the rise in direct marketing activity:

1 *Market fragmentation:* the trend towards market fragmentation has limited the application of mass marketing techniques. As market segments develop the capacity of direct marketing techniques to target distinct consumer groups is of increasing importance.
2 *Computer technology:* the rise in accessibility of computer technology and the increasing sophistication of software allowing the generation of personalised letters and messages has eased the task of direct marketing.
3 *The list explosion:* the increased supply of lists and their diversity (e.g. 25,000

Rolls Royce owners, 20,000 women executives, and 100,000 house improvers) has provided the raw data for direct marketing activities.

4 *Sophisticated analytical techniques:* by using geodemographic analysis, households can be classified into neighbourhood type, e.g. 'modern private housing, young families' or 'private flats, single people'. These in turn can be cross-referenced with product usage, media usage and life-style statements.

5 *Co-ordinated marketing systems:* the high costs of personal selling have led an increasing number of companies to take advantage of direct marketing techniques such as direct response advertising and telemarketing, to make the salesforce more cost-effective. For example, a coupon response advertisement or direct mail may generate leads that can be screened by outbound telemarketing, or inbound telemarketing can provide the mechanism for accommodating enquiries stimulated by other direct marketing activities.

As with all marketing communications, direct marketing campaigns should be integrated both within themselves and with other communication tools such as advertising, publicity and personal selling. Un-coordinated communication leads to blurred brand images, low impact and customer confusion.

The capability of direct marketing to transform markets is discussed in the following case history.

SELLING AND SALES MANAGEMENT IN ACTION

How direct marketing can change markets

The three classic cases of how direct marketing can transform markets are Dell Computers, First Direct's entry into banking and Direct Line's move into insurance.

Dell Computers was founded in 1984 by Michael Dell in the USA. His conception was to challenge existing players in the computer market by establishing a direct marketing operation that would allow customers to dial Dell to place an order for a computer. The computer, which was based upon customer specification, would be sent direct eliminating the need for a distributor. Just-in-time production means that computers can be manufactured in four hours. Dell moved into Internet marketing in 1996 and achieved over £14m worth of web-enabled revenue per day in 1999.

First Direct moved into telephone banking in 1989. Their success was based on customer dissatisfaction with traditional branch banks which offered short opening hours, queues and bank charges. By centralising banking operations and offering direct access by telephone, First Direct was able to offer high levels of customer service at low cost. The new service offered 24-hour access and free banking. The operation has proven to be a huge success with the number of customers far exceeding target, and the highest level of customer satisfaction of any bank.

Direct Line saw a market opportunity in motor insurance. Traditional insurance companies used insurance brokers situated in towns and cities to provide the link to customers. Direct line placed advertisements on television and in the print media to persuade prospects to phone their telemarketing operation with the inducement of a much cheaper quotation. All of the transaction is conducted over the telephone with the form being sent to the customer simply for signature. By eliminating the broker, Direct Line's cost structure enabled them to reduce costs and pass on some of the savings to its customers. The success of its motor insurance has led the company to move into related areas such as home and contents insurance.

Database marketing

Much direct marketing activity requires accurate information on customers so that they can be targeted through direct mail or telemarketing campaigns, for example. This information is stored on a marketing database which comprises an electronic filing cabinet containing a list of names, addresses and transactional behaviour. Information such as the types of purchase, frequency of purchase, purchase value and responsiveness to promotional offers may be held in the database. This allows future campaigns to be *targeted* at those people who are most likely to respond. For example, a special offer on garden tools from a mail order company can be targeted at those people who have purchased gardening products in the past. Another example would be a car dealer who, by holding a database of customer names and addresses and dates of car purchases, could use direct mail to promote service offers and new model launches.

By including postcodes in the address of customers and employing the services of an agency that conducts geodemographic analysis (such as ACORN), a customer profile can be built up. Direct mail can then be targeted at people with similar geodemographic profiles.

Database marketing is defined as an interactive approach to marketing which uses individually addressable marketing media and channels (such as mail, telephone and the salesforce) to

(i) provide information to a target audience;
(ii) stimulate demand; and
(iii) stay close to customers by recording and storing an electronic database memory of customers, prospects and all communication and transactional data.

Typical information stored on a database includes the following:

1 *Information on actual and potential customers.* Basic data such as names, addresses and telephone numbers enable customers to be contacted. This may be supplemented by psychographic and behavioural data. In business-to-

business markets, information on key decision-makers and their choice criteria may be held.

2 *Transactional information.* Such information as frequency of purchase, when the customer last bought, and how much was bought for each product category may be stored. Cross-analysing this type of data with customer type can throw light on the customer profile most likely to buy a particular product, and communications can be targeted accordingly.

3 *Promotional information.* Data covering what promotional campaigns have been run, customer response patterns, and results in terms of contacts, sales and profiles can be stored on a marketing database.

4 *Product Information.* Information relating to which products have been promoted, how, when, where and associated responses can be held.

5 *Geodemographic information.* Information about the geographical areas of customers and prospects and the social, life-style or business categories to which they belong can be stored. By including postcodes in the address of customers and employing the services of an agency that conducts geodemographic analysis (such as ACORN) a customer profile can be built up. Direct mail can then be targeted at people with similar geodemographic profiles.

We will now examine in more detail three of the most popular direct marketing techniques: direct mail, telemarketing and Internet marketing.

Direct mail

Direct mail is material sent by post to a home or business address with the purpose of promoting a product and/or maintaining an ongoing relationship.

An important factor in the effectiveness of a direct mail campaign is the quality of the mailing list. List-houses supply lists on a rental or purchase basis. Since lists become out of date quickly it is usually preferable to rent. **Consumer lists** may be compiled from subscriptions to magazines, catalogues, membership of organisations, etc. Alternatively, **consumer life-style lists** are compiled from questionnaires. The electoral roll can also be useful when combined with geodemographic analysis. For example, if a company wished to target households living in modern private housing with young families, the electoral roll can be used to provide names and addresses of people living in such areas. **Business-to-business lists** may be bought from directory producers such as the Kompass or Key British Enterprises directories, from trade magazine subscription lists (e.g. *Chemicals Monthly*, or *Purchasing Managers' Gazette*), or from exhibition lists (e.g. *Which Computer Show*). Perhaps the most productive mailing list is that of a company's own customers which is known as **the house list**. This is because of the existing relationship that a company enjoys with its own customers. Also of use would be names of past buyers who have become inactive, names of enquirers and of those who have been 'referred' or recommended by present customers of the company. It is not uncommon for a house list to be far more productive than an externally compiled list. Customer behaviour such as the products purchased, most recent purchase, frequency of purchase and expenditure can also be stored in an in-house database.

The management of direct mail involves asking five questions:

Who: Who is the target market? Who are we trying to influence?

What: What response is required? A sale, an enquiry?

Why: Why should they buy or make an enquiry? Is it because our product is faster, cheaper, etc?

Where: Where can they be reached? Can we obtain their home or working address?

When: When is the best time to reach them? Often this is at the weekend for consumers, and Tuesday, Wednesday or Thursday for business people (Monday can be dominated by planning meetings, and on Friday they may be busy clearing their desk for the weekend).

Other management issues include organisation for addressing and filling the envelopes. **Mailing houses** provide these services, and for large mailings the postal service needs to be notified in advance so that the mailing can be scheduled.

Direct mail allows *specific targeting to named individuals.* For example, by hiring lists of subscribers to gardening catalogues, a manufacturer of gardening equipment could target a specific group of people who would be more likely to be interested in a promotional offer than the general public. Elaborate personalisation is possible and the results directly measurable. Since the objective of direct mail is immediate – usually a sale or an enquiry – success can easily be measured. Some organisations such as the *Reader's Digest* spend money researching alternative creative approaches before embarking on a large-scale mailing. Such factors as type of promotional offer, headlines, visuals and copy can be varied in a systematic manner and by using code numbers on reply coupons, responses can be tied to the associated creative approach.

The effectiveness of direct mail relies heavily on the quality of the mailing list. Poor lists raise costs, and can contribute to the criticism of 'junk mail' since recipients are not interested in the contents of the mailing. Initial costs can be much higher than advertising in terms of cost per thousand people reached, and the response can be low (an average response rate of 2 per cent is often quoted). Added to these costs is the expense of setting up a database. In these terms direct mail should be viewed as a medium- to long-term tool for generating repeat business from a carefully targeted customer group. An important concept is the *lifetime value* of a customer which is the profit made on a customer's purchase over his/her lifetime.

Telemarketing

Telemarketing is a marketing communications system where trained specialists use telecommunications and information technologies to conduct marketing and sales activities.

In North America, sales prospects have long been solicited through the medium of the telephone for relatively expensive products such as cars, freezers and home improvements. Telephonists work from prepared scripts designed to give different selling approaches according to the circumstances of the prospect, these circumstances being established before the sales talk. The idea is to 'smooth the way' for a salesperson's visit following the telephone call. Success rates may appear low, but it is a very cost-effective method and eliminates a lot of 'cold canvassing' by salespeople. However, telephone selling can be a very demanding task for the person soliciting over the telephone, and this is reflected in the vernacular term applied to the location from which such solicitation takes place – 'the boiler room'.

Inbound telemarketing occurs when a prospect contacts the company by telephone, whereas outbound telemarketing involves the company calling the prospect. Developments in IT have affected both forms. For example, Quick Address is a package that enables telemarketing people handling inbound calls to quickly identify the address and account details of the caller with the minimum amount of typing time and also ensure it is accurate. The caller is asked for their name and postcode (either for the household or the company). From this the correct address will appear on the computer screen. If the caller wishes to purchase (e.g. using a credit card) over the telephone, the tedium of giving (and spelling) their address to allow postage is removed. This has gained penetration in such areas as selling football and theatre tickets. Even more sophisticated developments in telecommunications technology allow the caller to be identified even before the operator has answered the call. The caller's telephone number is relayed into the customer database and outlet details appear on the operator's screen before the call is picked up. This service (called *integrated telephony*) has gained penetration in the customer service area.

Computerisation can also enhance productivity in outbound telemarketing. Large databases can store information that can easily be accessed by telephone marketing operators. Call lists can be automatically allocated to operators. Scripts can be created and stored on the computer so that operators have ready and convenient access to them on screen. Orders can be automatically processed and follow-up actions (such as call-back in one month or send literature) can be recorded and stored. In addition, productivity can be raised by autodiallers.

Telemarketing automation also allows simple keystroke retrieval of critical information such as customer history, product information or schedules. If the prospect or customer is busy, automated systems can reschedule a call-back and allow the operator to recall the contact on screen at a later date simply by pressing a single key.

Telemarketing is often conducted from *call centres* where trained operators accept and send thousands of calls a day. This process is described in the following case discussion.

Telemarketing: the development of call centres

The development in telemarketing activity has led to a rapid expansion in call centres. These are huge offices where perhaps a hundred people operate telephones making and receiving calls. Their task is aided by automation, e.g. automatic dialling, computerised scripts, and automatic order/ticket processing and addressing.

Staff are trained to communicate effectively over the telephone. First Direct's call handlers, for example, are given seven weeks' training before they come into contact with customers. Some companies such as Virgin Direct, the financial services firm, only contact customers who have called them first and agreed to further calls. This builds up trust and places the customer in control.

Call centres are also used to check on service levels. For example, Kwik Fit, the tyres, brakes and exhausts chain, employs a vast telemarketing team that contacts customers within 72 hours of their visit to an outlet to ensure the service was satisfactory. Its call centre staff also telephone 5,500 potential buyers of their motor insurance a night, their details drawn from a database of 5 million people who have used their repair centres. They claim a one in four success rate.

Uses of telemarketing

McHatton (1988) has noted that when used professionally telemarketing can be a most cost-efficient, flexible and accountable medium. The telephone permits two-way dialogue that is instantaneous, personal and flexible, albeit not face-to-face.

As we have seen, telemarketing is often linked to field selling activities. The link between telemarketing and five field job types was developed by Moncrief (1986). The job types were described in terms of the amount of face-to-face contact required and the complexity of the selling process. The face-to-face contact (horizontal dimension) of Figure 8.1 is particularly useful to illustrate the possible roles of telemarketing in selling strategy.

The missionary seller (making new initial customer contact) and the order-taker job types offer potential opportunities of using telemarketers as the organisation's primary salesforce. The role of telemarketing in the institutional seller, trade servicer and trade seller job categories is to supplement field-selling efforts. The more routinised the selling process (the vertical dimension of Figure 8.1), the more likely telemarketing can make an important supplemental contribution to face-to-face selling.

An assessment of the need for face-to-face contact indicates whether telemarketing is appropriate in a supporting and/or a primary role in an organisation's selling strategy. In some selling situations, both primary and supporting telemarketing strategies may be appropriate.

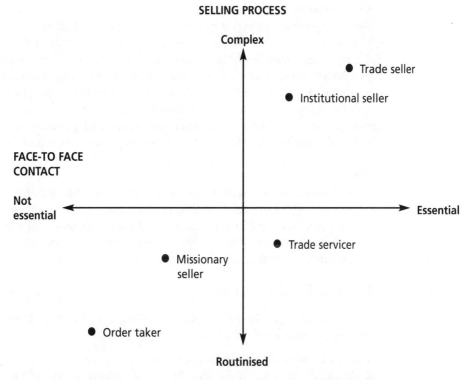

Figure 8.1   Selling process complexity and face-to-face contact dimensions of sales job types
(Source: Montcrieff, 1986)

Telemarketing as a supporting role

The need for this role occurs when face-to-face contact is required, but selected buyer/seller activities can be accomplished by telemarketing personnel. These activities may include taking orders and handling reorders. Successful implementation of a telemarketing support effort requires close co-ordination of field and telemarketing salespeople. Moncrief *et al.* (1989) point out that research suggests that the supporting role creates a major organisational design task and resistance from field personnel will be likely to occur. A carefully formulated plan is essential to assure co-operation of the telemarketing and the field salesforce. When face-to-face interaction is needed, telemarketing plays a secondary role in selling strategy.

Primary role

Telemarketing can provide a complete sales and customer support effort for selling situations in which face-to-face contact is not required. Conditions which suggest using telemarketing in a primary role include routinised selling process, low cash value of purchases, a large and widely dispersed customer base, and non-technical products. Regardless of other considerations, a significant factor in deciding not to use face-to-face contact lies in the cost of field sales calls and the margins available to cover these costs.

Combination role

Some companies have adopted selling strategies that utilise telemarketing in both supporting and primary roles. Organisations that may benefit from this strategy are ones with large and widely dispersed customer bases whose purchasers range from very small accounts to very large accounts. The accounts assigned to the primary telemarketing functions are those that cannot economically be served on a face-to-face basis. Telemarketers often have primary responsibility for smaller customers and provide backup services for other customers when face-to-face salespeople are not available.

No role

Importantly, certain selling situations are not appropriate for any type of telemarketing support. Conditions that may require face-to-face customer contact by a field salesperson greatly reduce or eliminate telemarketing's value, e.g. where the selling process complexity, contact requirements and importance of the purchase demand face-to-face contact.

Guidelines for telemarketing

An eight-step guide to telephone selling has been published by the Bell Telephone System of America:

1 Identify yourself and your company.
2 Establish rapport: this should come naturally since you have already researched your potential clients and their business.
3 Make an interesting comment (e.g. to do with cost savings or a special offer).
4 Deliver your sales message: emphasise benefits over features (e.g. your production people will like it because it helps to overcome downtime through waiting for the material to set).
5 Overcome objections: be skilled at objection-handling techniques.
6 Close the sale: when appropriate do not be afraid to ask for the order (e.g. 'Would you like to place an order now?') or fulfil another objective (e.g. 'Can I send you a sample?').
7 Action agreement: arrange for a sales call or the next telephone call.
8 Express your thanks.

Internet marketing

The Internet is a global web of over 50,000 computer networks which permit instantaneous global communications. Users from all over the world can send e-mail messages, shop for products, and access news, leisure and business information. A server is a computer that maintains an address book holding the addresses of every other server linked to the Internet. To access the Internet, users need to connect to one of these servers. These are normally owned by a communications company (called an Internet Service Provider) such as CompuServe or American On-Line. Users need to set up an account with one of these ISP companies and pay a monthly rental. However, free access is provided in the UK through Freeserve which was launched by Dixons, an electrical goods retailer. A glossary of Internet terms is given in Table 8.1.

The World Wide Web has changed the face of the Internet, breaking up long screeds of text with graphics, and allowing colour and sound to be used. This has led to an explosion in consumer and business-to-business use (see Figure 8.2 for the growth in global users). The original groups using the Internet were students and academics. However, use is more widespread now, particularly among more up-market, well-off and well-educated people making an attractive target market. Car companies such as Ford and Vauxhall (GM) use the Internet as part of their promotional strategy. For example, the Vectra's launch was accompanied by a multimedia campaign combining traditional media with Web addresses featured on print-based advertisements, website and Web-based advertising, a CD-ROM cover-mounted to Dennis Publishing's *CD-ROM* magazine and a card offering a CD-ROM in *Top Gear*'s (a UK car magazine) website.

Access to information on the Internet is facilitated by portals such as Yahoo! and Alta Vista which use search engines to search the Internet by means of keywords. These are vast online databases and libraries which can be used to locate the site that holds the information that is required. Yahoo! is available at www.yahoo.com and has one of the largest libraries of websites on the Internet. Alta Vista is available at www.altavista.com and is fast and comprehensive. Using both of these portals provides a vast coverage of the information domain under scrutiny. Use is normally free, with income for the providers being based on advertising revenue. Consequently these portal companies that guide millions

Table 8.1 Glossary of Internet Terms

Browser: computer software such as Netscape or Microsoft's Internet Explorer that guide users around the Internet.

Chatroom: a site that allows Internet users to communicate with each other about a topic. An example is the Motley Fool room where investors exchange information about shares.

Firewall: computer software that protects transactions over the Internet. Firewalls are embedded into on-line banking systems making it difficult for hackers to gain access.

Home page: a website's welcome page. It provides details of its content and offers directions to help users find their way around the site.

Internet service provider: companies (e.g. Dixon's Freeserve, AOL and Virgin Net) that allow users to access the Internet. ISP software can be obtained either over the Internet or from computer disks provided by an ISP.

Portal: a website that serves as an 'entry point' to the rest of the Web, often providing large amounts of information and ways to find other sites. They usually feature 'search engines' which allow users to search the Internet by using keywords. 'Yahoo!' and 'Alta Vista' are two examples of portals.

World Wide Web: a collection of millions of computer files that can be accessed via the Internet. A website is a WWW file that can contain text, pictures and sound.

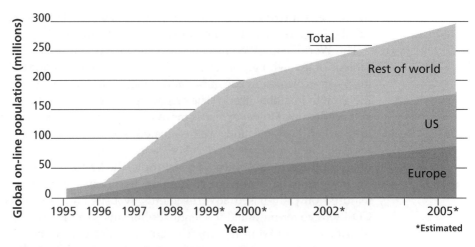

Figure 8.2 Growth of the global on-line population
(From Financial Times Survey, 1999)

of Internet users through the maze of the World Wide Web try to hold the users of their services for as long as possible. Users are encouraged to create their own home pages so that the information they previously sought regularly arrives on their screen without searching. For example, Yahoo! has created My Yahoo! for this purpose. New services have also been provided such as financial news, financial services, weather and stock prices in an effort to attract and hold users.

Two key capabilities of the Internet are the ability to send e-mail messages and to conduct e-commerce. Messages, files and documents can be sent by e-mail to any other user on the Internet anywhere in the world. They will receive the information instantly and it will be stored on their PC until they wish to access it. The benefits to salespeople in communicating with customers and head office are enormous. Quotations, queries and factual information can be transferred faster and cheaper than by mail, and without the need to talk to the recipient directly. The message will be waiting to be collected when the recipient next consults his/her computer.

E-commerce (electronic commerce) is any trading activity that is carried out over an electronic network such as the Internet. As such it is not unique to the Internet. For example, banks have been conducting business electronically for decades. Also electronic data interchange (EDI) has allowed customers to place orders and suppliers to send invoices electronically for many years. However, the growth of Internet use will see an accompanying expansion of e-commerce through this medium. The case study entitled 'E-commerce in action' discusses how e-commerce has contributed to the success of Amazon, Dell Computers, Wal-Mart and Cisco. This should not mislead anyone into believing that success on the Internet is guaranteed. For every success story there are hundreds of expensive e-commerce failures. Difficulties in locating websites, poor website design, reluctance to conduct transactions through a new medium, and security fears are barriers that hinder the faster adoption of e-commerce by consumers.

The business-to-business e-commerce market is already well established, however. For example, the majority of Dell Computers' Internet sales of over £14 million sales per day are business-to-business customers. This means that Dell's sales teams can be left to concentrate on selling to clients who require face-to-face interaction, typically large corporate accounts. Besides being convenient for purchasing, doing business on the Internet means driving down costs, e.g. by reducing the need for expensive salesforces and supplying product information without the need for multiple copies of catalogues.

E-commerce can take place on four levels (O'Connor and Galvin, 1998):

1 *Publish*. This is the provision of information to the customer electronically. It is one-way communication that may involve annual reports, press releases, information on products and services, recruitment opportunities and advertising.
2 *Interact*. The next level refers to interactive engagement with the user on the Internet. For example, Dell's website provides on-line technical support services including e-mail links to on-line technical support representatives.

E-commerce in action

Handling sales over the Internet is an exciting prospect with computers pioneering its successful use. The Internet automatically opens up a global market. Amazon, the US bookshop, sells around a quarter of its books abroad. The Internet makes buying and selling easy. By clicking the 'Buy a Dell' icon on the Dell website users can design and price customised computers. Then by clicking the 'purchase' icon an order can be submitted and a payment method (e.g. credit card) chosen. An electronic confirmation is sent out within five minutes.

Other companies such as Wal-Mart and Cisco are benefiting from the advantages the Internet provides. Wal-Mart is a leading US retailer that is constantly seeking to enlarge its customer base. It has developed a 'one-stop shopping' experience by partnering with other retailers to provide a wider range of products and services. By offering a range of over 140,000 items across 27 product categories on-line it has drawn in customers who do not live close to Wal-Mart stores and has attracted further customers who value the convenience of 'home-shopping'.

Cisco, a manufacturer of network products, also uses the Internet to handle sales. Over 500,000 customers access Cisco's website to download software and make technical inquiries. Over 40 per cent of Cisco's turnover is processed on the Internet and each customer's profile is recorded for future marketing use. The Internet not only makes doing business easy for customers, it also reduces Cisco's operating costs by around £170 million per year.

Based on O'Connor, J. and Galvin, E. (1998) '*Creating Value through E-commerce*,' Financial Times Management, London.

3 *Transact.* The third level of e-commerce allows products and services to be bought and sold over the Internet. Reaching this level can be costly in terms of initial investment, and although operating costs should be lower than more traditional ways of conducting business, usually costs need to be driven down in other areas of the business for cost savings overall to fall.

4 *Integrate.* The highest level of e-commerce is where integration of the computer systems and processes of traders is achieved to form a strong formalised relationship. This may involve the establishment of a business-to-business extranet which is an electronic network linking companies to their trading partners. Extranets allow partners to exchange information such as that relating to ordering, delivery and invoicing in a secure environment. For example, Mobil's extranet allows the oil company to accept orders from 300 distributors globally.

Benefits of the Internet and e-commerce

The advantages of the Internet and e-commerce to consumers are as follows:

1 *Convenience.* Customers can order products and services 24 hours a day. The chores of shopping, such as driving to stores, enduring traffic queues, parking, and searching through merchandise to find suitable products, disappear. On the Internet, products can be ordered immediately from home, unlike direct response advertising which requires a telephone call or mailing. This brings opportunities to supermarket chains such as Tesco who in 1999 announced the national roll-out of an Internet shopping service. After lengthy trials, Tesco has concluded that Internet ordering is the only way to make home delivery pay. Customers can specify a two-hour delivery slot between 10.00 am and 10.00 pm.

2 *Information.* Internet users can access detailed information about products without leaving the house or office. Prices, performance, quality and availability can be obtained. Services such as the Sabre on-line network scan prices to find the cheapest airfares available and InsWeb allows shoppers to compare quotes from sellers of life, vehicle and health insurance. Sampling can also occur: shoppers can listen to pieces of music on a CD before deciding to order it.

3 *Less hassle.* Electronic media avoid the necessity to negotiate and argue with salespeople when buying products.

4 *Multimedia.* The Internet is able to handle and transmit pictures, graphics, sound and video. Although the display of pictures and graphics affects the speed of loading a web page, it helps provide better understanding of the information and enhances its attractiveness. The use of 3D displays lets consumers examine items in detail, e.g. the interior of a car. Consumers can also use 3D for mixing and matching, e.g. how a blouse matches a skirt or how green sheets would look on a cherrywood bed.

5 *Creation of new products and services.* The development of the Internet has led to the creation of new services such as on-line financial services for managing bank accounts or trading shares, and on-line home grocery shopping. Also the ability to download audio, video and software will allow consumers to move away from the traditional physical products currently purchased.

The benefits to companies are as follows:

1 *Lower costs.* For high-street retailers the cost of running branches is eliminated and on-line catalogues can be produced much cheaper than the cost of printing and distributing paper catalogues. The establishment of extranets which allow the efficient placing of orders and receipt of invoices can slash order processing costs.

2 *Distribution.* For many products that can be digitised, such as text, pictures, music and videos, distance will no longer have any effect on the distribution costs of the product. Also products can be displayed around the clock, not just when shops are open for business. Location is irrelevant since products and services can be seen on a computer screen anywhere in the world.

3 *Face-to-face selling.* The Internet gives the seller the opportunity to come into direct contact with the buyer without the need for salespeople or distributors. The Internet will therefore continue the trend for salesforces to reduce in size, and distributors (e.g. insurance agents) to fall in number. Michael Dell once said that it was hard for any salesperson to compete in knowledge terms with what can be put on a website.

4 *Relationship building.* Marketers can establish a dialogue with customers and prospects via the Internet. Valuable information can be passed on to them and they can be encouraged to send information (including complaints) back to the company.

5 *Promotion.* The Internet offers major advantages for advertising compared with traditional media. For example, broadcast media can reach many people but cannot receive information to process transactions or offer any kind of customisation. On visiting the Del website customers can design their own computer, and information can be up-dated daily. The multimedia capability of a website allows marketers to use creative graphics, eye-catching images and sound to promote their products.

6 *Audience measurement.* Through on-line registration the number of people visiting a website and specific pages can be measured. The Electronic Telegraph, which claims to be the most popular website in Europe with 90,000 registered users and 100,000 pages requested daily, collects information on age, sex and occupation.

7 *Fast Changes to Catalogues.* Products, specifications and prices can be changed quickly without the need to reprint catalogues and distribute them to customers and prospects.

8 *New market opportunities.* The relatively low cost of establishing a website and the world-wide nature of the Internet means that there are exciting opportunities to reach new global markets. Small and medium-sized companies in particular can now reach customers they could not have communicated with using traditional methods.

9 *Marketing research.* Information that is available to potential customers on the Internet is also accessible to competitors. They can check product specifications, prices and company information. This kind of information is particularly useful for salespeople who can also conduct marketing research into new prospects so

that they are armed with essential background information before calling upon them. User groups (often called newsgroups) can also be researched; for example, their response to a new product idea could be assessed. Care has to be taken when surveying consumers as the profile of Internet users is biased towards better educated, more affluent and younger people. However, provided addresses are available, the potential of e-mail surveys as a low-cost method of questioning large samples remains. In the US, some marketing research agencies are experimenting with the use of on-line focus groups.

8.2 FURTHER INFORMATION APPLICATIONS IN SELLING AND SALES MANAGEMENT

Besides the effect that information technology has had on direct and database marketing, telemarketing and Internet marketing, it has also had a profound impact on salesforce productivity and management. Major applications include the following:

- *Remote access* through portable computers to branch office or headquarters' computer systems for up-to-the-minute information on order status, price, availability and competitive data allowing customers' queries to be answered immediately. Access is usually done by laptop or palmtop computers.
- *Electronic mail* to speed communications, facilitate links with hard-to-reach people and storing phone-in messages from customers.
- *Word processing and spreadsheet software* for customising sales letters and automating call reports, preparing budget quotas and proposals, and developing sales forecasting.
- *Time management software* to plan activities and automatically update call reports.
- *Database files* on suspects, prospects and customers for precalling, planning and account profiles.
- *Mobile phones* for creating productive time from often wasted travelling time.
- *Desktop publishing capabilities* that allow word-processed text and graphics to be laid out for maximum impact. Documents such as proposals, newsletters and brochures can be produced.
- *Presentation graphics software* such as Powerpoint for text and graphical presentations. Presentations can be stored on disk and projected onto a screen using a special projector with an LCD panel.
- *Diary packages* for reading appointments, preparing 'to do' lists, and storing telephone numbers and addresses.
- *Account management software* for storing account information such as contact names, telephone and fax numbers, type of business, purpose of last meeting, status of customer and details of previous orders.
- *Sales management software* for territory management and journey planning, recruitment and selection, training, sales forecasting, evaluation and control.

The extent to which information technology is affecting salespeople's jobs can be gauged by the following account from a national account manager of a major fast-moving goods company.

The IT revolution

Over the last five years, information technology has affected everyone's life. Whether it's the cashpoint machine, the video machine or the pocket calculator, we have all benefited from the advance in technology. Likewise many of us have experienced the transformation of our workplaces by the technological revolution.

In my work arena – sales – our job function is changing all the time as technology changes the environment in which we work, and reduces the number of employees required to complete the task. What do I mean by this?

Many years ago, a salesperson would visit an account and discuss business. At the end of the meeting they would return to their office and write a confirmation letter to the customer detailing the meeting and any associated information required. This would be to given to the secretary to type, which could take one to two days. The customer would receive a copy another two days later allowing for the vagaries of the post. At this point they might have additional questions for the salesperson, so they would write their own letter in reply, which took another two days to type and a further two days to navigate the postal system. Allowing time for thought, this whole process has taken two weeks to complete. When the 'fax' machine appeared this two week period was reduced to a couple of days by the removal of the postal system from the equation. Now this time has been reduced still further by the development of the 'e-mail' (electronic mail) which reduces the time taken to send messages to a matter of seconds. This effectively reduces the time available for thought and consideration as people demand immediate responses.

In addition to e-mail, the development of the mobile phone has had a similar effect, with the salesperson never being out of contact and always available to make a decision. I am not suggesting that these developments are negative, only that they need to be recognised as changes that have affected the way the salesperson works, and that they have altered the pressure under which the salesperson works.

Computers have affected our customers in a similar way. Much of the buying process is now computerised following the introduction of EPOS (electronic point of sale) systems. These allow buying teams to set certain parameters such as stock levels, size mix and seasonality, and leave the computer to reorder every time an item is purchased. This now goes one stage further with DDE (direct data entry), which permits computers at the customer's and supplier's offices to communicate directly, negating the need for large buying or selling teams. Finally, with computerised warehousing, where computer control maximises space and can even 'pick' items (full cases only), the number of people required to operate the supply chain is probably one-quarter what it was a few years ago.

To return to sales. The traditional role of the field salesperson is one of making regular calls to many customers. To perform this accurately, one would spend hours creating a 'journey plan' which in simple terms would ensure you called on each outlet at the same time once every so many weeks. This would take many hours and could not take into account rapid changes in priority, e.g. an Easter promotion targeted only at certain customers. Today the computer can cope with this and more. Databases holding all relevant information about the customer, their purchasing habits and history, can now be manipulated to ensure maximum use of the salesforce. These systems can analyse customers who buy your product regularly and therefore do not require targeting, lapsed customers who have purchased in the past who could perhaps be persuaded to purchase again by a promotional offer, and finally potential customers who have not yet purchased from you. They can also identify which salesperson to send, e.g. the nearest, the most effective, or the one who most needs experience. This information has always been available, but in reality no-one had the time to work it out. The real benefit of computers is that they can produce this information in a fraction of the time you or I would take to produce it.

It is in this time saving that computers have probably had most impact. The provision of data and general information is now controlled by perhaps one person and a computer rather than a team of people poring over books. This has likewise affected the number of salespeople required. The more effective one becomes, the more time one has to take on other accounts and responsibilities.

The next category of the working population to be affected are secretaries. The number of secretaries required will reduce as more workers become computer literate and able to produce their own presentations, and as e-mail takes over from the official letter. In addition, with the introduction of mobile phones, e-mail, faxes and answer machines, there are many alternatives to leaving a message with a secretary which may be mislaid or suffer from the 'Chinese whisper' syndrome.

The introduction of computers should enhance the customer's perception of the salesperson, making them more professional and effective. However, that relies on the big assumption that the salesperson is (a) ready for the technology; (b) capable of using it; and (c) wants it. If these three factors are absent the machine is a very costly white elephant.

In summary, computers have affected all areas of the work environment. They have taken the jobs of some people, and helped the jobs of others. The hardest element is estimated future change.

A perspective given by Mr Michael Coveney, Senior National Account Manager, Allied Domecq Ltd.

Establishing information technology in selling and sales management

Introducing information technology to a salesforce can be problematic since some salespeople (and managers) may lack essential computer skills and suffer from 'technophobia'. Also they may be reluctant to invest time in developing skills since to them 'time is money'. O'Connor and Galvin (1997) suggest a number of factors that can improve the chances of success for any salesforce automation programme:

1 *Introduce the salespeople in the design*: they should be consulted early in the design of the system so that they understand its purpose, and do not fear its implications. Salespeople must want to use the system rather than be forced to use it. Consequently they need to understand how it can enhance performance, and recognise that it is easy to use.
2 *Provide training*: some salespeople will not be computer literate and will believe that the paper-based methods they have used for years are adequate. A basic training course in computer skills will be required to enable them to gain confidence before they are introduced to the sales software on the new system.
3 *Select easy-to-use software*: this will reduce the costs of changing to new IT methods for salespeople .
4 *Avoid 'big bang' implementations*: software should be introduced gradually and new software tested on a small 'pilot' group before moving to the entire sales team. The initial group should consist of people with a positive attitude to IT and who will act as 'champions' during its roll-out.
5 *Provide a telephone helpdesk*: in order to cope with the inevitable teething problems, a telephone helpdesk should be set up to provide a quick response to problems and queries. If salespeople find that their problems are not being answered immediately they will revert to their old paper-based ways of working.
6 *Provide technical support*: backup support for laptops and palmtops is necessary. This includes the need to maintain and repair equipment that has been damaged in use, the issuing of new upgrades of software, and the carrying out of machine activities such as regularly backing up data.

We will now examine in more detail the potential of information technology developments in selling and account management, and sales management. We will also assess the impact of information technology on a key application, that of trade marketing.

Selling and account management applications

Improved communication via e-mail and fax means that salespeople can reach customers and sales offices much quicker than before. In addition, the development of the laptop computer means that a database of account information can be held and accessed easily.

This obviates the need to wade through masses of paper reports when planning a sales call, and allows the salesperson to access information at the touch of a button when face-to-face with a customer. A basic account management software package would provide the facility to record the following details:

- company name and address
- telephone and fax number
- e-mail address
- contact name(s) with position/job titles
- type of business
- size of business
- status (suspect, prospect, customer, client)
- personal interests
- date of last visit

The following case history illustrates an account management system for business-to-business markets produced and marketed by KMS London.

Managing accounts through IT

'Market-base' is a software package aimed at, among other things, account management in business-to-business environments. It enables suppliers to create an all-embracing database of contacts, customers, industries, locations, sales leads, product usage and computer activity. Supported by colour graphics, the package allows information to flow up and down a company from director and manager at the office, to field salespeople, and back again.

Salespeople can easily access the database to aid call prompting, call reporting, call planning, enquiry checking, lead tracking, sales planning and monitoring, and sales forecasting. An unlimited history can be stored for each client contact; event dates and details can be stored and browsed at will. A flexible report writer provides the ability to write reports, including graphics, specific to user needs. Targeted mailshots are also possible using the software.

Software programs such as Market-base are transforming the speed and quality of communication inside companies and between supplier and customer. By using laptop computers, salespeople can have information ready-to-hand when they need it in the field.

Based on information provided by Kensington Marketing Systems, Kensington, London and reproduced with permission.

In addition to basic account information, sophisticated software can provide information on customers, consumers and competitors, via a laptop. Table 8.2

provides a list of internal and external information that could be of immense value to an account handler.

Table 8.2   Information applications via the computer

Internal	External
Customer profitability by major customer by sector, by brand*	Market information (market size, structure, brand shares)
Product profitability	Consumer information (including brand information
Budgets and reports	information
Demand forecasting	Information on customers
Product information	Competitor intelligence
Shipments information	
Customer contact reports	
Database of retail outlets	

*Customer profitability which looks at returns from combinations of products and customers is particularly useful in terms of allocating resources to customers e.g. in promotional budgets or salesforce efforts.

Based on their ability to integrate information, managers and salespeople may be given a *workbench* or *toolbox*. This is a database of integrated information accessible on their own laptop computers. Much of the internal and external information listed previously is, using appropriate software, integrated to deliver information to aid decision-making.

The same toolbox can use software such as LotusNotes which, by allowing information to be shared, supports teamworking, e.g. electronically sharing the outcome of a customer meeting. This would remove the need to photocopy a contact report for all team members; instead the salient points of the meeting would be accessible to all via their individual laptop computers.

Laptop computers (or the account manager's workbench) also provide a valuable communication tool for personnel performing the sales function. Remote communications via electronic mail software enable on-line communications with head office, with other non-head-office personnel and with customers. (e-mail links with customers are very common.)

It is usual for this same workbench to offer access to office packages such as word processing, graphics and spreadsheets. Thus the account handler is self-sufficient in terms of preparing sales presentations and customer communiqués. An example of an integrated office package is: Lotus SmartSuite which incorporates the AmiPro (work processor), Lotus 1-2-3 (spreadsheet) and Freelance Graphics packages. Similarly the workbench could be loaded with Microsoft software, e.g. Word, PowerPoint and Excel.

One of the most recent innovations in corporate IT relates to the Internet. Referred to as 'intranet', the idea is a local company 'web' which allows access to information electronically. There is scope here to link account managers to this database via their remote communications facility on a laptop.

Productivity could be further enhanced by including an order-taking facility on a laptop. Instead of telephoning orders, the salesperson would link the laptop via a modem to head office. Information from head office, e.g. on product availability, could be downloaded in much the same way.

Sales management applications

IT applications in sales management can also improve efficiency in areas such as territory management and journey planning, recruitment and selection, sales training, sales forecasting, determining salesforce size and salesperson evaluation. We shall now examine how IT has affected the lives of sales managers in each of these areas.

Concern with the amount of time spent driving (one recent survey in the UK conducted by the Kinnair Group showed that 42 per cent of the average salesperson's time was spent at the wheel) means that any gains in productivity created by more efficient *territory management* and *journey planning* would be very worthwhile. Software that can design territories and create journey plans that minimise driving time is now available, so more time can be spent in face-to-face contact with customers. The following case shows how this can be achieved.

<table>
<tr><td>

SELLING
AND SALES
MANAGEMENT
IN ACTION

</td><td>

IT applications in territory management

Sales Performance and Analysis Ltd of Leamington Spa market two software packages designed to optimise territory design and journey planning. The first of these, TOTEM – Territory Optimisation and Territory Management – is a suite of computer software that creates efficient territories based upon workload potential and drivetime. The starting point is a comprehensive computerised road network of the UK. A computer program examines the network, allowing different speeds for different classes of road, urban areas, congested roads, etc. The country is divided into 'bricks' which are small geographical areas based on postcodes. The software calculates the shortest driving time from every brick to every other and creates a drivetime database of the time needed to complete millions of journeys. It can also work with other geographical units such as individual premises.

The software uses the drivetime database to build territories around home bases. A 'brick' is allocated to the person who can reach it in the shortest time. At the same time, data on workloads is used to calculate the workload potential allocated to each territory. The objective is to ensure that territories remain in balance in terms of workload. The result is the optimum territory plan, each 'brick' is on average 'nearer' to its home base, and workloads are equally balanced.

The second software package, JOURNEY PLAN, is a suite of software that relies on the same drivetime database to optimise call schedules, minimising the amount of driving time required to visit any given set of locations. It is designed for sales and service forces dealing with single and multi-frequency calls. Call Cycle Optimiser is a head office system which automatically

</td></tr>
</table>

generates the best journey plan for a salesforce with fixed territorial and pre-planned call cycles. Service Call Optimiser allocates a call to the best-placed engineer with the appropriate skills level, ignoring territory boundaries. The system can be set to balance workloads or to always choose the most appropriate engineer regardless of workload balance.

Drivetime Call Planner is a 'manual' system for use on the field salesperson's laptop. With knowledge of call locations and the drivetime database, calls can be placed in the diary using the 'drag and drop' technique. Driving time between calls is displayed and the system determines which calls will fit into any gap in the schedule. Finally, Drivetime Call Optimiser features schedule optimising. A number of calls can be selected and the software will automatically schedule them over the preferred time period so that drivetime is minimised.

Based on information provided by Sales Performance Analysis Ltd, Leamington Spa, Warwickshire, UK, and reproduced with permission.

Recruitment and selection decisions can also be facilitated by IT applications. Specific software packages have been developed to assess the suitability of sales personnel. For example, Un-Mask Ltd have developed a package that assesses candidates in terms of three critical attributes for a salesperson: intellect, motivation and sales ability. Intellect concentrates on verbal, numerical and spatial reasoning abilities. Motivation is measured by drive, ambition, energy level and need for recognition. Sales ability monitors ability in 12 skill areas which can be selected according to the nature of the sales job and includes prospecting, lead qualification, handling objections, presentation skills, closing, telephone technique and time management.

The software package can also be used in relation to the current sales team to diagnose under-performance and to identify training and motivational needs. For example, a sales manager can identify skills weaknesses and therefore focus on the area (e.g. presentation skills) in most need of attention. In relation to motivation, a manager can determine whether status is more important than money, and adjust incentives accordingly.

Implementation of training can also be assisted by IT. Computer-based training (CBT) packages can be used to deliver knowledge and develop skills in managing information. In particular, new product information can be delivered in this way. The software can be used to present information and challenge the salesperson to remember key points, or it can be used to monitor knowledge levels. Some companies, such as those in financial services (e.g. insurance), require their salespeople to achieve a minimum score before they are allowed to sell. A key advantage of computer-based training software is that it can be used at times and locations to suit the company and user.

There has been growing interest in multimedia training packages. As more and more portable computers have CD-ROMs and training organisations install multimedia labs, this application will grow. Some training organisations use

Philips CDi software which allows interactive responses in a group or classroom setting.

Computers have been used for sales forecasting purposes for many years. For example, the statistical software package SPSS can be used to forecast future sales using sophisticated techniques such as regression analysis. This takes account of variables such as advertising spend, disposable income and relative price levels to predict future sales. Without the power of the computer, the calculations would be time-consuming, tiresome and prone to error.

Software packages such as Microsoft Office or Lotus Smart Suite which contain spreadsheets can be used to calculate salesforce size and perform quantitative evaluations of salespeople. Spreadsheets describe computer packages that are used to record, present and calculate numerical data. Simple calculations such as totals and means can be carried out. For example, the value of orders received by the sales representative by customer could be totalled and compared with previous periods. Many of the quantitative measures of salespeople discussed in Chapter 14 could be entered onto a spreadsheet to facilitate evaluation.

In Chapter 14, the workload approach to determining salesforce size is described. It involves a calculation based on the number of accounts to be called upon, call frequency, average weekly call rate and number of working days per year. A spreadsheet package could be used to perform the necessary sums, and also to provide answers to 'what if' scenarios. For example, how many extra salespeople would be required if the number of accounts to call upon increased or call frequency was raised?

Application of IT in retailing and trade marketing

Major changes have taken place within the field of retailing which have had implications for the way in which business is conducted between suppliers and retailers. Suppliers need to be fully conversant with the technology employed by their trade customers, and to understand how they can fit with a customer's technology strategy and opportunities. Suppliers need to be sensitive to the impact their own actions can have on a customer's technology and should take advantage of opportunities to assist the customer through sharing of information and technological resources.

The power shift away from manufacturers towards retailers is due in large part to the technology, application and information used by retailers. The following is an account of some of the major IT developments.

Electronic point of sale (EPOS)

The main benefit of EPOS and retail scanner systems is the amount of timely and accurate information they deliver. Advances in technology have significantly aided the scope for data analysis. In addition to the original scanner-related data on sales rate, stock levels, stock turn, price and margin, retailers now have information about the demographics, socio-economic and lifestyle characteristics of consumers. They can also assess the impact of a whole host of variables, e.g. price, promotions, advertising, position in store, shelf position, number of facings, and so on. This information drives their choice of product mix, allocation of shelf-space and promotional tactics.

EPOS has certainly changed the relationship between buyer and seller. Before the availability of scanner data, the trading relationship depended on information provided by manufacturers from retail audits, information that was at least several weeks old. More detailed, accurate and timely data from scanner systems gives the retailer significant bargaining power. Not surprisingly, therefore, information finds itself on the negotiating agenda. Manufacturers do buy EPOS data from their customers but they can also trade the information and capabilities they have in exchange for it. Market knowledge is still the manufacturer's forte and this national market picture is of great use to the retailer. Additionally, armed with the retailer's EPOS data the manufacturer could deliver well-targeted trade marketing programmes beneficial to both sides. In true trade marketing spirit, co-operation is the overall preferred approach.

EPOS depends on the inclusion of bar-codes on all products to be scanned. This impacts directly on the manufacturer/supplier who should ensure that all packs carry a bar-code and that the bar-code for any new line listings or promotional packs is entered into the customer's system before any goods are shipped.

Space management systems

Maximising the sales and profitability of selling space is critical. Space management systems which try to systematise the retail merchandiser's decision-making processes are used widely by retailers and manufacturers alike. In many cases manufacturers have not only bought packages but have set up departments which specialise in space management. Opportunity exists for their proactive use by manufacturers, particularly in situations where the retailer is short of resources. More importantly, manufacturers can put themselves forward as produce category specialists. In the soft drinks sector, Coca Cola Schweppes Beverages act as the category specialist. A key function of the trade marketing role at CCSB is to advise the retail trade on the allocation of space to the soft drinks category in totality. An example of a software package that can accomplish this is Nielsen's Spaceman.

Direct product profitability

The output from direct product profitability (DPP) systems can affect retailer decisions on product stocking, store position, pricing and even trading terms demanded. It is vital therefore that the manufacturer understands DPP and the extent to and manner in which individual retailers use it.

DPP replaces gross margin as a much more accurate measure of a product's contribution to total company overhead and profit. It takes account of the fact that products differ with respect to the amount of resource they use; i.e., the amount of transport costs, warehouse and back-of-store space, staff handling time, share of shelf space, even head office costs. As a minimum, the manufacturer needs to be aware of how the retailer is using DPP and have sufficient expertise to question the results of the retailer's analysis. For example, a product with low DPP may still be essential to a retailer's success if it generates in-store customer flow, and if deleting it would lead to a loss of customers.

It can be used by manufacturers and retailers to examine the costs in their individual ends of the distribution chain, and by both to estimate the costs and profits in the other's field for use in negotiation. In some instances manufacturers have taken the lead in introducing DPP and in doing so have capitalised on the potential gains for both sides. Proctor and Gamble (USA) claims it would modify its packaging, its trading terms and other variables on the basis of DPP analysis. Proactive use of DPP by manufacturers works best with actual cost data from the retailer; without this only standard retail industry data can be used. In fact, to continue a theme already begun, manufacturer–retailer co-operation in the sharing of data is the preferred strategy in order to maximise gains for both parties.

Category management

Technology also enables category management. Scanning technology delivers information at a level of detail that allows customised merchandising strategies (tailored product assortments, space allocations, pricing, promotions) to be devised for categories or types of store. Furthermore, sophisticated computer modelling programs allow such marketing programmes to be pre-tested before they are implemented.

Retailers will best respond to those manufacturers who establish themselves as experts in the category. Manufacturers can step in to save the retailer's time, to analyse and identify significant consumer and category trends. The appointed 'category captain' is looked to for category insight and strategic recommendations. This, of course, presumes the adoption by the manufacturer of the relevant technology and applications, but the gains to the proactive manufacturer are substantial. Manufacturers may have extensive information on brand performance but would welcome any additional information on consumer behaviour and competitor activity which the retailers can share with them as category expert. The manufacturer would then be in a position to target merchandising and promotional efforts more adeptly.

Electronic data interchange

The direct linking of manufacture and retail computer systems is promoting wider co-operation between buyer and seller and creating gains in costs and efficiency too. EDI is used in the whole ordering–delivery–invoicing cycle to achieve a reduction in transaction costs, to assist in speeding up supply, and to minimise stock levels. Based on inventory control models, for example, EDI provides the means for automatic reordering.

In situations where a supplier manages a trade customer's inventory, electronic data links could be established to relay information on a customer's stock movements from customer to supplier. The opportunity to manage a trade customer's inventory is immensely beneficial to the manufacturer. By so doing, the manufacturer is able to improve demand forecasting, to minimise its own and its customer's inventory, and to minimise customer stock-outs.

8.3 CONCLUSIONS

This chapter has explored the new developments in selling such as the growth in direct marketing, database marketing, telemarketing, Internet marketing and other information technology applications in selling and sales management. Information technology is helping companies such as Direct Line, First Direct and Dell Computers to sell directly to customers without the need for salespeople or distributors. The use of direct mail and telemarketing is reducing the need for a field salesforce and the growth of Internet marketing is set to revolutionise the way in which transactions are completed.

Developments in information technology such as e-mail, fax and mobile telephones are improving the communication links between salespeople, customers and head office. They are also bringing pressures on salespeople who are now expected to respond faster because of the speed at which these new communication technologies operate.

Sales management has also benefited from these developments. Information technology has provided the platform for new territory management, journey planning, recruitment and selection, training, sales forecasting, salesforce size and evaluation models, as well as improving communication links with the field salesforce.

PRACTICAL EXERCISE

Yuletide Gems

'This particular snowman, will not be affected by heat and it certainly is not made of snow, stones and a carrot nose,' said Rosemary Vaux, Marketing Manager of Ireland-based jewellers Attwood & Sawyer.

The snowman has been created using the finest Chinese crystals and is only 3 cm high. The company, which produces a Christmas theme brooch every year, has this time decided on a snow man design. With a jaunty black enamel top hat, ruby crystal eyes, nose and buttons and a brilliant emerald enamelled scarf blowing in the wind, the Attwood snowman is set in 22 carat gold.

This hand-crafted piece of jewellery is shortly to be shown to the trade. It is then expected to be on sale from the end of October in London at Selfridges, Harrods and John Lewis as well as other selected jewellers and department stores throughout the UK and Ireland in particular, but also in other countries throughout the European Union.

'An awful lot of work has gone into this brooch,' said Rosemary Vaux, 'and it has been designed by our own people. We design our own products and every brooch is handmade, including putting in all the crystals. Already some of our brooches are collectors' items.'

Last year the firm, which has a 2,000 m² workshop in Cork, Ireland, produced a Christmas tree design for its Christmas brooch and the year before that, a teddy bear wearing ice skates. It is anticipated that the brooch should round off a good year's sales for the company.

For the fourth successive year the company has been named the most successful jewellery manufacturer for duty-free shops at airports all over the world, ahead of other famous names such as Dior and Givenchy. The company exports more than 80 per cent of its stock to 50 different countries and has designed and made the Miss World tiara. Its jewellery has also been seen in US 'soap operas' such as 'Dallas' and 'Dynasty', and the Oscar winning film 'Out of Africa'.

Although the company has established a very successful niche for itself in a competitive environment there is no room for complacency in such a business, and Rosemary Vaux feels that although sales are good, more channels of distribution should be opened up in order to expand its customer base. She has asked you, as her newly appointed Deputy Marketing Manager, to give your views, in the form of a report, addressing the following areas:

DISCUSSION QUESTIONS

1 The advantages and disadvantages, in the context of the product range specified, to a relatively small company like Attwood and Sawyer of using the Internet for promoting its full range of products.

2 The kind of research that should now be undertaken in order to assess the potential effectiveness of the Internet as a marketing and sales medium.

3 The company is currently viewed by the public and other companies as being an Irish company with its main market in the UK and to a lesser extent in the rest of Europe. In your report, suggest ways in which the Internet might ultimately make the company more of an international player.

EXAMINATION QUESTIONS

1 Compare the strengths and weaknesses of direct mail and telemarketing.

2 What is database marketing? Explain the types of information that are recorded on a database.

3 What is 'Internet marketing' and why is it growing? What are the barriers to its more rapid expansion?

Part Three

SALES ENVIRONMENT

SALES SETTINGS

OBJECTIVES   After studying this chapter, you should be able to:

1 Appreciate why channels are structured in different ways.

2 Evaluate push and pull promotional strategies and tactics.

3 Understand the unique problems and forces that surround organisational sales settings.

4 Evaluate the usefulness and application of exhibitions as a promotional medium.

5 Understand the nature and role of public relations as a selling tool.

KEY CONCEPTS
- environmental and managerial forces
- 'just-in-time' (JIT)
- market segmentation
- premium offers
- public relations
- exhibitions
- 'pull' techniques
- 'push' techniques
- sales promotions

It is appropriate in this first chapter in the 'Sales Environment' section of this book to analyse the major forces that are affecting selling and sales management. The chapter will then consider the specific sales settings such as sales channels, industrial/commercial/public authority, retail and services selling. It will also examine certain activities which support selling activities namely sales promotions, exhibitions and public relations.

9.1   ENVIRONMENTAL AND MANAGERIAL FORCES IMPACTING SALES

A number of major behavioural, technological and managerial forces are impacting on how selling and sales management are and will be carried out (Anderson, 1996; Magrath, 1997). These are outlined in Table 9.1.

Table 9.1   Forces affecting selling and sales management

Behavioural forces
  Rising customer expectations
  Customer avoidance of buyer–seller negotiations
  Expanding power of major buyers
  Globalisation of markets
  Fragmentation of markets
Technnological forces
  Sales force automation
  ● laptop computers and software
  ● electronic data interchange
  ● desktop videoconferencing
  Virtual sales offices
  Electronic sales channels
  ● internet
  ● television home shopping
Managerial forces
  Direct marketing
  ● direct mail
  ● telemarketing
  ● computer salespeople
  Blending of sales and marketing
  ● intranets
  Qualifications for salespeople and sales managers

Source: Adapted from Anderson (1996).

Behavioural forces

As customers adapt to their changing environment so the sales function has to adapt to the following forces: (i) rising customer expectations; (ii) customer avoidance of buyer–seller negotiations; (iii) the expanding power of major buyers; (iv) globalisation of markets; and (v) fragmentation of markets.

1 Rising customer expectations

As consumers experience higher standards of product quality and service so their expectations are fuelled to expect even higher levels in the future. This process may be accelerated by experiences abroad, and new entrants to industries (possibly from abroad) that set new standards of excellence. As an executive of the customer satisfaction research firm J.D. Power, explained, 'What makes customer satisfaction so difficult to achieve is that you constantly raise the bar and extend the finish line. You never stop. As your customers get better treatment, they demand better treatment.' The implication for salespeople is that they must accept that both consumer and organisational buyer expectations for product quality, customer service and value will continue to rise, and that they must respond to this challenge by advocating and implementing continuous improvements in quality standards.

2 Customer avoidance of buyer–seller negotiations

Studies have shown that the purchase of a car is the most anxiety-provoking and least satisfying experience in retail buying (*Business Week*, 1996). Some car salespeople are trained in the art of negotiation supported by high pressure sales tactics. Consequently, customers have taken to viewing the purchase as an ordeal to be tolerated rather than a pleasurable occasion to be savoured. In response, some car companies have moved to a fixed price, no pressure and full book-value for the trade-in approach. This was used for the successful launch of the Saturn by General Motors in the US and is the philosophy behind the marketing of Daewoo cars in the UK.

3 Expanding power of major buyers

The growing dominance of major players in many sectors (notably retailing) is having a profound influence on selling and sales management. Their enormous purchasing power means that they are able to demand and get special services, including special customer status (key account management), 'just-in-time' inventory control, category management, and joint funding of promotions. So keen is Hewlett Packard to provide fast, efficient service to its customers that it is prepared to rent an office in a key customer's headquarters and station an account manager there (Wood, 1994). Future success for salespeople will be dependent on their capabilities to respond to the increasing demands of major customers.

4 Globalisation of markets

As domestic markets saturate, companies are expanding abroad to achieve sales and profit growth. Large companies such as Coca Cola, Colgate-Palmolive and Avon Products now earn the largest proportion of their revenues in foreign markets. The challenges include the correct balance between expatriate and host-country sales personnel, adapting to different cultures, lifestyles and languages, competing against world class brands, and building global relationships with huge customers based in many countries. For example, 3M has a variety of global strategic accounts from industrial high-tech (e.g. Motorola, Hewlett Packard, IBM, Texas Instruments) to original equipment manufacturers in electronics, appliances, automotive, electrical, aerospace, furniture, consumer products and health care (Magrath, 1997). A major challenge for such a transnational corporation is the co-ordination of global sales teams which sell to the Nortels, Samsungs, Siemens or P&G's of this world, where the customer may be located in over 20 countries and require special terms of sale, technical support, pricing and customisation of products. This complexity means that strategic account managers require both enhanced teamwork and co-ordination skills to ensure that customers receive top quality service.

5 Fragmentation of markets

Driven by differences in income levels, lifestyles, personalities, experiences and race, markets are fragmenting to form market segments. For example, the Campbell Soup Company has divided the US into 22 distinct market segments based upon unique cultural and ethnic tastes for soups (Anderson and Rosenbloom, 1992). This means that markets are likely to become smaller with an increasing range of brands marketed to cater for the diverse requirements (both functional and psychological) of its customers. Marketing and sales managers need to be adept at identifying changes in consumer tastes and developing strategies that satisfy an increasingly varied and multicultural society.

Technological forces

The importance of technological forces on selling and sales management is reflected in the attention given to this topic in Chapter 8. Clearly three major forces are at play: (i) salesforce automation, (ii) virtual sales offices, and (iii) electronic sales channels.

Salesforce automation includes laptop and palmtop computers, mobile telephones, fax machines, e-mail and sophisticated sales-oriented software which aid such tasks as journey and account planning, and recruitment, selection and evaluation of sales personnel. In addition, electronic data interchange (EDI) provides computer links between manufacturers and resellers (retailers, wholesalers and distributors), allowing the exchange of information. For example, purchase orders, invoices, price quotes, delivery dates, reports and promotional information can be exchanged. Technological innovations have also made possible desktop videoconferencing, enabling sales meetings, training and customer interaction to take place without the need for people to leave their offices.

Improved technology has also encouraged the creation of virtual offices, allowing sales personnel to keep in contact with head office, customers and co-workers. The virtual office may be the home or even a car. This can mean massive cost and time savings, and enhanced job satisfaction for sales personnel who are spared some of the incessant traffic jams that are a part of the life of a field salesperson.

The fastest growing electronic sales channel is undoubtedly the Internet, which is discussed in detail in Chapter 8. However, another emerging channel is worthy of mention as it will reduce the need for field salesforces. This is television home shopping which is popular in the US. Viewers watch cable television presenters promote anything from jewellery to consumer electronics and order by telephone. In effect, the presenter is the salesperson.

Managerial forces

Managers are responding to the changes in the environment by developing new strategies to enhance effectiveness. These include (i) employing direct marketing techniques, (ii) improving the blend between sales and marketing, and (iii) encouraging salespeople to gain professional qualifications.

The increasing role of direct marketing, including direct mail and telemarketing, is discussed in Chapter 8. However, a third emerging change is the use of computer stations in US retail outlets to replace traditional salespeople. Although in Europe the use of computer-assisted sales in car showrooms has begun with Daewoo's employment of kiosks where customers can gather product and price information, the process has moved a stage further in the US where several Ford dealerships have installed computer stations which fully replace salespeople. Customers can compare features of competitive models, calculate running costs, compute monthly payments, and use the computer to write up the order and telephone to the factory, without the intervention of a salesperson.

Although the development of effective relationships between sales and marketing personnel is recognised by all, often in practice blending the two functions into an effective whole is hampered by, amongst other things, poor communication. The establishment of intranets, which are similar to the Internet except that they are proprietary company networks that link employees, suppliers and customers through their PCs, can improve links and improve information exchange. Intranets are used for such diverse functions as e-mail, team projects and desktop publishing. Clearly, the use of an intranet can enhance the effectiveness of a field salesforce which requires fast access to rapidly changing information such as product specifications, competitor news and price updates, and allow the sharing of information between sales and marketing.

Finally, sales management is responding to the new challenges by recognising the importance of professional qualifications. In the UK this has led to the formation of a new professional body, the Institute of Professional Sales. This body is charged with enhancing the profile of the sales function, promoting best practice, and developing education and training programmes to improve salespeople and sales manager's professionalism, skills and competence.

Having examined the major forces impacting the sales function, we will now consider the specific settings where selling takes place, and some of the activities such as sales promotions and exhibitions that support selling activities.

9.2 SALES CHANNELS

Before industrialisation, distribution was a simple matter, with producers selling to their immediate neighbours, who often collected the goods themselves. Modern-day manufacturing, more cosmopolitan consumers, better transportation and communications, and business specialisation has meant that channel decisions are now quite complex. Distribution costs have risen relative to production. In fact, as a result of automation and computerisation, production costs as a percentage of total cost are now considerably lower than they were only a few years ago. Marketing management must continually reappraise its channels of distribution in an attempt to effect cost savings. Company policy decides the marketing channels and this determines how the salesforce is organised.

A sales channel is merely the route that goods take through the selling process from a supplier to a customer. Sometimes the channel is direct, and the goods sold are incorporated into a manufacturing process which results in a different end-product. This, in turn, is sold through a different channel. Such a product example are carburettors, which are sold to automobile manufacturers; the automobiles are then sold to car distributors and the car distributors sell to the end consumers. When one considers a product from the raw material stage to the end product, many different sales channels can be involved at different stages in the manufacturing process. A sales channel can also be indirect, whereby a manufacturer sells to a wholesaler or agent, who sells in smaller lots to other customers. This process is known as 'breaking bulk'.

Selecting/reappraising sales channels

When selecting or reappraising channels, the company must take into consideration a number of factors, namely:

- the market
- channel costs
- the product
- profit potential
- channel structure
- product life-cycle
- non-marketing factors.

The market

This must be analysed with a view to ensuring that as many potential consumers as possible will have the opportunity to purchase the product or service. Channel compatibility with similar products in the marketplace is important; consumers are quite conservative and any radical move from the accepted norm can be viewed with suspicion. Unless there are sound reasons for so doing, it does not make sense to go outside the established channel. For instance, a canned-food processor would not normally consider selling through mail order unless the company was providing a very specialist type of food or perhaps providing it as part of a hamper pack. Instead, the company would use the traditional distribution outlets such as food multiples and cash and carry.

Channel costs

Generally the shortest channels are the costliest. Thus the company selling direct may achieve a large market coverage, but in addition to increased investment in the salesforce the firm will also incur heavier transportation and warehousing costs. However, against this must be balanced the fact that there will be a greater profit margin, by virtue of the fact that distributive intermediaries are obviated and their margins will not have to be met. In addition to these financial criteria, short channels have the advantage of being nearer to the end-users, which means that the company is in a better position to anticipate and meet their needs.

There has been a trend in recent years for manufacturers to shorten their channels in order to control more effectively the distribution of their products, particularly where expensive advertising has been used to pre-sell the goods to the consumer.

The product

Generally, low-cost, low-technology items are more suited to longer channels. More complex items, often requiring much after-sales service, tend to be sold through short channels. This is why most industrial products are sold direct from the producer to the user. The width of the product line is also important, in that a wide product line may make it worthwhile for the manufacturer to market direct because the salesperson has a larger product portfolio with which to interest the customer, and this makes for more profit-earning potential.

A narrow product line is more suited to a longer channel because, along the distribution chain, it can be combined with complementary products of other manufacturers, resulting in a wider range of items with which to interest the customer. In this particular case the distributive intermediaries, not the manufacturers, are performing the final selling function. A good illustration of the above is the manufacturer of bathroom fittings who would normally sell to builders' merchants. Builders' merchants then sell these fittings to builders alongside other merchandise that builders require.

Profit potential

There comes a point when the costs of attempting to obtain more sales through the channel outweigh the revenue and profits to be gained from those increased sales. For instance, a manufacturer of an exclusive and expensive perfume would not distribute through supermarkets or advertise during peak-time television viewing. If the company did, then sales would no doubt increase, but the costs of achieving those sales would make it an unprofitable exercise. It is really an accounting problem, and a balance must be struck between channel expense, profit and gross margins.

A manufacturer using short channels is more likely to have high gross margins, but equally higher channel expenses. The manufacturer using longer channels will have relatively lower gross margins, coupled with lower channel expenses.

Channel structure

To a great extent a manufacturer's choice of distributive intermediaries is governed by the members in that channel. If the members of the channel are strong (by virtue of, say, their size), then it will be difficult for the manufacturer to go outside the established channel.

In some cases it may be difficult to gain entry to the channel unless the product is somehow differentiated by way of uniqueness or lower price than those products already established in the channel. A good example here would be the potential difficulty that a new detergent manufacturer would have in attempting to sell products through the larger supermarkets. The manufacturer would have to convince members of the channel that the detergent was in some way better than those already on the market, or offer advantageous prices and terms. In addition, detergent is mainly marketed using a 'pull' strategy of marketing, relying upon consumer advertising to create brand loyalty and pre-sell the product. The manufacturer would thus have to spend a lot on mass advertising to create brand loyalty for the product, or attempt to 'push' the product through the channel by providing trade incentives, with probably a lower end price than competitive products coupled with a larger profit margin for retailers. It can, therefore, be seen that it would be a very daunting task for a new detergent manufacturer to enter the market in a big way without large cash resources at its disposal.

Product life-cycle

Considerations must be given to how far the product is along the product life-cycle. A new concept or product just entering the life-cycle may require intensive distribution to start with to launch it on to the market. As it becomes established it may be that after-sales service criteria become important, leading to a move to selective distribution, with only those dealers that are able to offer the necessary standard of after-sales service being allowed to sell the product.

In the case of television sets the wheel has turned full circle, from intensive distribution to selective distribution (for the reasons just mentioned) and back to intensive distribution. This is because the servicing of televisions has now become a relatively simple matter, in that televisions are now constructed similarly and standard units are replaced when repairs are needed. A television repairer no longer needs to be a specialist in one particular brand. Television manufacturers now realise that, with comparative parity between models, consumers are less likely to be drawn towards a particular brand because of its supposed technical superiority or standard of after-sales service. The most crucial factor now is ensuring that the customer is able to see the brand and compare it with competitors' brands. Thus, maximum exposure at the point of sale has become the manufacturer's objective.

Non-marketing factors

These usually relate to the amount of finance available. It may be, in the case of, say, an innovative product, that the firm is unable to exploit this to its fullest advantage because of financial constraints. In such a case the firm may have to distribute through a middleman because it cannot afford to employ a field salesforce. Conversely, the firm may use a non-conventional channel such as mail order which requires minimal investment in salespeople, although the physical characteristics of the product may not make it suitable for mail order.

Non-marketing factors often apply when selling internationally, since many companies unfortunately view export orders as a supplement to home trade and are prepared to offer an agency to anybody who is likely to obtain orders, irrespective of their commercial standing. A fuller discussion of international aspects takes place in Chapter 10, but it is worth noting that there are cases of companies who entered into export agency agreements when they were small and exporting was relatively unimportant to them. As the companies grew they came to regard exporting as being essential, but it proved difficult and expensive to unwind hastily entered-into agency agreements. The companies in many cases had to persevere with the original arrangements, often against long-term best interests.

Characteristics of sales channels

It should be realised that marketing channels are one of the more stable elements in the marketing mix. A channel is costly and complex to change, unlike, say, price which is relatively easy to manipulate. For instance, a switch from selective to intensive distribution is a top management policy decision that will have a direct effect upon salesforce numbers, and even upon the type of selling methods to be used.

The main problem that companies have to face is in choosing the most appropriate channel, and from the viewpoint of sales management this includes the type of sales outlet that must be serviced. Basically, a manufacturer has the choice of one of four types of distribution at its disposal:

1 *Direct*. Here the manufacturer does not use a middleman, and sells and delivers direct to the customer.
2 *Selective*. Here the manufacturer sells through a limited number of middlemen who are chosen because of their special abilities or facilities to enable the product to be marketed more effectively.
3 *Intensive*. The intention is to achieve maximum exposure at the point of sale, and the manufacturer will sell through as many outlets as possible. The servicing and after-sales aspects are probably not so important here. Product examples are cigarettes, breakfast cereals and detergents.
4 *Exclusive*. The manufacturer sells to a restricted number of dealers. An obvious example is the car industry, where distributive intermediaries must provide the levels of stockholding, after-sales service, etc., deemed appropriate by manufacturers; their reputations depend ultimately upon the service backup given by their distributors.

A discussion of other sales settings follows.

9.3 INDUSTRIAL/COMMERCIAL/PUBLIC AUTHORITY SELLING

These categories are grouped together because the selling approach to each is similar and the behavioural patterns exhibited by each conform to organisational behaviour (discussed in Chapter 2).

There are a number of characteristics in these types of market that distinguish them from consumer markets.

Fewer customers

Institutions and businesses purchase goods either for use in their own organisations or for use in the manufacture of other goods. There are consequently few potential purchasers, each making high-value purchases.

Concentrated markets

Industrial markets in particular are often highly concentrated, a good example being the textile industry in the United Kingdom which is centred in Lancashire and Yorkshire. An industrial salesperson who sells into one industry may deal with only a few customers in a restricted geographical area.

Complex purchasing decisions

Buying decisions often involve a large number of people, particularly in the case of a public authority where a purchasing committee may be involved in a major purchase.

Many industrial buying decisions involve more than the buyer; in some cases the technical specifier, production personnel and finance personnel are involved and this is where the decision-making unit can be seen in practice. This can lengthen the negotiation and decision-making process. Salespeople must be able to work and communicate with people in a variety of positions and be prepared to tailor their selling approaches to satisfy individual needs, e.g. specifiers will need to be convinced of the technical merits of the product, production people will want to be assured of guaranteed deliveries and buyers will be looking for value for money.

For technically complicated products, selling is sometimes performed by a sales team, with each member of the team working with his or her opposite number in the buying team, e.g. a sales engineer works with engineers in the buying company.

Long-term relationships

A life insurance policy or encyclopaedia salesperson makes a sale, and probably never meets the customer again. However, the nature of selling in industrial, commercial and public authority settings is that long-term relationships are established and both parties become dependent upon each other, one for reliable supplies and the other for regular custom.

There is thus a tendency to build up a strong personal relationship over a long time, and slick high-pressure selling techniques are unlikely to be of much help. A more considered approach which involves the salesperson identifying the needs of his individual customers and then selling the benefits of the product in order to satisfy those needs is more likely to be successful. The ability of salespeople to deal with complaints and provide a reliable after-sales service is very important. It has been suggested that increasingly the effective salesperson must understand how to develop and sustain relationships with key customer groups, along the lines of relationship selling.

Reciprocal trading

This is an arrangement whereby company A purchases certain commodities manufactured by company B and vice versa. Such arrangements tend to be made at board or director level and are often entered into when there is a financial link between the companies, such as companies within the same group of companies (sometimes referred to as intergroup trading) or between companies whose directors simply want to formalise an arrangement to purchase as much of each other's products as possible.

Such arrangements can be frustrating for salespeople and buyers alike, because they deter free competition; the buyer does not like to be told from where he or she must purchase, just the same as the salesperson does not relish the thought of having a large part of his or her potential market permanently excluded because of a reciprocal trading arrangement.

Types of production

This relates mainly to industrial sales. The type of production operated by the firm to whom the salesperson is selling can often determine the type of selling approach to be used. Basically, types of production can be as follows:

1 *Job (or unit specification) production.* An item is produced to an individual customer's requirements. It is difficult to forecast demand in industries with this type of production. Product examples are ships, tailor-made suits and hospital construction.
2 *Batch production.* A number of products or components are made at the same time, but not on a continuous basis. As with job production, batches are normally made to individual customer requirements, but sometimes batches are produced in anticipation of orders. Product examples are books, furniture and clothes.
3 *Flow (or mass or line) production.* There is continuous production of identical or similar products that are made in anticipation of sales. Product examples are motor cars, video recorders and washing machines.

4 *Process (or continuous) production*. The production unit has raw materials coming into the manufacturing process and a finished product emerging at the end of the process. Examples are chemicals, brewing and plastic processes.

Clearly, a salesperson selling in a combination of these settings will have to adopt a different approach for each. With flow production he or she will have to anticipate model changes in order to ensure that the firm is invited to quote at the outset, and then follow up this quotation in the expectation of securing an order which will be fulfilled over the life of the product. If the salesperson is unsuccessful at this stage, then he or she may not have the opportunity of selling to the firm again until the next model change (and even then it is difficult trying to dislodge established suppliers).

It is also important to realise that a number of flow production producers are now operating **'just-in-time' (JIT)** systems of production. Here, reliability of quality and delivery is of prime importance because the producer works on minimal stockholding of raw materials. Long-term relationships with suppliers are prevalent in these situations. 'Zero defects' are the goal that suppliers must strive to achieve in terms of quality.

With job production, losing an order is not quite so critical because, providing the firm is being correctly represented, it should be invited to quote for the next order and perhaps be successful then. Naturally, losing an order is a serious matter, but with job production it normally means waiting a short period before being asked to quote again for a different job, whereas with flow production it might be several years before the model is changed and the opportunity is provided to quote again (by which time the buyer might have forgotten the existence of the salesperson).

9.4 SELLING FOR RESALE

Selling for resale includes selling to retailers (some of whom own their own retail establishments and many of whom belong to groups) and selling to wholesalers. Much buying in this type of trade is centralised, and in many cases the potential buyer visits the seller (unlike industrial selling when the seller normally visits the buyer). A look at the changing patterns of retailing since the end of World War Two will illustrate how selling methods have been revolutionised.

Before examining these changing patterns of retailing, we must first categorise the different types of selling outlet:

1 *Multiples*. These are classed as belonging to a retail organisation with ten or more branches, each selling a similar range of merchandise. This has been one of the fastest growing areas of retailing, and in the United Kingdom multiples now dominate certain areas of retail trading.
2 *Variety chains* (sometimes called *variety multiples*). These are similar to multiples except that the qualifying number of stores is five and they sell a wider range of merchandise. Examples are mainly to be found in the grocery field.

3 *Co-operative societies*. These are owned and controlled by the people who shop there and each society is governed by a board of directors elected from its own members. Anybody can be a member by purchasing one share. The movement can be traced back to 1844 when it started in Rochdale. Its principles are as follows:

- open membership;
- democratic control (one man, one vote);
- payment of limited interest on capital;
- surplus arising out of the operation to be distributed to members in proportion to their purchases; this was originally distributed through dividends, later it was paid through trading stamps but is now increasingly being abandoned in favour of lower prices;
- provision of education;
- co-operation amongst societies, both nationally and internationally.

4 *Department stores*. These are stores that have five or more departments under one roof and at least 25 employees. Stores sell a wide range of commodities, including significant amounts of household goods and clothing.

5 *Independents*. As the term implies, these traders own their own retail outlets. There are, however, slight variations, the first being where the independent belongs to a retail buying association. This is an informal grouping whereby retailers (usually within a specific geographical area) group together to make bulk purchases. A more publicised arrangement is when a wholesaler or group of wholesalers invite retailers to affiliate to them and agree to take the bulk of their purchases from them. Such arrangements are termed voluntary groups (individual wholesaler sponsored) or voluntary chains (group wholesaler sponsored). Participating independent retailers have an identifying symbol, in addition to their customary title. Such retailers voluntarily agree to abide by the rules of the group or chain, which includes such matters as accounting procedures, standard facilities and group marketing/promotional schemes.

6 *Mail order*. Mail order has expanded significantly in recent years. The most popular type of trader in this section is the mail order warehouse, which carries a large range of goods. Such business is conducted through the medium of glossy catalogues held by appointed commission agents who sell to their families and friends. Mail order is also carried out by commodity specialists dealing in such items as gardening produce, military surplus and hi-fi. They tend to advertise in the appropriate specialist hobbies press and through the medium of direct mail. This type of business has expanded a lot in recent years, largely as a result of the expansion of the Sunday colour supplements. Many companies have been established that deal in more general ranges of goods and who use mainly such colour supplements to advertise their commodities. Some department stores also offer postal services and sometimes provide catalogues.

The success of the variety multiples has meant that manufacturers have had to reappraise their sales channels as it has meant a concentration of purchasing power into fewer hands. In the fast-moving consumer goods field, manufacturers have become increasingly involved in controlling the distribution of their products and have become involved in merchandising activities to support their 'pull' marketing strategies. This has meant heavy advertising expenditures, and the concurrent merchandising activities at point-of-sale have been necessary to ensure that the goods are promoted in-store to back up advertising. As a result of this, large manufacturers operating a 'pull' strategy have been able to exercise control over their distributive intermediaries; such intermediaries could only dismiss demand created through advertising and branding at the risk of losing custom. This control has meant lower margins for retailers, and manufacturers being able to dictate the in-store location of their particular products. The weight of advertising put behind major brands has given these manufacturers influence over their distributive outlets.

Although there was initially some resistance on the part of manufacturers to the development of the variety multiples, they eventually found it to their advantage to deal directly with them. This was because they purchased in bulk, often for delivery to a central depot, and placed large orders well in advance of the delivery date, thus enabling the manufacturer to organise production more efficiently.

The implications for selling as a result of these developments have been that salespeople of fast-moving consumer goods are no longer compelled to sell the products in the old-fashioned 'salesmanship' sense, as advertising has already pre-sold the goods for them. Selling to the variety multiples is more a matter of negotiation at higher levels whereby the buyer and the sales manager negotiate price and delivery and the salespeople merely provide an after-sales service at individual outlets. Sometimes the salespeople carry out merchandising activities such as building up shelf displays, providing window stickers and in-store advertising, although sometimes these duties are carried out by a separate merchandiser or team of merchandisers, particularly when some form of demonstration or product promotion is required.

The growing importance of retailers is being reflected in the formation of **trade marketing** teams to service their needs. A combination of key account management on the part of the salesforce, and the brand manager's lack of appreciation of what retailers actually want, has promoted many European consumer goods companies to set up a trade marketing organisation. A key role is to bridge the gap between key account management and the salesforce. Trade marketers focus on retailer needs: what kinds of products do they want, in which sizes, with which packaging, at what prices, and with what kind of promotion? Information on trade requirements is fed back to brand management who develop new products, and to the salesforce who can then better communicate with retailers. An important role for trade marketers is to develop tailored promotions for supermarkets. For example, a large supermarket chain also owned a group of hotels. It demanded from a drinks supplier that the next competition promotion offer holiday breaks in its hotels as prizes (paid for by the supplier).

Wholesalers of course have suffered during the post-war period, and many have gone out of business because their traditional outlet (the independent) has also suffered. In fact this is why wholesalers established voluntary groups or chains, in order to meet the challenge of the variety multiples and offer a similar type of image to the public. However, this seems to have largely failed, perhaps because of inferior purchasing power and because wholesalers must try to make their independent retailing members behave like variety multiples, using voluntary means. The wholesaler's only sanction against unco-operative members is to expel them from the group, whereas in the case of the variety multiples a recalcitrant manager can be quickly removed.

The post-war years have witnessed the growth of large-scale retailing, including a growth in the size of retailing establishments, first to supermarkets, then to superstores and eventually to hypermarkets. In addition, partly because of the large size of site required for such retail outlets, but mainly for customer convenience, the trend has been towards out-of-town sites where easy parking, etc., is facilitated. The pattern of shopping has also changed in that the shopper has, for most goods, been prepared to dispense with the personal service of the shopkeeper, and self-service and self-selection have been readily accepted in the interests of lower overheads and more competitive prices. There has been a growth in mass marketing because increased standards of living have meant that products which were once luxury goods are now utility goods and required by the bulk of the population, e.g. cars, foreign holidays, televisions and telephones. Because supply normally exceeds demand for the bulk of consumer goods, there has been a massive increase in advertising and other forms of promotion in an attempt to induce brand loyalty; the faster-moving forms of consumer goods are pre-sold to the consumer by means of 'pull' promotional strategies. Thus the retailing scene has been one of dynamic change which has affected ways in which salespeople now operate.

Franchising

A fast-growing trend in retailing in Europe has been the contractual system of franchising. It is sometimes referred to as a system of corporate vertical marketing (VMS) as its power is based at a point in the channel that is one or more stages removed from the end customer. The franchisor is the one who initiates the franchise and provides the link in the specific stages of the manufacturing/distribution process. Franchising is really an Amercian phenomenon and it was introduced into the UK in the 1950s. Since then it has grown enormously and it now has a code of conduct that is administered through a voluntary body called the British Franchising Association.

Franchising comes in a number of forms:

● From manufacturers to retailers, e.g. a car manufacturer (the franchisor) licenses car distributors (franchisees) to sell its products. In fact, the first franchising system in the world started in the United Kingdom through the 'tied public house' system. Landlords who owned their own premises were tied to a brewery under an agreement to purchase only that brewery's products. It was not, however, referred to as 'franchising' in those early days.
● From manufacturers to wholesalers, which is popular in the soft drinks

industry. Here manufacturers sometimes supply concentrate (i.e. the 'secret formula') which wholesalers then mix with water and bottle for distribution to local retail outlets (e.g. Pepsi Cola, Coca-Cola). Manufacturers are the driving force behind the brand image of the product and stringent consistency and control of quality is of paramount importance.

- From wholesalers to retailers, which has been in decline for a number of years as a result of the rise of the multiples mentioned in the previous section. The most successful example here is the voluntary group 'SPAR', which does not manufacture, but its large wholesale buying power means that it can pass on these cost savings to independent retailers who join the group and display the 'SPAR' logo. They must abide by the rules of the group in relation to such matters as price promotions, standards of store layout and opening hours which the group uses as part of its advertising: 'SPAR – your eight till late shop'.

- Service firms sponsored franchises to retailers is the area that has achieved the largest growth over recent years. Here, examples are to be found in the fast-food business (e.g. Burger King, McDonalds, Little Chef, Kentucky Fried Chicken, Spud-U-Like and Pizza Hut), car rentals (e.g. Avis, Budget and Hertz), office services (e.g. Prontaprint), hotels and resorts (e.g. some Sheraton and some Holiday Inn hotels are owned by individuals or groups of individuals who operate on a franchise basis).

All franchising arrangements have a common set of procedures for their operation:

1 The franchisor offers expert advice on such matters as location, finance, operational matters and marketing.
2 The franchisor promotes the image nationally or internationally, which promotes a well-recognised name for the franchisee.
3 Many franchise arrangements have a central purchasing system where franchisees buy at favourable rates or where a successful 'formula' is central to the operation of the franchise (e.g. Kentucky Fried Chicken).
4 The franchise agreement provides a binding contract to both sides. This contract governs such matters as hours of opening, hygiene and how the business is operated in terms of its dealings with customers. Indeed, on this latter point, organisations such as Little Chef employ 'mystery shoppers' who call unannounced and then order a meal anonymously. They check up on the operation of franchisees to ensure that they are following the rules of the operation of the franchise. The mystery shopper investigates matters such as how the customer is greeted; whether or not they were kept waiting; whether or not certain extra items of food were offered; cleanliness of restroom facilities and if such facilities were checked in the last two hours from a chart that is displayed on the wall.
5 The franchisor often provides initial start-up and then continuous training to the franchisee.
6 The franchise normally requires the franchisee to pay a royalty or franchise fee to the franchisor. However, the franchisee owns the business and is not employed by the franchisor.

This system of marketing has been very popular over recent years. It provides an advantage to both large-scale business (the franchisor) and the small-scale business (the franchisee). In the case of the latter, the opportunity to become self-employed and be in control of their own destiny is a strong motivating factor to work hard and make a success of the business.

9.5 SELLING SERVICES

Just like a tangible product, a service must satisfy the needs of buyers. However, their benefits are much less tangible than a physical product in that they cannot be stored or displayed and satisfaction is achieved through activities (e.g. transportation from one place to another rather than, say, a seat on a train).

Services can come in many forms and some of the more obvious examples include the following:

1 Transportation – air, sea, rail and road.
2 Power – electricity, gas and coal.
3 Hotels and accommodation.
4 Restaurants.
5 Communications – telephone, fax and e-mail.
6 Television and radio services.
7 Banking.
8 Insurance.
9 Clubs – social, keep fit, sporting and special interests.
10 Repair and maintenance.
11 Travel agencies.
12 Accounting services.
13 Business consultancy – advertising, marketing research and strategic planning.
14 Architectural.
15 Cleaning.
16 Library.
17 Public (local) authority services and undertakings – disposal of refuse and repair of roads.
18 Computing services.
19 Stockbroking services.

There are, of course, many more and they can be applied to both consumer and industrial users. The selling approach to each category will tend to differ, depending upon customer needs, just as selling approaches differ when considering physical products.

In the UK, the service sector has grown tremendously over the past decade, so much so that, like the United States, the UK is now primarily a service rather than a manufacturing economy. There are many reasons for this. For example, more women work full-time, and the division of responsibilities between men and women is breaking down into more equitable shares. This has put pressure on the service sector to provide services that can perform tasks that have hitherto been seen as the province of being provided in the home (e.g. more eating out in restaurants and more holidays – often two per year – because of increased disposable income).

Better technology, too, has assisted in the development and provision of a more comprehensive range of services (e.g. banks offer credit cards, 'instant' statements, quicker decisions on loans and longer term services such as mortgages). Building societies also provide a broader range of services and have moved into areas traditionally viewed as the province of the banks, more so after the recent 'liberalisation' of their activities through the Financial Services Act (1986). In addition to an expansion of existing services in the financial sector, many more services are now available (e.g. professional drain clearing through the franchise operation 'Dyno-rod').

Public services have become more marketing orientated and have to be seen to be more accountable to their 'publics' (e.g. the police service which is now more public relations conscious than in the past). Local authorities spend the money that is raised through council tax, and the public is beginning to question more closely how this money that they have contributed is being spent. Thus, local authority departments have to be seen to be spending money wisely as they are more publicly accountable. They have to communicate to their public and explain how the services they provide are of value.

Special characteristics of services include the following:

1 Intangibility.
2 It is difficult to separate production from consumption in that many services are consumed as they are produced.
3 Services are not as 'standard' as products and are thus more difficult to assess (in terms of value).
4 It is not possible to 'stock' services, unlike products.

Table 9.2 illustrates these characteristics more graphically.

Table 9.2   Characteristics of services and products

Products		Services
Low	Intangibility	High
Low	Inseparability	High
Low	Variability (i.e. non-standard)	High
Low	Perishability (i.e. inability to stock)	High
Yes	Ownership	No

The final crierion, ownership, shows that unlike a product the consumer does not secure ownership of the service but pays to secure access to the use of the service (e.g. a recreational facility like exercise in a gymnasium).

The notion of the 'four Ps' has now been extended to include an extra three Ps, and we now have what is referred to as the 'seven Ps' of service marketing. The extra three Ps are people, process and physical evidence.

People are an important element in carrying out the service, especially those who are directly involved with customers, and such employees must be considered in terms of their training and general demeanour in handling customers when developing a marketing mix.

Process relates to how the service is provided and it deals with customers at the point of contact in the supply of the service itself. Consistency and quality of service must clearly be planned and managed.

Physical evidence is also included because of the intangibility of services. Marketing should therefore highlight the nature of the service being offered. This should be communicated to the customer by emphasising such matters as levels of quality, types of equipment and physical facilities.

With the above background in mind, the task of selling services is perhaps more difficult than that of selling products because of their more abstract nature. A distinguishing feature is that those who provide the service are often the ones who sell that service. Thus, providers of services must be more highly trained in sales technique, and sales negotiation forms an important part of such interaction. It is important, too, that close attention is paid to image building (e.g. banks and insurance companies must be seen to be stable, reliable institutions, but with a friendly, non-intimidating attitude – an image which banks in particular have spent a lot of money fostering over the past decade). Perhaps above all, as McDonald (1988) has pointed out, because unlike a physical product it is never possible to know precisely what will be received until the service is rendered, the element of trust is essential in selling services. The seller of services must be an expert in creating an atmosphere of trust between buyer and seller.

9.6 SALES PROMOTIONS

Sales promotions embrace a variety of techniques that organisations can use as part of their total marketing effort. Examples of possible objectives that may be achieved through sales promotional activities include the following:

● the encouragement of repeat purchases
● the building of long-term customer loyalty
● the encouragement of consumers to visit a particular sales outlet
● the building up of retail stock levels
● the widening or increasing of the distribution of a product or brand.

Sales promotions include the following:

● price reductions
● vouchers or coupons
● gifts
● competitions
● lotteries
● cash bonuses.

In turn, the techniques can cover the following:

- consumer promotions
- trade promotions
- salesforce promotions.

The importance of sales promotions has increased steadily since the 1960s, as has the sophistication of methods used. It is sometimes implied that sales promotion is a second-rate or peripheral marketing activity, but companies are increasingly realising the importance of a well-planned and co-ordinated programme of sales promotion.

Within the United Kingdom, sales promotional activities have matured since the 1970s. At that time few attempts were made to measure the effectiveness of such activity, and advertising agencies tended to branch out into sales promotions with the aim of offering an all-inclusive package to their clients in an attempt to combat competition from the emerging sales promotion agencies. The mid-1980s brought increased economic pressure to bear on all business activities, and this had the effect of making advertising agencies become more concerned about reductions in company advertising budgets. They began to pay greater attention to the effectiveness of sales promotions, and began to adopt a more integrated approach to advertising and sales promotion. There was also a move towards fee-based sales promotional agencies, which implied a longer-term relationship between agency and client, rather than the *ad hoc* commission structure that had existed before.

As a result of this increased competition from sales promotional agencies, advertising agencies have tended, since the mid-1980s, to take sales promotion seriously and have begun to offer sales promotion alongside advertising as an integrated promotional package. Hence, since the late 1970s there has been a gradual erosion of the line between sales promotion and advertising.

Sales promotions can be divided into three main areas of activity:

1 consumer promotions
2 trade promotions
3 personnel motivation.

Each of these is examined separately.

Consumer promotions

These are often referred to as **'pull' techniques**, in that they are designed to stimulate final demand and move products through the sales channel, with the consumer providing the impetus.

The most widely used consumer promotion is the price reduction or price promotion. There are various techniques which fall into this category.

1 The item is marked '*x* pence off'. This can be manufacturer or retailer organised. This technique now has to be used with caution by UK manufacturers, as recent legislation now makes it illegal to state this, unless the previous price has been applied for a substantial period of time.
2 An additional quantity is offered for the normal price, e.g. 'two for the price of one' or '10 per cent bigger – same price as before'.

3 Price-off coupons, either in or on the pack, may be redeemed against future purchase of the product.
4 Introductory discount price offers on new products.

A view held by many organisers of such promotions is that the consumer, in economically difficult times, is more likely to be attracted by the opportunity to save money than by incidental free offers or competitions. Price promotions are predominantly used by fast-moving consumer goods producers, especially in the grocery trade.

Premium offers are marketing techniques that give extra value to goods or services in the short term as part of a promotional package. Under this category are the following:

1 *Self-liquidating premiums*. An offer of merchandise is communicated to the customer in, on or off the pack. The price charged to the customer covers the cost of the item to the promoter. The promoter is able to purchase such merchandise in bulk and thereby pass savings on to the customers who feel that they are getting good value for money. Such promotions are usually linked with the necessity to collect labels or cut out tokens, etc., from a number of purchases of the same, or same range of, products. Thus the premium need not necessarily be connected with the product that carried the premium; the idea is to stimulate purchases of the product – selling the premium is of secondary importance.
2 *On-pack gifts*. Here the premium is usually attached to the product. The premium may be product-related, e.g. a toothbrush attached to toothpaste, or not product-related, e.g. an item of merchandise such as shampoo taped to a magazine.
3 *Continuities*. These are sets of merchandise that can be collected through a series of purchases, e.g. picture cards, chinaware, glassware, etc., forming part of a set. The premium is either with the product or the purchaser has to send off for the premium.
4 *Coupon plans*. Coupons, contained within the pack, may be collected over time and exchanged for a variety of products in a catalogue. Coupon techniques may be used by one producer or supplier as a promotion for its goods or services, or the plan may include a number of different producers' products under one name. These schemes have largely replaced trading stamps, which were used in a similar way, although trading stamps and purchase vouchers that can be redeemed for cash or goods, are now making a comeback in a specialist way (e.g. for petrol purchases).
5 *Free samples*. These are sample packs of products offered with brand-related products, attached to magazines, given away separately in retail outlets, delivered door-to-door, etc.

Merchandise as a premium does not have the universal appeal of money, but it may have a more pointed appeal than cash or a price reduction. The premium chosen, and the way in which it is offered, may pre-select a specific type of customer, but the offer can at least be targeted at the right market segment. Providing the additional response generated more than covers the cost of the premium and the administration/distribution costs, the promotion will be cost effective.

The choice of premium and sales promotional technique is a crucial decision, and the problem is to find a premium that is 'different' or unusual, has broad customer appeal and is available in sufficient quantity to meet demand.

Competitions are popular in the United Kingdom and Germany. The advantage of running a competition is that it should be cost-effective if the cost of the prizes is spread over a large enough number of entrants.

Competitions for consumer goods are usually promoted on the pack concurrent with in-store promotion. The entry form is usually located on or near the product and it is usually required that each entry is accompanied by proof of purchase. More recently, free draws have become popular whereby a purchase is not necessary and the shopper merely fills in his or her name on an entry form and 'posts' it in an entry box in the retail outlet.

There is much scope for individuality and creativity in this method of promotion. It does, however, need much pre-planning and administration, which is probably the reason why competitions tend to be aimed at the national level, and involve high value prizes such as holidays and cars, so that consumer response is great enough to cover the costs of the promotion. Lotteries and sweepstakes are also used as promotional techniques, particularly by retail outlets, which use them to attract custom into the store.

Joint promotions are not specific to consumer goods, but are to be seen more often as companies attempt to find new promotional techniques. They may involve two or more companies, which tend to be related not by product type but rather by similar customer profits. There are a number of such arrangements:

1 Between a retailer and a producer, where a branded good may carry a voucher redeemable at a particular store or chain.
2 Between two or more producers, where one manufacturer's product carries a promotion for the other, and vice versa. Here the relation by customer profile and not product similarities becomes evident.
3 Between a service organisation and a producer, e.g. between a travel company and a breakfast cereal manufacturer, or a dry cleaner and a clothes manufacturer.

Trade promotions

The aim of trade promotions is usually to 'push' products (**'push' techniques**) through the sales channel towards the customer. Similar to consumer promotions, incentives are offered in the form of extra rewards such as cash discounts, increased margins on sales, dealer competitions, exhibitions, provision of demonstrators, holidays (often in the guise of a conference or product launch), etc.

The objectives of retailer–distributor promotions are as follows:

● to achieve widespread distribution of a new brand

- to move excess stocks on to retailers' shelves
- to achieve the required display levels of a product
- to encourage greater overall stockholding of a product
- particularly in the case of non-consumer products, to encourage salespeople at distributor level to recommend the brand
- to encourage support for overall promotional strategy.

There are a number of problems associated with trade promotions. Too frequent use of promotions can mean that a salesperson directs his or her attention to the one product involved and neglects other products in the product line. The objectives of the promoter may conflict with those of the retailer or distributor; consequently some sales employees are not permitted to accept incentives or participate in trade contests because their management wishes to maintain strict control over their selling activities. There is also a danger that a trade promotion may be used to push an uncompetitive brand or inferior product. Therefore, long-term measures to promote sales are not feasible, and the manufacturer would be better advised to look to product improvement as part of long-term strategy. The British Code of Sales Promotion Practice states:

> No promotion directed towards employees should be such as to cause any conflict with their loyalty to their employer. In case of doubt, the prior permission of the employer, or the responsible manager, should be obtained.

Although business gifts are not strictly speaking sales promotions, they are relevant to this section. The business gift sector is characterised by seasonal demand, and it is estimated that 80 per cent of this business is conducted in the last two months of every year. Apart from the obvious connotation that it puts the recipient under some moral obligation to purchase, it also serves as an advertising medium if the company logo is incorporated in the gift. From as early as 1981 the Chartered Institute of Purchasing and Supply took a serious and critical interest in the use of business gifts, especially where the 'giving' was tied to the placing of orders. They argued that such gifts could influence the buyer's objectivity, and that they should be restricted to such nominal items as calendars, diaries, pens, etc. Recently, the giving of business gifts has declined, as employers have placed restrictions upon what their employees may receive, and the Chartered Institute of Purchasing and Supply has published a 'blacklist' of companies operating what they consider to be gift schemes over and above items of nominal value.

Personnel motivation

These are essentially promotions to the salesforce, but many apply to distributors and retailers. The most widely used salesforce promotion is the sales incentives scheme. Rewards are offered to all participants on an equal basis and these rewards are over and above the normal sales compensation. Such rewards are offered as prizes in a competition to those individuals or groups who perform best against a specific set of objectives. The problem is that average or below-average performers may not feel sufficiently motivated to put in any extra effort if they consider that only top performers are likely to win. Thus, competitions tend to be used for group or area salesforce motivation.

When establishing a salesforce incentive scheme one must consider objectives, timing, scoring methods and prizes/rewards. Typical objectives of such a scheme may include the following:

- the introduction of a new product line
- the movement of slow-selling items
- to obtain wider territory coverage
- to develop new prospects
- to overcome seasonal sales slumps
- to obtain display
- to develop new sales skills.

The timing of the scheme may depend upon the size of the salesforce, the immediacy of action required and the nature of the objectives to be achieved. An incentive programme runs on average for between two and six months.

Scoring, or measuring performance, may be simply based upon value or unit sales. In order to overcome territorial differences, quotas may be established for individual regions, areas or salespeople. Points, stamps, vouchers, etc., may be awarded on the achievement of a pre-stated percentage of quotas or level of sales, and continue to be awarded as higher levels are achieved. These tokens, etc., may then be exchanged for merchandise, cash, etc., by the recipient. Frequently catalogues are supplied giving a range of merchandise for the salesperson or their family to choose from. Vouchers for redemption or exchange in retail stores are also used as prizes or rewards.

During a scheme additional bonus points may be awarded for the attainment of more specific short-term objectives such as increased sales of a particular product, increased number of new customers, training and display objectives. In this way a long-running scheme can be kept active and exciting for participants.

Another form of salesforce motivation is the award of recognition in the form of a trophy or 'salesperson of the year' award.

9.7   EXHIBITIONS

Exhibitions are not strictly speaking sales settings because the prime objective is not to sell from display stands. Their main function is to build up goodwill and pave the way for future sales. They do, however, cover all branches of selling and cover most types of goods, and thus merit separate attention.

Exhibitions were often regarded as a luxury item in a company's marketing budget, and exhibition stand personnel often looked upon manning an exhibition stand as an easy option to their normal duties. Companies are now more aware of the importance and value of exhibitions to their overall marketing and sales efforts and are beginning to organise and evaluate this valuable selling mechanism in a more professional manner. A study was undertaken by one of the authors to investigate how trade exhibitions could be used more effectively as part of a communications programme, and a summary of the results of this study forms the remainder of this section (Lancaster and Baron, 1977).

Characteristics of a good exhibition were deemed to be

● a wide range of products
● a large number of competitors
● a good amount of information on the products on show should be available beforehand (emphasising the importance of pre-exhibition mailing)
● a large number of new products
● nearness to the buyer's home base
● good exhibition hall facilities.

Characteristics of a good exhibitor were deemed to be

● exhibiting a full range of products, particularly large items that cannot be demonstrated by a travelling representative
● stand always manned
● well-informed stand staff
● informative literature available
● seating area or an office provided on the stand
● refreshments provided.

More recent research has shown that these basic characteristics of a good exhibition and a good exhibitor remain unchanged. Use of trade exhibitions is on the increase and firms increasingly need to establish a more scientific method of managing this function as it requires an understanding of how an exhibition stand communicates itself to the public. Setting exhibition objectives and measuring results are therefore important, as is the identification and comprehension of the elements within the exhibition effort. There is a need for the establishment of a managerial system to plan, co-ordinate and control the exhibition mix. Before a function can be managed, one must understand how it works and Figure 9.1 suggests how the exhibition communication process works.

Different communication problems exist for different types of product, including materials, services and small or large, simple or complex machinery.

With materials the selling feature or **unique selling proposition (USP)** may be communicated quite simply or through a low-communication medium, e.g. the written word. The USP of a large piece of complex machinery can possibly only be communicated by the potential customer viewing the machinery working. The different methods of communicating the USP of different types of product are termed communication strata; a product with a simple USP can be communicated through a low-communication stratum, whereas a product with a complex USP can best be communicated through a high-communication stratum.

Having selected the stratum needed to put across the USP, the other methods of communication used must be organised to complement the selected stratum. For example, if trade exhibitions are selected as the ultimate communication medium, all other marketing inputs, e.g. salesforce and media advertising, must be co-ordinated with the programmed trade exhibition. If strata 5 or 6 (see

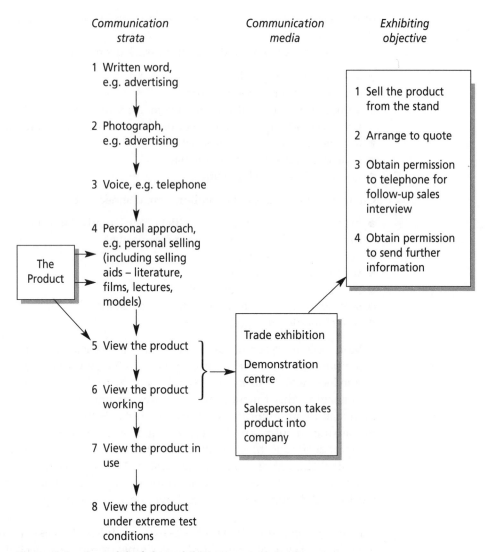

Figure 9.1   A model of the exhibition communication process

Figure 9.1) are needed, there are three communication media that can be used, i.e. trade exhibitions, demonstration centres or the salesperson taking the product into the firm.

In the management of any function, the setting of objectives is vital; without this, there is no basis for planning, co-ordination, control or measurement of results. Such objectives can be enumerated as follows:

1 Define the market with which it is intended to communicate by region, by product or by any other segmentation method.

2 Define the value of potential purchases. Is the exhibition effort to be aimed at potentially small or large users?

3 Define the status of contact at which to aim, e.g. purchasing manager, managing director, etc. High-status contacts cannot normally be attracted to small exhibitions – they may wish to speak to top management or require personal invitation plus entertainment.

4 Define the preference towards company products. Is the exhibition effort to be aimed at present customers? The danger here is that stand personnel's time can be taken up talking to the converted, whereas the objective should be to interest potential customers.

5 Define the communication level at which to aim:
   ● the ultimate (to sell the product from the stand)
   ● to obtain permission to quote
   ● to obtain permission to telephone for a follow-up sales interview
   ● to obtain permission to send further information.

Methods used to attract visitors to a particular stand include the following:

● direct mail
● telephoning
● a personal sales call before the event
● an advertisement in the technical or trade press.

Once there, attractions can include the following:

● a buffet
● give-aways
● advertising material
● films and seminars at the exhibition
● attention-gaining exhibits on the stand.

The exhibition stand itself should have a number of elements:

1 Products on show will depend upon the target market. The more products, the higher the number of prospects that will be interested, although a balance has to be struck so as not to provide so wide a range as to make it confusing.

2 Literature should not be on a self-service display. When a prospect comes to the stand looking for literature, this should be an ideal opportunity for the salesperson to establish contact and obtain details of the prospect.

3 Graphics should include at least a display board featuring the product literature. Such aids make the stand look more attractive. Models of the item being marketed are useful when the product being sold is too large or bulky to be physically displayed.

4 An office or interview room can take up a lot of expensive display space. An alternative is to demonstrate the product and then ask the visitor to a nearby seating area to conduct the interview.

5 Refreshment facilities on the stand are good attractors, and from the results of the study this was deemed to be a major drawing force.

6 An area should be designated for storage of coats, briefcases, literature, materials, etc., to avoid clutter and distractions from the main aim of the exhibition.

7 An expensive, eye-catching stand can be a double-edged weapon. It might attract visitors, but the study indicated that visitors' attitudes towards such ostentation were that it would be reflected in the price of the products.

The stand should be planned as early as possible by drawing up a checklist of everything required, checking limitations on stand design, drawing up a checklist of stand services required and a progress chart for the preparation of all products and exhibits, including their manufacture, transportation to the exhibition, assembly and dismantling.

Exhibition stand personnel must be able to communicate the USP of the products and have a sound commercial and technical knowledge. They may come from a variety of backgrounds such as sales, marketing and technical, and should be briefed upon a number of areas beforehand:

1 Objectives of the exhibition and set procedures to be used in achieving these objectives.
2 Features of the stand, who else is on the stand and the geography of the stand in the exhibition complex. Who is the exhibition stand manager?
3 How to approach stand visitors, how to interview them and how to deal with irrelevant visitors.
4 Tips on physical appearance before manning the exhibition stand.

Thus it has been shown that with professional pre-planning and management, exhibitions can be a powerful sales tool and not the expensive luxury that many companies at one time regarded them to be.

9.8   PUBLIC RELATIONS

Nature and role of public relations

Public relations covers a wider field than selling or, indeed, marketing. Its application is much wider and encompasses the entire organisation and its various external and internal 'publics'.

Its role, however, is increasingly important as an ancillary to selling both in the receiving and giving senses. Selling needs public relations to assist it in its everyday operation and selling is often called upon to disseminate a public relations message. Since the first edition of this book was written, there has been a general recognition of the strategic role of public relations; no longer is it viewed as a means of 'covering up' when something has gone wrong. It has a positive role to play in an organisation, and that role is particularly emphasised in this chapter.

The public relations practitioner has to conduct activities which concern every public with which the organisation has contact. The specific nature of such groups will vary according to circumstances.

Jefkins (1989) identifies seven basic publics:

● the community

- employees
- government
- the financial community
- distributors
- consumers
- opinion leaders.

Definition

The task of defining the exact nature of PR is difficult. Many definitions exist, each one emphasising a slightly different approach and each one attempting to arrive at a simple, yet brief and accurate, form of words. The difficulty in developing a single acceptable definition reflects the complexity and diversity of the subject. We will look at two definitions:

> PR practice is the deliberate, planned and sustained effort to establish and maintain mutual understanding between an organisation and its public.
> (Institute of Public Relations [IPR])

The essential features of this definition are firstly that PR practice should be *deliberate, planned* and *sustained* – not haphazard (e.g. when responding to the accidental pollution of a river). Second, *mutual understanding* is necessary in order to ensure that the communication between the organisation and its 'publics' is clear (i.e. the receiver perceives the same meaning as the sender intended).

An alternative definition is given by Frank Jefkins (1989), an acknowledged UK authority on the subject:

> PR consists of all forms of planned communication, outwards and inwards, between an organisation and its publics for the purpose of achieving specific objectives concerning mutual understanding.

This modified version of the IPR definition adds two dimensions:

- 'Public' becomes 'publics', since PR addresses a number of audiences.
- The inclusion of 'specific objectives' makes PR a tangible activity.

Communication is central to PR. The purpose of PR is to establish a two-way communication process to resolve conflicts by seeking common ground or areas of mutual interest. This is, of course, best achieved by word of mouth and is why the role of selling as the communication medium is so potentially important for PR to be successful.

If we accept the Jefkins definition, then we must also accept its further implication – that PR exists whether an organisation likes it or not. Simply by carrying out its day-to-day operations, an organisation necessarily communicates certain messages to those who interact with it. Everyday opinions are formed about the organisation and its activities. It is thus necessary that PR orchestrates these messages in order to help develop a *corporate identity* or *personality*.

Corporate identity

The concept of corporate identity or personality is inextricably linked to PR. All PR activities must be carried out within the framework of an agreed and understood corporate personality. This personality must develop to reflect the style of the top management, since they control the organisation's policy and activities.

A corporate personality can become a tangible asset if it is managed properly and consistently. However, it cannot be assumed that all managers will consider the role of personality when they make decisions. A PR executive thus needs to be placed so that he or she is aware of all issues, policies, attitudes and opinions that exist in the organisation that have a bearing upon how it is perceived by the organisation's publics.

The use of the word 'personality', rather than 'image', is deliberate. An image is a reflection or an impression which may be a little too polished or perfect. True PR is deeper than this. To use a common denigrating quote of a 'PR job', implies that somehow the truth is being hidden behind a glossy or false facade. Properly conducted, PR emphasises the need for *truth* and full information.

The public relations executive, as a manager of the corporate personality, can only sustain in the *long term* an identity that is based upon reality.

What public relations is *not*

Misunderstanding and ignorance as to the nature of PR has led to confusion about its role. Certain distinctions are now clarified:

*PR is **not** free advertising.*
1 Advertising complements selling. PR is informative, educational and creates understanding through knowledge.
2 PR is not free. It is time-consuming and costs money in terms of management expertise.
3 Editorial space and broadcasting time are unbiased and have more credibility than advertisements.
4 Every organisation, consciously or unconsciously, has PR.
5 PR involves communications with many groups and audiences, not just potential customers.

*PR is **not** propaganda.* Propaganda is designed to indoctrinate in order to attract followers. It does not necessarily call for an ethical content, so facts are often distorted or falsified for self-interest. PR seeks to persuade by securing the willing acceptance of attitudes and ideas.

*PR is **not** publicity.* Publicity is a result of information being made known. The result may be uncontrollable and either good or bad. PR is concerned with the behaviour of an organisation, product or individual that leads to publicity. It will clearly seek to control behaviour in such a way as to attempt to ensure that the publicity is good.

Objectives of public relations

PR is used in order to create a better environment for the organisation and its activities. The objectives may include the following:

- attract sales inquiries,
- reinforce customer loyalty,
- attract investors,
- attract merger partners or smooth the way for acquisition,
- attract better employees,
- dissolve or block union problems,
- minimise competitor advantage while you catch up,
- open a new market,
- launch a new product,
- reward key people with recognition,
- bring about favourable legislation.

In order to achieve such objectives, PR is viewed as part of the total marketing communications strategy, the principal part of which is the selling function. At any point in a marketing exercise there can be PR activity, for the simple reason that PR is concerned with human relations and is a two-way process. There is a PR element in every facet of marketing (e.g. a salesperson who exaggerates, cheats or lets down customers is a PR liability).

Manufacturers have to get 'closer' to people. In order to reach the different groups, each with separate interests, they must employ the techniques of press relations, house journals, seminars, works visits, private demonstrations, exhibitions, videos and other aids. Moreover, they have to consider those who influence opinion, sales channels and all communication media that express ideas and news.

Corporate public relations

This is concerned with group image and is based on a long-term, carefully planned programme designed to achieve maximum recognition and understanding of the organisation's objectives and performance which is in keeping with realistic expectations.

The main medium for corporate PR is prestige advertising (e.g. ICI's 'pathfinders' which present to the public a progressive image of the huge conglomerate). Another medium is house-style (e.g. a specific 'logo' like the woolmark sign devised by the International Wool Secretariat and displayed on hats and uniforms worn by the people they sponsor). Sponsorship is important for such sporting activities as golf, football, cricket and motor racing. Sponsorship can also include partial funding for, and the resultant publicity of, such events as concerts and community projects.

Effective public relations

Effective PR depends on the following:

● Setting specific objectives that are capable of evaluation.
● Fully integrating the PR function into the organisation.
● Selecting the right personnel to carry out the PR function.

We shall now examine each in more detail.

Objective setting

This is an essential requirement of PR practice. Bowman and Ellis (1982) state:

> If a PR programme is to be effective, then it is vital that its objectives be defined; that means of achieving them shall then be determined ... and that progress, success and failure be reviewed.

Although it is sometimes difficult to decide how an objective can be measured, an obvious objective can be cited in terms of increased sales, although it is sometimes difficult to determine whether such an increase in sales was due to PR activity or to some other marketing activity.

Crisis PR tends to dictate its own objectives. If information is to be prevented from reaching the press, then the yardstick that determines success or failure is whether that information reaches the press or not! If the objective is to maintain the company's reputation, then some attempt must be made to define 'reputation' in useful terms such that it can be measured and evaluated.

A traditional method of measuring PR activity is in terms of column centimetres gained from press coverage. This method does not, however, account for the quality of such coverage. Furthermore, the value of editorial cannot be quantified against equivalent advertising cost because of the greater credibility of editorial.

As PR matures, the call for more objectivity is likely to become greater. As Worcester and English (1985) state:

> Just as it is now difficult to conceive of marketing without measurement, a PR agency seeking to change the perception of its clients ... will begin by quantifying the scale of the problem ... and the effect of its activities over time.

Integration

The integration of the PR function into the organisation is important. It should be decided whether PR should act in a 'technician' or 'policy-making' role, the implication being that a technician simply carries out top management orders whereas the policy-maker inputs into corporate strategic plans. Modern thinking favours the latter role because every decision has PR implications. If PR is not involved in policy formation, then top management is implicitly assuming the PR mantle.

The role that is suggested for PR is a far-reaching one, involving communication with large numbers of people. This requires co-operation with other organisational functions. PR must then be a reasonably autonomous unit so that it can serve all departments equally. A staff function should be positioned so that it can funnel its services to the organisational levels who may be the public face of the organisation to outside groups. The importance of PR at lower hierarchical levels cannot be over-stated (e.g. from the way the secretary answers the telephone to the attitude of the company's delivery person).

The extent of PR responsibility has to be established initially by senior management and this can be achieved by objective-setting and well-defined job analyses. PR as a staff function exists to serve and facilitate line functions. Such lack of PR authority is desirable since it minimises conflict and ensures that the emphasis is upon co-operation and consultation between line and staff. It also recognises that day-to-day business and executive authority is vested in line management. It does, however, mean that it is essential that PR has direct access to the board in order that PR programmes can be sanctioned and executed with full backing from top management.

Selection

The selection of the 'right' personnel is especially important for potential PR practitioners. The practice of PR covers such a wide diversity of tasks that flexibility is very important. The Institute of Public Relations (IPR) recognises:

There is no single set of ideal qualifications and no formal path into the profession.

The IPR even states that formal qualifications are not necessary for PR personnel. It may be that PR as a profession has 'come of age' because Stirling University introduced a Master's degree in Public Relations in 1988 and Bournemouth University introduced a Bachelor's degree in 1989.

Practitioners have identified a number of skills and attributes necessary to be successful, including the following:

- sound judgment
- personal integrity
- communications skills
- organisational ability
- strong personality
- team player.

The traditional importance of media relations has resulted in a strong journalist contingent in the PR profession. However, some find it hard to adapt as the required writing style is different as are planning horizons and work routines. As the wide range of qualities and skills quoted above illustrate, relevant experience can be obtained from almost any background; personality is really of far more importance, together with a sense of empathy and the ability to be adaptable. It goes without saying that an ability to write and speak fluently is vital.

The use of public relations consultancies

In some situations, it is more cost-effective to use a PR consultancy, especially in areas where the organisation is inexperienced (e.g. the City or Parliament). Quite often larger companies find that a better interaction comes from an in-house PR department and an external specialist. Consultancies are an integral part of the PR industry and they do possess certain advantages of experience, independence and specialist skills that may not be evident internally.

External PR activities can be grouped as follows:

1 Freelance writers/consultants – who are generally technical authors able to produce PR feature articles.
2 PR departments of advertising agencies, which can vary from a small press office handling product publicity to augment an advertising campaign, to a large comprehensive PR department not unlike the agency setup itself.
3 PR subsidiary of an advertising agency, where there is a desire to permit a fuller development of PR activity on the part of the advertising agency and indeed whose clients will provide a useful source of potential business. Its association with an advertising agency can have benefits through shared services such as art studios and production.
4 Independent PR consultants usually specialise in a particular class of business, and clients can take advantage of this for *ad hoc*, or short-term assignments. Such consultants specialise in charities and appeals, the theatre, finance, agriculture, building, shipping, travel, fashion, etc.
5 PR counsellors are people who advise, but do not carry out the PR work.

9.9 CONCLUSIONS

This has been a relatively lengthy chapter of necessity and it has placed sales settings in their respective contexts. It has been shown that different selling approaches must be adopted, depending upon the situation in which one is selling.

Environmental and managerial forces have been discussed and their importance illustrated. Various sales settings including sales channels, industrial/commercial/public authority, reseller and services selling have been examined.

Sales promotions relate to all types of sales setting, and their growth and importance have been shown in respect of consumer markets, trade markets and as an aid to sales personnel motivation. The role of exhibitions has also been examined.

Public relations has been looked at in some detail, because this area has expanded most over recent years and its relationship to the selling function is a very direct one as the salesforce is increasingly being called upon to carry out PR activity.

Three practical exercises follow: two deal with sales setting problems (Argent

Distributors Ltd and Yee W. Plastic Piping Components Ltd) and the other deals more specifically with public relations (Quality Chilled Foods Ltd).

The next chapter is concerned with international selling. Although this is perhaps another example of a sales setting, it is treated separately because of its diversity and ever-increasing importance, especially in view of developing European Union legislation and changes as they will affect the selling function.

PRACTICAL EXERCISE

Argent Distributors Ltd

Argent Distributors Ltd markets washing machines and dryers which it imports from a medium-sized Italian manufacturer. The selling franchise arrangement has operated quite successfully for the past eight years, and Argent Distributors have grown at a steady pace during this period, as can be seen from the sales turnover figures:

Argent Distributors Ltd sales (£000)

1987	1988	1989	1990	1991	1992	1993	1994	1995	1996
135	1,238	1,464	1,824	2,936	3,542	4,162	4,948	5,340	5,338

The Italian manufacturer seems to be happy with the arrangement because, being a medium-sized manufacturer, it is considered that it would be too expensive to set up their own distribution facilities in the United Kingdom, and Argent Distributors seem to have performed a reasonable selling job on their behalf.

The selling operation within the United Kingdom is essentially direct to the end user, and the machines undercut equivalent popular makes of machine by 10 to 15 per cent. Householders are thus tempted to purchase this less well-known brand more upon the basis of price than comparative performance. Advertisements are placed in the press, and potential purchasers are invited to telephone or fill in a coupon for further details. All such potential customer inquiries are followed up with a visit from a sales representative.

Sales representatives are employed on a low level of basic salary plus commission, and they are given the sales leads from the head office on a weekly basis. These sales leads are closely monitored from the head office and, if the salesperson consistently falls below the average success rate of converting leads into orders, then he or she is dismissed. Such leads are usually obtained through responses from advertisements placed in the press.

The selling process essentially follows a set pattern which the salesperson learns from a manual. It is designed to suit every type of circumstance and to overcome every type of objection the potential customer might place in the way of the salesperson. Before a salesperson is allowed in the field, he or she must pass a test in the presence of the field sales manager. Basically, the test is designed to cover every selling circumstance and is set to ensure that the knowledge has been successfully acquired. Upon successful completion, the salesperson is then entrusted to sell the washing machines and dryers unaided.

Sales representatives are engaged on a self-employed basis. They are supplied with a demonstration kit of a washer and dryer plus a small van painted with the company logo. The van is maintained by the company, but the representative pays for the petrol. The basic salary in 1999 was £10,000 per annum, rising by £500 per annum for every year of service to a maximum of £12,000. Commission boosted these earnings, and during 1999 the lowest-earning salesperson achieved £10,000 basic plus £8,700 commission. They were subsequently dismissed for not turning sufficient enquiries into sales. The highest-earning salesperson had been with the company for seven years and his earnings were £12,000 basic plus £32,850 commission in 1999. The average basic plus commission in 1999 was £21,075. Fuel and subsistence expenses had to be met out of this.

The company believed in survival of the fittest and during 1998/9 turnover in salespersons was just over two years on average; four years previously the turnover period had been three years.

For the first time in the company's history, sales had actually fallen from those of the previous year. It was felt that this had been actuated by some bad (and in the company's opinion, unfair) publicity. One of the company's washing machines had been featured on a well-known consumer affairs television programme, and some of the selling tactics used by Argent Distributors' salespersons were deemed to be rather suspect. In addition, it was concluded that once the sale had been made, the company no longer retained an interest by way of an adequate after-sales service. In some instances, parts were not available for more than four weeks after the machine had broken down.

The company viewed this fall in sales seriously, and was also aware of a growing disaffection amongst the sales staff. It had been content to leave the service arrangements to a network of service engineers who serviced other makes of machine as well as those provided by Argent Distributors (on the premise that one machine is very much like another) and Argent Distributors carried and provided the stock of spare parts that were unique to their machines. They also used this network of service engineers to provide the backup for the warranty work during the first year of the machine's use. It was expected that these service engineers would have sufficient parts from their own stocks to do simple repairs, and the theory was that major parts could be provided from Argent Distributors' warehouse within 48 hours. However, on some of the older machines, stocks of major component parts were not kept and had to be ordered from Italy; hence the instances of four-weeks-plus deliveries of certain components that were highlighted on the television programme. The salesforce had found that many potential customers were using the sales objection of 'Is this the machine that you cannot provide parts for?' Although salespersons had been told to counter this objection with the fact that this was a single instance or two of older machines and new machines could be serviced almost immediately, this did not altogether convince a potential customer and it was felt that many sales had been lost.

DISCUSSION QUESTIONS

1 What advice would you proffer to Argent Distributors Ltd to:
   (a) counter their fall in sales
   (b) offer a better spares/after-sales service
   (c) remotivate their salesforce.

2 What are the dangers of such a distribution arrangement to:
   (a) the Italian manufacturer
   (b) Argent Distributors Ltd.

3 What is the implication to a company using such a non-traditional distribution channel as this for the sale of its goods?

4 What are the advantages and disadvantages of employing salespersons on such a 'high risk', low salary plus commission basis?

5 In which areas of operation and marketing is it more costly, and in which is it less costly, when adopting this direct type of distribution arrangement?

6 Are the sales figures put forward in the case study really as good as implied? In what other form(s) could the sales statistics have been more meaningfully presented?

PRACTICAL EXERCISE

Yee Wo Plastic Piping Components Ltd

Johnny Tan is the sales manager for Yee Wo Plastic Piping Components Ltd, which is a subsidiary of a Taiwanese multinational that manufactures a large range of diverse products. Their markets are mainly in the civil and chemical engineering industries.

Yee Wo Plastic Piping Components is solely involved in the manufacture and sale of plastic pumps, valves, fittings, pipes and gauges. Such products have applications in, for example, chemical plants, dyehouses and swimming baths. Their growth in the marketplace is virtually assured because they are largely replacing steel and malleable cast iron products at less cost and with greater efficiency.

In the ASEAN region, five manufacturers market similar products. The two largest are Yee Wo Plastic Piping Components and Shun Tak Fittings, each with about 40 per cent of the ASEAN market, with the remaining 20 percent being shared amongst the other three. Each of the five manufacturers charges around the same price for their products, but the smaller companies are more prone to negotiation downwards on the factory price.

Distribution is almost wholly through stockists, and the sales representatives' tasks are twofold:

1 to persuade stockists to hold a full range of the company's products to ensure a complete service to the end user;
2 to persuafe end users to specify the company's products when purchasing from distributors.

Only Yee Wo Plastic Piping Components and Shun Tak Fittings provide a complete product range and this probably accounts for their success. However, a disturbing trend has emerged amongst the smaller distributors, and this has been to stock only the fastest moving lines from marginally cheaper sources from smaller manufacturers. Yee Wo's representatives are increasingly being called upon to supply less popular lines at very short notice.

Several of Johnny Tan's representatives have become disturbed by this trend and two have recently resigned because of the adverse effects upon their sales commission. Replacing these with the right calibre people will be difficult, and Johnny realises that there are a number of opportunities open to him to help solve this problem.

● restrict supplies to licensed distributors only;
● persuade representatives to concentrate more upon the productive market sectors (e.g. large chemical plants);
● sell direct and cut out distributors.

DISCUSSION QUESTIONS

1 What can Johnny Tan do to revitalise his demoralised sales force?
2 What are the implications of pursuing each of the three courses of action suggested by Johnny Tan?

PRACTICAL EXERCISE

Quality Chilled Foods Ltd

The company manufactures a range of up-market chilled foods in a market that covers the counties of Norfolk, Suffolk, Essex, parts of Cambridgeshire and parts of North East London. The region consists of more than 10 million people. The company's customers are quality delicatessens and some of the smaller 'non-chain' supermarkets.

The following report has been published in the *East Anglian Times*, a newspaper that more or less covers the area in which the company's products are sold. This paper is an evening paper and has a very high readership.

Listeria bacteria have been found in a high percentage of chilled foods throughout East Anglia. This information comes from a report published by Essex County Council and it is confirmed by Norfolk and Cambridgeshire County Councils.

The report says that the virulent bacteria – which is particularly dangerous to children, elderly people and pregnant women – has been found in food such as cooked chickens, cooked meats and pâtés in supermarkets and stores. The report is to be studied in more detail later in the month by Essex authority's environmental health sub-committee.

It has been drawn up following a widespread survey in the towns of

Chelmsford, Southend and Colchester. At the same time similar surveys have been conducted in Ipswich and Cambridge, and although these results are not fully confirmed, their respective county councils state that their findings are likely to be similar to the findings from Essex.

It concludes, 'The relatively high percentage of commercial chilled foods which were positive gives cause for concern – not least because the large majority of these foods were ready to eat without further cooking or reheating.'

The Chief Environmental Health Officer for Essex said, 'The report is hardly a shock – it confirms a similar government finding of last year.'

DISCUSSION QUESTIONS

Quality Chilled Foods have asked you, a public relations consultant, to advise them what to do in relation to their retail customers in particular and the public in general. The company has absolute proof that none of their products will contain listeria bacteria because their chilling process is unique and has in-built safety checks to ensure against this kind of eventuality.

Prepare your advice in the form of a report, with special reference to the role which could be played by the salesforce.

EXAMINATION QUESTIONS

1 How important is the concept of segmentation in the area of selling?

2 Using examples explain how sales promotion techniques can be used to help the selling and marketing effort.

3 Using appropriate illustrations explain how PR assists the sales function.

4 Explain the meaning of 'push' and 'pull' promotional techniques. How can each help the salesperson to plan sales more effectively?

5 What is meant by the USP? How is it of use to the salesperson?

6 Explain the distinction between
   (a) segmentation
   (b) targeting
   (c) positioning.

CHAPTER 10

INTERNATIONAL SELLING

OBJECTIVES   After studying this chapter, you should be able to:

1 Understand key economic terms relating to international trade.

2 Appreciate the nature of different types of overseas representational arrangements.

3 Have a working knowledge of many of the world's trading blocs.

4 Evaluate the role of culture in international selling.

5 Know how to organise for international selling.

KEY CONCEPTS

- agent
- balance of payments
- culture
- distributor
- export houses

- indirect and direct (selling) methods
- joint venture
- licensing
- theory of comparative costs

10.1 INTRODUCTION

The key objective of this chapter is to summarise the most important facets of international selling. In a chapter of this length it is not possible to produce a comprehensive guide to the practice of international selling and exporting, and indeed this is not the objective. It is, however, appropriate to explore some of the key steps in international selling and to examine some of the issues and problems which stem from these.

A number of the key areas outlined in the chapter, e.g. the selection and use of agents and product policy, are sufficiently involved and complex, not to say important, to warrant separate treatment. Companies contemplating entering overseas markets will need, and are advised to seek or develop, specialist knowledge and expertise in these areas.

It should not be felt that selling overseas is such a specialist and complex area that the uninitiated must for ever be excluded, or that membership can only be purchased at the expense of having very costly specialist services. Some sales managers feel that selling abroad is impossibly difficult, but those who try it feel that it is no more difficult than selling to the home market.

One thing for certain is that selling abroad is 'different'. Whether it is more difficult than selling only to the domestic market is a debatable point, but success depends to a large extent on the attitude and approach of the firm and the personal qualities of the salespeople – not every salesperson is suited to such a task from the point of view of understanding and empathy with the foreign market concerned. While it is hoped that this text as a whole will contribute to the development of the personal qualities necessary for successful salesmanship, this chapter concentrates specifically on those aspects of international selling with which a firm either exporting or contemplating the same should be familiar.

Every year companies that have never been involved in selling abroad join the important, and often highly profitable, league of exporters or licensors and some even establish joint ventures or subsidiary companies in overseas countries. As will be seen, one of the problems for the United Kingdom economy is that, despite government exhortations for companies to become involved in selling overseas, many executives remain apprehensive because of the mystique with which the subject often surrounds itself. We shall now attempt to dispel some of this mystique by examining some of the more important economic aspects of international selling.

10.2 ECONOMIC ASPECTS

Many goods that we purchase are imported, and everywhere we read that industrialists are striving to increase exports. Successive governments have in their turn exhorted, threatened and promised, in order to persuade the business community to become involved in foreign markets and export more. As far as the United Kingdom is concerned there is one major and very simple reason for this – exporting is necessary for our economic survival.

It is perhaps an unfortunate truth that the United Kingdom is *not* self-supporting. Much of our raw materials and our food must be purchased in world markets and imported. In turn, if we are to be able to pay for these commodities, we must export. The ledger for these transactions is represented by the balance of trade accounts which show the difference between our overseas earnings and overseas expenditure. In fact the difference between our export earnings and our import expenditure (including 'invisibles', dealt with later) is often referred to as the **'balance of payments'**. We shall now take a more detailed look at what is meant by this term.

The balance of payments

Goods passing from one country to another have to be paid for; trading between countries thus involves the creation of debts between countries. Over a period of, say, one year, a country will add up how much it has paid or still owes for goods imported from foreign countries. In the same way, the country will add up how much has been paid or is still owed from overseas countries for goods exported to them. When the amount exported exceeds the amount imported the country is said to have a favourable balance of trade or a **trade surplus.** If the import of goods exceeds exports, then the country is said to have an adverse balance of trade or a trading deficit.

Payments for actual physical goods are not the only items involved in international trade. Debts also arise between countries because of services performed by one country for another. Because one cannot actually see such services they are referred to as 'invisible' exports or imports. For example, the UK performs insurance services for other countries and the premiums are payments due from those countries to the UK. Payment for shipping services, income from tourism, banking services and interest payments from international loans are other examples of invisibles.

To find how a country stands in respect of international trade, i.e. its balance of payments, we must compare the country's total exports (visible and invisible) with its total imports (visible and invisible). In the long term, a country's payments for imports and receipts for exports must balance.

If a country finds itself in deficit it can really only do one of two things to put matters right:

1 Reduce expenditure on imported foreign goods, reduce expenditure overseas on such items as defence and foreign aid, and attempt to discourage its citizens from travelling overseas to stop money being spent abroad.
2 Sell more goods and services overseas to increase foreign revenue. It can encourage foreign tourists to spend their money or it can encourage foreign investment which will provide income.

While the first alternative can be effective to some extent, there is a limit to which expenditure of this kind can be reduced. It is therefore to the second alternative – selling goods and services overseas – that countries must look if they are to maintain and improve their living standards and avoid a balance of payments crisis. We shall look briefly at the issues involved to fully understand these points.

A country that has a balance of payments surplus may receive payment from the debtor's foreign exchange reserves, receive the balance in gold, leave the money in the debtor country and use it to purchase goods and services in the future, or lend the debtor country the money to pay off the debt and receive interest on the loan in the meantime. In the same way, a country that has a deficit on its balance of payments will either have to run down its foreign exchange reserves, pay over gold, borrow the money to pay off the debt from other countries or hold money, in terms of credit, that the creditor country can use to purchase goods and services in the future.

A more technical explanation is that in essence the balance of payments is an accounting record, with information from various sources being entered on the basis of double entry book-keeping. If there is a deficit on the current account, i.e. if we import more goods and services than we export, this deficit must be matched by a surplus on the capital account to make the account balance. The capital account records purchases and sales of assets such as stocks, bonds, land, etc. There is a capital account surplus, or a net capital inflow, if our receipts from the sale of stocks, bonds, land, bank deposits and other assets exceed our payments for our own purchase of foreign assets.

If the government is to achieve a balance in the accounts in a current account deficit, it means either borrowing from abroad or reducing the government's stocks of gold and/or foreign exchange reserves. These borrowings and/or reductions are entered in the capital accounts as a positive figure and hence counteract the negative entry represented by a current account deficit, and hence the books balance.

As the reader will appreciate, a country can fund a continuing current account deficit only if it has limitless reserves of gold and foreign exchange or unlimited foreign borrowing power. In the long run, persistent current account deficits are difficult and costly to sustain, and are damaging to an economy. Total exports must pay for total imports, and if a country's exports fall then imports will also fall unless the deficiency in exports can be made good in the ways specified. We can now understand the importance to a country of keeping up the volume of exports.

United Kingdom share of international trade

The United Kingdom's share of exports by the main manufacturing nations has declined dramatically in recent years. On the other hand some of our major competitors such as Japan and Germany have increased their share. The problems this has given rise to are compounded when one examines our import record. On the import side there has been a disturbing trend comprising two related factors:

● the tendency for real imports per unit of real gross domestic product to increase;
● the rising share of manufactured goods accounted for by imports.

The effect of such trends on British manufacturing industry has been very serious.

In the late 1980s to the present day the UK has experienced an imbalance in the balance of payments. In fact, the cost of physical imports has exceeded the value of exported products for over a century. This has been undesirable, but not of critical importance because our income from invisible exports has made good the difference. However, for a variety of reasons, income from invisible exports has failed to keep pace with expenditure on physical imports, resulting in an overall deficit throughout this period.

Whatever the reasons for the current state of affairs, and there are many, selling overseas has been, and always will remain, one of the keystones of our national prosperity. Not only is it in the national interest, but it is in the interest of every industry, company, employer and employee.

Further economic factors

It is appropriate to consider briefly some of the more important developments in world trade over the past fifteen years or so. It is difficult to comment on the general effect of these developments as different industries and individual companies have been affected in different ways. Some companies feel that they have had a beneficial effect on their trading situation, while others feel that their competitive position has been seriously undermined.

The European Union (EU)

The EU was at first called the Common Market, and indeed reference is often made to this title even today. The Common Market was legally established on 25 March 1957 by the signing of the 'Treaty of Rome' between the governments of France, West Germany, Italy, the Netherlands, Belgium and Luxembourg. Since then, the ranks of Europeans have been swelled by the accession of Ireland, Denmark, Greece, Spain, Portugal and the United Kingdom, to be joined later by the former East Germany following the reunification of Germany. More recently, Austria, Sweden and Finland have been admitted to membership. The Common Market was also known as the European Economic Community (EEC), and then subsequently as the European Community (EC). These name changes resulted from the fact that, as the organisation expanded and matured, it began to see its role as being more of a political union than merely a trading bloc. More recently, its title has been changed yet again to the European Union (EU) which is a reflection of its current influential political role.

The initial objective of the treaty was to remove all restrictions on the free movement of goods and services and individuals within 12 years (i.e. by 1969), by removing taxation differentials, frontier controls and other forms of restriction. Since those early days, the movement towards this goal has been very slow for economic and political reasons. In fact, it was this political aspect that kept the United Kingdom out of the EC for many years. The UK was not seen to be truly 'European' – a contention which many would say holds true today – and it tends to view the EU as an economic, rather than as a political union.

By 1982 (the EU's 25th birthday) the momentum for a Single European Market had come to a virtual standstill. Many non-tariff barriers remained. The free movement of goods was hindered by varying taxation systems, public procurement restrictions (to only include tenders from domestic providers) and different technical and consumer protection standards. For example, at the time of writing, rates of value-added tax differ widely between individual countries.

A turning point came in 1984 when Jacques Delors (former French finance minister) assumed the presidency of what was then the EC. He developed the concept of an open market within the Community to create the largest single market in the Western world. Although there was essentially nothing 'new' in what he said, his statement came at the end of the economic recession of the late 1970s and early 1980s, during which time member states had turned economically 'inwards', defending their national markets against European competition.

A programme for removing all remaining obstacles to trade by 31 December 1992 was drawn up by Lord Cockfield, EC Commissioner in charge of the internal market portfolio. The programme was presented to the Heads of Government at a summit meeting in Milan in June 1985, and eventually the Single European Act came into force in July 1987. This Act lists 300 measures which were to be completed if the single market philosophy was to proceed to schedule. In order to hasten the decision-making process, the power of veto was removed and these resolutions could be passed by a 'qualified majority'. These 300 initial proposals were subsequently reduced to 279 by the withdrawal of certain proposals, and the grouping of others into single proposals.

The main features of the Single European Act (SEA) are as follows:

● the establishment of a Single European Market;
● products approved in any one EU country can be freely marketed throughout the EU;
● progressive opening up of government and public body contracts to all EU contractors on an equal basis;
● more competitive and efficient Europe-wide services in telecommunications and information technology;
● removal of 'red tape' on road haulage and shipping services between member countries should be provided on equal terms, and more competition on air routes with lower overall fares;
● banks should be free to provide banking and investment services anywhere within the EU; insurers should have greater freedom to cover risks in member countries;
● restrictions on the movement of capital to be abolished;
● harmonisation of national laws on patents and trade marks;
● professional qualifications gained in one country to be acceptable throughout the EU.

There are, of course, many other features, but for our purposes these are the most significant ones.

A pamphlet produced by the Department of Trade and Industry (1989) perhaps best summed up how companies could take advantage of the Single Market in terms of protecting their existing markets and developing new markets. This is quite poignant, because other members of the EU have more of a European 'mentality'. They tend to regard each others' markets as their own 'home' markets, whereas UK companies still tend to regard selling to EU countries as exporting. This is perhaps borne out by the fact that since the UK joined the EU with its current population of 320 million people, it has always operated with a net deficit on its balance of trade with its European partners. The pamphlet recommended that companies should ask a number of key questions in relation to their businesses:

● How has the market changed our business?

- Should we become a European business, looking upon Europe as our primary market rather than just the UK?
- Would becoming a European business alter the scale of the targets in our plans?
- In what ways will we be vulnerable to more competition in our present markets?
- Should we form links, merge or acquire business to strengthen our market presence, broaden our range of products and services, and spread our financial risk?
- Is our management and structure appropriate to exploit new opportunities or defend our position?
- What training, in languages and other skills, do we need to be ready for this Single Market?
- Who in our firm is going to be responsible for deciding how to make the most of the Single Market?

To a certain extent the pamphlet stated the obvious, but it did at least focus thinking in a formal manner to the issues of 1992. More specifically, it recommended that in the field of *selling* the company ask five key questions. The solution to each of these key questions was proffered through a list of suggestions:

1 How do you reach the customers?
   - investigate the trade structure such as wholesalers and retailers
   - identify buying points
   - find out about buying procedures, terms and practices, such as the preferred currency of invoicing
   - consider how far you need to know the local language
   - examine different selling approaches, including brokers and agents
   - find out how your competitors are using advertising, promotion and trade discounts
2 How can you sell into this market?
   - consider regional test marketing
   - establish your sales targets
   - decide on your total sales and promotion budget
   - decide on your selling organisation
3 What sales literature is necessary?
   - assess suitability of existing material for European markets
   - consider the need to redesign to appeal to new customers
   - arrange translation where necessary
4 How should you advertise?
   - examine your existing advertising
   - assess differences in national media availability and costs
   - decide on your advertising budget
5 How will you provide after-sales service?
   - consider relative merits and costs of direct provision or subcontracting

Needless to say, 1992 and the prospect of a Single Market is no longer a scenario for the future, but a reality. Companies that have failed to plan for the changes which the Single Market has brought, and will continue to bring, find themselves faced with increased competition for which they are ill-prepared. Successful companies will increasingly be those who prepared for the Single Market some years ago. In fact, it is heartening that a Confederation of British Industry survey of 200 companies, undertaken in 1990, found that three-quarters had undertaken strategic reviews in response to 1992. It is also important to remember that in many ways 1992 represented just one more step, albeit a major one, in what has been a 40-year journey towards genuine free trade within the European Union.

At a more general level, by the terms of the Treaty of Rome that first initiated the EU in 1957, member countries are independent of their national governments and are not able to accept instructions from them. Their proposals are subject to the official sanctions of the (European) Council of Ministers and the democratically elected members of the European Parliament. This means that many of the decisions which ultimately affect UK industry are outside the direct control of the UK government and, in many areas of trade, negotiations are carried out on our behalf by the EU as a whole. This process of Europeanisation is of course taken much further by the terms of the Maastricht Treaty which was so controversial in the domestic political arena of the United Kingdom. Indeed there is still deep division even within political parties as to the relative merits of the proposals in the treaty. Many still believe that the effects are so far reaching that the treaty should be put to a referendum for all the country to decide. Whether one agrees or disagrees with this contention is immaterial. The point being made is that although it is ultimately envisaged that the EU will be similar to the USA, with each member country being akin to a state and is even being billed as the 'United States of Europe', can it ever be a reality when one considers differences in attitude, culture, language and even religion? It will indeed be difficult to envisage a homogeneous pan-European marketing programme not unlike that of the USA. Clearly, a continuing trend towards political and economic unity will pose many opportunities (and threats) to companies within the EU, but it is felt that things will not change overnight; it will be more of a slow transitionary period and it could well take decades before we see an integration similar to that in the USA today. We have indeed now seen the first steps towards this goal, with the introduction of a common monetary unit – the Euro – that has been accepted by all except three member countries including Britain.

An interesting proposition is that postulated by Charles Betz of the European consultancy organisation Carré Orban and Paul Ray International that each European country will adopt a particular expertise as follows:

Germany will specialise in high technology engineering.
The Netherlands will concentrate on service industries (e.g. storage and distribution of petrochemicals).
Belgium will form the hub of the community through Brussels and theirs will be a bureaucratic role.

France will become more technical.

Switzerland will remain outside the EU and will be the financial centre and act as the neutral protector of money.

Austria has much potential and could play a major role as the bridge between the EU and Eastern European countries.

Greece and Turkey will become cheap manufacturing bases producing goods for the Middle East and North Africa.

Italy and Spain will be the 'winners' as they have reasonable levels of readily available, cost-effective labour.

Portugal has low labour costs and is basically an agrarian economy, making it a natural country from which to sell winter-grown vegetables to the more affluent Northern countries.

Denmark has traded its Scandinavian independence for an ability to trade within the EU and should do well for innovative designs.

Ireland will hopefully solve its political problems with the North and its low labour costs will put it in a good position to compete in manufacturing and assembly.

United Kingdom will show leadership in financing the consolidation of industries across national boundaries.

Sweden and Finland will develop their established expertise in precision machinery and telecommunications equipment.

This is merely one expert's conjecture, but clearly there will be some movement towards specialisation by individual member countries of the EU.

WTO (World Trade Organisation)

Perhaps one of the most important developments of the last few years has been a steady but widespread trend towards protectionism.

The greater part of world trade is subject to the General Agreement on Tariffs and Trade (GATT). Basically this is a complex agreement, but its most important features can be summarised in four fundamental principles:

1 *Non-discrimination.* Each member country agrees that any tariff concession or trade advantage granted to one country, whether or not a member of GATT, shall be granted to all member countries.
2 *Consultation.* Member countries are required to meet under GATT auspices to discuss any trade problems that may arise.
3 *Tariff negotiation.* That tariffs should be open to negotiation is the idea that originally inspired GATT. The hope was that these negotiations would be aimed at reducing and eventually removing customs duties.
4 *Trade liberalisation.* The overriding aim of the WTO, and from which the principles described above derive, is the continuing liberalisation of world trade. With this aim in mind, import quotas and licensing requirements, restrictions which nations have traditionally used to limit the volume and types of imports entering their countries, are prohibited. The idea is that temporary protection shall be afforded to each nation's domestic industry exclusively through the customs tariff.

There is no doubt that the effect of GATT over most of the post-war years has been to remove some of the protection afforded to national markets. As a result the GATT agreements have been responsible – at least in part – for the considerable growth in world trade referred to earlier. Recently this liberalisation of trade has been checked, or at least slowed, by a whole series of actions. It is well known that there has been widespread acceptance of restrictive trade measures falling outside the formal GATT rules, e.g. voluntary export restraints and anti-dumping legislation.

The Director-General of the WTO has suggested that, excluding agricultural products, the volume of international trade so affected now represents more than 5 per cent of the total volume of world trade and is expanding steadily.

However, the WTO principles resulted in the average tariff on manufactured goods falling from 40 per cent in 1947 to only 4.7 per cent in 1979, and it has edged down more gradually since then.

Such tariff reductions are negotiated in so called 'GATT rounds' – the eighth and most recent of which began in Uruguay in 1986 and was originally set for completion in December 1990. The fact that this round only finished in 1995 reflects the lengthy and difficult negotiations involved. The Uruguay round made slow progress on new rules and tariff reductions including a new general agreement on Trade in Services. However, a major stumbling block to reaching an agreement was the dispute between the United States and the members of the European Union regarding the Common Agricultural Policy. The US insisted that reform of the subsidies allocated to EU farmers was essential to a GATT agreement and called for the abolition of all farming subsidies over a period of ten years. Initially, it seemed that the US and the EU would not be able to agree on the farm subsidies issue, and that the Uruguay round would degenerate into a stalemate with a return to protectionist policies, especially on the part of the US. However, after intensive talks and diplomacy, the issues were largely resolved and the WTO is now able to move forward, albeit somewhat haltingly.

Eastern Europe

A further significant development in recent years has been the collapse of Communism and the changes in Eastern Europe which this has precipitated. This is not the place to discuss the nature and significance of these changes, but suffice it to say that many of the previously 'closed' Eastern European countries are now open to trade with their Western European neighbours, and with countries world-wide for that matter. In an effort to develop their economies, many of these previously centrally planned members of Europe represent eager and willing trade partners for those companies able to organise themselves to do business with them.

The continuing need to export

There is little doubt that the world economy is experiencing basic changes in the composition and direction of international trade, the terms of trade, and in the size, direction and character of capital movements. In a decade the UK has moved from being heavily reliant on oil imports to self-sufficiency. Related to this, our balance of payments accounts showed a surplus until the 1980s when they fell back into deficit again. Despite this, the imperative need to export remains as strong as ever. While these changes pose a formidable challenge to exporters, it can only be hoped that the response they evoke will be conducive to the well-being and prosperity of all.

Although increased exports of goods and services is in the national interest, individual firms have more selfish objectives, and the most positive inducement to them to sell overseas is the existence of potential profitable opportunities. However there are other factors that an individual firm must consider and these are discussed in the next section.

10.3 INTERNATIONAL SELLING AND THE INDIVIDUAL COMPANY

While the fact that our national economic prosperity depends upon selling overseas is not without relevance to individual companies, there are a number of more pressing reasons why companies benefit from selling overseas. Broadly, there are three reasons:

1 *Trade due to non-availability of a particular product.* Such trade is clearly beneficial when a country is able to import a commodity it could not possibly produce itself. For example, some countries need to import coal because there are no indigenous supplies. The UK has to import rubber because it cannot be grown here. It may be that a product or process is protected by a patent and can only be produced if a firm purchases the patent right or enters a licensing agreement.

2 *Trade due to international differences in competitive costs.* The basis for international trade between countries can be explained in terms of the economist David Ricardo's theory of comparative costs. Quite simply, this theory states that countries will gain if each country exports a product in which costs of production are, comparatively, lower and imports a product in which its costs of production are, comparatively, higher. Although this principle of comparative costs is applied mainly in connection with international trade, one can see it in operation in all forms of production. It is a similar concept to the benefit of the division of labour, in that benefits are to be gained, not by persons doing what they can do best, but by persons doing what they can do *relatively* better than other people. The more productive country would still benefit from specialisation in those goods it produces best, and should then import those goods it is comparatively worse at producing.

3 *Trade due to product differentiation.* In a number of industries each firm's product has some point of difference that distinguishs it in some way from the products manufactured by other firms; differentiation may be in terms of quality, design or even an intangible difference such as customers' perceived image of the product. This latter factor is very much in evidence in relation to

cars; this explains why the UK both imports cars from, and exports cars to, other countries.

It is important to note that the decision to export and import in a free market economy is not made by the country as a collective unit. It is made by individual firms who hope to benefit through foreign trade. We have looked at three broad economic reasons why individual firms may become involved in selling overseas, but there are other reasons that are more situation specific:

1 To become less vulnerable to the effects of economic recession, particularly in the home market, and/or market fluctuations.
2 Loss of domestic market share due to increased competition.
3 To take advantage of faster rates of growth in demand in other markets.
4 To dispose of surplus or to take up excess capacity in production.
5 Loss of domestic market share due to product obsolescence. Products that become technically obsolete in the more developed economies may still be 'appropriate technology' in less advanced economies. For example, the old type of fly paper has been replaced by aerosol fly killers, but fly paper is relatively inexpensive and is still very much in demand in developing countries.
6 To achieve the benefits of long production runs and to gain economies of scale. If the firm can expand its production it will lead to a reduction in average cost and hence a reduction in price, not only in the overseas market but also in the home market, which may lead to further domestic market expansion.
7 The firm has special expertise or knowledge of producing a product that is not available in a foreign market.
8 Finally, simply the existence of potential demand backed by purchasing power. This is probably the strongest incentive of all.

So far we have looked at some of the main economic factors concerned with selling overseas. The coverage does not claim to be exhaustive and, indeed, entire texts have been written upon the economics of international trade. However it is hoped that this has given the reader an appreciation of some of the issues involved.

At the beginning of the chapter it was stated that selling overseas was 'different' to selling in the home market. Whilst economic factors are important, only non-economic factors can explain the different patterns of consumption of two different countries with similar per capita incomes. Selling overseas is a cultural as well as an economic phenomenon, and it is to the important area of cultural influences in overseas markets that we now turn.

10.4 CULTURAL FACTORS IN INTERNATIONAL SELLING

In essence, **culture** is a distinctive way of life of a people, not biologically transmitted but learned behaviour that is passed on from one generation to the next, evolving and changing over time. A society organises itself in such a way that people adhering to cultural norms are rewarded while those that deviate are 'punished', to a greater or lesser degree depending upon the culture. As a society's needs change and evolve, so will the cultural norms change and certain old patterns of behaviour will no longer be rewarded whereas new patterns will. In this way, society sustains itself and produces the type of behaviour and responses it needs to survive.

This reward and punishment principle of culture is important for selling overseas. The culture in which a person lives affects his or her consumption patterns and affects perceptions of specific products and the meaning attached to them. Because of this, only certain types of products and selling practices that the individual perceives as normal and acceptable to his particular culture will be acceptable. It follows that overseas salespeople need to understand how culture functions in individual overseas markets in order that the selling approach can be tailored accordingly. In order to be able to offer value to the market, a salesperson must understand the value system of the foreign market and this means a knowledge of the influence of cultural factors.

Culture includes both abstract and material elements. Abstract elements include values, attitudes, ideas and religion. These are learned patterns of behaviour that are transmitted from one generation to another. Material elements of the culture are levels and type of technology and the consumption patterns within that society.

An understanding of the way a society organises its economic activities and the type of technology used is important for selling overseas. It stands to reason that a firm would find difficulty selling advanced microelectronic machinery to a culture with a primitive agriculturally-based economy. In such a case 'appropriate' technology will have a greater chance of being accepted.

Just as people can develop good social skills so salespeople should strive for good cultural skills. These provide them with the ability to relate to a different culture even when they do not know the elements of the culture in detail. Cateora and Graham (1996) suggest that people with cultural skills can

- convey respect and communicate verbally and non-verbally a positive attitude and interest in people and their culture;
- cope with ambiguity and the frustrations that sometimes occur when faced with an unfamiliar culture;
- show empathy by understanding other people's needs and viewpoints;
- avoid judging other people by their own value systems;
- control the use of self-reference criteria whereby assumptions are made based upon one's own culture and values;
- use humour to prevent frustration levels rising when things do not work out as planned;

We shall now explore some of these abstract and material elements within cultures in the knowledge that in some countries factors like religion have inhibited the acceptance of Western materialism and industrialisation.

Aesthetics

A non-material cultural factor which may have an influence on the development of overseas markets is aesthetics. This refers to a culture's ideas concerning beauty and good taste, together with an appreciation of colour and form. The exporter must be aware of the positive and negative aspects of its designs, its packaging, advertising, etc. The company needs to be sensitive to local preferences and tastes, and such things as company logos should incorporate local preferences.

Colour is important, the most quoted example being that black represents mourning in the West, whereas in Eastern countries the colour of mourning is white. This has obvious implications for pack design. Music is also important, particularly when used in advertising and promotion. Many non-Western cultures use a type of music, not used in the West, which has symbolic meaning to the members of the culture; an attempt should be made to understand this symbolism and turn it to positive selling advantage.

Religion

Material culture and aesthetics are outward manifestations of a culture, and these give an indication of how consumers in a particular culture behave. However, the firm selling overseas needs an understanding of why they behave in that way. The religion practised by a culture can give insights into its members' behaviour.

There is not space here to give a detailed account of all religions, nor is it the purpose of this text to do this. Clearly such matters are a specialist business and one should take detailed local advice before making any decisions. For illustrative purposes, two of the largest religions – Hinduism and Islam – are now discussed.

Hinduism is followed by 85 per cent of India's population and is as much a way of life as a religion. An understanding of the tenets of Hinduism is thus necessary for an understanding of the Indian culture. Important doctrines of Hinduism include the caste system, the joint family, the veneration of the cow and the restriction of women. Any product or selling activity which offends the tenets of Hinduism would have small chance of success because such views are deep-rooted in the Indian culture.

Islam takes the Koran as its ultimate guide, and anything not mentioned in the Koran is likely to be rejected by the faithful. An important element in Islamic belief is that everything that happens proceeds from the divine will. This belief restricts any attempt to bring about change because to attempt to change may be a rejection of, or contrary to, what Allah has ordained. Thus, firms entering overseas markets must bear this in mind when introducing new products or services.

A company must, therefore, be aware of religious differences in its foreign markets and be prepared to make adaptations where necessary, both in selling operations and in the products themselves.

Education

Analysing educational information for relevant markets gives the firm an insight into the nature and sophistication of consumers in different countries. It must be remembered that in some countries many of the population are not formally educated in the three Rs, although they may be very educated in the ways of their culture.

In attempting to market a new product in a foreign country, the firm is itself trying to educate consumers as to the uses and benefits of the product. The success of this sales communication will be constrained by the general level of education within the culture. If consumers are largely illiterate, then the firm's advertising, packaging and labelling will need to be adapted. Complex products that need written instructions may need to be modified to meet the educational level and skills of the particular culture.

Language

The language of a particular culture is also an important factor. For example, a literal translation by someone not familiar with its deeper cultural meaning may result in serious mistakes. If the brand name is standardised world-wide in English it may be found to have an unfavourable meaning in some countries, or it may not be pronounceable in other countries that lack certain letters of the alphabet. A good example of the latter is Signal toothpaste which was called Shield toothpaste. A now famed example of the former (and we understand that it is now denied by Rolls Royce) is that the Rolls Royce Silver Shadow was nearly called the Silver Mist which would have been most unfortunate when selling to the German market.

SELLING AND SALES MANAGEMENT IN ACTION

Understanding language in international selling

A key ingredient in international selling is a command of foreign languages. As the former German Chancellor Willy Brandt once said, 'If I am selling to you I will speak English, but if you are selling to me dann mussen Sie Deutsch sprechen!'

Salespeople also need to understand both the nuances of the foreign language and the silent language. A salesperson needs to know that Japanese 'yes' often means 'no', but that a Chinese 'no' often means 'yes'! Silent languages are also important as the following example illustrates.

A European salesperson visits a Saudi businessperson to sell him machinery. The Saudi offers the salesperson coffee which is politely refused (he had been drinking coffee earlier); he sits down and crosses his legs exposing the sole of his shoe; he passes sales literature to the Saudi with his left hand; asks about the Saudi's wife and stresses the need to make a quick decision.

Unwittingly, the European has offended the Saudi five times. He turned down his host's hospitality, showed disrespect, used an 'unclean' hand, was over-familiar and showed impatience with his host. Although the Saudi may realise that the actions were unintentional, the salesperson is left in a weakened position.

Based on Cateora, P.R. (1998) 'International Marketing', Irwin, Boston; Egan, C. and McKiernan, P. (1994) 'Inside Fortress Europe: Strategies for the Single Market', Addison Wesley, Wokingham.

Social organisation

Social organisation also differs between cultures. The primary kind of social organisation is based on kinship, and in many less-developed nations this takes the form of a very large extended family. A company operating in such a society must realise that the extended family means that the decisions on consumption are taken in a larger unit and in different ways. A firm selling overseas may find difficulty determining the relevant consuming unit (e.g. is it the family, the household or an individual?).

In many Asian and African countries, social organisation is in tribal groupings which may be a clue to effective market segmentation. Social class is more important and more rigid in many foreign countries, e.g. the Indian caste system. The selling firm must be aware of the cultural variations in social organisation when targeting sales efforts on to a particular social segment of the population.

Political

Culture includes all activities which characterise the behaviour of particular communities of people, such as legal, political and economic factors. Nationalism and dealings with governments are often considered to be the major problems facing a firm trying to sell overseas. Most governments play either participating or regulatory roles in their economies. In India, for example, certain sectors of the economy are reserved exclusively for government enterprise.

Government legislation and economic policy may affect a firm's pricing and credit policy and often there are regulations concerning products, promotions, etc. Factors such as nationalism, international relations, political stability and the level of capitalism and democracy in the foreign country will all have an impact on the overseas sales strategy (see Chapter 3).

General attitudes and values of a culture

In some cultures selling and trade in general have low social approval; a company selling overseas may thus have difficulty in recruiting appropriate sales personnel and difficulty selling the products through the channel of distribution. Many Eastern cultures put spiritual values before material values.

Different cultures also have different 'time values'. A much quoted example is in Latin American cultures, where sales representatives are often kept waiting a long time for a business appointment; in our culture this would be unorthodox, and at best it would be seen as being very bad mannered. A delay in answering correspondence in the UK usually indicates that the matter has low priority. A similar delay in Spain could mean something altogether different because there close family relatives take absolute priority and, no matter how important other business is, all non-relatives are kept waiting. In the West we are used to business deadlines, but in many Middle Eastern cultures a deadline is taken as an insult, and such business behaviour may well lose business for the overseas salesperson.

The concept of space has a different meaning to different cultures. In the West the size of an executive's office is often an indication of his or her status. In the Arab world this is not so; the managing director may use the same office as the general clerks, so the salesperson must be careful how he or she speaks to people! In the West, business agreements are carried out at a distance, say two metres or more. In the Middle East and Latin American countries, business discussions are carried out in very close proximity, involving physical contact, which many Western salespeople find strange.

In the West, business is discussed over lunch or at dinner in the businessman's home. In India, to discuss business at home or at any social occasion is a violation of hospitality rules. In the West we rely on the law of contract for all business agreements, but in the Moslem culture a man's word is just as binding. In fact, a written contract often violates a Moslem's sensitivities because it challenges his honour.

Sub-cultural influences must not be overlooked, because these are sometimes the dominant force in the country. Examples include the following:

- nationality groups, e.g. French- and English-speaking Canadians
- religious groups, e.g. Protestant and Catholic groupings in Northern Ireland
- geographical areas, e.g. the North and South of England may be thought of as separate markets for many products
- racial groups, e.g. in South Africa
- social stratification, e.g. the caste system in India

SELLING
AND SALES
MANAGEMENT
IN ACTION

The Chinese culture and sales negotiations

Cultural differences mean that salespeople need to understand and respect the values of overseas customers and alter their expectations and behaviour accordingly. Visiting salespeople may be required to attend long banquets when engaging in negotiations with Chinese people. The banquets may begin in either the late morning or early evening. Frequent toasts are usual and some Chinese hosts regard the visitor as having a good time if he or she becomes a little intoxicated.

In China, negotiations often take much longer than in many Western countries and arriving late for a business appointment is deemed acceptable behaviour. To do so in Hong Kong, however, would result in the visitor 'losing face', an extremely serious issue in the Chinese culture. When conducting sales negotiations, visiting salespeople should avoid creating a position where a Chinese person might 'lose face' by finding themselves in an embarrassing situation (e.g. by displaying lack of knowledge or understanding). Chinese people tend to elicit as much information as possible before disclosing their hand to avoid losing face or displaying ignorance. Business relations should be built on the basis of harmony and friendship. Contracts are accepted as much as a basis for business relationships as a legal document.

Many salespeople fall into the trap of using 'self-reference' criteria when selling abroad. They assume that what is acceptable and highly valued in their own country is equally valued in all cultures. To avoid this fallacy, salespeople need training in the special skills of selling to people from different cultures.

Based on: Bradley, F. (1998) 'International Marketing Strategy', Prentice-Hall, London; Jeannet, J.P. and Hennessey, H.D. (1995) 'Global Marketing Strategies', Houghton Mifflin, Boston.

Cultural change

A company following the marketing concept overseas, i.e. trying to satisfy the needs and wants of target markets at a profit, must keep abreast of changes in the cultural environment which affect people's attitudes and values, and hence, indirectly, their needs and wants of products and services. In our own society, for example, our cultural values towards debt have changed. Debt has lost its stigma and is now a part of everyday life, with the universal acceptance and use of credit cards. Our society's moral values have also changed and we are more liberal and tolerant of such matters as entertainment. Thus the products and services demanded have reflected this change in cultural values.

A firm must, therefore, be aware that its products may face obsolescence in overseas markets, not necessarily because of any technical advance, but because of cultural change.

Not only are a firm's existing products vulnerable to cultural change, but it may miss new, lucrative opportunities by not being informed of changes in culture. The impact of culture is particularly important if the company is dealing with a foreign culture seeking rapid industrialisation. It is, therefore, necessary for a company operating in this type of environment to monitor trends and adapt as necessary. Not only must the firm contemplating selling overseas be versed in the economics, law and politics of a foreign country, but it will also have to understand the more subtle, less tangible, meanings, values and languages of the culture itself.

10.5 ORGANISATION FOR INTERNATIONAL SELLING

The organisation required to implement international sales operations can be complex. Decisions have to be made on how to arrange the interface between manufacturing and sales, and in the area of delegating responsibility for international operations. Each of these problems can have alternative solutions and an optimal decision must be tailored for each individual firm. Whatever the form of organisation for overseas selling, it is important that there should be a senior manager charged, if only in part, with the responsibility for exporting. This manager should be able, through his or her position, to advise and influence colleagues at the highest level.

In choosing how to organise for international selling there is a broad division into **indirect and direct methods**. Some of the more common forms of overseas sales organisation are described in this chapter. The choice of organisation will depend upon a number of factors: the proportion of total turnover accounted for by overseas business, the nature of the product, the relative advantages and disadvantages of each form of organisation. What is important is that there is no single rigid uniform approach to the task. The keynote should always be flexibility and adaptability.

We shall first consider the indirect approaches to international selling.

Types of intermediary and their selection

It has been estimated that agents and distributors alone, acting on behalf of overseas companies, handle over half of the world's overseas trade. The term 'intermediary' is used to describe all those persons and organisations providing the service of representation between sellers and buyers.

Few manufacturers are able to cover a market adequately and satisfactorily without the service of some form of intermediary. The decision faced by firms as to which intermediary to use, and the policies to be adopted at this point, are critical to the firm's future in the market.

Agents

An **agent** is a firm or individual acting on behalf of another. This is one of the main forms of overseas representation. The most common form of agency is where the agents, acting as independent operators, obtain orders on behalf of the exporter on a commission basis and the exporter acts as principal. Agents also work on behalf of purchasers and some specialise in certain tasks, e.g. transport and distribution, advertising and market research.

Care should be exercised in appointing the right agent, and any company entering overseas markets should satisfy itself as to the agent's reputation and financial position. The agent may have other interests, and the firm should ensure that these interests do not conflict with its own. Agents are often key figures in a firm's overseas operations and success overseas will depend on the ability and commitment of the agent. Care therefore needs to be exercised in the choice of an agent and organisations such as banks will advise and assist in their selection.

In assessing the suitability of an agent, the principal will need clear answers to the following:

- When was the agency founded?
- What other interests does the agency have, i.e. what other agencies are held?
- Does the agent provide the required coverage for your market?
- What is the agent's standing in the business community of the market in terms of professional integrity and reputation, reliability, etc.?
- Is the agent the type of person or company that will fit in with the way your company carries out its business? Will you be able to work with the agency?

- Does the agent possess the resources necessary to carry out the task adequately, i.e. financial resources, transport, offices, warehouses and human resources?
- Is the agent able to provide technical support or after-sales service arrangements if this is necessary?

This list is not exhaustive and more specific details may be necessary depending on the market, the industry and the type of product. Once a suitable agent has been found, progress should be carefully monitored. Agents are usually appointed for a trial period at first, with extensions to the contract after that.

The training of agents is important to indirect selling in overseas markets, particularly if the products are technically complex. Without proper product knowledge and technical appreciation of the product range, the agent will be ill-equipped to conduct negotiations with professional buyers who may be experts in their field. Training may have to take place at the principal's manufacturing plant and such training should form a compulsory part of any agreement. Training may need to be a continuous activity, with periodic updating sessions and refresher courses, especially if the firm is involved in new product development or if technology is changing rapidly.

Sales meetings and conferences in the principal's own country can be used for training purposes and these can be used as a forum for tackling specific problems and for discussing future promotional strategies. Such meetings will also have a social function, bringing agents together for a few days to exchange ideas, discuss common problems and be made to feel part of the company.

Once the correct agent has been found, the right kind of working relationship must be nurtured. Many companies feel that the appointment of a good overseas agent is an alternative to involvement in the market themselves. This is *not* so and the principal has to be actively involved; if the relationship is to be successful then it must be based upon partnership and co-operation. The principal should also visit the agent in the market as this will give the agent a sense of value, importance, belonging and encouragement. It also keeps the agent well informed of developments in the principal's country and of the principal's products. The principal will gain valuable market information on competitive actions, the overseas business environment and feedback on promotions and new products. All of this will lead to a better understanding of the dynamics of the overseas market and an improvement in the overall sales strategy.

The principal can also give assistance to the agent by helping in the commercial negotiations between the agent and important customers, helping with special discounts or credit arrangements in order to secure business. Frequency of visiting abroad by the principal will depend on the importance of the particular market, the competence of the agent and the distance from the home base. Important markets should be visited more frequently, particularly if technical assistance or after-sales service is required.

In many cases, agents feel insecure because companies often regard them as being a temporary method of servicing overseas markets. Once the market expands and matures, many companies dismiss their agents and enter direct selling or open a subsidiary company. Therefore the very success of an agent can sometimes mean his downfall. In anticipation of this eventuality, agents sometimes collect a large number of agencies, resulting in a diffusion of effort and possible conflict of interests. This problem can be overcome by negotiating a long-term arrangement once the agent has proved himself, or by inserting a gradual run-down clause into the agency agreement. In the latter case, the agent can often make a valuable contribution to, say, the setting up of a new overseas subsidiary company, or even become managing director of the subsidiary. Thus, fair treatment of agents and ex-agents cultivates a reputation as a good and fair employer and this, in turn, will probably be reflected in future dealings in that country.

Distributors

The **distributor** acts in a different capacity to that of an agent because the distributor is the actual buyer and seller of the goods, whereas the agent works principally on commission. Like an agent, a distributor will usually be a local firm or individual and a specialist in the requirements of the local market. He or she should be familiar with the business practices of the area, the structure of the market, local customs, and the various socio-cultural factors pertaining to the market.

Distributors differ from agents in the following ways:

1 They will be able to finance their own stockholding of goods.
2 They will usually be able to purchase in larger quantities, thus saving on delivery costs.
3 Acting as principal, they will be commercially and legally responsible for all business transactions in the market.
4 They are entrepreneurs, and accept risks involved in the purchase and re-selling of goods, such as local falls in demand and currency fluctuations.
5 In some cases they may provide an after-sales service.

A frequent complaint from companies using distributors is that, because they are independent businesses acting independently, they can decide the final selling price to the customer. If price is thought to be a significant factor in the product's success, then the manufacturer should only deal with distributors who are willing to agree a mark-up and selling price with the manufacturer.

As with agents, it is important for the manufacturer to develop a good working relationship with the overseas distributor as commitment to the commercial relationship is needed from both sides. Although distributors actually purchase goods from the manufacturer to resell on their own account, they are much more than just another customer. The manufacturer is relying on the distributor to achieve his/her objectives, but the manufacturer must remember that distributors have objectives and interests of their own. It is, therefore, in the firm's own interest to give the distributor as much technical and sales assistance as possible. As with agents, distributors can be used in an information gathering capacity to report on trends and developments in the marketplace.

A decision will also have to be made whether to use a number of smaller local distributors or a small number of large national distributors. Using a number of small distributors has the advantage of good coverage, and is advantageous where there are regional differences in culture or business practices. However, large national distributors give economies of scale as goods can be shipped in bulk.

In some cases it may be desirable to have an exclusive agreement with the distributor, otherwise he or she might offer competitors' products to customers if they offer a higher margin. If such an exclusive arrangement is agreed, then it should also ensure that the distributor does not sell competing goods.

Licensing

Licensing is another alternative open to a firm that is contemplating an indirect venture into overseas markets. It does, of course, assume that the company has some unique product or process (preferably protected by patent) that an overseas company will want to manufacture. This is a particularly good way of entering and remaining in more distant markets, or in any market where it is difficult or impossible to export finished goods. In such markets, direct selling or control of agents or distributors might be impractical, or it may be the case that import duties or other non-tariff barriers might present obstacles to exporters.

The costs of setting up a manufacturing subsidiary might be prohibitive or the foreign country might be politically unstable. Licensing avoids the danger of the firm's overseas assets being expropriated and, in some situations, repatriation of profits is sometimes difficult for a manufacturing subsidiary. Where the product is bulky and expensive to transport relative to its value, licensing might be the only way to produce that good at a competitive price. If a firm has a good product idea, but is short of capital to expand and exploit the commercial opportunity itself, licensing allows the earning of at least some profit, or more precisely, royalty, without having to commit scarce financial resources.

The main problem is that if one has a licensing arrangement with a company in a politically sensitive area then, for one reason or another, royalties due might not be paid. This is one of the dangers of licensing and obviously the licensee will have to be chosen with great care. There are two possible suggestions to try to overcome this type of situation. One is to ensure that the licensing arrangement means the acceptance of certain component parts from the licensor and if there are problems in payment then components can be withheld. The other suggestion is that where the product under licence is technically advanced it is likely that it will be continually improved through innovation; the sanction here is that if there are royalty payment problems then the latest innovation can be withheld. However, these suggestions indicate a negative aspect of licensing, and the vast majority of such arrangements are successful. The obvious answer is to choose a licensee of undoubted integrity in a politically stable country (the only problem is that in such a situation there are probably more lucrative export arrangements than licensing).

Assuming that a licensing arrangement is agreed, then regular checks must be made as to the quality of the licensee's finished products and defined quality standards should be part of the licensing agreement.

Export houses

The use of **export houses** is an alternative to the manufacturer having his own export department. Export houses are usually home-based organisations which carry out some or all of the overseas activities in place of the manufacturer, often using their own agents, distributors or other intermediary. They are a useful alternative for small companies whose overseas operations are limited, not warranting the expense of direct involvement. They are also used by larger firms who are only marginally involved in smaller markets, or use export houses until such markets have expanded sufficiently to warrant their own overseas operation.

Manufacturers can delegate some or all of their overseas operations to an export house or they may delegate parts of the actual selling task to the export house. Thus, export houses offer flexibility, and they offer a range of services, including the following:

● Export factoring – handling finance and credit arrangements on behalf of the manufacturer.
● Factory representation – a sales supervisor supervising the sales activities of distributors or dealers on behalf of the manufacturer.
● Market intelligence gathering in overseas markets.
● Handling export procedures and documentation.
● Help in selecting agents, distributors and dealers.
● Confirming orders – paying the manufacturer on confirmation of an order from an overseas buyer and receiving commission, although here the export house is not actually paying the manufacturer but merely confirming liability for payment.

Having looked at the services export houses have to offer, we shall now look at a number of reasons why a manufacturer might want to use one:

1 Lack of resources to carry out overseas operations by the manufacturer.
2 When overseas selling operations are only small scale and it would not make economic sense to carry out such operations oneself.
3 Where the export house has particular expertise in a country or an industry.
4 Where the manufacturing company is predominantly production orientated and lacks the marketing expertise.

There are, however, a number of disadvantages, the main one being lack of direct contact with the market. The manufacturer may also experience difficulty in monitoring developments and changes in the overseas market and adapting to these changes in good time.

Having examined the indirect approaches to selling, we shall now look at the more direct methods.

Direct methods of overseas selling

Subsidiary companies

The subsidiary may be a selling or manufacturing organisation or both. The selling subsidiary usually replaces agents and distributors with the company's own permanent staff. In certain cases it is possible for a firm to start its own sales organisation with little investment. The usual way, however, is to start by using an agent, then open its own sales office with a limited number of staff and, once profits start to show, allow the unit to become self-sufficient and expand ultimately into manufacturing.

The above is, however, a generalisation and sales subsidiaries may require a larger investment than many companies can afford, especially where an after-sales service has to be offered and where the stocking of a large volume of spare parts is necessary. Manufacturing subsidiaries range from simple assembly plants to complete production units.

A simple assembly plant subsidiary is particularly useful where the product is bulky and freight costs are high. By using local assembly, the final cost of transport may be reduced as it is often more economical to ship containers of parts for assembly than to ship the finished bulky manufactured product. In addition, local employment is created and this promotes goodwill towards the company, which in itself assists in developing markets further.

Reasons for establishing overseas manufacturing subsidiaries differ from company to company, but the following factors are important:

1 *Production capacity.* Where overseas markets are expanding, a firm may find problems in serving the market from the home base.
2 *Non-tariff restrictions.* Where such restrictions exist, the setting up of a subsidiary may be the only way around them. Many foreign governments give grants and incentives to firms to set up manufacturing bases in their country and their purchasing strategy favours goods made at home. In some cases restrictions placed against imports may take the form of complex (and unnecessarily prohibitive) safety or packaging regulations.
3 *Costs.* Labour and manufacturing facilities are often quite economical in overseas countries and setting up a manufacturing base saves transportation costs.
4 *Explicit import restrictions.* Where these exist, the setting up of a manufacturing subsidiary may be the only way to enter or stay in the market.

When establishing a subsidiary, local legal and taxation regulations must make it possible to set up a profitable subsidiary and allow the parent company to extract profits from the country. It may be prudent for a firm to gain experience in the market through agents and distributors before venturing directly into setting up a manufacturing subsidiary. Many firms employ the staff of a previous agent or distributor to form the basis of the new company.

Although it may seem that the establishment of a foreign subsidiary exposes a firm to many of the risks which licensing minimises, a venture of this kind may offer the greatest potential. Not only may local employment and production be beneficial for the reasons mentioned, but the parent company can offer the subsidiary the wealth of its business experience and resources. Other advantages are that employees working direct for a company are often better motivated than those of an intermediary and it is easier to control a subsidiary because it is under the parent company's direct control. The main disadvantage is that political or economic instability within the country may cause problems outside the control of the parent company.

Joint ventures

A **joint venture** is where usually two, but sometimes more, firms manufacture and sell products on a joint basis. As such it can be an indirect as well as direct method of exporting, depending upon the arrangement. It is quite common in the transport, construction and high technology sectors of business.

Such agreements have financial benefits as the cost of development is shared, but friction and disagreement can sometimes arise between members of the agreement.

Direct selling

Despite the strengths already outlined of using intermediaries, some companies find that selling direct from the home country to overseas markets offers more advantages. Direct selling requires the firm to take full responsibility for establishing contact with potential customers.

Direct selling provides a degree of control that is impossible to achieve through intermediaries over such matters as price, credit, after-sales service, etc. The chief disadvantage is that more frequent travel is involved, and a lack of a permanent presence in the market can cause problems. The firm may find difficulty keeping abreast of developments in the market and will have to rely on customers to provide market information. Customers may also view this lack of permanent presence as a lack of definite commitment to the market. Firms supplying technically complex products that require technical service and advice often place a sales engineer in the market on a semi-permanent basis, which does tend to obviate the lack of commitment criticism somewhat.

The following are guidelines as to where direct selling is most appropriate:

1 *Buyer-specified work*. Where individual orders are large and custom-made it may be necessary for the manufacturer and purchaser to get together to discuss each job as a unique contract.
2 *Continuous supply*. Once set in motion this requires only a periodic visit to negotiate such matters as price changes. Such contracts are normally able to

run smoothly without a permanent overseas presence.

3 *Products are technically complex with a clearly defined market.* Here problems can be discussed directly between the supplier and user.

4 *Geographical proximity.* Countries in Western Europe can sometimes be serviced direct from the UK because of good communication facilities.

5 *Few customers but large or high-value orders.* In such situations time and expense involved travelling abroad is sometimes small compared with the size and value of the potential order.

In selling direct to a customer overseas, there is the opportunity to build up close relationships with individual customers, based upon trust, commitment and understanding. A close interactive commercial relationship is beneficial, particularly if the exporting company is unfamiliar with the market. Speaking the language of the country is more important in direct selling than if the firm is dealing through an intermediary. If the salesperson is to build up a close personal relationship with his or her customers, he or she must understand the cultural, religious and business practices of the country. There may be many mental barriers to a foreign buyer placing an order with an overseas salesperson, and patience will be required to break down these barriers. Thus, emphasis must be placed upon gradual acceptance rather than the expectation of instant success. This involves careful planning in building up contacts and nurturing them and not taking the first 'no' for an answer.

10.6 PRICING

Freight considerations

Pricing as an element of the marketing mix has already been covered in the first chapter, and indeed when considering pricing decisions for international markets the same rationale applies. There are, however, a number of additional factors that must be considered, the most significant of which is the potentially greater logistical problem of getting the goods to their destination. This normally involves extra packaging to withstand lengthy sea journeys, although advances in containerisation have now made it possible to rent either a full or a partial container, so this is less of a problem for those goods where containerisation is possible. Air freight is also an increasingly popular medium of quick transport to overseas destinations especially in relation to goods that are perishable, or where their weight is low in relation to their volume.

However, this adds to costs and this must be considered in relation to the price at which the goods will be charged when they reach their ultimate market. For this reason many manufacturers tend to accept a lower margin for export orders so that they will still be competitively priced. Quotations for export orders are sometimes the simple ex-works price which does not include freight charges to the end customer. At the other extreme, the price can include delivery to the customers' works. These various price quotations form part of the legal document of contract and they are considered in detail in the next chapter.

Import considerations

Another factor when calculating price is that of tariffs that might be levied on goods entering the customer's country. This too will have to be considered in the light of an additional cost before the goods reach the marketplace. Import considerations might also include a quota restriction on particular goods, which means that a numerical restriction is placed upon the amount that can be imported during a particular period. In such cases the importing country sometimes raises extra revenue by selling off these quotas to the highest bidder. An import licence is sometimes required, which apart from costing money, sometimes entails a lengthy process in terms of negotiating with the authorities in the country concerned. This process is detailed and complicated, and only companies with large international trading departments would be able to handle such detail internally. For smaller companies the services of shipping and handling agents would certainly be necessary, all of which adds to the landed cost of goods.

Transfer pricing

This is perhaps one of the most intriguing aspects of pricing, and it can be quite controversial in that it often involves detailed investigation by the customs and excise and taxation authorities if they feel that companies are abusing positions of relative privilege. It is of particular benefit to large international companies with manufacturing and assembly bases situated in different countries around the world.

Transfer pricing works when component parts and finished products are moved between manufacturing or assembly plants in different countries as part of the manufacturing or marketing process. Different countries have different rates of corporation tax, and import duties also vary between countries. There is, therefore, an incentive to an international company to make as much profit as possible in a country with a low rate of corporation tax. In fact, some countries offer 'tax-free holidays' for a specific period to a company that will set up a manufacturing base there.

What happens is that component parts from one country can be transferred to a high duty country in which the company also has a manufacturing base at a low transfer price to minimise import duty. Components can also be transferred into countries with higher rates of corporation tax at high transfer prices in order to minimise profits. In addition, parts or finished products can be transferred at high prices into a country from which transfer of profits is difficult owing to currency restrictions, or perhaps where there is an unstable currency, and so depress the profits of the manufacturing or assembly plant in that country.

In view of possible abuses of the transfer pricing system it can be seen why customs and excise and tax authorities tend to view such arrangements with a certain amount of suspicion.

10.7 A SPECIFIC STUDY IN INTERNATIONAL SELLING – JAPAN

It was stated at the beginning of this chapter that the objective was not to provide a comprehensive guide to international selling and exporting. The general case for exporting for the good of the economy and for the good of individual companies has been covered, together with an overview of organisational and cultural issues. The specific type of information that is of direct use to a potential exporter is that which follows in respect of exporting to Japan. This information has been taken from an article (Saunders and Hon-Chung, 1984) in the *Journal of Sales Management* for which the second author was then editor.

Successful selling to Japan requires patience and a sensitivity to customs and business practices not altogether appreciated by Westerners. Business in Japan is still conducted in a traditional Confucian manner where civility, politeness and the search for constructive relationships are of the essence, and successful business follows the establishment of such relationships.

In many ways the Japanese do not respond in the same way as Westerners. For the most part, the Japanese keep their emotions under control, and culture demands that a person of virtue will not show a negative emotion when shocked or upset by sudden bad news. This ideal of an expressionless face in situations of great anxiety was strongly emphasised in *bushido* (the way of the warrior) which was the guideline for *samurai* and the ideal for many others. Furthermore, not only are negative emotions suppressed, but the control of an outward show of pleasant emotions in public is also rarely relaxed in Japan. Women tend to cover their mouths while laughing, and males show true merriment (and true anger) mainly after hours when their culture allows them greater freedom of behaviour while drinking alcohol. Thus the poker-faced ideal is very common in public settings in Japan. The moral of these observations is that one must develop a sensitivity to the reactions of the Japanese because of the difficulty of telling how they are reacting.

Another noteworthy aspect is that shame is intolerable in Japan. This means that one should never put one's Japanese counterpart in a position that will force him or her to accept blame for a project going wrong, being delayed, etc. This characteristic has important implications for two elements of the sales process: handling objections and the close. The Japanese may avoid explicit objections because politeness demands that the seller does not lose face. Similarly, an attempted close may put the Japanese in a position where they are concerned for the seller's loss of face if the answer is to be negative. The deft footwork associated with the persuasion approach to selling clashes with the Japanese character and is completely opposed to the spirit of Japanese negotiations.

In some countries it is considered socially acceptable to compliment someone directly on his or her business accomplishments or the accomplishment of the company, but in Japan anything in the way of a compliment is made indirectly. Instead, say, of complimenting someone directly on his or her taste and sophistication, the Japanese practice is often to approach this particular problem indirectly, and pick out some aspect of the room which reflects the other person's taste and sophistication and comment on that.

With regard to business correspondence, Japanese companies may fail to answer written inquiries concerning possible business relationships. This does not necessarily mean a lack of interest. There can be a number of reasons for a slow response. Decision-making tends to be much slower and this is often the reason. Most Japanese companies are also accustomed to being able to talk face to face with suppliers and it is the usual way of conducting business in Japan.

Personal introductions are commonly executed by a third party rather than through, say, the medium of a telephone call requesting a meeting. The person making the introduction will explain to the person one wishes to meet approximately what subjects are to be discussed, what company one comes from and one's position within that company. Because there will usually be a common understanding between the two Japanese, the Japanese businessperson whom one wishes to meet will generally be more favourably disposed to hearing one's opinion than if one walks in without an introduction.

The key to a successful business relationship in Japan is a successful personal relationship and nowhere in the world are business and personal relationships so intertwined. However, such friendship only opens the door; thereafter the hard reality of the benefits to be gained and the risks to be run will take over. Friendships in Japan take more time to form, are deeper and last longer than those in the West and often these obligations extend to business relationships. For example, during a recession, a large firm will commit itself to its suppliers and subcontractors for continued orders to tide them over. The lesson of these observations is that one must be prepared to operate within this two tier business structure; establish friendship first and then move to the second stage of actual business negotiations.

To Westerners, Japanese business seems formal and ritualistic. To a degree this is true, but business relationships do no more than reflect the formality of relationships generally. As in all societies, ritual is particularly important when meeting someone for the first time. It is used to establish and signal that one has identified initial relationships. The first meeting is also a time when transgressions are most likely to cause lasting damage.

One of the most powerful forms of non-verbal communication is dress. The usual dress for Japanese businesspeople is a dark suit for men and sober dress for women. However, most Japanese businesspeople acquainted with foreigners have come to expect a certain variety within reasonable limits in the dress of foreign businessmen. It is not, therefore, expected that one should imitate the Japanese mode of dress. However, one should avoid extremes in dress which may cause uneasiness. For example, loud clothing will create the disturbing feeling among the Japanese businesspeople that the foreigner has perhaps failed to take them as seriously as he or she might have, by failing to observe that the common practice in dress in Japan is some degree of formality.

At the beginning and end of every meeting, the Japanese businessperson will bow very formally to the members of the other side in the negotiations. This is generally observed at the first meeting and to a somewhat lesser extent at subsequent meetings. Most Japanese with experience in dealing with Westerners will be expecting to use a handshake rather than a bow. The appropriate strategy is perhaps to wait to determine whether the Japanese businessperson is prepared to offer his hand for a handshake or whether he is going to bow. The question of whether the non-Japanese should imitate the bow of the Japanese is controversial within Japan itself. Generally, a nod of the head or a slight bow is considered acceptable for the non-Japanese party. One should be aware that reciprocal bowing behaviour is dependent on the status relationship of participants; the inferior must begin the bow, and his bow is deeper, while the superior determines when the bow is complete. When participants are of equal status, they must both bow the same way and begin and end the bow at the same time.

One of the most obvious differences between Japanese and Western business practices is the use of business calling cards or *meishi*. These are exchanged on every occasion where one business person meets another. The prime purpose is to enable the recipients of the cards to know the other's status so that not only do they bow correctly, but also use the proper form of language. Japan is a hierarchical society and the Japanese are very status conscious in that they use different forms of language and bow in different manners according to the status relationship with another individual. Business cards also serve the function of not having to memorise instantaneously the names and positions of one's business counterparts and they provide a record for future reference.

Such cards are a standard pattern and size, so that they will fit in the Japanese filing systems. They must have square corners for males and round corners for females. The typical business card that the non-Japanese businessman or businesswoman should have will show the Japanese translation of the individual's name on one side, along with his/her company, its address and the person's title. The other side will have the same information in English (which is the most common foreign language used in Japanese business).

The exchange of business cards is a very important part of the process of introduction in Japan. For this reason, cards should be exchanged one at a time and with some care. The courteous method is to present it, Japanese side up, with the printing facing the receiver.

One of the peculiarities of these business cards is that there is no single standard set of English translations for the ranks and positions in Japanese companies. As mentioned earlier, Japan is a very hierarchical and status-conscious society, so an understanding of the ranks in business is very important. Table 10.1 (Japanese External Trade Organisation, 1976) translates some of the more common Japanese business titles.

The basic titles in a Japanese firm are usually very clear, and the level of the position within a company, as indicated by the title, is usually closely related to the age of the individual. This system of ranking and responsibility, corresponding closely with age and years of service in the company, is one unique characteristic of Japanese organisations.

Table 10.1   Translations of common Japanese business titles

Japanese title	Description and/or usual translation
No title	New graduate, aged 23–33
Kakaricho	Manager, aged 34–43
Kacho	Section chief, aged 44–47
Bucho	Bureau chief, aged 48+, senior manager
Torishimariyaku	Director
Fuku Shacho	Vice-president (more senior director)
Shacho or Daihyo Torishimariyaku	President (managing director)
Kaicho	Chairman

While the details of negotiations may be left to a representative in Japan, the managing director of the foreign firm (or some other high official in the company) should establish an initial contact with his or her equal in the Japanese firm. This is termed the *aisatsu* or the greeting. The purpose of this is to establish a presence.

The Japanese term *hai* is literally translated as 'yes', although it can also mean 'I see' or 'I understand' and does not necessarily mean agreement. Furthermore, the Japanese are very reluctant to give a direct 'no' answer, because Japanese culture emphasises harmony rather than confrontation. Instead of the answer 'no', one is more likely to hear something non-committal such as 'Let me think.' One must, therefore, learn to read the negative response signs such as hesitancy or an unwillingness to be more specific.

Postponements of negotiations are common in Japan, largely because decision-making follows a prescribed process called the *ringi* system. This means that a proposal must be circulated among various sections and departments that will be affected by the proposal, with much discussion and correction ensuing. The *ringisho* (request for a decision) goes back and forth and eventually a consensus is achieved among the interested parties, with the president giving final approval.

During negotiations long periods of total silence are common. This is because the Japanese like time to think over what has been said and what alternatives are open to them when they next speak. Silence is also part of the Japanese communication procedure and they tend to rely heavily upon non-verbal communication. Westerners often find such silences embarrassing and feel obliged to say something unnecessary to relieve the supposed tension. The best way to handle such silences is to exercise restraint and outwait the silence.

Japanese businesspeople have little confidence in detailed contracts which attempt to provide for all possible contingencies. Their preference is for broad agreements and mutual understanding. Contracts are drawn up with an eye to flexibility and a contract is often considered an agreement to enter into a general course of conduct rather than something fixing precise terms. The Japanese like to negotiate each issue as it arises and there is an assumption that each party is prepared to make substantial accommodations to the other. This should not be interpreted as an attempt to violate the contract, but rather the desire of the Japanese to allow both sides the ability to adjust to unforeseen circumstances. One should not expect to obtain a detailed contract, but once a commitment is made it is for the long term. Japanese firms prefer long-term reliable and exclusive business relationships and they tend to turn to established channels to develop new business initiatives.

Because of the consciousness of using the correct level of language in a conversation or discussion, any interpreter one engages may unconsciously modify statements going from English to Japanese and back to English again, according to the rank of the people involved. For example, if a senior official of a Western company is speaking with a high-level Japanese manager, the interpreter will feel in an inferior position to both of them. The statement that the senior official intends to have translated verbatim for a Japanese counterpart may end up as being something quite different.

Entertainment in Japan plays a major role in establishing personal and business relationships. Unlike the West, business luncheons are a rarity and evening entertainment almost never takes place in the home. The typical pattern is for the Japanese businessperson to eat at a restaurant in the evening and thereafter go to a bar or cabaret. Such evenings are for cementing business relationships rather than for discussing specific aspects of business.

The personal skills necessary to conclude negotiations successfully in Japan do not come naturally to the Westerner. What is perhaps even more disturbing is the inappropriateness of much sales training to the Japanese situation. Many skills such as reading body language are culture bound. The persuasion approach to selling seems diametrically opposed to the Japanese character and perception of the role of negotiations.

Eight recommendations put forward by Bruderev (1993) for selling to people in Japanese organisations are as follows:

1 *Describe your organisation in detail.* Japanese businesspeople welcome pamphlets and brochures that describe your organisation, its location, its products, and your objectives for being in Japan. Ideally these should be in Japanese; if not, the main points should be summarised in Japanese.

2 *Manage meetings Japanese-style.* Get a mutual acquaintance to introduce you, don't be late or change appointments, leave plenty of time for travel between meetings and bring a small gift (e.g. a modest novelty item made in your country, but not something made by your firm as this would be viewed as a paltry give-away).

3 *Recognise that decisions are often made by middle management.* On your first call you may meet the president, but this is a formality. The important person is probably the head of a department or division.

4 *Do not push for a close.* Even with the most attractive product and effective sales propositions, Japanese businesspeople will not make a decision at that meeting. They will want time to assess your proposal, your company and you personally. They will be thinking about establishing a long-term relationship, and so will demand time to consider all aspects of the sale. If they do not like your proposal, courtesy rules out their saying 'no' to your face.

5 *Use Japanese whenever possible.* Write sales and promotional material in Japanese using a native-born translator. If you have to write in English this will damage your image. Many Japanese businesspeople have a limited knowledge of English, so if you have to speak in English, speak slowly, using simple words. Learn some common Japanese expressions; the effort you have made will be appreciated.

6 *Make sales presentations low key.* Use a moderate, low key, deliberate style to reflect their preferred manner of doing business.

7 *Establish a strong relationship.* Japanese people follow formal rules when beginning a relationship (e.g. the introduction, exchange of business cards, the gradual beginning of business talks) and expect you to cultivate relationships through sales calls, courtesy visits and the occasional lunch and other social events.

8 *Dress conservatively.* Japanese prefer plain, undemonstrative business dress. The objective should be to blend in quietly.

10.8 CONCLUSIONS

This chapter has examined international selling. The broad economic aspects were first discussed, including balance of payments and the United Kingdom's share of international trade. Britain's entry into the European Union (EU) was examined, together with the effects of the General Agreement on Tariffs and Trade (GATT).

The advantages to the individual company entering international selling were discussed and this was followed by aspects of how different cultures affect the sales approach. More specifically, this included aesthetics, religion, education, language, social organisation and political factors.

Different types of organisation for international selling were considered, including agents, distributors, licensing and export houses under indirect methods. Direct methods included subsidiary companies, joint ventures and direct selling. This was concluded by a specific description of the problems involved in selling to Japan.

The next chapter considers the legal and social aspects of selling which then concludes the section on the sales environment.

PRACTICAL EXERCISE

Wardley Investment Services (Hong Kong)

Private banking has been one of the main growth areas of the banking industry in the ASEAN (Association of South East Asian Nations) region over the last few years, but private bankers have found that the newly rich ASEAN clientele can be quite a different market from the traditional customer in Europe and North America.

Mr Robert Bunker and Mr John Cheung, directors of Wardley Investment Services (Hong Kong) said both Wardley and its corporate parent, the Hongkong & Shanghai Bank Group, have adopted what has been described as the American interpretation of private banking in their approach to the ASEAN marketplace.

Mr Bunker explained: 'We provide a one-stop shop for financial services to high net worth individuals, drawing on the wide range of services available in the Group. There are many smaller banks which have seen private banking as a profitable growth area, but it is difficult for them to provide the breadth of services with just a small representative office in the region. As a result, they struggle to develop the mass of business necessary to make a living.'

And the demands of ASEAN customers do tend to differ from those of their counterparts in Europe and North America.

Mr Cheung said that in Asia as a whole, private banking is not as tax driven as it is in much of the West. 'There are other differences. For example, the division of corporate and private wealth in Asia is often blurred, and some Asian clients are very aggressive in the way they like to invest. Again, such tendencies can mean a different attitude on the part of the private bank,' he said.

Mr Bunker added: 'I think that you will notice in the marketing strategy of the Group that we are trying to shrug off our traditional image and create a more adventurous and aggressive picture.'

He said the infrastructure of the Group provides a great boon. In the ASEAN region, the Bank has a presence in one form or another in Singapore, Thailand and Indonesia.

European banks entering the ASEAN market find it a lot more difficult to rely on name or reputation to build their market share, particularly when many potential customers are not familiar with their names. A bank such as Banca della Svizzera Italiana (BSI), for example, despite its size and reputation in Europe, has to fight hard to get noticed in the already crowded marketplace.

But Mr Anton Jecker, BSI's chief representative in Hong Kong, believes his bank can offer a competitive service for its clients. He said: 'We see private banking as just that, knowing the individual needs and requirements of a customer and servicing those needs. We provide individually serviced accounts with an emphasis on the personal nature of banking. We provide safety and confidentiality as a Swiss bank, and investors do not put their money with us for us to speculate. So we do not target the entrepreneur so much and tend to go for personal assets on the whole. We make it clear where we can help from the beginning, and we do not do everything in the wide spectrum of banking services.'

Although BSI has a different emphasis to the Hongkong Bank Group, Mr Jecker still feels that there is a great future for private banking in the region. 'But it is difficult for European banks to enter such markets, especially given the dominance of US banks in the last 30 to 40 years. The same can be said for the Philippines which, despite its economic and political problems, still has a lot of potential for private banking.'

DISCUSSION QUESTIONS

1 Give advice to a United Kingdom bank that has not previously been engaged in the ASEAN region as to what problems it might face when setting up in the area.

2 What segmentation possibilities might exist for a smaller bank in the region?

3 What research would you advise a small bank to undertake before setting up in the region for the first time?

4 Assume that a small bank you are advising has decided to set up in the region. What strategic guidelines would you give to the bank in so far as organising its selling activities is concerned?

PRACTICAL EXERCISE

Sapporo (Hong Kong) Ltd

Sapporo is part of a major Japanese conglomerate. They manufacture in Hong Kong, but mainly buy in from their own factory in China a range of consumable cleaning items including household brushes, mops and cleaning cloths as well as similar products designed for industrial markets.

The raw material used is principally high-density woven material that has a relatively long lifespan. The company is regarded as being at the 'quality' end of the market for such products. Their goods are packaged and branded so as to make them stand out from the more traditional generic unbranded products.

Both industrial and consumer products are distributed through intermediaries and not direct. The salesforce sells to distributors for industrial products and to wholesalers for consumer products. Advertising plays a key role in the company's marketing efforts and products are brand managed in order to create an element of internal marketing competition.

Hong Kong sales for the past three years have been increasing steadily from HK$17.4 million in 1996/7, to HK$21.2 million in 1997/8 to HK$26.9 million in 1998/9. Press and television advertising (above-the-line) and sales promotional spending (below-the-line) has been about 5 per cent of sales during this period with 60 per cent of this being spent on television campaigns. The remainder has been spent on leaflets, in-store campaigns, trade magazines and the press.

The parent company had made a decision to expand more into the ASEAN market and has encouraged Sapporo to open up satellite manufacturing and distribution plants in the region. They are concerned that Sapporo chooses the right advertising agency for this planned expansion. The parent company uses two agencies in the ASEAN region and at one point they attempted to impose one of these agencies on

Sapporo's Hong Kong operations. Sapporo (Hong Kong) Ltd resisted, saying that another country's agency would not understand the Hong Kong market. Now the Japanese parent company is using this same argument against Sapporo taking its Hong Kong advertising campaign (and Hong Kong advertising agency) into the ASEAN region.

DISCUSSION QUESTIONS

1 In view of the sales turnover figures, is the company justified in engaging in so much above-the-line advertising, especially in view of its expansion into other ASEAN countries? Would it not be better to engage in more direct selling?

2 Advise Sapporo on how it should go about switching its promotional mix away from above-the-line promotion and more towards selling, particularly in view of the planned ASEAN expansion. In your answer, comment on the potential problems in relation to the choice of advertising agency and the possibility of incorporating a pan-ASEAN theme into its promotion

PRACTICAL EXERCISE

Quality Kraft Carpets Ltd

This company was founded in 1987 by William Jackson and John Turner in Kidderminster, a town in the UK with a tradition of carpet-making going back hundreds of years. Carpet manufacture and related activities had been the major provider of employment in the area up until the late 1960s. However, since that date, the carpet industry, like many other areas of British textiles, faced problems and decline.

Paradoxically, it was this decline that brought Quality Kraft Carpets into existence. William Jackson had been production manager with one of the largest carpet manufacturing firms in the area, with a world-wide reputation for quality carpets. John Turner had been a loom tuner (a maintenance engineer) responsible for maintaining over one hundred carpet looms for another large company. Jackson had been made redundant as a result of a drastic decline in orders and Turner's company had gone into liquidation. Both of them were very good friends, and since their respective demises had come together they decided to start their own small company, specialising in the product they knew best – traditional, woven, good quality, Axminster carpets.

Because so many firms in the area were either closing down or cutting back production, there was a steady supply of textile machinery being sold very cheaply by local auctioneers. By pooling their respective resources, plus help from the bank, they were able to acquire a 15-year lease on a small factory and purchase enough equipment to enable them to commence production.

Their policy was to weave best-quality carpets made of 80 per cent wool and 20 per cent nylon. The market was good-quality carpet shops and the contract market, especially hotels, restaurants, offices and large stores. They made a conscious decision not to deal with the new carpet superstores, largely because profit margins would be so low, in that their bulk purchasing power made them able to demand low margins. In addition, these carpet superstores predominantly sold cheaper carpets, mainly tufted synthetic carpets purchased from North America. It was contended that purchasers looking for a good-quality carpet would go to a conventional carpet shop and not to a carpet superstore which they considered was more applicable to the lower end of the market.

At the time of setting up, the main problems facing UK carpet manufacturers were the depressed state of the economy and the fact that imports of carpets were taking an increasing share of a diminishing market. Thus, the recession made carpet purchasing a lower priority matter for those who already had carpets and the attitude was to make them last longer.

Nowadays, imports account for almost 35 per cent of the UK carpet market and this percentage is increasing. The main imports are synthetic tufted carpets, mainly from North America but increasingly from EU countries – Belgium followed by Germany and Holland. Nylon carpet is basically oil based, which gave the Americans a significant advantage until the late 1980s because of the cheapness of their oil. However, since then their oil prices have increased and the strength of the US dollar has made their exports to the UK less competitive.

Despite the apparently depressing picture for UK manufacturers, the UK carpet industry is still amongst the largest in the world, particularly the high-quality woven carpet sector. The UK has always been a net exporter of carpets and its reputation for quality has world-wide acclaim.

Since Quality Kraft Carpets commenced, its total sales have been as follows:

Quality Kraft Carpets Ltd sales (£000)

1987	1988	1989	1990	1991	1992	1993	1994	1995	1996	1997	1998	1999
500	640	820	1,280	1,760	2,300	2,900	2,100	2,000	1,970	1,950	1,960	1,990

These sales are to two distinct markets:

● direct to quality retailers
● the contract market.

The percentage of sales accounted for by each of these market segments is given below:

Percentage of sales to each segment

	1987	1988	1989	1990	1991	1992	1993	1994	1995	1996	1997	1998	1999
Retail	78	76	70	66	63	60	60	58	56	52	52	50	50
Contract	22	24	30	34	37	40	40	42	44	48	48	50	50

At the 1993 level of demand the company was operating at full capacity, but today it has an excess of manufacturing capacity. The company has not laid off any employees, but overtime has been cut out and some work that was given to outside contractors, e.g. final 'shearing' up of carpets, is now done in the company. An interesting facet of contract sales is that much of it is for customised carpet, often incorporating the customer's company logo in the design.

The company now feels that the industry is likely to remain depressed and foreign competition in the UK market is likely to increase further. The company has not attempted to sell its products abroad, but feels that if it is ever to expand again, then overseas markets are the only feasible method. William Jackson and John Turner had a long discussion about exporting, as they were both inexperienced in such matters, and they listed the strengths and weaknesses of Quality Kraft Carpets in order to arrive at a decision as to which would be the most appropriate overseas market to enter. Their conclusions were as follows:

1 *Weaknesses*
   ● Small and relatively new without the reputation of a long-established firm.
   ● Management has no knowledge of selling overseas and, although educated by experience, has little knowledge of finance, economics, languages, etc., which are of help when selling overseas.
   ● The more popular types of tufted carpets are not manufactured.
   ● The company cannot compete on price in the volume markets because of outdated equipment and small purchasing power.
   ● Although products are first class, they are expensive.
   ● The company does not directly employ such specialists as designers, but operates on a freelance/contractual basis.
2 *Strengths*
   ● Expertise in the manufacture of good-quality conventionally-woven Axminster carpets.
   ● The company is small and flexible and can easily cope with new trends in designs.
   ● Proficiency is increasing in contract work and staff have specialist knowledge of such one-off tasks. Much repeat business is coming from satisfied contract customers.
   ● There is a loyal workforce who have flexible working arrangements in that the workers can each carry out a number of different jobs without demarcation disputes.
   ● The company is reasonably profitable and it has very little long-term debt.
   ● The retail part of the business contains loyal customers with much repeat business.

After discussions with the bank and advice from the British Overseas Trade Board, it was decided that the USA offered most potential for the immediate future. The Middle East and Japan also showed promise in the medium term. It was also decided that they should concentrate on the contract market. These decisions were based upon the following criteria:

1 The USA is now an established market for best quality Axminster carpet.
2 Although the USA does manufacture some conventionally woven Wilton carpet, it does not manufacture much good-quality Axminster carpet.
3 In the contract market, quality seems to be more important than price and it would seem to be good for the company to concentrate on contract carpet sales.

4 Import tariffs into the USA from the UK are 9½ per cent *ad valorem* (on top of the imported cost) for Axminster and 19½ per cent for Wilton (the latter being higher to protect the USA producers). This gives an undoubted advantage for the export of Axminster carpets.

5 A market research survey conducted in the USA had indicated that their interior designers liked Axminster because of the fact that any pattern or logo could be woven into the design. Most contract carpet in the USA is tufted and printed which only makes mass production runs feasible. This printing process, although much cheaper, is inferior to the design being actually woven into the carpet as is the case with Axminster.

6 The pound is relatively good value against the United States dollar, and this makes the product good value in the USA.

7 Advice from the British Overseas Trade Board has indicated that the UK has a high reputation in the USA for quality carpets, that they appreciate personal service and good delivery and that British carpet might be seen as a status symbol.

Quality Kraft Carpets Ltd decided that they would immediately enter the North American market, but did not want to commit too much money to the venture in case it failed. On the other hand, if it was successful, they were prepared to commit more resources.

DISCUSSION QUESTIONS

1 Draw up a short-, medium- and long-term sales strategy upon how Quality Kraft Carpets can enter, develop and remain in the United States market.

2 What form of representation would you recommend for this new market – or would you consider setting up a manufacturing subsidiary? Give reasons for your decision.

3 How might your various strategies change and what further considerations would need to be made if, after initial success in the United States market, the Middle East and Japan offered good export opportunities?

4 What would be your marketing communications and sales promotional strategies for the company in the USA? More specifically, outline your sales 'message' and the type of media you would use to communicate this message.

5 What, if any, further research needs to be undertaken before attempting to export to the USA?

EXAMINATION QUESTIONS

1 Discuss the contention that there is no such thing as 'overseas selling'; it is merely an extension of selling to the home market.

2 How does the role of an export agent differ from the role of an export salesperson?

3 Discuss the contribution that the WTO has made to a freeing up of international sales negotiations.

4 What are the differences that should be considered when international sales managers draw up their export plans?

5 How is the world-wide trend towards urbanisation and greater overseas travel affecting the opportunities for international selling?

LAW AND ETHICAL ISSUES

OBJECTIVES   After studying this chapter, you should be able to:

1 Understand the importance of consumer protection in the context of selling.

2 Apply appropriate terms and conditions to a contract of sale.

3 Appreciate how legal controls affect sales activities.

4 Make voluntary and legal restraints work to the advantage of both the buyer *and* the seller.

KEY CONCEPTS
- collusion
- consumer credit
- consumer protection
- contract
- exclusion clauses
- false trade descriptions
- faulty goods
- inertia selling
- terms and conditions
- terms of trade
- unit pricing

Consumer protection by the law is very much a twentieth century phenomenon. Before that the prevailing attitude can be described by the phrase *caveat emptor* – let the buyer beware. Much of the legislation has been drawn up since 1970 when there was a recognition that sellers may have an unfair advantage compared with consumers when entering into a contract of sale. The major laws controlling selling activity in Britain include the following:

- Weights and Measures Acts 1878, 1963, 1979
- Sale of Goods Acts 1893, 1979
- Resale Prices Acts 1964, 1976
- Restrictive Trade Practices Acts 1956, 1968, 1976
- Misrepresentation Act 1967
- Trade Descriptions Acts 1968, 1972
- Unsolicited Goods and Services Acts 1971, 1975
- Supply of Goods (Implied Terms) Acts 1973, 1982
- Fair Trading Act 1973

- Hire Purchase Act 1973
- Consumer Credit Act 1974
- Unfair Contract Terms Act 1977
- Consumer Safety Act 1978
- Consumer Protection Act 1987

In addition to these Acts, consumers are protected by a range of codes of practice covering such activities as advertising, market research and direct selling. Trade associations such as the Association of British Travel Agents, the Society of Motor Manufacturers and Traders, and the Radio, Electrical and Television Retailers' Association have also drawn up codes of practice which have been approved by the Office of Fair Trading.

The consumers' interest is also protected by the Consumers' Association which campaigns for consumers and provides information about products, often on a comparative basis, which allows consumers to make a more informed, rational choice between products and brands. This information is published in their magazine *Which?* The National Consumer Council was established in 1975 to represent the consumer interest at national level and to issue reports on various topics of consumer concern, e.g. consumer credit.

Since a Conservative Government came to power in 1979, there has been a certain amount of reining back in relation to consumer protection. The first indication of this was the dissolution of the post of Minister for Consumer Affairs and this was followed by the merging of Consumer Advice Centres with Citizens' Advice Bureaux. The feeling was that consumer protection had gone too far and it was time to give power back to manufacturers. However, more fundamental was the notion that market forces would keep 'good' manufacturers in business and force 'bad' ones out. Thus the age of the so-called 'consumerist movement' effectively lost its momentum at the end of the 1970s.

11.1 THE CONTRACT

All this activity is centred upon the contract entered into when a seller agrees to part with a good, or provide a service, in exchange for monetary payment.

A contract is made when a deal is agreed. This can be accomplished verbally or in writing. Once an offer has been accepted a contract is formed and is legally binding. Thus if a builder offers to build a garage for £1,000 and this offer is accepted, the builder is obliged to carry out the work and the householder is under an obligation to pay the agreed sum upon completion. Although contracts do not have to be in writing – except, for example, house purchase – to place an offer and acceptance in writing can minimise the likelihood of misunderstanding over the nature of the agreement which has been struck and provide tangible evidence in the event of legal action. Important in written contracts are the terms and conditions which apply. This aspect of the contract will now be considered, before an examination of some business practices, and the way in which they are controlled by law, is undertaken.

In a binding contract, one party should have made a firm offer and the offer should have received an unequivocal acceptance. An offer should be distinguished from 'an invitation to treat'. An invitation to treat (negotiate) is not an offer. For example, the display of goods at a certain price in a shop is not an offer by the shopkeeper to sell. Rather it is an invitation to shoppers to make an offer to buy. Thus if a product is accidentally priced too low, the customer cannot demand to buy at that price.

11.2 TERMS AND CONDITIONS

As the name suggests, **terms and conditions** state the circumstances under which the buyer is prepared to purchase and the seller is prepared to sell. They define the limit of responsibility for both buyer and seller. Thus both buyer and seller are at liberty to state their terms and conditions. Usually the buyer will state his on the back of his order form and the seller will do so on the reverse of his quotation form. Often a note is typed on the front of the form in red ink: 'Your attention is drawn to our standard terms and conditions on the reverse of this order.'

Typical clauses incorporated into the conditions of a purchase order include the following:

1 Only orders issued on the company's printed order form and signed on behalf of the company will be respected.
2 Alterations to orders must be confirmed by official amendment and signed.
3 Delivery must be within the specified time period. The right to cancel is reserved for late delivery.
4 Faulty goods will be returned and expenses charged to the supplier.
5 All insurance of goods in transit shall be paid for by the supplier.
6 This order is subject to a cash discount of 2½ per cent, unless otherwise arranged, for payment within twenty-eight days of receipt. Any payment made is without prejudice to our rights if the goods supplied prove to be unsatisfactory or not in accordance with our agreed specification or sample.
7 Tools supplied by us for the execution of this order must not be used in the service of any other firm without permission.

Careful drawing up of terms and conditions are essential in business since they provide protection against claims made by the other party should problems arise in fulfilment of the contract.

An example of a conditions of sale document for a seller is given in Figure 11.1.

CONDITIONS OF SALE

These Conditions apply except so far as they are inconsistent with any express agreement entered into between the Seller and the Buyer before the delivery.

1 Where the Seller delivers in bulk it is the Buyer's responsibility
  (a) to provide a safe and suitable bulk storage which complies in all respects with all relevant regulations made by H.M. Government or other competent authority.
  (b) to ensure that the storage into which delivery is to be made will accommodate the full quantity ordered and in the case of Petroleum Spirit to procure certification to this effect and also to the effect that the connecting hose is properly and securely connected to the filling point. In this regard the Buyer is referred to the regulations currently in force relating to the storage and use of petroleum spirit.
  (c) in the case of highly inflammable products and where otherwise applicable, strictly to observe any regulations laid down by H.M. Government or other competent authority in respect of the avoidance of smoking, naked lights, fires, stoves or heating appliances of any description in the vicinity of the storage and the fill, dip and vent pipes connected thereto.
  The Buyer will indemnify the Supplier against any damages, claims, expenses or costs which may arise as a result of the Buyer's non-observance of these conditions.
2 It is a condition of every bulk sale that the quantity shown by any measuring devices employed by the Seller shall for the purpose of accounts be accepted by the Buyer as the quantity delivered but the Buyer may be represented at the taking of these measurements in order to verify them if he so desires. The Seller cannot accept any responsibility whatever for discrepancies in the Buyer's tanks, dip rods or other measuring devices.
3 Prices include any Government Tax (other than Value Added Tax) in force at the time of supply. Any variation in the rate of existing tax, or any additional taxation, is for Buyer's account.
4 All products supplied are chargeable at the price ruling on the day of despatch irrespective of the date of the order or the amount of cash sent with order.
5 In the event of missing consignments, short delivery or damage the Seller can only investigate the circumstances if
  (a) In the case of damage the Buyer notifies the Railway or other Carrier and the Seller of the damage immediately upon receipt of the damaged goods, such notices to be in writing and quoting the invoice number;
  (b) In the case of non-receipt or short delivery the Buyer notifies the Seller in writing of non-receipt or short delivery. Such notice, quoting the invoice number, should be sent within 21 days of date of despatch.
6 Acceptance of goods will be treated as acceptance of the Seller's conditions.

Figure 11.1 Example of conditions of sale document

11.3   TERMS OF TRADE

In addition to the tactical and strategic aspects of international selling discussed in Chapter 10, sellers and buyers need to be aware of the **terms of trade** which apply when trading overseas. Differences in the terms of trade can have serious profit consequences for the unwary. Terms of trade are used to define the following:

1 who is responsible for control over the transfer of goods between importer and exporter; and
2 who is responsible for each part of the cost incurred in moving the goods between importer and exporter.

A number of terms are used to cover these aspects of delivery and cost. Variations in definitions led to the International Chamber of Commerce drawing up formal definitions in 1936. These were published under the title of INCOTERMS and have since been subject to update. For example, in 1980 a new edition of INCOTERMS covered two new terms which were required because of the increasing importance of container transportation.

Terms of trade are useful in that they cover a range of situations extending from the case where exporters merely make their goods available for collection by importers or their agents at their factory (ex works) to the case where the exporter agrees to deliver the goods to the importer's factory thereby taking responsibility for the costs and administration of that delivery (free delivered).

The following sections list the more commonly used terms.

Bills of lading

A bill of lading is a receipt for goods received on board a ship which is signed by the shipper (or agent) and states the terms on which the goods were delivered to and received by the ship. The Bills of Lading Act 1855 laid down the following principles:

1 It maintained the right of the shipper to 'stoppage in transit'. Thus an unpaid exporter could reclaim the goods during shipping.
2 It set up the principle of transferability which allowed the transfer of the bill of lading from the holder to a third person who then assumed ownership of the goods as well as any rights and liabilities stated in the bill.
3 It stated that the bill of lading was *prima-facie* evidence that the goods had been shipped.

The bill of lading thus acts as evidence that the goods have been received by the shipper. It can also act as part of the contract between the shipper and the person or organisation who is paying for the shipping. For example, if the goods are damaged upon arrival at the port of departure, a shipper can 'clause' the bill of lading to that effect.

A bill of lading will usually cover the following details:

- the name of the shipper
- the ship's name
- a description of the cargo
- payment details, e.g. whether freight has been paid or is payable at destination
- name of consignee
- terms of the carriage contract
- the date when the goods were loaded in the ship
- who is to be notified on the arrival of the shipment at its destination
- the ports of departure and final destination.

In summary, the bill of lading is a receipt for the goods shipped, a transferable document of title to the goods allowing the holder to claim his or her goods, and evidence of the terms of the contract of shipping.

Ex works

An exporter may quote a price to an importer 'ex works'. This places the exporter's liability for loss or damage to the goods at a minimum and also means that the exporter's duties in delivering the goods are minimal. Ownership of the goods passes to the buyer once it leaves the factory and the buyer pays all costs of exporting and accepts the risks once the goods pass through the factory gates. Quoting ex works may make sense if the goods are to be combined with those of another organisation to form a joint export cargo, or when the buyer has well-developed transportation facilities, e.g. buyers of commodity items such as tea and coffee beans. However, for other customers, quoting an ex works price may not meet their needs, since they cannot easily compare the actual cost of such goods against buying in their own country where prices are quoted with delivery.

Free on board (FOB)

This extends the responsibility, liability and costs of delivery for the exporter until the goods have been loaded on to the ship ('passed the ship's rail'). From this point, the importer pays the costs of insurance and freight. However, the exporter still has the right of 'stoppage in transit' should the importer fail to pay for those goods. Variations for land transport are 'free on rail' (FOR) and 'free on wagon' (FOW) which mean that the seller has the responsibility and cost of delivering goods on board a railway transporter or wagon.

Free alongside ship (FAS)

This term means that the exporter is responsible for and must pay all the costs of transport up to the point of placing the goods alongside the ship. A provision should be made covering who is responsible for any loss or damage before the goods are actually loaded on to the ship. The importer thus pays for the loading of the cargo and the cost of insurance and freight to its destination.

Cost, insurance and freight (CIF)

If a cost, insurance and freight agreement is reached, the exporter is responsible for the delivery of the goods on to the ship and pays the insurance on the part of the buyer against loss or damage while on ship. Should any loss or damage occur after the shipping company has received the goods and given the shipment a clean bill of lading, the buyer can take action against the ship owner or underwriter. Thus responsibility has passed from the exporter once the cargo is aboard ship although it is the exporter who pays for the shipping to the importer's port.

The term cost and freight (C & F) is similar to CIF except, as its name suggests, the exporter is not responsible for insurance during shipping. Instead the importer incurs the cost of this insurance.

Free delivered

This places maximum responsibility and cost on the exporter since he undertakes to deliver the goods to the importer with all costs paid and all of the administrative duties (e.g. obtaining an import licence) carried out by the exporter. From a marketing perspective, quoting a delivered price has the advantage that it minimises customer uncertainty and workload since the costs of transport, obtaining documentation, arranging shipping, etc., are borne by the seller. Furthermore, it allows the customer to compare actual prices from a foreign source with local prices where delivery costs are included or are of minimal amount. However, customers who have an efficient importing system may prefer to pay 'ex works' or 'free on board' and organise carriage themselves rather than pay the higher 'free delivered' price.

11.4 BUSINESS PRACTICES AND LEGAL CONTROLS

False descriptions

Unscrupulous salespeople may be tempted to mislead potential buyers through inaccurate statements about the product or service they are selling. In the UK the consumer is protected from such practice by the Trade Descriptions Act 1968. The Act covers descriptions of products, prices and services and includes both oral and written descriptions.

Businesses are prohibited from applying a **false trade description** to products and from supplying falsely described products. The false description must be false to a material degree, and the Act also covers 'misleading' statements. Not only would a salesperson be contravening the Act if he or she described a car as achieving 50 miles per gallon when, in fact, it only achieved 30 miles per gallon, he would also be guilty of putting a false trade description if he or she described a car as 'beautiful' if it proved to be unroadworthy.

The Trade Descriptions (Place of Production) (Marking) Order 1988 requires that where products are marked in such a way as to suggest they were made elsewhere than is the case, a clear statement of the actual place of manufacture must be made.

Misleading price indications are covered by the Consumer Protection Act 1987. This Act states that it is an offence to give a misleading indication of the price at which goods, services, accommodation or facilities are available. Agents, publishers and advertisers are covered by the Act as well as the person or organisation offering the goods or services.

Prices can be misleading when

- it is suggested that a price is less than it actually is;
- it is suggested that other charges are included in the price when in fact they are not;
- it is misleadingly suggested that prices will increase, decrease or stay the same;
- it is misleadingly suggested that the price depends on certain circumstances or particular facts;
- consumers are encouraged to depend on the truth of the price indication by circumstances which do not apply.

The Act covers both products and services.

Confusion over value for money due to differing pack sizes can be reduced by unit pricing whereby packs are marked with a price per litre or kilogram, etc. An EU Directive which came fully into force in 1994 requires that many supermarket products, for example, must be marked with a unit price unless packed in EU-approved pack sizes.

Faulty goods

The principal protection for the buyer against the sale of **faulty goods** is to be found within the Sale of Goods Act 1979. This Act states that a product must correspond to its description and must be of merchantable quality, i.e. 'fit for the purpose for which goods of that kind are commonly bought as it is reasonable to expect.' An example is a second-hand car which is found to be unroadworthy after purchase; it clearly is not of merchantable quality, unless bought for scrap! Finally a product must be fit for a particular purpose which may be specified by the buyer and agreed by the seller. If, for example, a buyer bought a car in this country with the expressed desire to use it in Africa, a retailer may be committing an offence if he or she agrees that the car is fit to be used when in fact, because of the higher temperatures, it is not.

The condition that products must correspond to their description covers both private and business sales, whereas the merchantability and fitness for purpose conditions apply to sales in the course of a business only. The latter two conditions apply not only at the time of purchase but for a reasonable time afterwards. What exactly constitutes 'reasonable' is open to interpretation and will depend upon the nature of the product.

In order to protect the consumer against faulty goods, some companies give guarantees in which they agree to replace or repair those goods should the fault become apparent within a specified period. Unfortunately, before the passing of the Supply of Goods (Implied Terms) Act 1973, these so-called guarantees often removed more rights than they gave. However, since the passing of that Act it has been unlawful for a seller to contract out of the conditions that goods should be merchantable and fit for their purpose. Buyers can now be confident that signing a guarantee will not result in them signing away their rights under the Sale of Goods Act 1979.

The Consumer Protection Act 1987 came into operation in response to a European Union Directive. This protects buyers if they suffer damage (e.g. death, personal injury, or damage to goods for private use). They must be able to prove that the good was defective and that the damage was caused by the defect in the product. Usually liability falls on the manufacturer or importer of the finished product or of the defective component or raw material. A product is considered to be defective when it does not provide the safety which a person is entitled to expect (including instruction for use). A major defence against claims is the 'development defence' where the manufacturer proves that the state of technical knowledge when the product was launched did not enable the existence of the defect to be discovered.

Further consumer protection is provided by the Consumer Safety Act 1978 which prohibits the sale of dangerous products, and by various EU regulations. For example, the EU mark can only be used on aerosol containers if they conform to EU regulations regarding dimensions, strength, etc.

Inertia selling

Inertia selling involves the sending of unsolicited goods or the providing of unsolicited services to people who, having received them, may feel an obligation to buy. For example, a book might be sent to people, who would be told that they had been specially chosen to receive it. They would be asked to send money in payment or return the book within a given period, after which they would become liable for payment. Non-payment and failure to return the good would result in letters demanding payment, sometimes in quite threatening terms.

The growing use of this technique during the 1960s led to a campaign organised by the Consumers' Association demanding that legislation be enacted curbing the use of the technique. As a result the Unsolicited Goods and Services Act 1971 was passed, followed by the Unsolicited Goods and Services (Amendment) Act 1975.

These Acts have not prohibited the use of the technique but have created certain rights for consumers which makes the use of the method ineffective. Unsolicited goods can be treated as a free gift after a period of six months from receipt if the sender has not reclaimed them. Further, if the recipient notifies the sender that they are unsolicited, the sender must collect them within 30 days or they become the property of the recipient. The 30-day rule was felt to be a fair compromise between the rights of the recipient and the rights of the sender who may be the subject of a false order placed by a third party.

The practice of sending threatening letters demanding payment has been outlawed, as have the threats of legal proceedings or placing of names on a published list of defaulters.

Unsolicited services have also been controlled by law. For example, the practice of placing unsolicited entries of names of firms in business directories and then demanding payment has been controlled.

The law therefore gives sufficient rights to consumers effectively to deter the practice of inertia selling. Fortunately for the consumer the trouble and costs involved in using this technique nowadays outweigh the benefits to be gained.

Exclusion clauses

Another practice which some sellers have employed in order to limit their liability is the use of an **exclusion clause**. For example, a restaurant or discotheque might display a sign stating that coats are left at the owner's risk, or a dry cleaners might display a sign excluding themselves from blame should clothes be damaged. This practice is now controlled by the Unfair Contract Terms Act 1977. A seller is not permitted to limit liability or contract out of his liability for death or injury arising from negligence or breach of contract or duty.

For other situations, where loss does not include death or injury, an exclusion clause is only valid if it satisfies the requirement of 'reasonableness'. This means that it is fair taking into account the circumstances prevailing when the sale was made. Relevant factors which are taken into account when making a judgement about 'reasonableness' include the following:

● the strength of the bargaining positions of the relevant parties;
● whether the customer received an inducement to agree to the exclusion clause;
● whether the customer knew or ought to have known of the existence of the exclusion clause;
● whether the goods were produced to the special order of the customer;
● for an exclusion clause which applies when some condition is not complied with, whether it was practicable for the condition to be met.

Buying by credit

Before 1974 obtaining **consumer credit** through a hire-purchase agreement was treated differently, under the law, to consumer credit by means of a bank loan.

However, from the consumer's point of view there is very little difference between paying for a good by instalments (hire purchase) or paying in cash through a bank loan which is itself repayable by instalments. The Consumer Credit Act 1974 effectively abolished this distinction. Almost all consumer credit agreements up to £15,000 are termed **regulated agreements**. A notable exception is a building society mortgage. Regulations concerned with 'truth in lending' provisions of the Act came into operation in 1985. The Act now replaces all former statutes concerning credit (e.g. hire purchase).

An important consumer protection measure which resulted from the Act was that a lender should disclose the true interest rate in advertisements and sales literature. This true rate now appears in advertisements as the APR (annual percentage rate) and enables consumers to compare rates of interest charged on a common basis. Prior to this Act, cleverly worded advertisements and sales literature could give the impression that the scale of charges was much lower than was the true case.

Control of credit trading was achieved by a system of licensing which is placed in the hands of the Director-General of Fair Trading. This system was designed to ensure that only people with a sound trading record are able to deal in credit. Not only finance companies but also retailers who arrange credit in order to sell their products must have a licence. Exempt from the Act, however, is weekly or monthly credit. Thus, many credit card agreements are exempt since total repayment is often required at the end of each month.

People entering credit agreements are entitled to receive at least one copy of the agreement so that they are informed of their rights and obligations. A 'cooling off' period is provided for in the Act when the agreement is preceded by 'oral representations' (sales talk) and the agreement was not signed on business premises. This provision was designed to control doorstep selling through credit arrangements. A consumer who wishes to cancel must serve notice of cancellation within five days of the date of receiving the copy of the signed agreement.

The Consumer Credit (Advertisements) Regulations 1989 laid down the minimum and maximum information which may be given in credit or hire advertisements. Advertisements are categorised as being simple, intermediate or full advertisements and the information content is regulated accordingly.

Collusion between sellers

In certain circumstances it may be in the sellers' interest to collude with one another in order to restrict supply, agree upon prices (price fixing) or share out the market in some mutually beneficial way. The Restrictive Trade Practices Act 1979 requires that any such trade agreement must be registered with the Director-General of Fair Trading, a post established under the Fair Trading Act 1973. If the Director-General of Fair Trading considers that the registered agreement is contrary to the public interest, he is empowered to refer it to the Restrictive Practices Court. If the Court agrees, the agreement may be declared void. The EU Commission also has powers over collusion and has had notable successes in breaking down price cartels, for example in plastics.

11.5 CONCLUSIONS

This chapter has examined some of the laws and organisations which have been established to protect consumer interests. Unfortunately the unscrupulous few have made it necessary to enact laws which provide consumer protection.

Central to the study of the sale is an understanding of a contract and its associated terms and conditions. Finally, a number of business practices and their related legal controls are described.

Part Four examines the issues and methods relevant to the management of a salesforce.

PRACTICAL EXERCISE

Kwiksell Cars Ltd

John Perry spent £1,500 on a second-hand car bought from Roy Clarke, Kwiksell Cars' salesperson. He is rueing his decision. Perry had never bought a car before but believed that he was smart enough to tell a good car from a bad one. After several weekends of trying to buy a car from private sellers, he decided that to go to a dealer was the only sensible option left to him if he wanted to buy one quickly.

A four-year-old Austin Astrada 1100 in the forecourt of Kwiksell Cars had caught his eye as he travelled to work by bus. It was advertised at £1,800 and looked in good condition.

When Perry and his girlfriend visited Kwiksell Cars the following Saturday he was greeted by Roy Clarke, who asked him which car he was interested in and took him to see the Astrada. Clarke described the car as 'in lovely condition', the mechanics having been overhauled recently and the engine tuned. Perry was concerned about petrol consumption and was told that he could expect around 40 mpg around town, increasing to nearly 55 mpg on long runs. Perry was very impressed but he was a little worried about the car's capacity to pull his father's caravan. 'There's no problem there,' said Clarke. 'The Astrada might have a small engine but the carburettor has been souped up and it will cope with a caravan. No problem!'

Clarke asked Perry if he and his young lady would like a test drive. Perry agreed and found the car quite good on acceleration, although the engine was a bit noisier than his father's car. 'That's the souped up engine,' said Clarke. 'It makes it sound a bit racey, doesn't it?'

To Perry, the car looked like the solution to his long search but he knew that, as a cash purchaser, he might be able to negotiate a lower price.

'The car seems to suit my purposes but the price is a little higher than I would be prepared to pay.'

'Yes, but it's not often a car in this condition comes on to the market, sir,' retorted Clarke.

'What would you be prepared to knock off the price for a cash deal?' asked Perry.

'Usually, the maximum I am allowed to go is £200, but if you are prepared to pay a deposit now, with the remainder on, say, Tuesday when you collect the car, I'm willing to reduce the price to £1,500.'

Perry felt pleased with himself, and in front of his girlfriend, too! He agreed. He wrote a cheque for £500 and agreed to bring the balance in cash on the following Tuesday. Clarke asked him to sign a contract of sale and promised that the car and all the necessary documents would be ready by Tuesday.

Perry was pleased with his new purchase at first, but the following weekend when he was on a long run, Perry noticed a knocking noise coming from the engine. The car also appeared to be using much more petrol than he expected. He decided to buy a car guide from WHSmiths and check the petrol consumption figures. The guide stated that the Austin Astrada would achieve 30 mpg on the urban cycle and 40 mpg at a steady 56 mph. Perry was livid!

The knocking noise was still to be heard, so he took the car to his father's garage. The mechanic told Perry that the car's big ends were worn badly. It would cost £300 to be repaired. 'The engine's not souped up,' he said, 'it's kaput!'

'But I need the car next weekend; I'm going on holiday in my father's caravan,' said Perry.

'Well, I hope you're thinking of using your father's car,' said the mechanic. 'You'd blow the engine for sure with a car like the Astrada. It's only got an 1100 engine.'

Perry stormed into Clarke's office.

'I'm sorry you've had these problems but engine troubles are common with Astradas,' explained Clarke. 'I'd like to help but I did take you for a test drive.'

'You conned me!' shouted Perry.

'Not at all. You will see that the contract you signed clearly states that the responsibility to check for defects was the buyer's. That means that any faults which appear after sale are your responsibility to put right. You told me you knew a bit about cars. If you didn't you should have brought a mechanic with you. I knocked £300 off the price. That was to cover for any problems like this.'

DISCUSSION QUESTIONS

1 Did Clarke break the law regarding the sale of the car? Which laws are relevant to this case?

EXAMINATION QUESTIONS

1 What is a contract? Of what significance are contracts in buyer–seller relationships?

2 How well protected are customers from false trade descriptions and faulty goods?

3 How does the external legal environment affect the role of sales management?

SALES
MANAGEMENT

RECRUITMENT AND SELECTION

OBJECTIVES   After studying this chapter, you should be able to:

1 Appreciate that salesperson selection is a key to ultimate selling success.

2 Apply interview and selection procedures in the context of recruiting salespeople.

3 Understand the advantages and drawbacks of certain tests and procedures related to selection.

KEY CONCEPTS
- empathy and ego drive
- interviewing
- job description
- personnel specification
- psychological tests

- recruitment
- role playing
- salesforce selection
- short-listing

12.1   THE IMPORTANCE OF SELECTION

In attempting to recruit and select a new sales representative, sales managers find themselves in an unaccustomed role. Instead of being a seller he or she, for once, takes on the role of buyer. It is crucial that this transition is carried out effectively because the future success of the salesforce depends upon the infusion of high-calibre personnel. There are a number of facts which emphasise the importance of effective **salesforce selection**:

1 There is wide variability in the sales effectiveness of salespeople. In 1979, the Institute of Marketing commissioned a study (PA Consultants, 1979) into salesforce practice. In this study, the following question was asked of sales managers: 'If you were to put your most successful salesperson into the territory of one of your average salespeople, and made no other changes, what increases in sales would you expect after, say, two years?' The most commonly expected increased was 16-20 per cent, and one-fifth of all sales managers said they would expect an increase of 30 per cent or over. It must be emphasised that the comparison was between the top and *average* salesperson, not top and

worst salesperson. Clearly, the quality of the sales representatives which sales managers recruit can have a substantial effect on sales turnover.

2 Salespeople are very costly. If a company decides to employ extra sales personnel, the cost will be much higher than just basic salary (and commission). Most companies provide a car if travel is required, and travel expenses will also be paid by the company. The special skills necessary to make a sale, rather than to receive an order, imply that training will be required. No company will want to incur all of these costs in order to employ a poor performer.

3 Other important determinants of success, such as training and motivation, are heavily dependent on the intrinsic qualities of the recruit. Although sales effectiveness can be improved by training, it is limited by innate ability. Like other activities where skill is required, such as cricket, soccer and athletics, ultimate achievement in selling is highly associated with personal characteristics. Similarly, motivational techniques may stimulate the salesperson to achieve higher sales but they can do only so much. A lot will be dependent on the inborn motivation of the salesperson himself to complete a difficult sale or visit another prospect instead of returning home.

A study by Galbraith *et al.* (1991) examined the features that attracted salespeople into selling and what they valued most about their work. The results are given in Table 12.1.

Table 12.1   Features of most interest and most value

Most interest	%	Most value	%
Working methods	60	Independence	40
Independence	13	Earnings	18
Earnings	12	Providing a service	14
Company status	5	Freedom	11
Good training	4	Dealing with people	8
Promotion chances	2	Job satisfaction	6
Professional status	2	Status	3
Exclusive territory	2	Promotion prospects	1

The table shows that working methods and independence are more important than earnings as the attraction for entering selling. This challenges the assumption made by many companies that money is the main reason for embarking on a sales career. Independence is also highly valued when doing the selling job. The implication of these findings is that sales management should understand the reasons why people are attracted to selling in their industry to develop effective recruitment strategies. They certainly should not blindly assume that earnings are always paramount.

Sales managers are clearly faced with a difficult and yet vitally important task. However, many of them believe that the outcome of the selection process is far from satisfactory. In the Institute of Marketing survey, nearly half of the sales managers reported that fewer than seven out of ten of the salespeople they had recruited were satisfactory.

Recruitment and selection is a particularly difficult task when operating in overseas markets. The following case discussion identifies some of the key issues.

Recruiting and selecting an international salesforce

A company wishing to recruit an international sales team has a range of options. Recruits could be expatriates, host-country nationals or third-country nationals. Expatriates (home-country salespeople) are well regarded by technical companies selling expensive products because they tend to possess a high level of product knowledge and the ability and willingness to provide follow-up service. Work overseas also provides companies with the opportunity to train managers and prepare junior executives for promotion. Furthermore, expatriates allow international companies to maintain a high degree of control over global marketing and sales activities. However, there are drawbacks. Expatriates are usually more expensive than local salespeople, they may not settle in the new country, and may fail to understand the cultural nuances required to sell successfully abroad.

The second option is to hire host-country nationals. The advantages are that they bring cultural and market knowledge, language skills and familiarity with local business tradition. This often means a shorter adjustment period for a company wanting to be active in a new overseas market. However, these benefits must be assessed in the light of several potential disadvantages. Often host-country nationals require extensive product training together with knowledge about the company, its history and philosophies. Second, in some countries such as Thailand, Malaysia and India salespeople are not held in high esteem. This restricts the supply of well-educated people into sales jobs and makes the task of recruiting local people more difficult. Finally, loyalty to a foreign company may be less than from expatriates.

The third option is to hire third-country nationals. When hired from similar countries in a particular region, they provide cultural sensitivity and language skills while allowing access to a more skilled and/or less costly salesforce than is available in the target country. Particularly for regionally-focused companies, third-country nationals can be an effective compromise between expatriates and host-country nationals. However the drawbacks are that the third-country national may have difficulty identifying with where and for whom they work. They sometimes suffer from blocked promotions, lower salaries and difficulties in adapting to new environments.

Based on Boyacigiller, N. (1990) 'The role of expatriates in the management of interdependence, complexity and risk in multinational corporations', *Journal of International Business Studies*, 21(3), pp. 357–381; Honeycutt, Jr., E.D. and Ford, J.B. (1995) 'Guidelines for managing an international sales force', *Industrial Marketing Management*, 24, pp. 135–144; Zeira, Y. and Harari, E. (1977) 'Managing third country nationals in multinational corporations', *Business Horizons*, October, pp. 83–88.

There are a number of stages in the recruitment and selection process:

1 Preparation of the job description and personnel specification.
2 Identification of sources of recruitment and methods of communication.
3 Designing an effective application form and preparing a short-list.
4 Interviewing.
5 Supplementary selection aids – psychological tests, role playing.

An understanding of each stage and the correct procedures to be followed will maximise the chances of selecting the right applicant.

12.2 PREPARATION OF THE JOB DESCRIPTION AND SPECIFICATION

The production of an accurate **job description** should prove of little difficulty for the sales manager. He or she has intimate knowledge of what is required, having been a salesperson himself or herself and having been out on the road with his or her salespeople during training and evaluation exercises. Generally a job description will cover the following factors:

1 The title of the job.
2 Duties and responsibilities – the tasks which will be expected of the new recruit, e.g. selling, after-sales service, information feedback, and the range of products/markets/type of customer with which he or she will be associated.
3 To whom he or she will report.
4 Technical requirements, e.g. the degree to which the salesperson needs to understand the technical aspects of the products he or she is selling.
5 Location and geographical area to be covered.
6 Degree of autonomy – the degree to which the salesperson will be able to control his or her own work programme.

Once generated, the job description will act as the blueprint for the **personnel specification** which outlines the type of applicant the company is seeking. The technical requirements of the job, for example, and the nature of the customers which the salespeople will meet, will be factors which influence the level of education and, possibly, the age of the required recruit.

The construction of the personnel specification is more difficult for the sales manager than that of the job description. Some of the questions posed lead to highly subjective responses. Must the recruit have selling experience? Should such experience be within the markets that the company serves? Should he be within a certain age range? Is it essential that the salesperson holds certain technical qualifications? If the answer to all of these question is yes, then the number of possible applicants who qualify is reduced.

The danger is that applicants of high potential in selling may be excluded. Graduates at universities often complain that jobs which they are confident that they are capable of doing well are denied them because of the 'two years experience in selling' clause in the advertisements. The implications of this are that the job specification should be drawn up bearing in mind the type of person who would be *excluded* from applying if conditions are laid down with regard to such factors as previous experience. Is it really necessary or just more convenient since less training may then be required?

Another aspect of the personnel specification is the determination of qualities looked for in the new salesperson. This is a much more nebulous concept than the level of technical qualifications, age or previous experience. The qualities themselves may depend on the nature of the job, the personal prejudices of the sales manager (a good rule of thumb is that many managers favour people who are like themselves) or be based on more objective research which has been conducted into attributes associated with successful salespeople. A survey (Jobber and Millar, 1984) which investigated selection practice amongst sales managers in large UK companies produced a plethora of qualities deemed to be important. Figure 12.1 lists the top 20 characteristics and the percentage mentioning each.

Mayer and Greenberg (1964) produced a more manageable list. Extensive research amongst over 1,000 companies in the USA revealed only two qualities essential to selling – empathy and ego drive. **Empathy** is defined as the ability to feel as the buyer does; to be able to understand the customers' problems and needs. This is distinct from sympathy. A salesperson can feel and understand without agreeing with that feeling. The other basic determinant of sales success, **ego drive**, is defined as the need to make a sale in a personal way not merely for money.

Mayer and Greenberg claim that when an applicant has a large measure of both of these qualities he will be successful at selling anything. Their research led them to believe that sales ability is fundamental, not the product being sold:

> Many sales executives feel that the type of selling in their industry (and even in their particular company) is somehow completely special and unique. This is true to an extent. There is no question that a data-processing equipment salesperson needs somewhat different training and background than does an automobile salesperson. Differences in requirements are obvious, and whether or not the applicant meets the special qualifications for a particular job can easily be seen in the applicant's biography or readily measured. What is not so easily seen, however, are the basic sales dynamics we have been discussing, which permit an individual to sell successfully, almost regardless of what he is selling.

Certainly, the evidence which they have provided, which groups salespersons into four categories (highly recommended, recommended, not recommended, and virtually no chance of success) according to the degree to which they possess empathy and ego drive, correlated well with sales success in three industries – cars, mutual funds and insurance. Their measures of empathy and ego drive were derived from the use of a psychological test, the multiple personal inventory, which will be discussed in the section covering psychological tests (see section 12.6).

Percentage of respondents mentioning:

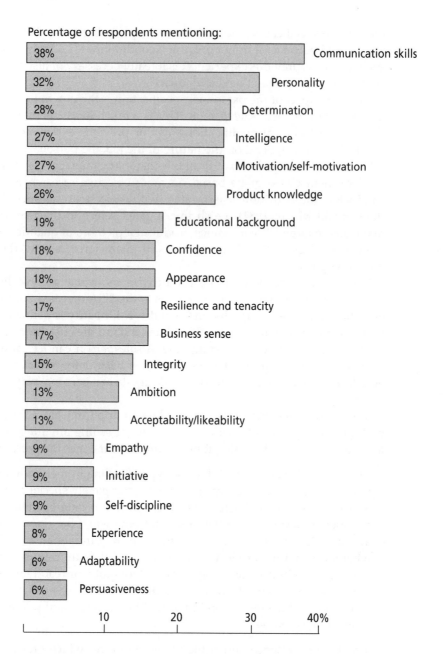

Figure 12.1   Important qualities of salespeople

(Source: Jobber and Millar, 1984)

In summary, a personnel specification may contain all or some of the following factors:

1 Physical requirements, e.g. speech, appearance.
2 Attainments, e.g. standard of education and qualifications, experience and successes.

3 Aptitudes and qualities, e.g. ability to communicate, self-motivation.
4 Disposition, e.g. maturity, sense of responsibility.
5 Interests, e.g. degree to which interests are social, active, inactive.
6 Personal circumstances, e.g. married, single, etc.

The factors chosen to define the personnel specification will be used as criteria of selection in the interview itself.

12.3 IDENTIFICATION OF SOURCES OF RECRUITMENT AND METHODS OF COMMUNICATION

Sources

There are six main sources of recruitment:

● from inside – the company's own staff
● recruitment agencies
● educational establishments
● competitors
● other industries
● unemployed.

Company's own staff

The advantage of this source is that the candidate will know the company and its products. The company will also know the candidate much more intimately than an outsider. A certain amount of risk is thereby reduced in that first-hand experience of the candidate's personal characteristics is available. However, there is no guarantee that he or she has selling ability.

Recruitment agencies

Recruitment agencies will provide lists of potential recruits for a fee. In order to be entered on such a list, reputable agencies screen applicants for suitability for sales positions. It is in the long-term interests of the agencies to provide only strong candidates. The question remains, however, as to the likelihood of top salespeople needing to use agencies to find a suitable job.

Educational establishments

It is possible to recruit, straight from higher education, personnel who have, as part of their degree, worked in industry and commerce. Most business degree students in the UK have to undergo one year's industrial training. Some of these students may have worked in selling, others may have worked in marketing. The advantage of recruiting from universities is that the candidate is likely to be intelligent and may possess the required technical qualifications. It should be borne in mind that the applicant may not see his or her long-term future in selling, however. Rather, they may see a sales representative's position as a preliminary step to marketing management.

Competitors

The advantage of this source is that the salesperson knows the market and its customers, and the ability of the salesperson may be known to the recruiting company, thus reducing risk.

Other industries and unemployed

Both of these categories may provide applicants with sales experience. Obviously careful screening will need to take place in order to assess sales ability.

Communication

Although some sales positions are filled as a result of personal contact, the bulk of recruitment uses advertisements as the major communication tool. Figure 12.2 shows how large companies attract applicants from outside the company. It is advisable to be aware of a number of principles which can improve the communication effectiveness of advertisements.

There is a wide selection of national and regional newspapers for the advertiser to consider when placing an advertisement. A major problem with

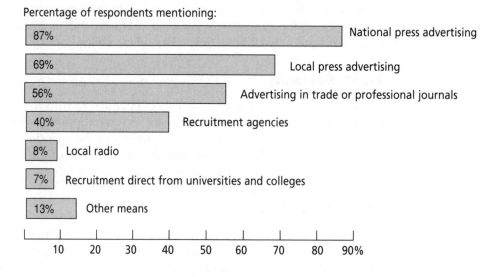

Percentage of respondents mentioning:

- 87% National press advertising
- 69% Local press advertising
- 56% Advertising in trade or professional journals
- 40% Recruitment agencies
- 8% Local radio
- 7% Recruitment direct from universities and colleges
- 13% Other means

10 20 30 40 50 60 70 80 90%

Figure 12.2 How companies attract applicants from outside the company
(Source: Jobber and Millar, 1984)

such classified recruitment advertising is impact. One method of achieving impact is size. The trick here is to select the newspaper(s), check the normal size of advertisement which appears in it, then simply make your advertisement a little bigger than the largest. This should ensure a good position and its size will give the advertisement impact. This method assumes, of course, adequate funds, although compared with selecting a lower-quality salesperson, the extra cost to many companies is small.

The other component of impact is the content of the advertisement, of which the headline is the most important ingredient simply because if it does not attract and is not read, then it is very unlikely that *any* of the advertisement will be read. An inspection of any Friday night regional newspaper will highlight the lack of imagination employed in designing the average sales representative recruitment advertisement. There is plenty of scope, therefore, to attract attention by being different. As in the case of size, look at the newspaper which is to be used and ask the question 'If I were contemplating changing jobs, what headline would attract my attention?'

Finally, if imagination is low and funds are high, it is worth considering employing a recruitment advertising specialist who will produce the advertisement and advise on media.

Whether the advertisement is produced by the company itself or by a recruitment specialist, it is important to ensure that all of the major attractions (not just features) of the job are included in the advertisement. This is necessary to attract applicants – the object of the exercise.

12.4 DESIGNING AN EFFECTIVE APPLICATION FORM AND PREPARING A SHORT-LIST

The application form is a quick and inexpensive method of screening out applicants in order to produce a **short-list** of candidates for interview. The questions on the form should enable the sales manager to check if the applicant is qualified *vis-à-vis* the personnel specification. Questions relating to age, education, previous work experience and leisure interests are often included. Besides giving such factual information, the application form also reveals defects such as an inability to spell, poor grammar or carelessness in following instructions.

The application form can reveal much about the person who is applying. Some applicants may be inveterate job-hoppers; others may have inadequate educational qualifications. Whatever the criteria, the application form will often be the initial screening device used to produce a short-list. Its careful design should, therefore, be a high priority for those involved in selection.

Four categories of information are usual on application forms:

1 *Personal*
- name
- address and telephone number
- sex
- marital status
- date of birth and age

2 *Education*
- schools: primary/secondary
- further and higher education: institutions, courses taken
- qualifications
- specialised training, e.g. apprenticeships, sales training
- membership of professional bodies, e.g. Chartered Institute of Marketing

3 *Employment history*
- companies worked for
- dates of employment
- positions, duties and responsibilities held
- military service

4 *Other interests*
- sports
- hobbies
- membership of societies/clubs

Such an application form will achieve a number of purposes:

- to give a common basis for drawing up a short-list;
- to provide a foundation of knowledge which can be used as the starting point for the interview;
- to aid in the post-interview decision-making stage.

Having eliminated a number of applicants on the basis of the application form, an initial or final short-list will be drawn up depending on whether the interviewing procedure involves two stages or only one stage. References may be sought for short-listed candidates or simply for the successful candidate.

12.5 THE INTERVIEW

The survey into the selection processes for salespeople of large UK companies (Jobber and Millar, 1984) identified a number of facts pertinent to the **interview**:

1 Most companies (80 per cent) employ two-stage interviews.
2 In only one-fifth of the cases does the sales manager alone hold the initial interview. In the majority of cases it is the personnel manager or the personnel manager and the sales manager together who conduct the initial interview. This tends to be the case at the final interview also.
3 In 40 per cent of the cases the personnel manager and the sales manager together make the final choice, and in 37 per cent of the cases the sales manager only makes the final decision. In other cases, marketing directors and other senior management may also be involved.

These facts highlight the importance of the sales manager in the selection process and indicate that selection normally follows two interviews – the screening interview and the selection interview. Already, if the procedures described so far have been followed, the sales manager will have produced a personnel specification including some or all of the factors outlined above and repeated here for convenience.

1 Physical requirements, e.g. speech, appearance, manner, fitness.
2 Attainments, e.g. standard of education, qualifications, sales experience and successes.
3 Aptitudes and qualities, e.g. ability to communicate, empathy, self-motivation.
4 Disposition, e.g. maturity, sense of responsibility.
5 Interests, e.g. identification of social interests, interests which are related to products which are being sold, active versus inactive interests.

The job specification will be used as a means of evaluating each of the short-listed candidates. In reality other, more personal considerations, will also play a part in the decision. A candidate whom the sales manager believes would be difficult to work with or might be a troublemaker is unlikely to be employed. Thus, inevitably, the decision will be based upon a combination of formal criteria and other more personal factors which the sales manager is unable or unwilling to express at the personnel specification stage.

Having carried out the essential preparation necessary to form the basis of selection, what are the objectives and principles of interviewing? The overall objective is to enable the interviewers to form a clear and valid impression of the strengths and weaknesses of the candidates in terms of the selection criteria. In order to do this all applicants must be encouraged to talk freely and openly about themselves. However, at the same time the interviewer(s) must exercise a degree of control in order that the candidate does not talk at too great length on one or two issues, leaving insufficient time for other equally important factors (possibly where the candidate is weaker) to be adequately discussed.

The interview setting

The interview setting will have a direct bearing on the outcome of the interview. A number of examples will illustrate this point:

1 A room where the sales manager is likely to be interrupted by colleagues or telephone calls is not ideal for interviewing. If such a room has to be used, visitors and telephone calls should be barred.
2 A very large room with just two or three people occupying it may not have the intimacy required to obtain a free, natural discussion.
3 A large desk situated between candidate and interviewer, particularly if littered with filing trays and desk calendars, can have the psychological effect of distancing the two parties involved, creating too formal an atmosphere and inhibiting rapport. A more relaxed, informal setting away from the manager's work desk is likely to enable the interviewee to relax more easily. The use of a

low table which interviewers and interviewee can sit around (rather than sitting face-to-face) is a common method for achieving this effect.

Conducting the interview

Besides creating the right atmosphere by the judicious selection of the interview setting, the interviewers themselves can do much to help establish rapport.

What happens at the beginning of the interview is crucial to subsequent events. The objective at this stage is to set the candidate at ease. Most interviewees are naturally anxious before the interview and when they first enter the interview setting. They may feel embarrassed or be worried about exposing weaknesses; they may feel inadequate and lack confidence; and above all they may feel worried about rejection. This anxiety is compounded by the fact that the candidate may never have met his interviewers before and may thus be uncertain about how aggressive they will be, the degree of pressure which will be applied and the types of question they are likely to ask. Some sales managers may argue that the salesperson is likely to meet this situation out in the field and therefore needs to be able to deal with it without the use of anxiety-reducing techniques on the part of the interviewers. A valid response to this viewpoint is that the objective of the interview is to get to know the candidate in terms of the criteria laid down in the personnel specification, or 'profile' as it is sometimes called. In order to do this candidates must be *encouraged* to talk about themselves. If sales ability under stress is to be tested, role playing can be used as part of the selection procedure.

There are a number of guidelines which, if followed, should reduce anxiety and establish rapport:

1 One of the interviewers (preferably the sales manager) should bring the candidate into the room, rather than the candidate being sent for through a secretary or junior administrator. This reduces status differentials and hence encourages rapport.
2 Open the conversation with a few easy-to-answer questions which, although not directly pertinent to the job, allow the candidate to talk to the interviewers and gain confidence.
3 Continuing in this vein, questions early in the interview should be, if possible, open-ended rather than closed. Open-ended questions allow the applicant scope for talking at some length on the topic, e.g. 'Can you tell me about your experiences selling pharmaceuticals?' Closed questions, on the other hand, invite a short answer, e.g. 'Can you tell me how long you worked for Beechams?' Some closed questions are inevitable but a series of them makes it difficult for the candidate to relax and gain confidence. Indeed, such questions may give the impression that the applicant is uncommunicative, when really the problem lies with the interviewer.
4 Interviewers should appear relaxed and adopt a friendly, easy manner.
5 They should be courteous and appear interested in what the applicant says.

Having successfully established rapport and reduced anxiety, the interviewer will wish to encourage candidates to talk about themselves, their experiences, attitudes, behaviour and expectations. To do this the interviewer not only needs to develop the art of being a good listener but also needs to develop skills in making people talk. The skills required in the needs analysis stage of the selling process discussed in Chapter 5 may be used in an interview to good effect. Specifically, the interviewer can use the following techniques:

● the 'playback' technique
● the use of rewards
● the use of silence
● the use of probes
● summarising
● the use of neutral questions.

The 'playback' technique

The interviewer repeats the last few words of the candidate's sentence in order to elicit the reason for what has been said. For example, the candidate might say 'I worked for XYZ Company for two years, but I didn't like it very much.' The interviewer follows with 'You didn't like it very much?' Candidate: 'No, the sales manager was always on my back, checking to see that I was making my calls.'

Use of rewards

Obvious interest in the candidate's views, experiences and knowledge shown by the interviewer confers its own reward. This can be supplemented by what can only be described as encouraging noises such as 'Uh uh' or 'Mmm, yes, I see.' The confidence which is instilled in the candidate will encourage further comment and, perhaps, revelations.

A further method of reward is through 'eye behaviour'. The subtle narrowing of the eyes, together with a slight nodding of the head can convey the message 'Yes, I see.' The correct use of such rewards comes only with experience, but their application is undoubtedly an aid in encouraging the candidate to talk freely.

The use of silence

Silence can be a very powerful ally of the interviewer. However, silence must be used with discretion, otherwise rapport may be lost and candidates may raise their barriers to open expression.

Its most common use is after the candidate has given a neutral, uninformative reply to an important question. A candidate, eager to impress, will feel uncomfortable, interpreting silence as an indication that the interview is not going well. In such a situation he or she will normally attempt to fill the void, and it may be that the only way he or she can do this is by revealing attitudes or behaviour patterns which otherwise he or she would have been happy to have kept hidden. Alternatively, the pause may allow the candidate to formulate his/her thoughts and thus stimulate a more considered reply. Continuing with a follow-up question without a pause would have precluded this happening. Either way, extra potentially revealing information can be collected by the discriminate use of silence.

The use of probes

The salesperson who is adept at needs analysis will be well acquainted with the use of probes. In an interview, comments will be made which require further explanation. For example, the applicant might say 'The time I spent on a sales training course was a waste of time,' to which the interviewer might say 'Why do you think that was?' or 'That's interesting, why do you say that?' or 'Can you explain a little more why you think that?' Such phrases are to be preferred to the blunt 'Why?' and are really alternatives to the 'playback' technique mentioned earlier.

A choice of phrases and techniques allows the interviewer to vary his approach to probing during the course of the interview. Although it may not always be possible to guarantee, probing of particularly embarrassing events such as the breakup of an applicant's marriage (if thought relevant to job performance) or failure in examinations, should be left until the interview is well under way and should certainly not be the subject of scrutiny at the start of the interview.

Summarising

During an interview, the interviewer will inevitably be attempting to draw together points which have been made by the applicant at various times during the interview in order to come to some opinion about the person under scrutiny. A useful device for checking if these impressions are valid in the subject's eyes is to summarise them and ask for his or her corroboration.

After a period of questioning and probing the interviewer might say 'So, as I understand it, your first period in sales was not a success because the firm you worked for produced poor-quality products, inferior in terms of technical specifications compared to competition and you felt inexperienced, but your second job, working with a larger, more well-known company, was more satisfactory, having received proper sales training and having the advantage of selling a recognised high-quality product line. Would you say that this was a fair summary?' Having obtained agreement, the interviewer can then move to another area of interest or continue to investigate the same area with the certainty that there has been no earlier misunderstanding.

The use of neutral questions

A basic principle of good interviewing is to use neutral rather than leading questions. The question, 'Can you tell me about the sales training you received at your previous employer?' is likely to lead to rather different, less biased responses than 'I'm sure you learnt a lot from your sales training courses, didn't you?' Again, 'What do you feel about dealing with the type of customer we have?' is more neutral than 'I'm sure you wouldn't have any problems dealing with our customers, would you?'

Other considerations

There are other considerations which an interviewer is wise to bear in mind. First, he must not talk too much. The object is for most of the time spent interviewing to be used to evaluate the candidates. Second, part of the interview will be a selling task in order to ensure that the chosen applicant accepts. The balance between evaluation and selling is largely based upon judgement, and no hard and fast rules apply, but obviously the competitive situation and the strength of the candidate will be two factors which affect the decision.

Third, the interviewer must discreetly control the interview. A certain amount of time will be allocated to each candidate and it is the interviewer's responsibility to ensure that all salient dimensions of the candidate are covered, not only those about which the candidate wishes to talk. Some of the earlier techniques, used in reverse, may be necessary to discourage the candidate from rambling on. For example, the interviewer may look uninterested, or ask a few closed questions to discourage verbosity. Alternatively, the interviewer can simply interrupt with 'That's fine. I think we're quite clear on that point now,' at an appropriate moment.

Finally, the interviewer will need to close the interview when sufficient information has been obtained. Usually, the candidate is forewarned of this by the interviewer saying 'OK, we've asked you about yourself, are there any questions you would like to ask me (us)?' At the end of this session, the interviewer explains when the decision will be made and how it will be communicated to the candidate and then thanks him or her for attending the interview. They both stand, shake hands and the candidate is shown to the door.

12.6 SUPPLEMENTARY SELECTION AIDS

Psychological tests

Although success at the interview is always an important determinant of selection, some firms employ supplementary techniques to provide a valid measure of potential. A number of large firms use **psychological tests** in this way. However, care has to be taken when using these tests and a trained psychologist is usually needed to administer and interpret the results. Further, there are a number of criticisms which have been levelled at the tests:

1 It is easy to cheat. The applicant, having an idea of the type of person who is likely to be successful at selling, does not respond truly but 'fakes' the test in

order to give a 'correct' profile. For example, in response to a question such as 'Who is of more value to society – the practical man or the thinker?' they answer 'the practical man' no matter what their true convictions may be.

2 Many tests measure interest rather than sales ability. The sales manager knows the interests of his/her successful salespeople and uses tests to discover if potential new recruits have similar interest patterns. The assumption here is that sales success can be predicted by the type of interests which a person has. This is as unlikely as discovering a new George Best by measuring the interests of young footballers.

3 Tests have been used to identify individual personality traits which may not be associated with sales success. Factors such as how sociable, dominant, friendly and loyal a person is have been measured in order to predict sales success. While some of these factors may be useful attributes for a salesperson to possess, they have failed to distinguish between high- and low-performing sales personnel.

Earlier in the chapter, reference was made to the use of the multiple personal inventory in order to predict the degrees of empathy and ego drive which a person possesses. Mayer and Greenberg have shown that sales success can be reasonably accurately predicted once these characteristics are known. The ideal is a person who possesses a high degree of both. A high degree of empathy (an ability to feel as the customer feels) and ego drive (the need to make a sale in a personal way) are usually associated with high sales performance. Plenty of empathy but little ego drive means that the salesperson is liked by the customers but sales are not made because of an inability to close the sale purposefully. A person with little empathy but much drive will tend to bulldoze his or her way through a sale without considering the individual needs of customers. Finally, the person with little empathy and ego drive will be a complete failure. Too many salespeople, say Mayer and Greenberg, fall into this last group.

The test itself – the multiple personal inventory – is based on the forced choice technique. The subject picks those statements which are most like and least like himself/herself from a choice of four. Two of these statements may be termed favourable and the other two unfavourable. Mayer and Greenberg claim that the test is difficult to fake, since the two favourable statements are chosen to be equally favourable and the two unfavourable ones are equally unfavourable. The subject, then, is likely to be truthful. Since it is very difficult to produce statements which are *equally* favourable or unfavourable, the cautious conclusion is that the forced choice technique minimises cheating rather than completely eliminating it. The test also overcomes the criticism that psychological tests measure personality traits which may not be correlated with performance. Mayer and Greenberg describe empathy and ego drive as the 'central dynamics' of sales ability and produce evidence that scores on these characteristics correlate well with performance in the car, insurance and mutual funds fields.

If the multiple personal inventory, or any other psychological test, is to be used as a basis for selection of sales personnel, a sensible procedure would be to validate the test beforehand. Research has shown that other personality tests correlate with performance and that different types of people do well in different selling situations. Randall (1975), for example, has shown that the type of person who was most successful selling tyres could be summarised as a 'grey man'. His characteristics were those of a humble, shy, tender-minded person of below-average intelligence, quite unlike the stereotyped extrovert, happy-go-lucky, fast-talking salesperson. The explanation of why such a person was successful was to be found in the selling situation. Being in the position of selling a brand of tyre that was not widely advertised and that had only a small market share, the salesperson had to hang around tyre depots hoping to make sales by solving some of the supply problems of the depot manager in meeting urgent orders. He was able to do this because his company provided a quicker service than many of its competitors. Thus, the personality of the man had to be such that he was prepared to wait around the depot merging into the background, rather than by using persuasive selling techniques.

This rather extreme example demonstrates how varied the sales situation can be. Contrast that situation with the skills and personality required to sell hi-fi equipment, and it becomes immediately apparent that successful selection should focus on matching particular types of people to particular types of selling occupations. Indeed Greenberg, since his earlier study, does seem to have moved position and recognised that successful selling depends on other personality dynamics 'which come into play depending on the specific sales situation' (Greenberg and Greenberg, 1976). Consequently different psychological tests may be required for different situations.

Validation requires the identification of the psychological test or tests which best distinguish between a company's above-average and below-average existing salespeople. Further validation would test how the predictions made by the test results correlate with performance of new recruits. Recent research has cast doubt on the general applicability of the empathy/ego drive theory of sales success, but certainly the multiple personal inventory could be one psychological test used in this validation exercise, although it must be carried out under the supervision of a psychologist.

Finally, it must be stressed that the proper place of psychological tests is alongside the interview, as a basis for selection, rather than in place of it.

Role-playing

Another aid in the selection of salespeople is the use of **role-playing** in order to gauge the selling potential of candidates. This involves placing them individually in selling situations and assessing how well they perform.

The problem with this technique is that, at best, it measures sales ability at that moment. This may depend, among other things, on previous sales experience. Correct assessment of salespeople, however, should be measuring *potential*. Further, role-playing cannot assess the candidate's ability to establish and handle long-term relationships with buyers and so is more applicable to those selling jobs where the salesperson/buyer relationship is likely to be short-term, and the sale a one-off. Role-playing may, however, be valuable in identifying the 'hopeless case', whose personal characteristics, e.g. an inability to communicate or to keep his/her temper under stress, may preclude them from successful selling.

12.7 CONCLUSIONS

The selection of salespeople, while of obvious importance to the long-term future of the business, is a task which does not always receive the attention it should from sales managers. All too often, the 'person profile' is ill-defined and the selection procedure designed for maximum convenience rather than optimal choice. The assumption is that the right candidate should emerge whatever procedure is used. Consequently the interview is poorly handled, the smooth talker gets the job, and another mediocre salesperson emerges.

This chapter has outlined a number of techniques which, if applied, should minimise this result. Specifically, a sales manager should decide on the requirements of the job and the type of person who should be able to fulfil them. He or she should also be aware of the techniques of interviewing and the necessity of evaluating the candidates, in line with the criteria established during the personnel specification stage. Finally, the sales manager should consider the use of psychological tests (under the guidance of a psychologist) and role playing as further dimensions of the assessment procedure.

The next chapter examines two further key areas of sales management: motivation and training.

PRACTICAL EXERCISE

Plastic Products Ltd

Plastic Products Ltd is a company that produces and markets plastic cups, teaspoons, knives and forks for the catering industry. The company was established in 1974 in response to the changes taking place in the catering industry. The growth of the fast-food sector of the market was seen as an opportunity to provide disposable eating utensils which would save on human resources and allow the speedy provision of utensils for fast customer flow. In addition, Plastic Products has benefited from the growth in supermarkets and sells 'consumer packs' through four of the large supermarket groups.

The expansion of sales and outlets has led Jim Spencer, the sales manager, to recommend to Bill Preedy, the general manager, that the present salesforce of two regional representatives be increased to four.

Spencer believes that the new recruits should have experience of selling fast-moving consumer goods since essentially that is what his products are.

Preedy believes that the new recruits should be familiar with plastic products since that is what they are selling. He favours recruiting from within the plastics industry, since such people are familiar with the supply, production and properties of plastic and are likely to talk the same language as other people working at the firm.

DISCUSSION QUESTIONS

1 What general factors should be taken into account when recruiting salespeople?

2 Do you agree with Spencer or Preedy or neither?

EXAMINATION QUESTIONS

1 Distinguish between the job description and the personnel specification. For an industry of your choice, write a suitable job description and personnel specification for a salesperson.

2 Discuss the role of psychological testing in the selection process for salespeople.

13

MOTIVATION AND TRAINING

OBJECTIVES After studying this chapter, you should be able to:

1 Understand certain motivation theories in the context of selling.

2 Apply motivation in practice.

3 Set sales targets and quotas.

4 Organise suitable sales training programmes and evaluate their usefulness.

KEY CONCEPTS
- group meetings
- Herzberg's dual factor theory
- Likert's sales management theory
- Maslow's hierarchy of needs
- merit-based promotion system
- sales contests
- sales quotas
- sales targets
- training programmes
- Vroom's expectancy theory

13.1 MOTIVATION

Creating and maintaining a well-motivated salesforce is a challenging task. The confidence and motivation of salespeople are being constantly worn down by the inevitable rejections they suffer from buyers as part of everyday activities. In some fields, notably life insurance and double glazing, rejections may greatly outnumber successes; thus motivation may be a major problem. This is compounded by the fact that salesperson and supervisor are normally geographically separated, so that the salesperson may feel isolated, even neglected, unless management pays particular attention to motivational strategies which take account of his or her needs.

It is critical that sales managers appreciate that motivation is far more sophisticated than the view that all salespeople need is a 'kick up the pants'. Effective motivation requires a deep understanding of salespeople as individuals, their personalities and value systems. In a sense, sales managers do not motivate salespeople; what they do is provide the circumstances that will encourage salespeople to motivate themselves.

An understanding of motivation lies in the relationship between needs, drives and goals. 'The basic process involves needs (deprivations) which set drives in motion (deprivations with direction) to accomplish goals (anything which alleviates a need and reduces a drive)' (Luthans, 1981). Thus a need resulting from a lack of friends, sets up a drive for affiliation which is designed to obtain friends. In a work context, the need for more money may result in a drive to work harder in order to obtain increased pay.

In this chapter both applied theory and practice will be evaluated in order to identify the means of motivating a salesforce.

Motivational theories

Motivation has been researched by psychologists and others for many years. A number of theories have evolved which are pertinent to the motivation of salespeople. These are the theories of Maslow (1943), Herzberg *et al.* (1959), Vroom (1964), Adams (1965) and Likert (1961).

Maslow's hierarchy of needs

Maslow's classic **hierarchy of needs** model proposed that there are five fundamental needs which are arranged in a 'hierarchy of prepotency'. Table 13.1 shows this hierarchy.

Table 13.1 Maslow's hierarchy of needs

Category	Type	Characteristics
Physical	1 Physiological	The fundamentals of survival, e.g. hunger, thirst
	2 Safety	Protection from the unpredictable happenings in life, e.g. accidents, ill health
Social	3 Belongingness and love	Striving to be accepted by those to whom we feel close (especially one's family) and to be an important person to them
	4 Esteem and status	Striving to achieve a high standing relative to other people; a desire for prestige and a high reputation
Self	5 Self-actualisation	The desire for self-fulfilment in achieving what one is capable of for one's own sake – 'Actualised in what he is potentially' (Maslow)

Maslow argued that needs form a hierarchy in the sense that, when no needs are fulfilled, a person concentrates upon his or her physiological needs. When these needs are fulfilled, safety needs become preponderant and become important determinants of behaviour. When these are satisfied, belongingness becomes important – and so on up the hierarchy.

Although Maslow's belief that one set of needs only becomes important after lower-order needs have been completely satisfied, has been criticised, the theory does have relevance to salesforce motivation. First, it highlights the perhaps obvious point that a satisfied need is not a motivator of behaviour. Thus, for a salesperson who already receives a more than adequate level of remuneration, additional payments may have no effect on motivation. Second, the theory implies that what may act as a motivator for one salesperson may not be effective with another. This follows from the likelihood that different salespeople will have different combinations of needs.

Effective motivation results from an accurate assessment of the needs of the individual salespeople under the manager's supervision. The overriding need for one salesperson may be reassurance and the building of confidence; this may act to motivate him or her. For another, with a great need for esteem but a problem regarding work rate, the sales manager may motivate by displaying to colleagues at a sales meeting his or her relatively poor sales performance.

Herzberg

Herzberg's **dual factor theory** distinguished factors which can cause dissatisfaction but cannot motivate (hygiene factors) and factors which can cause positive motivation. Hygiene factors included physical working conditions, security, salary and interpersonal relationships. Directing managerial attention to these factors, postulated Herzberg, would bring motivation up to a 'theoretical zero' but would not result in positive motivation. If this were to be achieved, attention would have to be given to true motivators. These included the nature of the work itself which allows the person to make some concrete *achievement*, *recognition* of achievement, the *responsibility* exercised by the person, and the *interest value* of the work itself.

The inclusion of salary as a hygiene factor rather than as a motivator was subject to criticisms from sales managers whose experience led them to believe that commission paid to their salespeople was a powerful motivator in practice. Herzberg accommodated their view to some extent by arguing that increased salary through higher commission was a motivator through the automatic recognition it gave to sales achievement.

The salesperson is fortunate that achievement is directly observable in terms of higher sales (except in missionary selling, where orders are not taken, e.g. pharmaceuticals, beer and selling to specifiers). However, the degree of responsibility afforded to salespeople varies a great deal. Opportunities for giving a greater degree of responsibility to (and hence motivating) salespeople include giving authority to grant credit (up to a certain value), discretion to offer discounts, and handing over responsibility for calling frequencies to the salespeople. The results of an experiment with a group of British salespeople by Paul, Robertson and Herzberg (1969) showed that greater responsibility given to salespeople by such changes resulted in higher sales success.

Herzberg's theory has been well received, in general, by practitioners, although academics have criticised it in terms of methodology and oversimplification (see Dessler, 1979). The theory has undoubtedly made a substantial contribution to the understanding of motivation at work, particularly in extending Maslow's theory to the work situation, and highlighting the importance of job content factors which had hitherto been badly neglected.

Vroom's expectancy theory

Basically this theory assumes that a person's motivation to exert effort is dependent upon his expectations for success. Vroom (1964) based his theory on three concepts – **expectancy**, **instrumentality** and **valence**.

1 *Expectancy*. This refers to a person's perceived relationship between effort and performance, i.e. to the extent to which a person believes that increased effort will lead to higher performance.
2 *Instrumentality*. This reflects the person's perception of the relationship between performance and reward; for example, it reflects the extent to which a person believes that higher performance will lead to promotion.
3 *Valence*. This represents the value placed upon a particular reward by a person. For some individuals promotion may be highly valued, for others it may have little value.

Thus, according to the theory, if a salesperson believes that by working harder he or she will achieve increased sales (high expectancy), and that higher sales will lead to greater commission (high instrumentality) and higher commission is very important (high valence), a high level of motivation should result. The nature of the relationships in the sales setting is depicted in Figure 13.1.

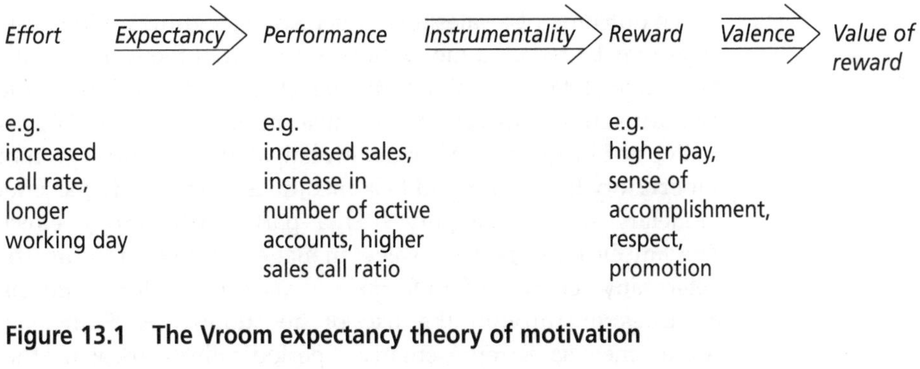

Effort → *Expectancy* → Performance → *Instrumentality* → Reward → *Valence* → Value of reward

e.g.	e.g.	e.g.
increased call rate, longer working day	increased sales, increase in number of active accounts, higher sales call ratio	higher pay, sense of accomplishment, respect, promotion

Figure 13.1   The Vroom expectancy theory of motivation

Clearly, different salespeople will have different valences (values) for the same reward. Some might value increased pay very highly, while for others higher pay may have less value; for some the sense of accomplishment and recognition may be very important, for others much less so. Also, different salespeople may view the relationship between performance and reward, and between effort and performance, in quite different ways. A task of sales management is to specify and communicate to the salesforce these performance criteria, which are important in helping to achieve company objectives, and to relate rewards to these criteria. Further, this theory supports the notion that performance targets, e.g. sales quotas, to be effective motivators, should be regarded as attainable (high expectancy) by each salesperson, otherwise the first link in the expectancy model will be severed. Finally, this model provides a diagnostic framework for analysing motivational problems with individual salespeople and provides an explanation of why certain managerial activities can improve motivation. Training in sales skills, for example, can improve motivation by raising expectancy levels.

Adams's inequity theory

Feelings of inequity (unfairness) can arise when an individual's effort or performance on the job exceeds the reward which he or she receives. Salespeople who feel they contribute more than others to the organisation expect to receive proportionately greater rewards. This is the essence of Adams's **inequity theory**. For a salesperson inequity can be felt in the following areas:

● monetary rewards
● workload
● promotion
● degree of recognition
● supervisory behaviour
● targets
● tasks.

The outcome of a salesperson perceiving significant inequities in any of these areas may be reduced motivation as a result of the feeling of unfairness. A study by Tyagi (1990) examined the effect of perceived inequities (rewards and favouritism) on motivation of life insurance salespeople. The results showed that feelings of inequity in all areas investigated (monetary, promotion, recognition, supervisory behaviour and task inequities) had an adverse effect on motivation. Monetary reward inequity had a particularly strong effect on motivation. The implication is that sales managers must monitor their salesforce to detect any feelings of unfairness. This can be done informally during sales meetings or through the use of questionnaires. Some sales organisations survey their sales representatives periodically to measure their perceptions of inequity and the effectiveness of the company's motivational programme in general.

Motivation is often equated with incentives but Adams's work emphasises that the elimination of disincentives (e.g. injustices, unfair treatment) may be an equally powerful influence.

Likert's sales management theory

Unlike Herzberg, Maslow and Vroom, who developed 'general' theories of motivation, Likert (1961) based his theories on research which looked specifically at the motivation of salespeople. His research related differing **characteristics and styles of supervision** to performance. One of the hypotheses he tested was that the sales managers' own behaviour provides a set of standards which, in themselves, will affect the behaviour of their salespeople. He found that there was a link. High performing sales teams usually had sales managers who themselves had high performance goals.

His research also investigated the methods used by sales managers in the running of sales meetings. Two alternative styles were compared (see Figure 13.2). Sales managers who used the group method of leading sales meetings encouraged their team both to discuss sales problems which had arisen in the field and to learn from one another. Sales managers who monopolised the meeting discouraged interaction between salespeople and used the meeting as an opportunity to lecture them rather than to stimulate discussion. There was a strong tendency for higher-producing sales teams to use the group method.

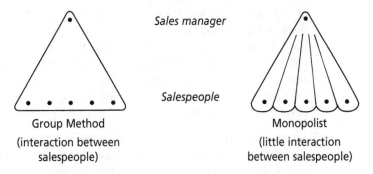

Sales manager

Salespeople

Group Method
(interaction between
salespeople)

Monopolist
(little interaction
between salespeople)

Figure 13.2   Methods of conducting sales meetings

Several reasons can be put forward to explain this. First, it is likely that a problem faced by one salesperson has been met previously by another who may have found a way of overcoming it; for example, a troublesome objection to one salesperson may have been successfully dealt with by another. The group method of leading a sales meeting, then, encourages problem-solving and stimulates communication. Second, the more open style of meeting enables the sales manager to gain a greater understanding of the needs and problems of the salesforce. Finally, the group method promotes a feeling of group loyalty since it fosters a spirit of co-operation.

The research conducted by Likert, then, suggests that, to produce a highly motivated salesforce, the sales manager himself/herself should have high performance goals and encourage analysis and discussion of salespeople's performance and problems through the group method of conducting sales meetings.

The Churchill, Ford and Walker model of salesforce motivation

Churchill, Ford and Walker (1992) developed a model of salesforce motivation that integrated some of the ideas of Herzberg and Vroom (see Figure 13.3). This suggests that the higher the salesperson's motivation, the greater the effort, leading to higher performance. This enhanced performance will lead to greater rewards which will bring about higher job satisfaction. The circle will be completed by the enhanced satisfaction causing still higher motivation.

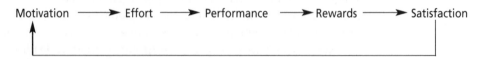

Figure 13.3   Salesforce motivation

The implications for sales managers are as follows:

1 they should convince salespeople that they will sell more by working harder or by being trained to work 'smarter' (e.g. more efficient call planning, developing selling skills);
2 they should convince salespeople that the rewards for better performance are worth the extra effort. This implies that the sales manager should give rewards that are valued, and attempt to 'sell' the worth of those rewards to the salesforce. For example, a sales manager might build up the worth of a holiday prize by stating what a good time he or she personally had when there.

They also found that the value of rewards differed according to salesperson type. Older salespeople who had large families valued financial rewards more. Younger, better educated salespeople who had no or small families tended to value higher-order rewards (recognition, liking and respect, sense of accomplishment) more.

Motivation in practice

A study into salesforce practice commissioned by the Chartered Institute of Marketing (PA Consultants, 1979) asked sales managers to rank eight factors (excluding salary, bonus or commission) which could be effective in stimulating their salespeople to better their usual performance. The results of this research are given in Figure 13.4.

Figure 13.4 illustrates the importance of the manager/salesperson relationship in motivation. Individual meetings between sales manager and salesperson were thought to be the most effective of the eight factors investigated. Sales contests and competitions were ranked only sixth in importance, although a more detailed analysis of the answers revealed that this form of motivation was ranked first among the consumer goods companies replying to the questionnaire.

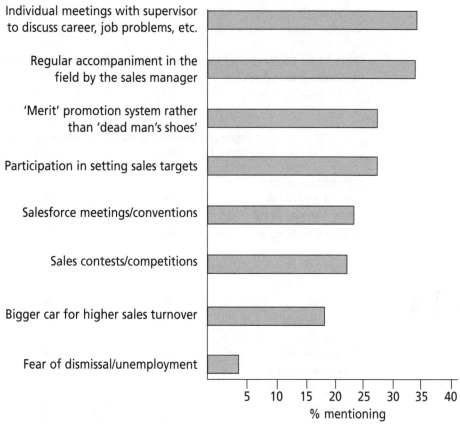

Figure 13.4 Motivating factors for salespeople

More recent surveys by Shipley and Kiely (1988) and Coulaux and Jobber (1989) investigated factors which motivated industrial and consumer goods salespeople. In both surveys self-satisfaction from doing a good job was ranked as the top motivator; achieving targets and acknowledgement of effort were also highly ranked by both industrial and consumer salespeople. However, a major difference was the factor 'satisfy customer needs' with industrial salespeople ranking it second while their consumer counterparts ranked it only sixth. The difference between industrial and consumer products and customers probably explains the discrepancy with the former selling more technical products to customers with more complex needs (see Table 13.2).

Some of these factors, along with financial incentives, will now be evaluated in terms of their potential to motivate.

Financial incentives

Most companies, whether they be selling consumer or industrial goods, pay commission or bonus to their salespeople. The most usual form of payment is the salary plus commission system since this provides a level of security plus the incentive of higher earnings for higher sales. However, in some instances salespeople are paid on a straight commission basis so that earnings are entirely dependent upon achievement.

Table 13.2 Motivational factors for salespeople in industrial and consumer goods markets

	Industrial			Consumer		
	Extremely strong	Moderately strong	Ranking*	Extremely strong	Moderately strong	Ranking*
Self-satisfaction from doing a good job	75	24	1	75	21	1
Satisfy customer needs	51	39	2	36	46	6
Achieve sales budgets	35	46	3	58	35	2
Acknowledgement of effort	36	43	3	50	37	4
Increase chance of promotion	89	29	5	58	31	3
Improve lifestyle	34	35	6	42	33	6
Meet family responsibilities	40	22	6	44	25	8
Make more money	38	22	8	46	33	5
Satisfy sales manager's expectations	24	32	9	29	35	9

*Note that the ranking is based on the sum of responses to extremely strong and moderately strong motivator with double weighting to the former category.

Sources: Industrial – Shipley and Kiely (1988); Consumer – Coulaux and Jobber (1989)

There are a number of variants of the commission system, each depending on the outcome of the following decisions (Kotler, 1999):

1 the commission base, e.g. sales revenue, or profits;
2 the commission rate, e.g. a set percentage of all sales or different for various products;
3 the starting point for commission, e.g. the first sale, or at some predetermined sales level.

A commission system may thus comprise a given percentage, e.g. 1½ per cent of total sales revenue generated per salesperson, or a percentage, e.g. 5 per cent of sales revenue for all sales in excess of a sales quota. Some companies may construct more complicated commission systems whereby different products have varying commission rates. Higher rates may be paid on higher-profit items, lines which are regarded as being harder to sell or products with high inventory levels. Thus the commission system can be used not only to stimulate greater effort in general but also to direct salespeople towards expending greater energy on those products the company particularly wants to sell.

Commission may work in motivating salespeople through providing a direct reward for extra effort (Vroom) and by giving recognition for achievement (Herzberg).

Setting sales targets or quotas

If a **sales target** or **quota** is to be effective in motivating a salesperson it must be regarded as fair and attainable and yet offer a challenge to him/her. Because the salesperson should regard the quota as fair, it is usually sensible to allow him or her to participate in the setting of the quota. However, the establishment of the quotas is ultimately the sales manager's responsibility and he or she will inevitably be constrained by overall company objectives. If sales are planned to increase by 10 per cent, then salespeople's quotas must be consistent with this. Variations around this average figure will arise through the sales manager's knowledge of individual sales personnel and changes in commercial activity within each territory; for example, the liquidation of a key customer in a territory may be reflected in a reduced quota. The attainment of a sales target usually results in some form of extra payment to the salesperson.

Meetings between manager and salespeople

These were highly regarded by sales managers in the motivation of their sales teams. Managers have the opportunity to meet their salespeople in the field, at head office and at sales meetings/conventions. They provide a number of opportunities for improving motivation.

First, they allow the sales manager to understand the personality, needs and problems of each salesperson. The manager can then better understand the causes of motivation and demotivation in individual salespeople and respond in a manner that takes into account the needs, problems and personality of the salesperson. A study by Jobber and Lee (1994) showed the extent to which the perceptions of sales management and salespeople towards motivation and demotivation can differ. They investigated the perceptions of what motivates and demotivates salespeople by asking a sample of life assurance salespeople and their sales directors. Figure 13.5 gives a summary of the results.

Sales management thought that competitions/prizes and incentives based on target setting motivated salespeople significantly more than the salespeople did themselves. Salespeople, on the other hand, valued fringe benefits higher than sales management. Perceptions of demotivating issues were also at variance. Sales management believed supervisory relations and personal problems demotivated salespeople significantly more than the salespeople did themselves, whereas the salespeople believed that lack of advancement, lack of security and long hours of work were more a source of demotivation than did sales management. Such misunderstandings can lead to wasted managerial effort devising motivational schemes and compensation plans which are not valued by salespeople. The remedy is to meet regularly with the salesforce to understand their value systems so that what is prescribed by management is effective in raising salesforce motivation.

	Motivators	Demotivators
Sales directors value these factors more highly	Competitions/prizes Incentives based on target setting	Supervisory relations Personal problems
Sales representatives value these factors more highly	Fringe benefits	Lack of advancement Lack of security Hours of work

Figure 13.5 Summary of differences between sales directors and sales representatives

Second, meetings in the field, which may form part of an evaluation and training programme, can also provide an opportunity to motivate. Sales technique can be improved and confidence boosted, both of which may motivate by restoring in the salesperson the belief that performance will improve through extra effort.

Third, **group meetings** can motivate, according to Likert, when the sales manager encourages an 'open' style of meeting. Salespeople are encouraged to discuss their sales problems and opportunities so that the entire sales team benefits from the experiences of each salesperson. This leads to a greater sense of group loyalty and improved performance. Finally, meetings between manager and salespeople provide the opportunity for performance feedback where weaknesses are identified and recognition for good work is given.

The study by Coulaux and Jobber (1989) found that almost half their sample of consumer salespeople wanted more meetings with their sales managers. Table 13.3 shows the topics which they would most like to discuss. Three-quarters of the salespeople said that they would like more opportunity to analyse job problems and try to find a solution with their sales managers. Sales targets were second on the list of issues which they would like to discuss.

The work by Herzberg highlights the importance of **recognition** as a positive motivator and Maslow suggests that many people have a need to be accepted. Thus what sales managers say to their salespeople can have both motivational and demotivational effects, by giving and/or taking away recognition and acceptance. Giving recognition and acceptance (by a pat on the back or praise, for example) are called *positive strokes* and can act as a motivator; withdrawing recognition and acceptance (for example by criticising or ignoring the person) are called *negative strokes* and can act as both a motivator or a demotivator depending on the circumstances. Such withdrawal can motivate when the

Table 13.3 Topics salespeople would like to discuss more with their sales managers

Matters	%
Analyse job problems and try to find solutions together	75
Sales targets	70
Job problems	68
Promotion	45
Job career	45
Review performance together	30
Remuneration	22
Personal problems	22

salesperson is underperforming through lack of effort and that person has a strong desire for recognition and acceptance. However, many managers can demotivate almost unknowingly by what they say and do. Outside factors such as domestic problems may cause managers to give out negative strokes to people who do not deserve them. Under such circumstances they can have a demotivational effect. Table 13.4 gives a few examples.

Table 13.4 Positive and negative strokes

Strokes	Physical contact	Psychological
Positive	Handshake Pat on the back	Praise, smile, appreciative glance
Negative	Push Slap	Criticism, ridicule, ignore, sideways glance, frown

A further example of the use of negative strokes was the sales manager of a financial services company who wanted to reduce his salesforce's expenses bill. The salespeople were provided with BMWs. To their astonishment the sales manager declared that from the following month the salesperson with the highest expenses would get to drive the company's new Skoda!

Promotion

Sales managers believe that a **merit-based promotional system** does act as a motivator. If the promotion is to a managerial position, there are grave dangers of promoting the company's best salesperson. The skills required of a sales manager are wider than those required of a salesperson. A sales manager must be able to analyse and control the performance of others, motivate and train them. These are skills which are not required to sell successfully.

If promotion is to be tied to sales performance, it is sensible to consider the creation of a dual promotional route. The first path follows the normal managerial career sequence. The other is created to reward outstanding sales success. An example of such a merit-based promotional ladder is:

Salesperson → Senior Salesperson → National Account Executive

Sales contests

Sales contests are a popular form of incentive for consumer salesforces. The purpose of the sales contest varies widely. It may be to encourage a higher level of sales in general, to increase the sales of a slow-moving product or to reward the generation of new customers. The strength of a sales contest lies in its ability to appeal to the competitive spirit of salespeople and to their need for achievement and recognition. As with other financial incentives, to be effective the contest must be seen to be fair and each salesperson must believe that he or she is capable of winning.

However, problems can occur. Contests can encourage cheating. In one company which used a sales contest to promote sales at a series of promotional events around the country with its dealers, salespeople 'stored up' orders achieved prior to the events in order to increase the apparent number of orders taken at the events. Also, contests, by pitching salesperson against salesperson, militate against the spirit of mutual help and co-operation which can improve salesforce performance.

Sales managers need to be sensitive to the differences in cultural ideas and expectations of overseas salespeople when devising motivational programmes. Examples of how such differences can impact on salesforce motivation are given in the following case discussion.

SELLING
AND SALES
MANAGEMENT
IN ACTION

Motivating international salespeople

The key to selecting appropriate salesperson motivation and compensation systems is to understand their values and expectations, and not assume that what works at home will work in foreign markets. For example, in Europe money is often viewed as a key motivator whereas in the Middle East and Japan commission is little used, and non-financial factors such as increased responsibilities or higher job security are more effective. An understanding of local customs is required. For example, in Japan salary increases are usually based on seniority. Political factors can also determine the fixed salary/commission split and the level of fringe benefits provided for employees.

Perceptions of unfairness can arise when the overseas salesforce consists of a mixture of expatriates and local sales people. Because a salary increase normally accompanies an expatriate's overseas move, they may be paid more than local recruits. If this becomes common knowledge, the motivation of locally recruited salespeople may suffer.

Based on: Cundiff, E. and Hilger, M.T. (1988) 'Marketing in the International Environment', Prentice-Hall, Englewood Cliffs N.J.; and Hill, J.S., Still, R.R. and Boya, U.O. (1991) 'Managing the multinational sales force', *International Marketing Review*, 8(1), pp. 19–31.

13.2 TRAINING

A study for the Learning International Organization (1988) revealed seven sales challenges that organisations must meet if they are going to survive in the competitive marketplace:

1 *Distinguish between similar products and services.* Success in sales requires more than just having an exceptional product or service. The proliferation of 'me too' products is causing buyers to become confused. Excellent salespeople are needed to capitalise on product differences: that their offerings are better than the competitor's.

2 *Putting together groups of products to form a business solution.* As customers' requirements are continually becoming more complex, single product or service selling is becoming obsolete. Their needs can only be met by a 'package' of products or services. The salesperson will have to be highly trained to put together a package to satisfy these needs.

3 *Handling the more educated buying population.* Today's customers are willing to work harder and take the time to shop around for what they need. They are also more aware of the product features, benefits, options and prices. Today's professional salesperson must thus work harder to close the sale.

4 *Mastering the art of consultative selling.* The salesperson now needs to understand the specific business issues and problems faced by customers. His or her role is to lessen customers' responsibility to discover their own needs, and show how the product and service being offered will fill these needs.

5 *Managing a team selling approach.* In the future a team selling approach will have to be adopted to satisfy customer needs. The salesperson will have to draw on knowledge of technical staff, marketing staff, and experts in other product areas.

6 *Knowing the customer's business.* Future sales will require in-depth knowledge of the customer's business, with salespeople well versed in the requirements of the market segment in which they sell. Relationship building with the customer is paramount and the customer's best interests are always placed at the forefront. Accurate marketing information is needed to provide each customer with the best possible service.

7 *Adding value through service.* When a product reaches a commodity status the salesperson's perceived value is diminished. They are reduced to 'order takers'. Companies must continue to build up their relationship with customers by adding value through services such as business consultations and ongoing product support.

These challenges have assumed greater importance since the advent of the Single European Market. For the first time there is easy access to the European markets. Thus competition has increased, and it is only companies who are prepared to meet these challenges that will survive.

Producing the best available product or service is not enough; it has to be sold. If companies are to survive they must attach the utmost importance to training their field salesforce, not just pay lip service to the concept. Top management must be totally committed to training and authorise sufficient investment for this to occur. They must also accept that the benefits deriving from sales training may not be immediate; they take time to show through.

On the whole, insufficient attention is paid to training. Presumably it is believed that salespeople will learn the necessary skills on the job. This approach ignores the benefits of a training programme which builds a reference frame within which learning can occur and provides the opportunity to practise skills with feedback which is necessary to identify the strengths and weaknesses of performance. For training to succeed the salesperson must accept that there is a problem with his or her performance, otherwise he/she is unlikely to try to rectify the problem.

Another approach to the training problem of new salespeople is to send them out with an experienced salesperson to observe how selling is done. This, in itself, is insufficient for successful sales training. Its virtues are that the trainee may gain insights not only into techniques which appear to be successful in selling, for example, certain closing techniques, but also into the kinds of objections which are raised by buyers. However, its value is greatly enhanced if supplemented by a formal sales training programme conducted by an experienced sales trainer who is skilled in lecturing, handling role-playing sessions and providing constructive feedback in such a way that it is accepted by the trainee.

Sales training provides particular challenges in the international environment. Differences in language and culture mean that care must be taken when training overseas sales teams. The following case discussion addresses some major points.

SELLING AND SALES MANAGEMENT IN ACTION

Training overseas salesforces

When training local salespeople cultural imperatives should be recognised. For example, when training Chinese and Japanese salespeople situations where 'loss of face' can occur should be avoided. Japanese salespeople receive on-the-job training in a ritualistic formal setting to ensure that constructive criticism does not result in 'loss of face' for the inexperienced salesperson. Also some selling approaches may not be applicable in certain cultures. For example, problem solving techniques may not be suitable for Chinese or Japanese salespeople. Finally, care needs to be exercised when translating sales manuals into foreign languages.

For local recruits, training will include product knowledge and an appreciation of the company, its history and philosophies. For expatriates, language training may be required and familiarity with foreign business etiquette. Often initial on-the-job training is with an experienced expatriate. Training in the language, lifestyle and culture of the people of the new country should include the salesperson's spouse and children to reduce early burnout.

Based on Hill, J.S., Still, R.R. and Boya, U.O. (1991) 'Managing the multinational sales force', *International Marketing Review*, 8(1) pp. 19–31; Honeycutt, Jr, E.D. and Ford, J.B. (1995) 'Guidelines for managing an international sales force', *Industrial Marketing Management*, 24, pp. 135–144.

Skill development

There are four classic stages to learning a skill. These are shown in Table 13.5.

Table 13.5   Skills development

Stage	Description
1 Unconsciously unable	Trainee does not think about skills
2 Consciously unable	Trainee reads about skills but cannot carry them out in practice
3 Consciously able	Trainee knows what to do and is reasonably proficient in individual skills but has difficulty putting them all into practice together
4 Unconsciously able	Trainee can perform the task without thinking about it; skills become automatic

The first stage defines the situation before a trainee decides to enter a career in selling. He or she is unable to carry out the skills and has not even thought about them. By reading or being told about the skills involved the trainee reaches the stage of being consciously unable. He or she knows what he or she is supposed to do but cannot successfully perform any of the skills.

At the next stage (consciously able) the trainee not only knows what to do but is reasonably proficient at putting the skills into practice individually. He/she is like a learner driver who can engage gear, release the clutch, look in the mirror, gently press the accelerator and release the handbrake as a series of separate operations, but not in a co-ordinated manner which successfully moves the car from a standing start. The trainee may be able to make a presentation successfully, to handle objections and to close a sale, but he or she may be hopelessly adrift when he/she needs to handle objections, continue making the presentation and all the while look for signs to close the sale.

A successful training programme takes the trainee through this difficult barrier to the final stage (unconsciously able) when he or she can perform all of the skills at once and has the ability to think a stage in advance so that he/she has control of the selling situation. A car driver reaches this stage when he/she can co-ordinate the skills necessary to start, move and stop a car without thinking; the timing of gear changes and braking, for example, become automatic, without conscious thought. Similarly, the salesperson can open the interview, move through the stages of need identification, presentation and handling objections in a natural manner, and can alter his or her approach as situations demand, before choosing the right moment and most appropriate technique to close the sale.

When a salesperson becomes unconsciously able he or she is likely to be a competent salesperson although, like a driver, football player or cricketer, there will always be room for further improvement and refinement of his or her skills.

Components of a training programme

A **training programme** will attempt to cover a combination of knowledge and skill development. Five components can be identified:

1 The company – objectives, policies and organisation.
2 Its products.
3 Its competitors and their products.
4 Selling procedure and techniques.
5 Work organisation and report preparation.

The first three components are essentially communicating the required level of knowledge to the salesperson. The first component will probably include a brief history of the company, how it has grown and where it intends to go in the future. Policies relevant to the selling function, for example how salespeople are evaluated, and the nature of the compensation system will be explained. The way in which the company is organised will be described and the relationship between sales and the marketing function, including advertising and market research, will be described so that the salesperson has an appreciation of the support he or she is receiving from headquarters.

The second component, product knowledge, will include a description of how the products are made and the implications for product quality and reliability, the features of the product and the benefits they confer on the consumer. Salespeople will be encouraged to carry out their own product analyses so that they will be able to identify key features and benefits of new products as they are launched. Competitors will be identified and competitors' products will also be analysed to spotlight differences between them and the company's products.

Some training programmes, particularly within the industrial selling arena, stop here, neglecting a major component of a training programme – selling procedures and techniques. This component involves an examination of the factors analysed in Chapter 5 and will include practical sessions where trainees develop skills through role-playing exercises.

The final component of the programme – work organisation and report writing – will endeavour to establish good habits among the trainees in areas which, because of day-to-day pressures, may be neglected. The importance of these activities on a salesperson's performance and, hence, earnings will be stressed.

Methods

The lecture

This method is useful in giving information and providing a frame of reference to aid the learning process. The lecture should be supported by the use of visual aids, for example professionally produced overhead projector transparencies. Trainees should be encouraged to participate so that the communication is not just one way. Discussion stimulates interest and allows misunderstandings to be identified and dealt with.

Films

These are a useful supplement to the lecture in giving information and showing how a skill should be performed. They add an extra dimension to a lecture by demonstrating how the principles can be applied in a selling situation. In terms of the stages of learning skills, lecture and films take the trainee up to the point of being consciously unable. They will show what he or she is required to do, but he/she will lack the experience to put the theory into practice successfully.

Role-playing

This learning method moves the trainee into the stage of being consciously able to perform a skill. It allows the trainee to learn by his or her own successes and failures in a buyer–seller situation. Feedback is provided by other group members, the sales trainer and by audio-visual means.

Seeing oneself perform is an enlightening and rewarding experience and can demonstrate to the trainee the points raised by other members of the group. Without this dimension some trainees may refuse to accept a fault, e.g. losing the buyer's interest, simply because in the heat of the selling discussion they genuinely do not notice it. Playback allows the trainee to see the situation through the eyes of a third person, and problems are more easily recognised and accepted.

Role-playing has its critics. Some say that trainees do not take it seriously enough and that by its very nature it is not totally realistic. Its main value is in teaching inexperienced salespeople the basic skills of selling in a less threatening environment than real selling. The selling process can be broken up into a series of activities, e.g. opening and need identification, sales presentation and overcoming objections, each of which requires a special set of skills. Role-playing can be used to develop each set of skills in a series of exercises which gradually build up to a full sales interview. A role-playing exercise designed to develop skills in need identification is given at the end of Chapter 5.

The degree of success achieved by role-playing is heavily dependent upon the skills of the sales trainer. When the trainees have at least a modicum of sales experience, it is good practice to allow them to devise their own sales situations based upon actual experiences. The briefs so produced are then exchanged between trainees so that each is presented with a situation which is new to them but which, at the same time, is realistic (Wilson, 1999).

Case studies

Case studies are particularly appropriate for developing analytical skills. Trainees are asked to analyse situations, identify problems and opportunities and make recommendations for dealing with them. They can be used, for example, in setting call objectives. A history of a buyer–seller relationship is given and the trainee is asked to develop a set of sensible objectives for his or her next visit.

In-the-field training

It is essential that initial training given to trainees is reinforced by on-the-job training. The experience gained by real-life selling situations plus the evaluation and feedback provided by the sales manager should mean that the salesperson moves solidly into the final stage of the learning skills process – unconsciously able. The salesperson does the right things automatically, just as a driver can co-ordinate the set of skills necessary to drive a car without consciously thinking.

Although unconsciously able is the final stage in the learning process, it does *not* describe a finite position beyond which improvement cannot take place. Field training is designed to improve the performance of the experienced as well as the newer salesperson. In order to do this the sales manager needs to do the following:

- analyse each salesperson's performance
- identify strengths and weaknesses
- gain agreement with the salesperson that a weakness exists
- teach the salesperson how to overcome the weaknesses
- monitor progress to check that an improvement has been realised.

There may be a strong temptation during a sales interview for a manager to step in when it is obvious that the salesperson is losing an order. Whether he or she succumbs to this temptation will depend upon the importance of the order, but to do so will undoubtedly reduce the effectiveness of the training session. Ideally, the sales manager should use the situation as an opportunity to observe and evaluate how the salesperson deals with the situation. Stepping in may save the order but cause resentment on the part of the salesperson, who loses face with the customer. This may jeopardise future sales and damage the manager's relationship with the salesperson.

Generally, a salesperson will respect criticism which he/she feels is fair and constructive. To achieve a sense of fairness, the sales manager should begin the post-interview assessment session by listing the positive points in the sales-person's performance. He/she should then ask the salesperson to relate any aspects of the sales interview which could be improved upon. If the salesperson himself/herself realises that he or she has a weakness, then the manager does not have the problem of convincing him or her that a difficulty exists.

It is inevitable that some weaknesses will not be exposed in this way and that the manager will have to explain them to the salesperson. However, since the manager has earlier praised other aspects of performance, the salesperson is unlikely to reject the manager's criticisms out of hand. Having gained agreement, the sales manager will then suggest methods to overcome the problem. Perhaps he or she will take the role of the buyer and engage in a role-playing exercise to rehearse the way in which a problem should be dealt with before the next call, or simply instruct the salesperson and suggest that he or she applies what has been said at his or her next call.

Evaluation of training courses

A study by Stamford-Bewley and Jobber (1989) sought to identify the methods used to evaluate training courses among a sample of companies in service, consumer and industrial sectors. The results appear in Figure 13.6. It appears that only 57 per cent attempt to measure changes in sales volume which may occur as a result of the course. More popular were field visits with salespeople (78 per cent) where the sales manager would subjectively gauge whether ability had improved as a result of the training course.

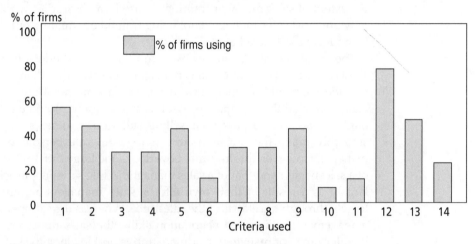

Key: Criteria used to evaluate training course
1. Change in sales net volume
2. Change in sales net value
3. Change in sales volume per call
4. Change in sales value per call
5. Number of new accounts gained
6. Number of old accounts lost
7. Order/Call rate
8. Order taken/Target
9. Coverage of territory
10. Length of time representatives spend with customer
11. Length of time representatives stay with company
12. Ability shown during field visits
13. Questionnaire at end of course
14. Questionnaire at some time in the future

Figure 13.6   Criteria used to evaluate training courses
(Stamford-Bewley and Jobber, 1989)

Training sales managers

To succeed as a sales manager requires a formidable set of skills and roles (Anderson, 1996), including the following:

● developing close relationships with customers and an in-depth understanding of customers' businesses;
● partnering salespeople to achieve sales, profitability and customer satisfaction goals;
● co-ordinating hybrid salesforces of telemarketers and field salespeople;
● keeping up-to-date with the latest technologies impacting the sales function.
● learning marketing skills to identify potential business opportunities and recommend strategies;
● working with other functional areas to achieve overall corporate goals through customer satisfaction;

- continually seeking ways to exceed customer expectations and create added value in buyer–seller relationships;
- creating a flexible, learning and adapting environment for the sales team;
- developing teaching, analytical, motivational, organisational, communicational, and planning skills.

The sales manager's job is becoming increasingly demanding because of the environmental changes discussed at the beginning of Chapter 9. Yet the training of sales managers appears to be neglected in many companies. Information on the extent of sales manager training is based on US studies which show that not only are most sales managers not being trained adequately but that most are not being formally trained at all.

The most recent US survey was conducted by Anderson *et al.* (1997) and showed that 57 per cent of sales managers reported that their company failed to provide them with formal sales management training. They speculate that one reason may be that companies assume that a newly promoted 'top salesperson' ought to be able to pass their selling skills on to other salespeople and thus smoothly make the transition from successful salesperson to successful sales manager. However, this argument overlooks the large differences between the job of a salesperson and that of a sales manager. While salespeople achieve their goals largely as a result of their own efforts, sales managers accomplish their goals largely through the efforts of the salesforce. Whereas the salesperson requires self-management, selling and negotiation skills, the sales manager requires a much broader range of managerial, administrative and leadership skills. Hence it is not surprising that top salespeople do not always make the best managers.

For those who did receive training, most tended to be on-the-job coaching by supervisors or peers backed up by a company-sponsored course or seminar at a college or university. Most of the training involved traditional training methods such as group discussions, role-playing, case studies and motivational speakers (see Table 13.6).

Table 13.6 Methods used to train sales managers

Method	%
Group discussions	72
Role-playing	64
Case studies	50
Motivational speakers	46
Computer simulation games	44
Seminars (up to four weeks long)	44
Videotapes/films	40
College courses	24
Correspondence courses	16
In basket exercises	10
Videoconferencing	8

Source: Anderson *et al.* (1997)

Table 13.7   Topics covered in sales training programmes

Topic	%
Motivating salespeople	82
Goal setting for salespeople	76
Leading salespeople	66
Training salespeople	64
Evaluating salespeople	64
Territory management	62
Time management	60
Developing sales strategies	58
Strategic sales planning	56
Recruiting new salespeople	52
Organizing salespeople	52
Sales forecasting	50

Source: Anderson *et al.* (1997)

The topics most frequently covered were motivation, goal setting for salespeople, leadership skills, training evaluation, territory management and time management (see Table 13.7). Very little attention was given to profitability analyses (by product category, market segment, salesperson, territory or customer type) indicating that sales managers were not being given essential financial skills to support their job.

13.3   CONCLUSIONS

This chapter considered motivational theory and practice as applied to the sales area. A number of theories were examined:

1 Maslow's hierarchy of needs theory;
2 Herzberg's motivator/hygiene theory;
3 Vroom's expectancy theory;
4 Adam's inequity theory;
5 Likert's sales management theory.

Motivation in practice is focused on the use of the following:

● financial incentives
● sales quotas or targets
● meetings between salesperson and manager
● sales contests.

Sales training involves the development of a programme which develops selling skills. The components of a training programme, and the methods used, were

PEN	Filling method	Price	Spare nibs	Spare cartridge cost	Nib size/ type	Construction material (all with pocket clips)	Shape	Colours	Other features
A	Capillary refillable	£15	£2.50	—	Medium/ gold	All-metal "gold" finish	Round	'Silver'/ 'gold' tops	Barrel has to be unscrewed to refil with an easy grip feature; guaranteed for 2 years; screw cap; spare italic nib supplied; made in the UK 
B	Cartridge, 3 spare	£12	£1.50	£1 for 4	Medium/ gold	Metal/ plastic tops	Round	Black/ 'silver'	Very slim enclosed nib; screw cap; guaranteed for 1 year; made in France 
C	Cartridge, 2 spare	£10	£1.50	£1 for 4	Medium/ steel	Metal/ plastic	Round	Various/ 'silver' tops	Bulky easy-to-hold style; screw cap; guaranteed for 1 year; made in Italy 
D	Cartridge, 4 spare	£10	£1.30	£1 for 6	Fine/ steel	Plastic with "silver" top tops	Round	Various/ 'silver'	Superslim variety; enclosed nib; screw cap; guaranteed for 2 years; made in France 
E	Cartridge, 1 spare	£9	£2.00	£1 for 6	Fine/ steel	Plastic	Tri-angular	Black/ red/ blue	Push-on cap; 1 year guarantee; made in Germany 
F	Cartridge, 1 spare	£7	£4.00	£0.60 for 4	Broad/ steel	Metalised plastic	Round	'Silver'	Choice of left/ right-hand nib; push-on cap; guaranteed for 6 months; made in the UK 

Figure 13.7   Fountain pen features

examined before the skills required for sales management were outlined.

The next chapter explores two other management considerations: sales organisation and compensation.

PRACTICAL EXERCISE

Selling fountain pens

This exercise can be used to develop the skills required for effective selling outlined in Chapter 5, i.e. need identification, presentation and demonstration, answering questions and handling objections, and closing the sale. The salesperson's profile is given below. The salesperson should be given at least fifteen minutes to study the range of pens on sale (see Figure 13.7). The role-play can be video-recorded and played back in front of the class to provide a focus for discussion.

Salesperson's profile

You are a salesperson in a stationery department of a small store. For a few minutes a customer has been looking at your range of quality pens. The person comes up to you saying, 'I'm looking for a good fountain pen.'

You take the interview from this point. You have a display of six fountain pens (A–F) with the features shown in Figure 13.7.

(The authors are grateful to Mr Robert Edwards, sales training manager, UKMP Department, ICI Pharmaceuticals, who devised this exercise, for permission to reprint it.)

EXAMINATION QUESTIONS

1 It is impossible to motivate, only to demotivate. Discuss.

2 You have recently been appointed sales manager of a company selling abrasives to the motor trade. Sales are declining and you believe that a major factor causing this decline is a lack of motivation amongst your salesforce. At present they are paid a straight salary, the size of which depends on length of service. Outline your thoughts regarding how you would approach this situation.

CHAPTER 14

ORGANISATION AND COMPENSATION

OBJECTIVES After studying this chapter, you should be able to:

1 Appreciate the advantages and disadvantages of different salesforce organisation structures.

2 Compute the numbers of salespeople needed for different selling situations.

3 Understand the factors to be considered when developing sales territories.

4 Strike a balance between various sales compensation plans.

5 Establish priorities in relation to customers, travelling time, and evolving call patterns.

KEY CONCEPTS

- compensation plans
- key account selling
- organising a salesforce
- team selling
- workload approach

14.1 ORGANISATIONAL STRUCTURE

Perhaps the classical form of **organising a salesforce** is along geographical lines, but the changing needs of customers and technological advances have led many companies to reconsider their salesforce organisation. The strengths and weaknesses of each type of organisational structure, as illustrated in Figure 14.1, will now be examined.

Geographical structure

An advantage of this form of organisation is its simplicity. Each salesperson is assigned a territory over which to have sole responsibility for sales achievement. His or her close geographical proximity to customers encourages the development of personal friendships which aids sales effectiveness. Also,

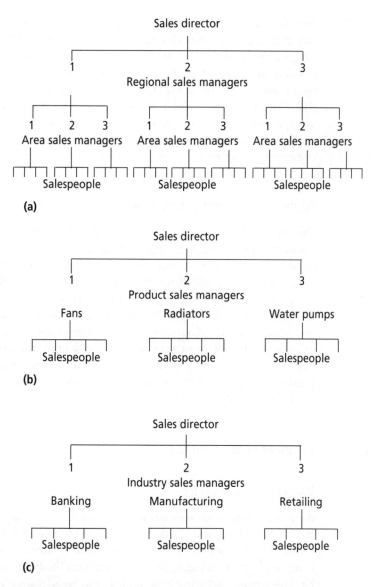

Fig. 14.1 Organisation structures: (a) geographical structure – the area sales manager level is optional: where the number of salespeople (span of control) under each regional manager exceeds eight, serious consideration may be given to appointing area managers; (b) product specialisation structure; (c) customer-based structure

compared with other organisational forms, e.g. product or market specialisation, travelling expenses are likely to be lower.

A potential weakness of the geographical structure is that the salesperson is required to sell the full range of the company's products. They may be very different technically and sell into a number of diverse markets. In such a situation it may be unreasonable to expect the salesperson to have the required depth of technical knowledge for each product and be conversant with the full range of potential applications within each market. This expertise can only be developed if the salesperson is given a more specialised role. A further related disadvantage of this method is that, according to Moss (1979), salespeople in discrete geographical territories, covering all types of customer, are relatively weak in interpreting buyer behaviour patterns and in reporting about changes in the operational circumstances of customers compared with salespeople organised along more specialised lines.

Product specialisation structure

One method of specialisation is along product lines. Conditions which are conducive to this form of organisation are where the company sells a wide range of technically complex and diverse products, and where key members of the decision-making unit of the buying organisations are different for each product group. However, if the company's products sell essentially to the same customers, problems of route duplication (and hence higher travel costs) and customer annoyance can arise. Inappropriate use of this method can lead to a customer being called upon by different salespeople representing the same company on the same day. When a company contemplates a move from a geographically-based to a product-based structure, some customer overlap is inevitable, but, if only of a limited extent, the problem should be manageable.

Customer-based structures

Market-centred structure

Another method of specialisation is by the type of market served. Often in industrial selling the market is defined by industry type. Thus, although the range of products sold is essentially the same, it might be sensible for a computer firm to allocate its salespeople on the basis of the industry served, e.g. banking, manufacturing companies, and retailers, given that different industry groups have widely varying needs, problems and potential applications. Specialisation by market served allows salespeople to gain greater insights into these factors for their particular industry, as well as to monitor changes and trends within the industry which might affect demand for their products. The cost of increased customer knowledge is increased travel expenses compared with geographically determined territories.

Magrath (1989) looked at the way industrial sales specialists levered up sales by virtue of applications expertise. Because they knew so much about the industry, they were welcomed as 'fraternity brothers' by customers.

Account-size structure

Some companies structure their salesforce by account size. The importance of a few large customers in many trade and industrial markets has given rise to the establishment of a **'key or major account' salesforce**. The team comprises senior salespeople who specialise in dealing with large customers who may have different buying habits and may demand more sophisticated sales arguments than smaller companies. The team will be conversant with negotiation skills since they are likely to be given a certain amount of discretion in terms of discounts, credit terms, etc., in order to secure large orders. The range of selling skills required is therefore wider than for the rest of the salesforce, who deal with the smaller accounts. Some organisations adopt a three-tier system, with senior salespeople negotiating with key accounts, ordinary salespeople selling to medium-sized accounts, and a telemarketing team dealing with small accounts.

A number of advantages are claimed for a key account salesforce structure:

1 Close working relationships with the customer – the salesperson knows who makes what decisions and who influences the various players involved in the decision. Technical specialists from the selling organisation can call on technical people (e.g. engineers) in the buying organisation, and salespeople can call upon administrators, buyers and financial people armed with the commercial arguments for buying.

2 Improved communication and co-ordination – the customer knows that a dedicated salesperson or sales team exists so that they know who to contact when a problem arises.

3 Better follow-up on sales and service – the extra resources devoted to the key account mean there is more time to follow-up and provide service after a major sale has been made.

4 More in-depth penetration of the DMU – there is more time to cultivate relationships within the key account. Salespeople can 'pull' the buying decision through the organisation from the users, deciders and influencers to the buyer, rather than the more difficult task of 'pushing' it through the buyer into the organisation, as is done with more traditional sales approaches.

5 Higher sales – most companies who have adopted key account selling claim that sales have risen as a result.

6 The provision of an opportunity for advancement for career salespeople – a tiered salesforce system with key (or national) account selling at the top provides promotional opportunities for salespeople who wish to advance within the salesforce rather than enter a traditional sales management position.

The term 'national account' is generally considered to refer to large and important customers who may have centralised purchasing departments that buy or co-ordinate buying for decentralised, geographically-dispersed branches that transcend sales territory boundaries. Selling to such firms often involves the following:

1 obtaining acceptance of the company's products at the buyer's headquarters.
2 negotiating long-term supply contracts;
3 maintaining favourable buyer–seller relationships at various levels in the buying organisation;
4 establishing first-class customer service.

The customer or small group of customers is given special attention by one key person (often known as a national account manager) or team headed by this person. This allows greater co-ordination than a geographically-based system where each branch would be called upon by a different salesperson as part of his or her job of covering their territory.

This depth of selling activity frequently calls for the expertise of a range of personnel in the supplying company in addition to the salesperson. It is for this reason that many companies serving national accounts employ **team selling**.

Team selling involves the combined efforts of such people as product specialists, engineers, sales managers and even directors if the buyer's decision-making unit includes personnel of equivalent rank. Team selling provides a method of responding to the various commercial, technical and psychological requirements of large buying organisations.

Companies are increasingly structuring both external and internal sales staff on the basis of specific responsibility for accounts. Examples of such companies are those in the electronics industry, where internal desk staff are teamed up with outside staff around 'key' customers. These company salesforces are able, with reasonable accuracy, to forecast future sales levels at these key locations. Further, an in-depth understanding of the buyer's decision-making unit is developed by the salesperson being able to develop a relationship with a large number of individual decision-makers. In this way, marketing staff can be kept informed of customer requirements, enabling them to improve products and plan effective communications.

New/existing account structure

A further method of sales organisation is to create two teams of salespeople. The first team services existing accounts, while the second concentrates upon seeking new accounts. This structure recognises the following:

1 Gaining new customers is a specialised activity demanding prospecting skills, patience, the ability to accept higher rejection rates than when calling upon existing customers, and the time to cultivate new relationships.
2 Placing this function in the hands of the regular salesforce may result in its neglect since the salespeople may view it as time which could be better spent with existing customers.
3 Salespeople may prefer to call upon long-established customers whom they know rather than prospects where they might face rejection and unpleasantness.

Pioneer salespeople were used successfully by trading stamp companies to prospect new customers. Once an account was obtained it was handed over to a maintenance salesperson who serviced the account. This form of salesforce organisation is used in the CCTV, freight and copier industries.

New account salespeople have been found to spend more time exploring the prospect's needs and provide more information to management regarding buyer behaviour and attitudes than salespeople working under a conventional system (Moss, 1979). The deployment of new account salesforces is feasible for large companies with many customers and where there is a continual turnover of key accounts which have to be replaced. The new account structure allows better planning of this vital function and eliminates competition between prospecting and servicing.

Functional specialisation

In industrial selling, companies sometimes separate their salesforces into development and maintenance sales teams. The development salespeople are highly trained in handling very technical new products. They will spend considerable time overcoming commercial, technical and installation problems for new customers.

A major reason why companies have moved to a development/maintenance structure is the belief that one of the causes of new product failure is the inadequacy of the salesforce to introduce the product. Perhaps the cause of this failure is the psychological block each salesperson faces in terms of possible future problems with the buyer–seller relationship if the product does not meet expectations. Because of this, the salesperson is likely to doubt the wisdom of giving an unproven product his/her unqualified support. Employment of a development sales team can reduce this problem, although it is often only large companies which can afford such a team. Its use can provide other advantages, including clarity of purpose, effective presentation and reliable feedback from the marketplace. Some pharmaceutical companies use this form of salesforce organisation.

Mixed organisation

This section has discussed the merits and weaknesses of the major sales organisational structures. In practice a combination may be used. For example, a company using a two-product group structure may, in order to minimise travelling expenses, divide the country into geographically-based territories with two salespeople operating within each one.

Like many selling decisions, the choice of sales organisation is not a black and white affair, which is why many salesforces are a blend of general territory representatives and specialists. Many companies use all forms of selling simultaneously: for very big accounts they use key account specialists; for the balance of small and medium accounts they use general territory representatives, perhaps supplemented by product application specialists who help generalists across several territories.

The challenge to any sales manager is to know how to assess the options. Financial, customer coverage and organisational flexibility trade-offs need to be made. The company must balance hard numbers with what the customer wants, which often means some form of specialisation, and what the competition are providing. Increasingly, the customer wants to buy total solutions, and demands value-added services rather than one-off transactions.

As companies internationalise, consideration of salesforce organisation on a global scale needs to be made. The following case discussion covers a number of relevant issues.

SELLING AND SALES MANAGEMENT IN ACTION

Organisation for international sales

A common approach to organising international salesforces is to adopt the same approach as that taken in the domestic market. Many multinational corporations use the simple geographical method within a given country or region. However, international companies that have wide product lines, large sales volumes, and/or operate in large developed markets prefer more specialised organisational forms such as customer- or product-based structures. For smaller markets such as those found in developing economies, such specialisation may not be economically viable leading to geographical organisation.

Language also affects international salesforce organisation. For example, territories in Belgium are often divided by language – French to the south, and Flemish in the north – or countries are combined as with Austria and Germany because both use the German language. Similarly, Switzerland is often organised into different regions based upon usage of the French, German and Italian languages, while some companies combine Central America into a single sales region.

Some considerations when deciding upon international salesforce organisation are as follows:

● geographical size
● sales potential
● customer expectations
● product line width
● current selling practices
● language spoken.

Geographical structures tend to be used in less developed markets, when a single product line is sold and for small sales volumes. Product- or customer-based organisation is more likely in large developed markets, for broad product lines, and where the large sales volume justifies specialisation.

Based on Hill, J.S. and Still, R.R. (1990) 'Organising the overseas sales force: how multinationals do it', *Journal of Personal Selling and Sales Management,* 10(2), pp. 57–66; Honeycutt, Jr, E.D. and Ford, J.B. (1995) 'Guidelines for managing an international sales force', *Industrial Marketing Management,* 24, pp. 135–144; Samli, A.C., Still, R.R. and Hill, J.S. (1993) '*International Marketing*', Macmillan: New York.

14.2 DETERMINING THE NUMBER OF SALES PEOPLE

The workload approach

The **workload method** allows the number of salespeople needed to be calculated, given that the company knows the number of calls per year it wishes its salespeople to make on different classes of customer. Talley (1961) showed how the number of salespeople could be calculated by following a series of steps:

1 Customers are grouped into categories according to the value of goods bought and potential for the future.
2 The call frequency (number of calls on an account per year) is assessed for each category of customer.
3 The total required workload per year is calculated by multiplying the call frequency and number of customers in each category and then summing for all categories.
4 The average number of calls per week per salesperson is estimated.
5 The number of working weeks per year is calculated.
6 The average number of calls a salesperson can make per year is calculated by multiplying (4) and (5).
7 The number of salespeople required is determined by dividing the total annual calls required by the average number of calls one salesperson can make per year.

Here is an example of such a calculation. The formula is:

$$\frac{\text{Number of}}{\text{salespeople}} = \frac{\text{Number of customers} \times \text{Call frequency}}{\text{Average weekly call rate} \times \text{Number of working weeks per year}}$$

Steps (1), (2) and (3) can be summarised as in the following table:

Customer groups	No. of firms		Call frequencies per year		
A (Over £1,000,000 per year)	200	×	12	=	2,400
B (£500,000–£1 m per year)	1,000	×	9	=	9,000
C (£150,000–£499,000 per year)	3,000	×	6	=	18,000
D (Less than £150,000)	6,000	×	3	=	18,000
Total annual workload				=	47,400

Step (4) gives:
Average number of calls per week per salesperson   = 30

Step (5) gives:
Number of weeks   = 52
Less:
   Holidays   4
   Illness   1

Conferences/meetings	3	
Training	1	9
Number of working weeks		= 43

Step (6) gives:

Average number of calls per salesperson per year	$= 43 \times 30$
	$= 1{,}290$

Step (7) gives:

$$\text{Salesforce size} = \frac{47{,}000}{1{,}290} = 37 \text{ salespeople}$$

When prospecting forms an important part of the salesperson's job, potential customers can be included in the customer categories according to potential. Alternatively, separate categories can be formed, with their own call rates, to give an estimation of the workload required to cover prospecting. This is then added to the workload estimate derived from actual customers to produce a total workload figure.

The applicability of this method is largely dependent upon the ability of management to assess confidently the number of calls to be made on each category of customer. Where optimum call rates on customers within a particular category vary considerably, management may be reluctant to generalise. However, in a company quoted by Wilson (1999), although call rates varied between one and ten calls per day, for 80 per cent of the days seven or eight calls were made.

The method is of particular relevance to companies who are expanding into new geographical territories. For example, a company expanding its sphere of operation from England to Scotland could use a blend of past experience and judgement to assess feasible call frequencies in Scotland. Market research could be used to identify potential customers. The workload approach could then be used to estimate the number of salespeople needed.

14.3 ESTABLISHING SALES TERRITORIES

There are two basic considerations which are used to allocate salespeople to territories. First, management may wish to balance workload between territories. Workload can be defined as follows:

$$W = n_i t_i + n t_k$$

where W = workload, n_i = number of calls to be made to customers in category i, t_i = average time required at call for each category i, n = total number of calls to be made and t_k = average time required to travel to each call. This equation is useful because it highlights the important factors which a sales manager must take into account when assessing workload. The number of calls to be made will be weighted by a time factor for each call. Major account calls are likely to be weighted higher than medium and small active accounts since, other things being equal, it makes sense to spend longer with customers who have higher potential. Also, calls on prospects may have a high weighting since salespeople need extra time to develop a new relationship and to sell themselves, their company and its products. In addition, the time required to travel to each customer must be taken into account. Territories vary in their customer density, and so travel time must be allowed for in the calculation of workload.

The data will be determined partly by executive judgement, e.g. how long to spend with each customer type on average, and, where a salesforce already exists, by observation, e.g. how long it takes to travel between customers in different existing territories. These data can be obtained during field visits with salespeople, and estimates of current workloads calculated. For new sales teams the input into the formula will, of necessity, be more judgemental, but the equation does provide a conceptual framework for assessing territory workload.

The second consideration management may wish to use in working out territories is sales potential. Equalising workload may result in territories of widely differing potential. This may be accepted as a fact of life by some companies and dealt with by assigning their best salespeople to the territories of higher potential. Indeed, moving salespeople from lower potential territories to ones of higher potential could be used as a form of promotion. If company policy dictates that all salespeople should be treated equally, then a commission scheme based upon the attainment of sales quotas which vary according to territory potential should establish a sense of fairness. However, if, after preliminary determination of territories by workload, sales potentials are widely disparate, it may be necessary to carry out some adjustment. It may be possible to modify adjacent territory boundaries so that a high potential territory surrenders a number of large accounts in return for gaining some smaller accounts from a neighbouring lower potential territory. In this way differences in sales potentials are reduced without altering workload dramatically. If this is not easily done it may be necessary to trade off workload for potential, making territories less similar in terms of workload but more balanced in terms of sales potential.

Designing territories calls for a blend of sound analysis and plain common sense. For example, it would be crazy to design territories purely on the basis of equalising sales potential if the result produced strips of territory which failed to recognise the road system (especially motorways) as it exists in the country today.

Territory revision

A sales territory should not be considered a permanent unit. The following factors may suggest the need for territory revision:

- change in consumer preference;
- competitive activity;
- diminution in the usefulness of chosen distribution channels;

- the complete closure of an outlet or group of stores;
- increases in the cost of covering territories;
- salesforce complacency.

Before deciding that changes are necessary, a number of aspects of the sales effort should be investigated. The most common indicators that something might be wrong with the territorial structure is falling sales volume. However, great care must be taken before accepting this as a reason for territory revision. Sales may be falling because the selling and promotion effort within the territory is not as effective as it should be. If this is the case, then it is not the boundaries of the sales area that are in need of revision.

Salespeople may be calling only on the prospects which offer the greatest potential. If there is no systematic plan for the territory, salespeople may make a poor job of planning their calls and this may result in an increase in non-selling time (e.g. travelling time). Furthermore, the supervision may be at fault. If sales personnel are not supervised properly, they may lose their enthusiasm for the job, or even for the product.

Before changes are implemented, a reappraisal of market potential should take place. It may be that the original distributors of the products are in need of replacement or motivation because they have become disenchanted with the company, its products, or its policies. Consumer acceptance of the product may need to be investigated before territories are revised. This may require a limited market survey. The current activities of competitors should also be investigated.

If territories are to be revised, the salesforce must be fully informed about the extent of the changes and the reasons behind them. The extent to which the boundaries are changed will be governed by the need to increase coverage, reduce costs, or increase sales. The sales manager should enlist the aid of his or her supervisors and salespeople when the task of altering territories begins.

While the overall design of territories, their size, number of customers, etc., is the responsibility of the sales manager, once allocated, the salesperson too (sometimes in conjunction with the sales manager) can play an important role in managing this territory such as to achieve maximum sales effectiveness. In fact, much of this aspect of territory management comes down to effective self-management on the part of the salesperson. Information technology can aid territory management and revision as discussed in Chapter 8.

14.4 COMPENSATION

Compensation objectives

Sales managers should consider carefully the type of **compensation plan** they wish to use. This is because there are a number of objectives which can be achieved through a compensation scheme. First, compensation can be used to motivate a salesforce by linking achievement to monetary reward. Second, it can be used to attract and hold successful salespeople by providing a good standard of living for them, by rewarding outstanding performance and providing regularity of income. Third, it is possible to design compensation schemes which allow selling costs to fluctuate in line with changes in sales revenue. Thus, in poor years lower sales are offset to some extent by lower commission payments, and in good years increased sales costs are financed by higher sales revenue. Fourth, compensation plans can be formulated to direct the attention of sales personnel to specific company sales objectives. Higher commission can be paid on product lines the company particularly wants to move; special commission can be paid to salespeople who generate new active accounts if this is believed to be important to the company. Thus, compensation plans can be used to control activities.

Types of compensation plan

When designing compensation plans, sales management need to recognise that not all of the sales team may be motivated by the thought of higher earnings. Darmon (1974) identified five types of salespeople:

1 *Creatures of habit*. These salespeople try to maintain their standard of living by earning a predetermined amount of money.
2 *Satisfiers*. These people perform at a level just sufficient to keep their jobs.
3 *Trade-offers*. These allocate their time based upon a personally determined ratio between work and leisure that is not influenced by the prospect of higher earnings.
4 *Goal-orientated*. These salespeople prefer recognition as achievers by their peers and superiors and tend to be sales quota orientated with money mainly serving as recognition of achievement.
5 *Money-orientated*. These people aim to maximise their earnings. Family relationships, leisure and even health may be sacrificed in the pursuit of money.

The implication is that sales management need to understand and categorise their salespeople in terms of their motives. Compensation plans can only be effectively designed with this understanding. For example, developing a new plan based upon greater opportunities to earn commission is unlikely to work if the sales team consists only of the first three categories of salesperson. Conversely, when a sales team is judged to be composed mainly of goal- and money-orientated salespeople, a move from a fixed salary to a salary and commission system is likely to prove effective.

There are, basically, three types of compensation plan:

● fixed salary
● commission only
● salary plus commission.

Each is evaluated below in terms of its benefits and drawbacks to management

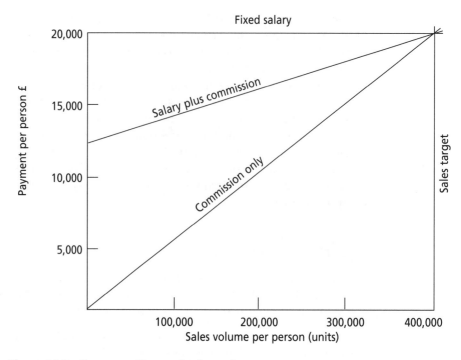

Figure 14.2 Compensation and sales volume

and salespeople, while Figure 14.2 shows how a sales target can be associated with a fixed salary, commission only, or salary plus commission system. If the target is achieved, sales costs are equal no matter which system is used.

Fixed salary

This method of payment encourages salespeople to consider all aspects of the selling function rather than just those which lead to a quick sales return. Salespeople who are paid on fixed salary are likely to be more willing to provide technical service, complete information feedback reports and carry out prospecting than if they were paid solely by commission. The system provides security to the salesperson who knows how much income he or she will receive each month and is relatively cheap to administer since calculation of commissions and bonuses is not required.

The system also overcomes the problem of deciding how much commission to give to each salesperson when a complex buying decision is made by a number of DMU members who have been influenced by different salespeople, perhaps in different parts of the country. Wilson (1999) cites the case of a sale of building materials to a local authority in Lancashire being the result of one salesperson influencing an architect in London, another calling on the contractor in Norwich and a third persuading the local authority itself.

However, the method does have a number of drawbacks. First, no direct financial incentive is provided for increasing sales (or profits). Second, high-performing salespeople may not be attracted, and holding on to them may be difficult using fixed salary since they may perceive the system as being unfair and may be tempted to apply for jobs where financial rewards are high for outstanding performers. Third, selling costs remain static in the short term when sales decrease; thus the system does not provide the inbuilt flexibility provided by the other compensation systems.

Because of its inherent characteristics it is used primarily in industrial selling where technical service is an important element in the selling task and the time necessary to conclude a sale may be long. It is particularly appropriate when the salesperson sells very high-value products at very low volumes. Under these conditions a commission-based compensation scheme would lead to widely varying monthly income levels depending on when orders were placed. A Chartered Institute of Marketing study (PA Consultants, 1979) found that roughly one-third of salespeople are paid by this method in the UK.

Commission only

The commission-only system of payment provides an obvious incentive to sell. However, since income is dependent on sales results, salespeople will be reluctant to spend time on tasks which they do not perceive as being directly related to sales. The result is that sales personnel may pursue short-term goals, to the detriment of activities which may have an effect in the longer term; salespeople may be reluctant to write reports providing market information to management and spend time out of the field to attend sales training courses, for example.

The system provides little security for those whose earnings may suffer through no fault of their own, and the pressure to sell may damage customer–salesperson relationships. This is particularly relevant in industrial selling, where the decision-making process may be long and pressure applied by the salesperson to close the sale prematurely may be detrimental.

From management's perspective the system not only has the advantage of directly financing costs automatically, but also allows some control over sales activities through the use of higher commission rates on products and accounts in which management is particularly interested.

It is most often used in situations where there are a large number of potential customers, the buying process is relatively short and technical assistance and service is not required. Insurance selling is an example where commission-only payments are often used.

Salary plus commission

This system attempts to combine the benefits of both of the previous methods in order to provide financial incentives with a level of security. Since income is not solely dependent upon commission, management gains a greater degree of control over the salesperson's time than under the commission-only system, and sales costs are, to some extent, related to revenue generated. The method is attractive to ambitious salespeople who wish to combine security with the capability of earning more by greater effort and ability.

For these reasons it is the most commonly used method of compensating salespeople, although the method of calculating commission may vary. Extra payment may be linked to profits or sales generated, at a constant rate for all sales or only after a certain level of sales has been generated. Payment may be based upon a fixed percentage for all products and customers or at a variable rate. Alternatively, a bonus (a given monetary sum) may be paid on the accomplishment of a particular task (e.g. achieving a sales target, opening a certain number of new accounts). The results of two surveys which have examined the use of salary, salary plus commission/bonus, and commission only (Avlonitis, *et al.* 1985; Shipley and Jobber, 1991) are shown in Table 14.1.

Table 14.1   The use of compensation methods in the UK

	Manufacturing firms (%)	Industrial distributors (%)
Salary only	34	15
Salary + commission/bonus	66	81
Commission only	–	4

Sources: Manufacturing firms – Avlonitis *et al.* (1985); Industrial distributors – Shipley and Jobber (1991)

14.5   CONCLUSIONS

Two management functions – organisation and compensation – have been discussed in this chapter. There are three methods of organising a salesforce:

● geographical
● product
● customer.

The customer-orientated approach has four variants:

● market-centred
● account size
● new/existing accounts
● functional.

Determining the number of salespeople needed may be accomplished by the workload approach.

Establishing sales territories will be determined by attempting to balance workload and sales potential.

Finally, the three major categories of compensation plan were examined. These are the fixed salary, commission only and salary plus commission.

The next part of the text looks at the final area of sales management – sales control.

PRACTICAL EXERCISE

The Silverton Confectionery Company

Silverton Confectionery is a growing Berkshire-based company specialising in selling quality chocolates and sweets at higher-than-average prices through newsagents and confectioners.

At present their span of operation is limited to England and Wales, which is covered by a salesforce organised along geographical lines. Each salesperson is responsible for sales of the entire product line in his territory and for seeking out new outlets in which to develop new business. The system works well with Silverton's salespeople, who are well known by their customers and, in most cases, well liked. The salesperson's responsibilities include both the selling and merchandising functions. They are paid on a salary plus commission system.

The success of this company, which has exploited a market niche neglected by the larger confectionery companies, has led Silverton management to expand into Scotland. You, as national sales manager, have been asked to recommend the appropriate number of salespeople required.

The coverage objective is to call upon all outlets with a turnover of over £200,000 three times a year, those between £100,000 and £200,000 twice a year and those below £100,000 once a year. As a first step, you have commissioned a market research report to identify the number of outlets within each size category. The results are given below:

Category	No. of outlets
Under £100,000	2,950
£100,000–200,000	1,700
Over £200,000	380

A salesperson can be expected to call upon an average of sixty outlets a week and a working year, after holidays, sales meetings, training, etc., can be assumed to be forty-three weeks.

DISCUSSION QUESTION

1 How many salespeople are required?

EXAMINATION QUESTIONS

1 The only sensible way to organise a salesforce is by geographical region. All other methods are not cost efficient. Discuss.

2 How practical is the workload approach to salesforce size determination?

Part Five

SALES
CONTROL

<table>
</table>

<table>
<thead>
<tr><th>CHAPTER
15</th><th># SALES FORECASTING</th></tr>
</thead>
</table>

CHAPTER 15

SALES FORECASTING

OBJECTIVES   After studying this chapter, you should be able to:

1 Appreciate the position of sales forecasting in the marketing planning system.

2 Understand qualitative forecasting techniques.

3 Understand quantitative forecasting techniques.

4 Appreciate how computer software is used in forecasting.

KEY CONCEPTS
- casual techniques
- diffusion models
- qualitative forecasting techniques
- quantitative forecasting techniques
- time series analysis

15.1   PURPOSE

It is of the utmost importance that the sales manager has some idea of what will happen in the future in order that he or she can make plans in anticipation of that happening. There would otherwise be no point in planning and all that has been said in Chapter 14 would be negated. Many sales managers do not recognise that sales forecasting is one of their responsibilities, and leave such matters to accountants, who need the forecast in order that they can prepare budgets (dealt with in Chapter 16). Perhaps sales managers do not see the immediate need for forecasting and think that selling is a more urgent task. Indeed, the task of forecasting by the sales manager is often pushed to one side and a hastily put together effort with no scientific base, little more than an educated guess, is the end result. The folly of such an attitude is examined during the course of this chapter.

When one is in a producer's market – similar to the situations in the immediate post-war years as was described in Chapter 1 – there is less of a need for forecasting as the market takes up all one's production; it is less a matter of selling and more a matter of allowing customers to purchase. However, in a buyer's market the situation is different, and the consequence of over-production is that one is left with unsold stock which is costly to finance in that such finance must come from working capital borrowings. The marginal money, i.e. the cost of borrowing the last pound of revenue, comes from the bank overdraft, which is at least base rate of borrowing plus 1 or 2 per cent. It can therefore be seen that over-production and stocking can be a costly business. Conversely, under-production can be a bad thing because sales opportunities might be missed due to long delivery times and the business might pass to a competitor who can offer quicker delivery.

Thus the purpose of the sales forecast is that it allows management to plan ahead and go about achieving the forecasted sales in what it considers to be the most effective manner. It is again emphasised that the sales manager is the person who should be responsible for this task. The accountant is not in a position to know whether the market is about to rise or fall; all that can be done is to extrapolate from previous sales, estimate the general trend and make a forecast based on this. The sales manager is the person who should know which way the market is moving, and it is a negation of a major part of his or her duty if the task of sales forecasting is left to the accountant. In addition, the sales forecasting procedure must be taken seriously, because from it stems business planning; if the forecast is erroneous then such plans will also be incorrect.

15.2 PLANNING

It has been established that planning stems from the sales forecast and that the purpose of planning is to allocate company resources in such a manner as to achieve these anticipated sales.

A company can forecast its sales either by forecasting the market sales (called **market forecasting**) and then determining what share of this will accrue to the company or by forecasting the company's sales directly. Techniques for doing this are dealt with later in the chapter. The point is that planners are only interested in forecasts when the forecast comes down to individual products in the company.

We shall now examine the applicability and usefulness of the short-, medium- and long-term forecasts in so far as company planners are concerned and shall then look at each from individual company departmental viewpoints.

1 *Short-term forecasts.* These are usually for periods up to three months ahead, and as such are really of use for tactical matters such as production planning. The general trend of sales is less important here than short-term fluctuations.
2 *Medium-term forecasts.* These have direct implications for planners. They are of most importance in the area of business budgeting, the starting point for which is the sales forecast. Thus if the sales forecast is incorrect, then the entire budget is incorrect. If the forecast is over-optimistic, then the company will have unsold stocks which must be financed out of working capital. If the forecast is pessimistic, then the firm may miss out on marketing opportunities because it is not geared up to produce the extra goods required by the market.

More to the point is that when forecasting is left to accountants, they will tend to err on the conservative side and will produce a forecast that is less than actual sales, the implications of which have just been described. This serves to re-emphasise the point that sales forecasting is the responsibility of the sales manager. Such medium-term forecasts are normally for one year ahead.

3 *Long-term forecasts*. These are usually for periods of three years and upwards depending upon the type of industry being considered. In industries such as computers three years is considered long term, whereas for steel manufacture ten years is a long-term horizon. They are worked out from macro-environmental factors such as government policy, economic trends, etc. Such forecasts are needed mainly by financial accountants for long-term resource implications, but such matters of course are board of directors' concerns. The board must decide what its policy is to be in establishing the levels of production needed to meet the forecasted demand; such decisions might mean the construction of a new factory and the training of a workforce.

In addition to the functions already mentioned under each of the three types of forecast, other functions can be directly and indirectly affected in their planning considerations as a result of the sales forecast. Such functions include the following:

1 It has already been mentioned that production need to know about sales forecasts so that they can arrange production planning. There will also need to be close and speedy liaison between production and the sales department to determine customer priorities in the short term. Production also needs long-term forecasts so that capital plant decisions can be made in order to meet anticipated sales.

2 Purchasing usually receives its cue to purchase from the production department via purchase requisitions or bills of material. However, in the case of strategic materials or long-delivery items it is useful for purchasing to have some advance warning of likely impending material or component purchases in order that they can better plan their purchases. Such advance warning will also enable purchasing to purchase more effectively from a price and delivery viewpoint.

3 Human resource management is interested in the sales forecast from the manpower planning viewpoint.

4 It has already been mentioned that the financial and, more specifically, the costing function needs the medium-term forecast in order to budget. The next chapter details how use is made of the sales forecast through the sales budget and how such a function operates. The long-term forecast is of value to financial accountants in that they can provide for long-range profit plans and income flows. They will also need to make provision for capital items such as plant and machinery needed in order to replace old plant and machinery and to meet anticipated sales in the longer term.

5 Research and development will need forecasts, although their needs will be more concerned with technological matters and not with actual projected sales figures. They will want to know the expected life of existing products

and what likely changes will have to be made to their function and design in order to keep them competitive. Market research reports will be of use to research and development in that they will be able to design and develop products suited to the marketplace; such a view reflects a marketing orientated approach to customer requirements. Here reports from salespeople in the field concerning the company's products and competitors' products will be useful in building up a general picture; such information will be collated and collected by the marketing research function.

6 Finally, marketing needs the sales forecast so that sales strategies and promotional plans can be formulated in order to achieve the forecasted sales. Such plans and strategies might include the recruitment of additional sales personnel, remuneration plans, promotional expenditures and other matters as detailed in Chapters 3 and 9.

A useful model was proposed by Hogarth (1975) involving three interactive forecasting components: the person performing the task of forecasting; the actions that are a consequence of that person's judgements; and the ultimate outcome of that judgement. This model is shown in Figure 15.1

The individual making the forecast is represented in the scheme in terms of beliefs relating to the forecasting task. This judgement relates to acquisition and processing of information and the output from this information. This is then translated into action which is the sales forecast. The outcome refers to action

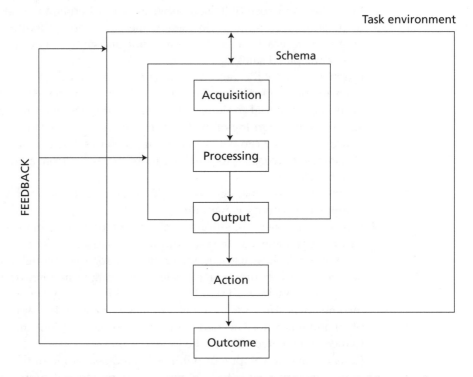

Figure 15.1   A conceptually based model of judgemental forecasting
(From Hogarth, 1975)

that along with external factors then produces the final forecast. Feedback points are included as corrective measures that might be needed as the forecast becomes reality.

It can thus be seen that an accurate forecast is important because all functions base their plans on such forecasts. The short-, medium- and long-term forecasts all have some relevance to some business function and, in the absence of reasonably accurate forecasting, where such plans are not based on a solid foundation, they will have to be modified later as sales turn out to be wide of those predicted in the sales forecast.

Now that the purpose of sales forecasting has been established, together with its role as a precursor to all planning activity, we can look at the different types of forecasting technique, bearing in mind that such forecasting is the responsibility of the sales function. Such techniques are logically split into two types, qualitative techniques and quantitative techniques, and each is dealt with in turn.

15.3 LEVELS OF FORECASTING

Forecasts can be produced for different horizons starting at an international level, and then ranging down to national levels, by industry and then by company levels until we reach individual product-by-product forecasts. This is then broken down seasonally over the time span of the forecasting period, and geographically right down to individual salesperson areas. It is these latter levels that are of specific interest to sales management, for it is from this level of forecasting that the sales budgeting and remuneration system stems, as we discuss in more detail in Chapter 16.

However, companies do not generally have to produce international or national forecasts as this information is usually available from recognised international and national sources. The company forecaster does, however, find such data useful for it is by using such information that product-by-product forecasts can be adjusted in the light of these macro-level predictions. It is also from these market forecasts that the company can determine what share of that forecast it will be able to achieve through its individual selling and marketing efforts. These marketing efforts involve manipulating the marketing mix in order to plan how to achieve these forecasted sales. Once it reaches a detailed level of product-by-product forecasting, geographically split over a time period, it is then termed the 'sales forecast', which is more meaningful to sales management. Indeed, it could be said that this is the means through which sales management exercises control over the field salesforce, and as we describe in the next chapter, this is the revenue generating mechanism for the entire sales organisation of a company.

15.4 QUALITATIVE TECHNIQUES

Qualitative forecasting techniques are sometimes referred to as judgemental or subjective techniques because they rely more upon opinion and less upon mathematics in their formulation. They are often used in conjunction with quantitative techniques which are described in section 15.5.

Consumer/user survey method

This method involves asking customers what their likely purchases are to be for the period it is wished to forecast; it is sometimes referred to as the market research method. For industrial products, where there are fewer customers, such research is often carried out by the salesforce on a face-to-face basis. The only problem is that then you have to ascertain what proportion of their likely purchases will accrue to your company. Another problem is that customers (and salespeople) tend to be optimistic when making predictions for the future. Both of these problems can therefore lead to the possibility of multiplied inaccuracies.

For consumer products it is not possible to canvass customers through the salesforce, and the best method is to interview them through a market research survey (probably coupled with other questions or through an omnibus survey where questions on a questionnaire are shared with other companies). Clearly, it will only be possible to interview a small sample of the total population and because of this the forecast will be less accurate. There is also a question of the type and number of questions one can ask on such a sample survey. It is better to canvass grades of opinion when embarking on such a study and these grades of opinion can reflect purchasing likelihoods. One can then go on to ask a question as to the likelihood of purchasing particular makes or brands which will, of course, include your own brand or model.

This method is of most value when there are a small number of users who are prepared to state their intentions with a reasonable degree of accuracy. It tends, therefore, to be limited to organisational buying. It is also a useful vehicle for collecting information of a technological nature which can be fed to one's own research and development function.

Panels of executive opinion

This is sometimes called the jury method, where specialists or experts are counselled who have knowledge of the industry being examined. Such people can come from inside the company and can include marketing or financial personnel or indeed any others who have a detailed knowledge of the industry. More often, the experts will come from outside the company and can include management consultants who operate within the particular industry, usually working as economists. Sometimes external people can include personnel from customer organisations who are in a position to advise from a buying company's viewpoint. The panel thus normally comprises a mixture of internal and external personnel.

These experts come with a prepared forecast and must defend their stance in committee among the other experts. Their individual stances may be altered following such discussions. In the end, if disagreement results, mathematical aggregation may be necessary to arrive at a final compromise.

This type of forecasting method is termed a 'top down' method whereby a forecast is produced for the industry, and the company must then determine what its share will be of the overall forecast. Because the statistics have not been collected from basic market data (from the 'bottom up') there is difficulty in allocating the forecast out amongst individual products and sales territories, and any such allocation will probably be a very arbitrary matter. Thus the forecast represents aggregate opinion and is only useful when developing a general, rather than specific product-by-product forecast.

A variation of this method is termed 'prudent manager forecasting' whereby company personnel are asked to assume the position of purchasers in customer companies. They must then look at company sales from a customer's viewpoint and 'prudently' evaluate these sales, taking into consideration such factors as external economic conditions, competitive offerings in terms of design, quality, delivery and price and whatever other factors are considered relevant to making an evaluation of the company's sales.

Salesforce composite

This method involves each salesperson making a product-by-product forecast for his or her particular sales territory. Thus individual forecasts are built up to produce a company forecast; one can thus perhaps appreciate why it is sometimes termed the 'grass roots' approach. Each salesperson's forecast must be agreed with his or her area manager, and the divisional manager where appropriate, and eventually the sales manager agrees the final forecast.

Such a method is very much a 'bottom up' approach. Where remuneration is linked to projected sales (through quotas or targets) then there can be less cause for complaint because the forecast upon which such remuneration is based has stemmed from the salesforce itself.

A variation of the above method is termed 'detecting differences in figures' and here each stage in the hierarchy produces a set of figures before meeting. The salesperson produces figures, broken down by product and by customer, and the area manager produces figures for the salesperson's territory. They then meet and must reconcile any differences in figures. The process goes on similarly with the area manager producing territory-by-territory figures and meeting with the regional manager who will have produced figures for his or her area, until it eventually reaches the sales manager and the entire forecast is ultimately agreed.

The immediate problem with the salesforce composite method of sales forecasting is that when the forecast is used for future remuneration (through the establishment of sales quotas or targets) there will be a natural tendency for salespeople to produce a pessimistic forecast. This can be alleviated to a certain extent by linking sales expenses to the forecast as well as future remuneration. On the other hand, when remuneration is not linked to the sales forecast there is perhaps a temptation to produce an optimistic forecast in view of what was said earlier about customers and salespeople tending to over-estimate. The consequence of the above is that a forecast might be produced that is biased either pessimistically or optimistically. As a corollary to the above it can also be argued that salespeople are too concerned with everyday events to enable them to produce objective forecasts and they are perhaps less aware of the wider or 'macro' factors affecting sales of their products. Thus their forecasts will tend to be subjective.

Delphi method

This method bears a resemblance to the 'panel of executive opinion' method and the forecasting team is chosen using a similar set of criteria. The main difference is that members do not meet in committee.

A project leader administers a questionnaire to each member of the team which asks questions, usually of a behavioural nature, e.g. 'Do you envisage new technology products supplanting our product lines in the next five years? If so, by what percentage market share?' The questioning then proceeds to a more detailed or pointed second stage which asks questions about the individual company, and the process can go on to further stages where appropriate. The ultimate objective is to translate opinion into some form of forecast. After each round of questionnaires the aggregate response from each round is circulated to members of the panel before they complete the questionnaire for the next round, so members are not completing their questionnaires in a void and they can moderate their response in the light of the averaged results.

The fact that members do not meet in committee means that they are not influenced by majority opinion and a more objective forecast might result. However, as a vehicle for producing a territory-by-territory or product-by-product forecast it has very limited value. It is of more use in providing general data about trends within the industry and is perhaps of greater value as a technological forecasting tool. It can also be useful for providing information about new products or processes which the company intends developing for ultimate manufacture and sale.

Bayesian decision theory

This technique has been placed under qualitative techniques, although it is really a mixture of subjective and objective techniques. It is not possible to describe the detailed workings of this method within the confines of this text; indeed it is possible to devote a whole text to the Bayesian technique alone!

The technique is similar to critical path analysis in that it uses a network diagram, and probabilities must be estimated for each event over the network. The basis of the technique can best be described by reference to a simple example. Owing to the fact that this chapter does not easily lend itself to the provision of a case study that can encompass most or all of the areas covered in the chapter, a detailed practical exercise, followed by appropriate questions covering the Bayesian decision theory technique, has been included at the end of the chapter, and this should give the reader an insight into its workings.

Product testing and test marketing

This technique is of value for new or modified products for which no previous sales figures exist and for which it is difficult to estimate likely demand. It is therefore prudent to estimate likely demand for the product by testing it on a sample of the market beforehand.

Product testing involves placing the pre-production model(s) with a sample of potential users beforehand and noting their reactions to the product over a period of time by asking them to fill in a diary noting product deficiencies, how it was working, general reactions, etc. The type of products that can be tested in this fashion can range from household durables, e.g. vacuum cleaners, to canned foods, e.g. soups. However, there is a limit to the number of pre-production items that can be supplied (particularly for consumer durables) and the technique is really of value in deciding between a 'go' or 'no go' decision.

Test marketing is perhaps of more value for forecasting purposes. It simply involves the limited launch of a product in a closely defined geographical test area, e.g. a test town such as Bristol or a larger area such as the Tyne-Tees Television area. Thus a national launch is simulated in a small area, obviously at less expense. It is of particular value for branded foodstuffs, and the test market results can be grossed up to predict the national launch outcome. However, the estimate can only cover the launch and, over time, the novelty factor of a new product might wear off. In addition, it gives competitors an advantage because they can observe the product being test marketed and any potential surprise advantage will be lost. It has also been known for competitors to deliberately attempt to foul up a test marketing campaign by increasing their promotional activity in the area over the period of the test market.

15.5 QUANTITATIVE TECNHIQUES

Quantitative forecasting techniques are sometimes termed objective or mathematical techniques in that they rely more upon mathematics and less upon judgement in their computation. These techniques are becoming very popular with the onset of sophisticated computer packages, some tailor-made for the company needing the forecast.

It is not proposed to go into the detailed working of such techniques because they require specialist skills in their own right; indeed it would be possible to devote a textbook to one technique alone! Some quantitative techniques are very simple while others are extremely complex. The remainder of this chapter attempts to explain such techniques so that the reader will at least have an appreciation of their usefulness and applicability to his or her individual forecasting problems. If the problem calls for one of the specialist mathematical techniques then the answer must be to consult a specialist and not attempt it on the basis of the incomplete information given here.

Quantitative techniques can be divided into two types:

1 *Time series analysis*. The only variable that the forecaster considers is time. These techniques are relatively simple to apply, but the danger is that too much emphasis might be placed upon past events to predict the future. The techniques are useful in predicting sales in markets that are relatively stable and not susceptible to sudden irrational changes in demand. In other words, it is not possible to predict downturns or upturns in the market, unless the forecaster deliberately manipulates the forecast to incorporate such a downturn or upturn.

2 *Causal techniques*. It is assumed that there is a relationship between the measurable independent variable and the forecasted dependent variable. The forecast is produced by putting the value of the independent variable into the calculation. One must choose a suitable independent variable and the period of the forecast to be produced must be considered most carefully. The techniques are thus concerned with cause and effect. The problem arises when one attempts to establish reasons behind these cause and effect relationships; in many cases there is no logical explanation. Indeed, there is quite often nothing to suppose that the relationship should hold good in the future. This reasoning behind causal relationships may not be too clear at this stage, but once the techniques are examined later in the chapter it should become self-evident.

The first set of techniques that are examined are those concerned with **time series analysis.**

Quantitative techniques (time series)

Moving averages

This method averages out and smooths data in a time series. The longer the time series, the greater will be the smoothing. The principle is that one subtracts the earliest sales figure and adds the latest sales figure. The technique is best explained through the simple example given in Table 15.1; it can be seen that using a longer moving average produces a smoother trend line than using a shorter moving average.

Table 15.1 **Office Goods Supplies Ltd: annual sales of briefcases, moving average**

Year	Number	Three year Total	Three year Average	Five year Total	Five year Average
1985	1,446	–	–	–	–
1986	1,324	4,179	1,393	–	–
1987	1,409	3,951	1,317	6,543	1,309
1988	1,218	3,773	1,258	6,032	1,206
1989	1,146	3,299	1,100	5,855	1,171
1990	935	3,228	1,076	5,391	1,078
1991	1,147	3,027	1,009	4,953	991
1992	945	2,872	957	4,810	962
1993	780	2,728	927	5,049	1,008
1994	1,003	2,957	986	4,706	941
1995	1,174	2,981	994	4,805	961
1996	804	3,022	1,007	5,186	1,037
1997	1,044	3,009	1,003	5,470	1,094
1998	1,161	3,492	1,164	–	–
1999	1,287	–	–	–	–

These data are reproduced graphically (see Figure 15.2) and it can be seen that averaging smooths out the annual sales figures. The five-year averaging produces a smoother line than the three-year averaging. One can then produce a forecast by extending the trend line, and it is up to the individual forecaster to decide whether three-year or five-year averaging is better. Indeed, it is sometimes unnecessary to smooth the data (in the case of a steady trend) and in such a case the technique is termed trend projection. Generally speaking, the more the data fluctuate, the more expedient it is to have a longer averaging period.

Exponential smoothing

This is a technique that apportions varying weightings to different parts of the data from which the forecast is to be calculated. The problem with moving averages and straightforward trend projection is that it is unable to predict a downturn or upturn in the market (unless the forecaster deliberately places a downturn or upturn in the data). In this technique the forecaster apportions appropriate degrees of 'typicality' to different parts of the time series.

It is not proposed to explain the detailed mathematics behind the technique, because this is not a sales forecasting textbook. Instead, the statistics used in the previous example have been taken and, from these, weightings have been applied to earlier parts of the series. These weightings are applied by the forecaster according to his or her own judgement as to how 'typical' earlier parts of the data are in the production of a forecast (although there is a mathematical technique for deciding this if necessary). The result is shown in Figure 15.3.

Number

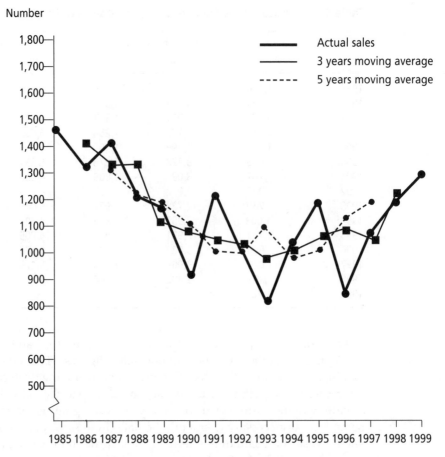

Figure 15.2   Office Goods Supplies Ltd: annual sales of briefcases, moving averages

In the moving averages technique the forecast will take some time to respond to a downturn or upturn, whereas with the exponential smoothing method the response can be immediate. In this example the forecaster has apportioned greater weightings to downturn periods of trade than to upturn periods, and the forecast will thus reflect another downturn period for 2000. Had a moving averages forecast been used, this would have produced a less steep continuum of the 1998–9 upturn trend.

In practice the technique is simple to operate, but it is essentially a computer technique. The forecaster can very simply alter the smoothing constant for different periods to produce a number of alternative forecasts; the skill lies in determining the degree of weightings for earlier and later parts of the time series.

Time series analysis

This technique is useful when seasonality occurs in a data pattern. It is of particular use for fashion products and for products that respond to seasonal

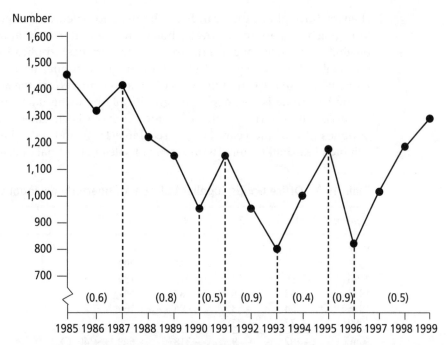

Figure 15.3 Office Goods Supplies Ltd: annual sales of briefcases, exponential smoothing (weighting shown in brackets)

Table 15.2 Office Goods Supplies Ltd: quarterly sales of briefcases

Year	Quarter	Unit sales	Quarterly moving total	Sum of pairs	Divided by 8 to find trend	Deviations from trend
1995	1	207				
	2	268	= 1,174	= 2,295	287	– 64
	3	223	1,121	2,136	267	+209
	4	476	1,015	= 1,934	242	– 88
1996	1	154	919	1,723	215	– 53
	2	162	= 804	= 1,643	205	– 78
	3	127	839	1,779	222	+139
	4	361	940	= 1,935	242	– 53
1997	1	189	995	2,039	255	+ 8
	2	263	= 1,044	= 2,110	264	– 82
	3	182	1,066	2,156	269	+141
	4	410	1,090	= 2,197	275	– 64
1998	1	211	1,107	2,268	284	+ 3
	2	287	= 1,161	= 2,346	293	– 94
	3	199	1,185	2,433	304	+160
	4	464	1,248	= 2,497	312	– 77
1999	1	235	1,249	2,536	317	+ 33
	2	350	= 1,287			
	3	200				
	4	502				

changes throughout the year. It can be used for cyclical changes in the longer term (such as patterns of trade) but there are better techniques available for dealing with such longer-term trends. Thus its best application is where the seasonal pattern is repeated on a fairly regular annual basis. These seasonal movements are measured in terms of their deviation from the aggregate trend.

The technique is best explained graphically by using data from the previous example. The quarterly sales of briefcases have been taken for Office Goods Supplies Ltd for the years 1995–9 (see Table 15.2), and it can be seen that sales exhibit a seasonal pattern, with a peak of sales in the final quarter of each year.

Table 15.3 Office Goods Supplies Ltd: sum of quarterly deviations from trend

Quarter	1	2	3	4	
Year					
1995	–	–	– 64	+ 209	
1996	– 88	– 53	– 78	+ 139	
1997	– 53	+ 8	– 82	+ 141	
1998	– 64	+ 3	– 94	+ 160	
1999	– 77	+ 33	–	–	
Sum	– 282	– 9	– 318	+ 649 = + 40	

When the sums of quarterly deviations from the trend are added, the resultant sum is +40 in this particular case (see Table 15.3). The total sum must equal zero, otherwise it would mean that a positive bias would be built into the forecast. However, this correction must come from all figures equally, and is calculated as:

$$40/4 = +10$$

Therefore +10 must be subtracted from each quarter's figures. The corrected figures are then:

Quarter	1	2	3	4
Corrected deviations	–292	–19	–328	+639 = 0

In this particular example these figures must now be divided by 4 to produce a yearly aggregate (because four years' data have been used in their compilation) and the figures from which the forecast will be derived are as follows:

Quarter	1	2	3	4
Deviations	–73	–5	–82	+160 = 0

The figures in Table 15.4 were derived as follows. Unit sales are added to provide a one-year total. This total then summates the one-year moving sales by taking off the old quarter and adding on the new quarter. The quarterly moving totals are then paired in the next column (to provide greater smoothing) and this sum is then divided by 8 to ascertain the quarterly trend. Finally, the deviations

Table 15.4   Office Goods Supplies Ltd: forecasted trend figures and deviations from trend that have been applied

Year	Period	Trend	Deviation	Forecast
1999	3	326	− 82	244
	4	334	+ 160	494
2000	1	343	− 73	270
	2	352	− 5	347
	3	360	− 82	278
	4	369	+ 160	529

from trend are calculated by taking the actual figure (in unit sales) from the trend, and these are represented in the final column as deviations from the trend.

The statistics are then incorporated into a graph and the unit sales and trend are drawn in as in Figure 15.4. The trend line is extended by sight (and it is here that the forecaster's skill and intuition must come in). The deviations from trend are then applied to the trend line, and this provides the sales forecast.

In this particular example it can be seen that the trend line has been extended on a slow upwards trend similar to previous years. The first two figures for periods 3 and 4 of 1999 are provided as a forecast, but these quarters have, of course, passed and the figures are disregarded. The four quarters of 2000 have been forecasted, and these are included in the graph.

The technique, like many similar techniques, suffers from the fact that downturns and upturns cannot be predicted, and such data must be subjectively entered by the forecaster through manipulation of the extension to the trend line.

Z (or Zee) charts

This technique is merely a furtherance of the moving averages technique. In addition to providing the moving annual total, it also shows the monthly sales and the cumulative sales; an illustration of the technique shows why it is termed Z chart. Each Z chart represents one year's data and it is best applied using monthly sales data. As a vehicle for forecasting it provides a useful medium where sales for one year can be compared with previous years using three criteria (monthly, cumulative and moving annual).

The sales of briefcases for Office Goods Supplies Ltd have been provided for each month of 1998 and 1999 and this is sufficient to provide data for the Z chart as can be seen in Table 15.5. The figures in Table 15.5 are then transposed graphically in Figure 15.5.

Moving annual sales are obtained by adding on the new month's figure and taking off the old month's figure, twelve months previously. The cumulative sales are obtained by adding each month to the next month, and the bottom line of the Z is the monthly sales.

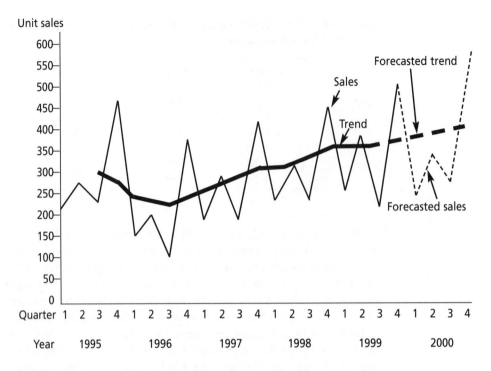

Figure 15.4 Office Goods Supplies Ltd: quarterly sales of briefcases and one-year forecast

Table 15.5 Office Goods Supplies Ltd: monthly sales of briefcases 1998/9

| Month | Unit sales | | Cumulative | Moving annual |
	1998	1999	sales 1999	total
Jan	58	66	66	1,169
Feb	67	70	136	1,172
Mar	86	99	235	1,185
Apr	89	102	337	1,198
May	94	121	458	1,225
Jun	104	127	585	1,248
Jul	59	58	643	1,247
Aug	62	69	712	1,254
Sep	78	73	785	1,249
Oct	94	118	903	1,273
Nov	178	184	1,087	1,279
Dec	192	200	1,287	1,287

The method is very much a comparison by sight method and in this case would be used for the medium-term (one year) sales forecast. However, as a serious method for prediction its uses are limited; its main use is for comparison.

Unit sales

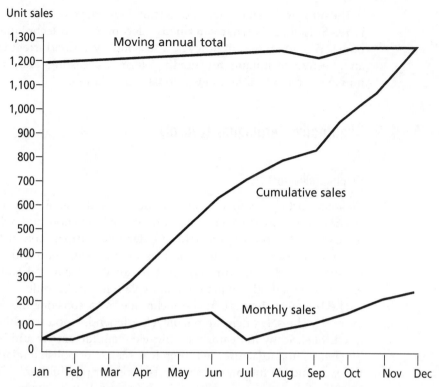

Figure 15.5   Office Goods Supplies Ltd: monthly sales of briefcases, Z-chart for 1999

Miscellaneous

This final section very briefly describes two techniques that are very much computer techniques; to describe their workings in detail would take a disproportionate amount of space together with a detailed knowledge of mathematics. They rely in their application upon sophisticated computer packages, and if the reader wishes to pursue the techniques further then the advice would be to go to a software specialist who can advise as to their applicability and to their degree of accuracy for the desired intention. This is not to say that the forecaster (say the sales manager) should necessarily need to have a detailed knowledge of the technique that is being applied; all he or she needs to know is what the forecast will do and its degree of likely correctness.

The first of these techniques is Box-Jenkins, named after the people who developed it. It is a sophistication of the exponential smoothing technique which applies different weightings to different parts of the time series. In the case of this technique, the computer package takes earlier parts of the time series and manipulates and weights parts of this against known sales from later parts of the time series. The weighting that provides the best fit is finally deduced and this can then be used for the forecast. It is reasonably accurate for short- and medium-term forecasting, and it is predicted that its application will increase as more powerful personal computers are developed.

The other technique is termed X-11 and was developed by an American called Julius Shiskin. It is what is termed a decomposition technique and it breaks a time series down into trend cycles, seasonal cycles and irregular elements. It is an effective technique for medium-term forecasting and it incorporates a number of analytical methods into its computation.

Quantitative techniques (causal)

Leading indicators

This forecasting method seeks to define and establish a linear regression relationship between some measurable phenomenon and whatever is to be forecasted. It is not appropriate to enter into a discussion of the technique of linear regression within the confines of this text; should the reader wish to pursue the technique further, most reasonably advanced statistical texts will explain the method adequately and explain its applicability.

The best way to explain the technique is to consider the following simple example. The sale of children's bicycles depends upon the child population, so a sensible leading indicator for a bicycle manufacturer would be birth statistics. The bicycle manufacturer will therefore seek to establish a relationship between the two and, if the manufacturer is considering children's first two-wheeler bicycles (say, at age 3 years old, on average), then births will precede first bicycles by three years. In other words first bicycles will lag births by three years.

The example is obviously an over-simplification, and there are forecasting packages available that permute a number of leading indicators, i.e. they are indicators that are ahead of actual sales, and it is possible to provide the permutation that best fits known sales, where the sales are lagged in time and the indicator is leading. The permutation that best fits the known sales to the indicator (or permutation of indicators) is the one to use in the forecast. Thus the permutation is constantly under review as time goes on. As forecasts pass into actual sales, so the forecasting permutation is modified to take account of the most recent sales.

This more sophisticated type of forecasting just described uses what is known as correlation analysis to establish the relationship, and again the reader is directed to any reasonably advanced statistics textbook for a fuller explanation of its workings and its implications.

Simulation

This forecasting methodology has only become possible with the widespread use of the digital computer. Leading indicator forecasting establishes relationships between some measurable phenomenon and whatever is to be forecasted, whilst simulation uses a process of iteration, or trial and error, to arrive at the forecasting relationship. In a reasonably complicated forecasting problem (which most are that utilise this technique) the number of alternative possibilities and outcomes is vast. When probabilities of various outcomes are known, the technique is known as Monte Carlo simulation and it depends upon a predetermined chance of a particular event occurring (it is no coincidence that the technique derives from probabilities worked out for gambling games).

It is difficult to explain the technique further without entering into complex mathematical discussions and explanations. In so far as this text is concerned, it is sufficient that the reader is aware of such a technique; if further information is to be sought, a professional forecaster must be consulted. It is essentially a digital computer technique, and to apply it successfully requires the help of an expert.

Diffusion models

Most of the techniques that have been discussed so far have depended upon a series of past sales for the company and the industry to be available before a forecast can be calculated. However, when new products are introduced to the market, and the products are not simply extensions or redesigns of old products, then the technique for estimating sales comes from a body of theory called the diffusion of innovations. One of the authors has already made a study of the subject and has produced a forecast for video-recorders which utilised the Bass **diffusion model** (Lancaster and Wright, 1983).

Again, as with most of these causal techniques, the mathematics are complicated and the best advice for the sales manager seeking to apply such a technique to a new product would be to seek the advice of a specialist. This is essentially a digital computer technique and it is complicated in its computation.

Basically, diffusion theory assumes that the new product has four basic units:

- the innovation
- the communication of the innovation among individuals
- the social system
- time.

The theory goes on to say that the innovation can be categorised into one of the following groupings:

- continuous
- dynamically continuous
- discontinuous.

This latter is a hierarchical listing, with the innovations being more widely removed from previous technology as one moves further down the list. This means that the further down the hierarchy the innovation is placed, the lower will be the degree of likely acceptance. In the early days of a product innovation, knowledge must be communicated to as many individuals as possible, especially those who are likely to be influential in gaining wider appeal for the innovation. This communication process is broken down into formal and informal communication. It is these two elements that are fed into the forecasting model and as such the model can be applied without large amounts of past sales data. The formal communication is controlled by the company and includes such data as advertising expenditure and sales support for the launch and the informal element relates to such matters as family and reference group influences.

Once the innovation has been launched, a measure of the rate of adoption is needed in order to produce a useful forecast. Products are born, they mature and eventually die, and it is important to the forecaster using this technique that the first few points of the launch sales are known in order to be able to determine the rate of adoption. Thus a forecast can be made using only a small amount of data covering the early launch period. An assumption is therefore made that the product being considered has a life-cycle curve and that new product acceptance is through a process of imitation, i.e. later purchasers will follow the innovators.

The use of computer software in sales forecasting

Much software has been written designed specifically for forecasting purposes. The problem with any listing of such software is that it quickly dates, so if it is proposed to use a software package then the best advice is to consult an up-to-date listing. The following is a list of more generalised packages that have withstood the test of time.

EXEC*U*STAT from Mercia Software Ltd. Combines business statistics with high quality graphics output. It provides for quick analysis of data.

FOCA from Timberlake Clark Ltd. Offers modern quantitative forecasting of time series using exponential smoothing, spectral analysis, Box-Jenkins and adaptive filtering.

MINITAB from CLE. COM Ltd. A general-purpose data analysis system that is easy to use. Its features include descriptive statistics, regression analysis with diagnostics, residual analysis and step-wise procedures, time series analysis including robust smoothers and Box-Jenkins operations.

RATS from Timberlake Clark Ltd. An econometric package that performs time series and cross-sectional regression. It is designed for forecasting of time series, although small cross-sectional and panel data may also be used.

SAS/ETS from SAS Software Ltd. An econometrics and time series library which provides forecasting, planning and financial reporting. It contains procedures for time series analysis, linear and non-linear systems simulation, and seasonal adjustments and its applications include econometric modelling and cash-flow planning as well as sales forecasting.

SORITEC from Timberlake Clark Ltd. Includes non-linear and simultaneous estimation techniques, simultaneous non-linear simulation and solution, a full matrix processing language and transfer function estimation.

SPSS-PC+ from SPSS (UK) Ltd. A fully interactive data analysis package with full screen editing facilities, data entry and validation and a range of analytical and reporting procedures.

SPSS-X from SPSS (UK) Ltd. A simple statistical and reporting package. It provides a wide range of facilities from data validation to sophisticated tables, graphics and mapping.

STATGRAPHICS from Cocking & Drury Ltd. A statistical and graphics package that includes plotting functions (2D and 3D), descriptive methods, estimation and testing, distribution fitting, exploratory data analysis, analysis and variance, regression analysis, time series analysis including Box-Jenkins ARIMA modelling, multivariate and non-parametric methods and experimental design.

STATPAC GOLD from Molimerx Ltd with batch and interactive processing and good graphics which requires less memory than most other packages.

This listing only documents those packages that are available in the United Kingdom; many more are available in the USA.

15.6 CONCLUSIONS

The purpose of sales forecasting has been explained and it has been emphasised that this function rests with sales management. Its importance to the planning process has been established; without reasonably accurate forecasting, planning will be in vain. The purpose of forecasting has been considered in the short-, medium- and long-term, and the usefulness of each has been established within the major functions of any manufacturing or service concern.

Forecasting has been considered under the headings of qualitative and quantitative techniques, with the latter being split into time series methods and causal methods. Qualitative techniques and time series methods have been explained in the amount of detail required to give the reader a working knowledge of their application. However, causal methods depend largely upon the use of the digital computer, and their computation relies to a great extent upon advanced mathematics. As such, the techniques have been described but not explained in workable detail.

The next chapter is concerned with sales budgets, taking the sales forecasting procedure to its next logical step.

PRACTICAL EXERCISE

Classical Reproductions Ltd

Background to the application of Bayesian decision theory

It has been pointed out throughout the chapter that since the 1960s we have seen the development of sophisticated statistical techniques for problem-solving where information is incomplete or uncertain. The new area of statistics has a variety of names – statistical decision theory, simple decision theory and Bayesian decision theory (after the Reverend Thomas Bayes, 1702–61). These names can be used inter-changeably, but for the purposes of this case we shall use the term Bayesian decision theory.

Bayesian decision theory is a relatively new, and somewhat controversial, method for dealing with future uncertainties. Applied to forecasting, the technique incorporates the firm's own guesses as data inputs into the calculation of a sales forecast. There are essentially two ways of conceiving probability:

1 as a physical property, inherent to a physical system
2 as a measure of belief in the truth of some statement.

Until the late 1950s most statisticians held the first view of probability, with the probability of an event being the relative frequency with which the event might occur. Since this period there has been a rethink on the meaning of probability, and it is now regarded more as a measure of belief. This latter approach is termed Bayesian statistics. The Bayesian view is that probability is a measure of our belief, and we can always express our degree of belief in terms of probability.

To use the Bayesian approach, the decision-maker must be able to assign a prob-ability to each specified event or state of nature. The sum of these probabilities must add to one. These probabilities represent the strength of the decision-maker's feeling regarding the likelihood of the occurrence of the various elements of the overall problem. It is because of the subjective nature of the process in generating these probabilities that Bayesian decision-making is so useful in solving business problems for which probabilities are often unknown. It is also the reason why many practitioners often reject the Bayesian approach; in fact some of the more conservative statisticians have termed it 'the quantification of error'!

In practical business problems, decisions are often delegated to persons whose levels of expertise should be such as to enable them to assign valid probabilities to the occurrences of various events. These probabilities will be subjective evaluations based on experience, intuition and other factors like available published data, all of which are acquired prior to the time that the decision is made. For this reason such subjective probability estimates are referred to as the prior probability of an event.

In business decision-making we must decide between alternatives by taking into account the monetary repercussions or expected value of our actions. A manager who must select from a number of available investments should consider the profit and loss that might result from each option. Applying Bayesian decision theory involves selecting an option and having a reasonable idea of the economic consequences of choosing that action.

Once the relevant future events have been identified and the respective subjective prior probabilities have been assigned, the decision-maker computes the expected payoff for each act and chooses the act with the most attractive expected payoff. If payoffs represent income or profit, the decision-maker chooses the act with the highest expected payoff.

The Bayesian technique can be used to solve quite complex problems, but in this example we use a relatively simple problem by way of illustration and explanation. However, the principles are similar for simple or difficult problems.

Bayesian decision theory applied to Classical Reproductions Ltd

This UK manufacturer of fine reproduction English furniture is considering venturing into the United States market. The company is to appoint an agent who will hold stock and sell the furniture to quality retail stores.

In order for the firm to gain economies in freight charges, consignments need to be fairly large, and it is planned that the first consignment will be £2 million worth of furniture.

This type of furniture is particularly fashionable in the USA at present and commands high prices. Classical Reproductions' management expect that this furniture will remain heavily in demand so long as the economic conditions in the USA remain buoyant. If economic conditions take a turn for the worse, then demand and prices will fall dramatically, because such products are a deferrable purchase.

To finance the manufacture, shipping, warehousing and other costs associated with the venture, the company is raising capital from a bank. Although the venture looks sound there is uncertainty as to the future direction of the US economy over the next twelve months. The decision facing management is whether to risk going ahead with the venture now, when demand for their products is going to be high, but with the possibility of the economy deteriorating, or to postpone the venture until the economic outlook in the USA is more certain, but during which time tastes might change.

Let us assume that the management feel that the direction of the United States economy could go in one of three ways in the next twelve months:

● continue to be buoyant
● a moderate downturn
● a serious recession.

The direction of the economy is an event (E) or a state of nature that is completely outside the control of the company.

Let us also assume that management has decided on three possible courses of action (A):

● export now while demand is high
● delay the venture by 1 year
● delay the venture by 2 years.

Management has made a forecast of the likely expected profit for each of the possible courses of action for each of the three possible events, and this information is shown in the table below.

Events (E)	Actions (A)	Export now (£)	Delay 1 year (£)	Delay 2 years (£)
Economic conditions remain good		800,000	600,000	500,000
Moderate downturn in economy		450,000	370,000	200,000
Economic recession		–324,000	50,000	80,000

Management wishes to make the decision that will maximise the firm's expected profit. They assign subjective prior probabilities to each of the possible events:

Event	Probability
Economic conditions remain good (A)	0.4
Moderate downturn in economy (B)	0.3
Economic recession (C)	0.3
	1.0

These prior probabilities are now incorporated into a decision tree (see Figure 15.6) which is made up of a series of nodes and branches. The decision points are denoted by a square and chance events by circles. The node on the left (square) denotes the decision the firm has to make. Each branch represents an alternative course of action or decision. Each branch leads to a further node (circle) and from this, further branches denote the chance events.

The expected value (EV) should now be calculated for each forecast and then totalled for each alternative course of action. This is done in the 'payoff table' below by multiplying the expected profit for each event by their assigned probabilities and summing these products.

1 Action 1 – export now:

Event (E)	Probability	Expected profit (£)	Expected value (£)
A	0.4	800,000	320,000
B	0.3	450,000	135,000
C	0.3	−324,000	−97,200
Total EV for this alternative			£357,800

2 Action 2 – delay 1 year:

Event (E)	Probability	Expected profit (£)	Expected value (£)
A	0.4	600,000	240,000
B	0.3	370,000	111,000
C	0.3	50,000	15,000
Total EV for this alternative			£366,000

3 Action 3 – delay 2 years:

Event (E)	Probability	Expected profit (£)	Expected value (£)
A	0.4	500,000	200,000
B	0.3	200,000	60,000
C	0.3	80,000	24,000
Total EV for this alternative			£284,000

The firm decides to delay the venture by one year because the maximum expected payoff is associated with this. Since the act is selected under conditions of uncertainty, the EV of £366,000 is referred to as the EV under uncertainty and the act is referred to as the optimal act.

In this example the probabilities that have been assigned to events have been prior probabilities, so called because they have been arrived at prior to the acquisition of

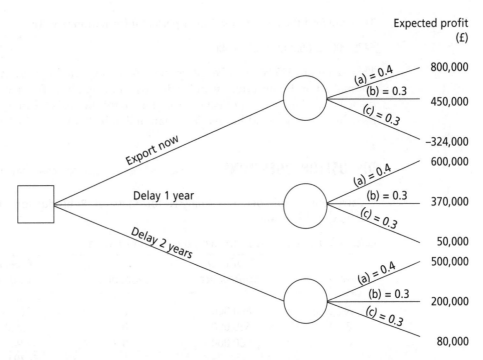

Expected profit
(£)

Figure 15.6 Decision tree for Classical Reproductions Ltd: (a) economy remains buoyant; (b) moderate downturn; (c) recession

sampling or experimental information. As a rule, these prior probabilities are subjective, representing the decision-maker's belief that various events will happen. The analysis which is carried out using these prior probabilities is called prior analysis. Following prior analysis, the decision-maker must decide whether to go ahead with the optimal act indicated by prior analysis, or to obtain further information in the hope of making a better and more certain decision.

Additional information may be obtained by conducting a survey, by carrying out an experiment or by some other means. If this additional information is acted upon, the decision-maker will have to substitute new probabilities for the prior probabilities. Another analysis will then have to be undertaken using this new information. These new probabilities are called posterior probabilities.

Naturally, generating further information can be costly and the decision-maker must decide if the potential result is worth the cost. To extend this final point, let us find the expected value with perfect information when the prior probabilities are as follows:

(A)   Economic conditions remain buoyant   = 0.4
(B)   Relative economic decline   = 0.3
(C)   Recession   = 0.3

If economic conditions remain buoyant, the optimum choice would be to export now. If there is a moderate downturn in the economy, the optimum choice would still be to export now. If there is a recession, the optimal choice will be to delay for two years.

Thus we find the expected value of perfect information (EVPI):

£479,000–£366,000 = £113,000

This value of £113,000 can be interpreted as the expected opportunity loss for the optimal act under uncertainty and is the cost of uncertainty. The decision-maker can do no better than obtain perfect information, so this figure is the maximum he would be willing to pay for additional information that he knows will be less than perfect.

DISCUSSION QUESTIONS

1 Carry out a full decision analysis for Classical Reproductions Ltd, using the following information.

Calculation of expected profit with perfect information

Event	Profit for optimal act	Probability	Expected value (£)
A	800,000	0.4	320,000
B	450,000	0.3	135,000
C	80,000	0.3	24,000
			£479,000

Prior probablities for the various events for the next twelve months are:

(A) = 0.3
(B) = 0.4
(C) = 0.3

2 Carry out a pre-posterior analysis and find the expected value of perfect information (EVPI).

3 Having applied Bayesian decision theory to this example, what do you consider are its advantages and disadvantages?

EXAMINATION QUESTIONS

1 What is the place of sales forecasting in the company planning process?

2 Distinguish between qualitative and quantitative forecasting techniques. What are the advantages and disadvantages associated with each approach?

3 Define the differences between a sales forecast and a market forecast.

4 How might a government forecast or a forecast from a trade association be of specific use to a medium-sized company?

16 BUDGETING AND EVALUATION

OBJECTIVES After studying this chapter, you should be able to:

1 Appreciate the part budgets play in the smooth running of an organisation.

2 Understand how the sales budget is derived and its purpose.

3 Know how standards of performance are set in order that sales can be achieved.

4 Set qualitative and quantitative measures of performance.

KEY CONCEPTS

- appraisal interviewing
- budget allocation
- budget determination
- performance measures
- sales budget
- salesforce evaluation
- standards of performance

16.1 PURPOSE OF BUDGETING

An organisation needs to budget in order to ensure that its expenditure does not exceed its planned income. It has already been shown that the sales forecast is the starting point for business planning activities. The company costing department takes the medium-term sales forecast as its starting point, and from this budgets are then apportioned to departments (or cost centres in accounting parlance). Budgets state limits of spending; they are thus a means of control. The company can plan its profits based upon anticipated sales, minus the cost of achieving those sales (which is represented in the total budget for the organisation).

The consequence of an incorrect medium-term forecast can be immediately seen because then the whole company profit plan will be incorrect. It has already been mentioned, but it is re-emphasised here, that if the forecast is pessimistic and the company achieves more sales than those forecast, then potential sales might be lost owing to unpreparedness and insufficient working finance and facilities being available to achieve those sales. On the other hand, if the sales forecast is optimistic and sales revenue does not match anticipated sales, then revenue problems will arise, with the company having to approach a lending institution – most probably a bank – to fund its short-term working capital requirements (which can be very expensive when interest rates are high). This latter factor is a prime cause of many business failures, not necessarily because of bad products or a bad salesforce, but through insufficient money being available to meet working capital requirements. These problems all stem from incorrect medium-term forecasting in the first place.

16.2 BUDGET DETERMINATION

Departmental budgets are not prepared by cost accountants. Cost accountants, in conjunction with general management, apportion overall budgets for individual departments. It is the departmental manager who determines how the overall departmental budget will be utilised in achieving the planned-for sales (and production). For instance, a marketing manager might decide that more needs to be apportioned to advertising and less to the physical effort of selling in order to achieve the forecasted sales. He or she will therefore apportion the budget accordingly and may concentrate upon image rather than product promotion; it is a matter of deciding beforehand where the priority must lie when planning for marketing.

Thus, the overall sales forecast is the basis for company plans and the sales department budget (other names include sales and marketing department budget and marketing department budget) is the basis for marketing plans in achieving those forecasted sales. The sales department budget is consequently a reflection of marketing's forthcoming expenditure in achieving those forecasted sales.

At this juncture it is useful to make a distinction between the sales department budget and the sales budget. The sales department budget is merely the budget for running the marketing function for the budget period ahead. Cost accountants split this budget into three elements of cost:

1 The selling expense budget includes those costs directly attributable to the selling process, e.g. sales personnel salaries and commission, sales expenses and training.
2 The advertising budget includes those expenses directly attributable to above-the-line promotion, e.g. television advertising, and below-the-line promotion, e.g. a coupon redemption scheme. Methods of ascertaining the level of such a budget are as follows:

- A percentage of last year's sales.
- Parity with competitors, whereby smaller manufacturers take their cue from a larger manufacturer and adjust their advertising budget in line with the market leader.
- The affordable method, where expenditure is allocated to advertising after other cost centres have received their budgets. In other words, if there is anything left over it goes to advertising.

- The objective and task method calls for an ascertainment of the advertising expenditure needed to reach marketing objectives that have been laid down in the marketing plan.
- The return on investment method assumes that advertising is a tangible item that extends beyond the budget period. It looks at advertising expenditures as longer-term investments and attempts to ascertain the return on such expenditures.
- The incremental method is similar to the previous method; it assumes that the last unit of money spent on advertising should bring in an equal unit of revenue.

The first method assumes that increasing sales will generate increasing promotion and vice versa, whereas the converse might be the remedy, i.e. a cure for falling sales might be to increase the advertising spend. The second method assumes status quo within the marketplace. The third method does not really commend itself because the assumption is that advertising is a necessary evil and should only be entered into when other expenditures have been met. It quite often happens in times of company squeezes that advertising is the first item to be cut because of its intangibility. The cure for the company ailment might rest in increased promotional awareness. The fourth method seems to make sense, but accountants contend that marketing personnel will state marketing objectives without due regard to their value, and such objectives may not sometimes be related to profits. The fifth and sixth methods seem to make sense, but the main difficulties are in measuring likely benefits such as increased brand loyalty resulting from such advertising expenditures, and determining when marginal revenue equals marginal expenditure. In practice, firms often use a combination of methods, e.g. the fourth and fifth methods, when deciding their advertising budget.

3 The administrative budget represents the expenditure to be incurred in running the sales office. Such expenses cover the costs of marketing research, sales administration and support staff.

The marketing manager (or whoever is responsible for the overall marketing and selling function) must then determine, based upon the marketing plan for the year ahead, what portion of the sales department budget must be allocated to each of the three parts of the budget described above. Such expenditure should of course ensure that the forecasted sales will be met as the forecasting period progresses.

What has been stated so far relates to the sales department budget; the sales budget itself has not been dealt with. The sales budget has far more implications for the company and this merits a separate section by way of explanation.

16.3 THE SALES BUDGET

The **sales budget** may be said to be the total revenue expected from all products that are sold, and as such this affects all other aspects of the business. Thus, the sales budget comes directly after the sales forecast.

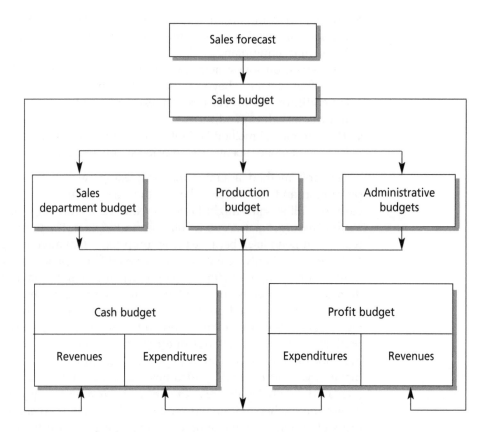

Figure 16.1   The budgetary process

It can therefore be said that the sales budget is the starting point of the company budgeting procedure because all other company activities are dependent upon sales and the total revenue anticipated from the various products that the company sells. This budget affects other functional areas of the business, namely finance and production, because these two functions are directly dependent upon sales. Figure 16.1 best explains the sales budgeting procedure.

Figure 16.1 represents the way cost accountants view the budgeting procedure. From the sales budget comes the sales department budget (or the total costs in administering the marketing function, which has been dealt with earlier in the chapter); the production budget covers all the costs involved in actually producing the products; and the administrative budget covers all other costs like personnel, finance, etc., and costs not directly attributable to the production and selling processes.

The sales budget is thus the revenue earner for the company and the other budgets represent expenditures incurred in achieving the sales. Cost accountants also have cash budgets and profit budgets, each with revenue provided from company sales. It is not proposed to go into why they split into cash and profit budgets; if the reader wishes to know more about the mechanism and thinking involved here, then any simple text on cost accountancy should provide an adequate explanation.

16.4 BUDGET ALLOCATION

The sales budget itself is a statement of projected sales by individual sales-people. The figure that reaches the individual salesperson is sometimes called the sales quota or sales target and this is the amount that must be sold in order to achieve the forecasted sales. Such quotas or targets are therefore performance targets that must be reached, and quite often incentives are linked to sales-people reaching (and surpassing) such quotas or targets. Such incentives have already been dealt with in Chapters 13 and 14.

Each salesperson knows the individual amount he or she must sell in order to achieve their quota, and such quotas are in effect performance targets. Quotas need not necessarily be individually based, but can be group based – say, collectively throughout a region – with everybody from the regional or area manager downwards equally sharing the sales commission. Quotas may also be for much shorter periods than the one year. The entire year's budget may be broken down in the same manner, say, month by month; when administered in this way the time horizon is more realistic and immediate than one year. Thus there is more of an incentive for a salesperson to achieve the quota or target.

For established firms the most common practice of budget allocation is simply to increase (or decrease) last year's individual budgets or quotas by the appropriate percentage, depending on the change in the overall sales budget. However, periodically it is sensible to review individual sales quotas in order to establish if they are reasonable given current market conditions.

The first step in this procedure is to attempt to determine the sales potential of territories. Usually surrogate measures will be employed to give at least relative measures of potential. For consumer products, disposable incomes and number of people in the target market may be used to assess relative potential. For industrial products, the number and size of potential customers may be used. Another factor to be taken into account is workload. Obviously two territories of equal potential may justify different quotas if one is compact while the other is more widespread. By assessing sales potential for territories and allowing for workload, the overall sales budget can be allocated in as fair a manner as possible between salespeople.

Not only does the sales quota act as an incentive to the salesforce; it also acts as a prime measure of performance. The following sections of this chapter look at the whole area of evaluation of sales personnel.

16.5 THE PURPOSE OF EVALUATION

The prime reason for evaluation is to attempt to attain company objectives. By measuring actual performance against objectives, shortfalls can be identified and appropriate action taken to improve performance. However, evaluation has other benefits. Evaluation can help improve an individual's motivation and skills. Motivation is affected since an evaluation programme will identify what is expected of him or her, and what is considered good performance. Second, it provides the opportunity for the recognition of above-average standards of work performance, which improves confidence and motivation. Skills are affected since carefully constructed evaluation allows areas of weakness to be identified, and effort to be directed to the improvement of skills in those areas.

Thus, evaluation is an important ingredient in an effective training programme. Further, evaluation may show weaknesses, perhaps in not devoting enough attention to selling certain product lines, which span most or all of the sales team. This information may lead to the development of a compensation plan designed to encourage salespeople to sell those products by means of higher commission rates.

Evaluation provides information which affects key decision areas within the sales management function. Training, compensation, motivation and objective setting are dependent on the information derived from evaluation, as illustrated in Figure 16.2. It is important, then, that sales management develop a system of information collection which allows fair and accurate evaluation to occur.

The level and type of control exercised over international salesforces will depend upon the culture of the company and its host nations. The following case discussion highlights some important points.

SELLING AND SALES MANAGEMENT IN ACTION

Controlling international salesforces

The degree to which sales teams are controlled may depend upon the culture of the employing company. Many European and US companies are profit-focused and so emphasise quantitative (e.g. sales and profit) control mechanisms. Many Japanese and Asian companies use less formal and less quantitative evaluation systems.

Control systems must take into account the local conditions in each overseas market. Furthermore, they should account for the type of salesforce employed (expatriates or foreign nationals). Systems that are used at home may be appropriate for expatriates, but for foreign nationals they may be alien to their culture and way of doing business.

Based on Honeycutt, Jr., E.D. and Ford, J.B. (1995) 'Guidelines for managing an international sales force', *Industrial Marketing Management*, 24, pp. 135–144.

16.6 SETTING STANDARDS OF PERFORMANCE

Evaluation implies the setting of standards of performance along certain lines which are believed to be important for sales success. The control process is based

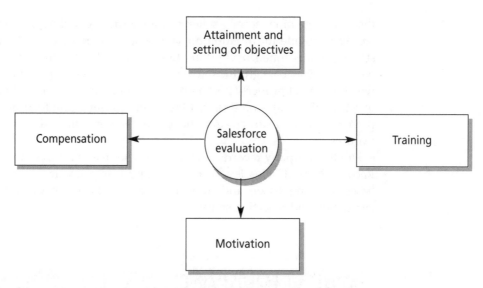

Figure 16.2   The central role of evaluation in sales management

upon the collection of information on performance so that actual results can be compared against those standards. For the sales team as a whole the sales budget will be the standard against which actual performance will be evaluated. This measure will be used to evaluate sales management as well as individual salespeople. For each salesperson, his or her sales quota will be a prime standard of sales success.

Standards provide a method of fairly assessing and comparing individual salespeople. Simply comparing levels of sales achieved by individual salespeople is unlikely to be fair since territories often have differing levels of sales potential and varying degrees of workload.

16.7 GATHERING INFORMATION

The individual salesperson will provide much of the information upon which evaluation will take place. He or she will provide head office with data relating to sales achieved by product/brand and customer, a daily or weekly report of the names of customers he or she has called on, and problems and opportunities revealed, together with expense claims.

Such information will be supplemented by sales management during field visits. These are important in providing more qualitative information on how the salesperson performs in front of customers as well as giving indications of general attitudes, work habits and degree of organisational ability, all of which supplement the more quantitative information provided by the salesperson himself/herself.

Market research projects can also provide information on the sales team from customers themselves. A specific project, or a more general one which focuses on the full range of customer–seller relationships, e.g. delivery, product reliability, etc., can provide information on salespeople's performance. A market research study commissioned by Perkins Engines (Reed, 1983) found that salespeople with technical backgrounds were basing their sales presentation on features which were not properly understood by their audience. This led Perkins Engines to retrain their salesforce so that their sales presentation focused upon a simple presentation of features and the customer benefits which arose from those features.

Finally, company records provide a rich source of information for evaluation. Records of past sales levels, calls achieved, expense levels, etc., can provide bases for comparison and indications of trends which can be used both for evaluation and objective setting.

16.8 MEASURES OF PERFORMANCE

Quantitative measures of performance

There are two fundamental groups of **performance measure**. For both groups, management may wish to set targets for their sales team. One group is a set of input measures which are essentially diagnostic in nature – they help to provide indications of why performance is below standard. Key output measures relate to sales and profit performance. Specific output measures for individual salespeople include the following:

- sales revenue achieved
- profits generated
- percentage gross profit margin achieved
- sales per potential account
- sales per active account
- sales revenue as a percentage of sales potential
- number of orders
- sales to new customers
- number of new customers.

All of these measures relate to output.

The second group of measures relates to input and includes:

- number of calls made
- calls per potential account
- calls per active account
- number of quotations (in part, an output measure also)
- number of calls on prospects.

By combining output and input measures a number of hybrid ratios can be determined. For example:

1 strike rate $= \dfrac{\text{Number of orders}}{\text{Number of quotations}}$

2 sales revenue per call ratio

3 profit per call ratio   call effectiveness

4 order per call ratio

5 average order value $= \dfrac{\text{Sales revenue}}{\text{Number of orders}}$

6 prospecting success ratio $= \dfrac{\text{Number of new customers}}{\text{Number of prospects visited}}$

7 average profit contribution per order $= \dfrac{\text{Profits generated}}{\text{Number of orders}}$

All of these ratios can be applied to individual product and customer types.

These ratios help to answer the following questions:

- Is the salesperson achieving a satisfactory level of sales?
- Is sales success reflected in profit achievement?
- Is the salesperson 'buying' sales by giving excessive discounts?
- Is the salesperson devoting sufficient time to prospecting?
- Is time spent prospecting being rewarded by orders?
- Does the salesperson appear to be making a satisfactory number of calls per week?
- Is he or she making enough repeat calls on different customer categories? Is he or she making too many calls on low-potential customers?
- Are calls being reflected in sales success?
- Are the number of quotations being made reflected in orders taken?
- How are sales being achieved – a large number of small orders or a few large orders?
- Are the profits generated per order sufficient to justify calling upon the account?

Many of these measures are clearly diagnostic. They provide pointers to possible reasons why a salesperson may not be reaching his or her sales quota. Perhaps he or she is lazy – not making enough calls. Perhaps call rate is satisfactory but call effectiveness, e.g. sales per call, is low, indicating a lack of sales skill. Maybe the salesperson is calling on too many established accounts and not enough new prospects.

Ratios also provide clues to problem areas which require further investigation. A low strike rate (order to quotations) suggests the need for an analysis of why orders are not following quotations. Poor call effectiveness suggests a close examination of sales technique to identify specific areas of weakness so that training can be applied more effectively.

A further group of quantitative measures will explore the remuneration which each salesperson receives. The focus will be on expenses and compensation. With respect to expenses, comparisons will be made between salespeople, and between current year and last year. Ratios which may be used include the following:

1 expenses/sales revenue generated
2 expenses/profit generated
3 expenses per call
4 expenses per square mile of territory.

Such measures should give an indication of when the level of expenses is becoming excessive.

Compensation analysis is particularly valuable when:

● a large part of salary is fixed
● salespeople are on different levels of fixed salary.

The latter situation will be found in companies which pay according to the number of years at the firm or according to age. Unfairness, in terms of sales results, can be exposed by calculating for each salesperson the following two ratios:

● total salary (including commission)/sales revenue
● total salary (including commission)/profits.

These ratios will reveal when a compensation plan has gone out of control, and will allow changes to be made before lower-paid higher-achievers leave for jobs which more closely relate pay to sales success.

A study by Jobber, Hooley and Shipley (1989) surveyed a sample of 450 industrial products organisations (i.e. firms manufacturing and selling repeat industrial goods such as components, and capital goods such as machinery). The objective was to discover the extent of usage of sales evaluation criteria among small (less than £3 million sales turnover) and large (greater than £3 million sales turnover) firms. Table 16.1 shows that there is a wide variation in the usage of output criteria among the sample of firms, and that large firms tend to use more output criteria than small organisations.

Table 16.2 shows that the usage of input criteria is also quite variable with statistics relating to calls the most frequently used by both large and small firms. Again, there is a tendency for large firms to use more input criteria when evaluating their salesforces.

The growth in the penetration of personal computers is mirrored by the development of **software packages** that provide the facilities for the simple compilation and analysis of salesforce evaluation measures. The creation of a databank of quantitative measures over time allows a rich source of information about how the salesforce is performing.

These quantitative measures cannot solely produce a complete evaluation of salespeople. In order to provide a wider perspective, qualitative measures will also be employed.

Table 16.1 A comparison of the usage of salesforce evaluation output criteria between small and large organisations

Evaluative criteria	Small firms %	Large firms %	Statistically significant difference
Sales			
Sales volume	87.2	93.1	
Sales volume by product or product line	61.2	80.3	✳
Sales volume by customer or customer type	48.2	59.5	
Sales volume per order	22.4	26.7	
Sales volume by outlet or outlet type	22.4	38.9	✳
Sales volume per call	12.9	24.4	✳
Market share	32.9	57.3	✳
Accounts			
Number of new accounts gained	58.8	55.7	
Number of accounts lost	44.7	42.7	
Amount of new account sales	57.6	54.2	
Number of accounts on which payment overdue	41.2	38.2	
Proportion/number of accounts buying full product line	14.1	16.0	
Profit			
Gross profit generated	58.8	48.9	
Net profit generated	38.8	42.7	
Gross profit as a percentage of sales volume	47.1	45.0	
Net profit as a percentage of sales volume	38.8	34.4	
Return on investment	28.2	26.7	
Profit per call ratio	12.9	12.2	
Orders			
Number of orders taken	48.2	38.2	
Number of orders cancelled	14.1	13.7	
Order per call ratio	25.9	29.0	
Strike rate (Number of orders) / (Number of quotations)	37.9	40.5	
Average order value	28.2	26.0	
Average profit contribution per order	21.2	16.8	
Value or orders to value of quotations ratio	29.4	21.4	
Other output criteria			
Number of customer complaints	23.5	22.3	

Note: ✳ indicates significant at p< 0.05.

Qualitative measures of performance

Assessment along qualitative lines will necessarily be more subjective and will take place, in the main, during field visits. The usual dimensions which are used are given in the following list:

Table 16.2 A comparison of the usage of salesforce evaluation input criteria between small and large organisations

Evaluative criteria	Small firms %	Large firms %	Statistically significant difference
Calls			
Number of calls per period	49.4	69.7	✳
Number of calls per customer or customer type	15.3	37.4	✳
Calls on potential new accounts	56.5	53.8	
Calls on existing accounts	55.3	61.8	
Prospecting success ratio:			
$\dfrac{\text{(Number of new customers)}}{\text{(Number of potential new customers visited)}}$	28.2	32.8	
Expenses			
Ratio of sales expense to sales volume	38.8	45.4	
Average cost per call	21.2	30.8	
Other input criteria			
Number of required reports sent in	42.0	42.0	
Number of demonstrations conducted	23.5	22.3	
Number of service calls made	21.2	23.1	
Number of letters/telephone calls to prospects	14.1	7.7	

Note: ✳ indicates significant at $p < 0.05$.

1 *Sales skills*. These may be rated using a number of sub-factors.
   ● Handling the opening and developing rapport.
   ● Identification of customer needs, questioning ability.
   ● Quality of sales presentation.
   ● Use of visual aids.
   ● Ability to overcome objections.
   ● Ability to close the sale.
2 *Customer relationships*.
   ● How well received is the salesperson?
   ● Are customers well satisfied with the service, advice, reliability of the salesperson, or are there frequent grumbles and complaints?
3 *Self-organisation*. How well does the salesperson carry out the following?
   ● Prepare calls.
   ● Organise routeing to minimise unproductive travelling.
   ● Keep customer records up to date.
   ● Provide market information to headquarters.
   ● Conduct self-analysis of performance in order to improve weaknesses.
4 *Product knowledge*. How well informed is the salesperson regarding the following?
   ● His or her own products and their customer benefits and applications.

- Competitive products and their benefits and applications.
- Relative strengths and weaknesses between his or her own and competitive offerings.

5 *Co-operation and attitudes.* To what extent will the salesperson do the following?:

- Respond to the objectives determined by management in order to improve performance, e.g. increase prospecting rate.
- Co-operate with suggestions made during field training for improved sales technique.
- Use his or her own initiative.

What are his or her attitudes towards the following:

- The company and its products.
- Hard work.

The study by Jobber *et al.*(1989) referred to earlier, also investigated the use of qualitative evaluative measures by industrial goods companies. Table 16.3 shows the results, with most criteria being used by the majority of the sales managers in the sample. Although differences between small and large firms were not so distinct as for quantitative measures, more detailed analysis of the results showed that managers of small firms tended to hold qualitative opinions 'in the

Table 16.3 A comparison of the usage of qualitative salesforce evaluation criteria between small and large organisations

Evaluative criteria	*Small firms %*	*Large firms %*	*Statistically significant difference*
Skills			
Selling skills	81.9	86.9	
Communication skills	77.1	85.4	
Knowledge			
Product knowledge	94.0	90.8	
Knowledge of competition	80.7	83.1	
Knowledge of company policies	56.6	68.5	
Self-management			
Planning ability	77.1	76.2	
Time management	54.2	61.5	
Judgement/decision-making ability	74.7	68.5	
Report preparation and submission	63.9	77.7	*
Personal characteristics			
Attitudes	91.6	88.5	
Initiative	92.8	83.1	
Appearance and manner	90.4	86.9	
Aggressiveness	45.8	50.8	
Creativity	49.4	56.9	

Note: * indicates significant at $p<0.05$.

head', whereas managers of large firms tended to produce more formal assessments, e.g. in an evaluation report.

As mentioned earlier, the use of quantitative and qualitative measures is interrelated. A poor sales per call ratio will inevitably result in close scrutiny of sales skills, customer relationships and degree of product knowledge in order to discover why performance is poor.

Sales management response to the results of carrying out salesforce evaluation is shown in Figure 16.3. Lynch (1992) suggests four scenarios with varying implications:

1 *Good quantitative/good qualitative evaluation.* The appropriate response would be praise and monetary reward. For suitable candidates promotion would follow.
2 *Good quantitative/poor qualitative evaluation.* The good quantitative results suggest that performance in front of customers is good, but certain aspects of qualitative evaluation, e.g. attitudes, report writing and market feedback, may warrant advice and education regarding company standards and requirements.
3 *Poor quantitative/good qualitative evaluation.* Good qualitative input is failing to be reflected in quantitative success. The specific causes need to be identified and training and guidance provided. Lack of persistence, poor closing technique or too many / too few calls might be possible causes of poor sales results.
4 *Poor quantitative/poor qualitative evaluation.* Critical discussion is required to agree problem areas. Training is required to improve standards. In other situations, punishment may be required or even dismissal.

For an evaluation and control system to work efficiently, it is important for the sales team to understand its purpose. For them to view it simply as a means for

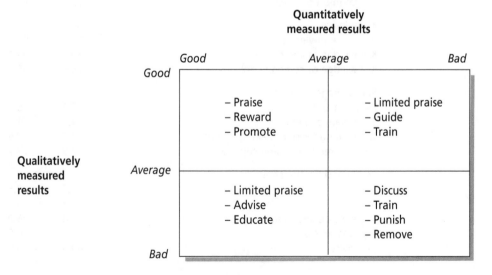

Figure 16.3 Salesperson evaluation matrix

management to catch them out and criticise performance is likely to breed resentment. It should be used, and be perceived, as a means of assisting salespeople in improving performance. Indeed, the quantitative output measures themselves can be used as a basis for rewarding performance when targets are met. In essence, controls should be viewed in a positive manner, not a negative one.

Winning or losing major orders

A key qualitative evaluation question that sales managers have to ask is 'Does it appear that we are going to win or lose this order?' This is particularly important for major sales. For example, a sales manager may be asked by the managing director, 'Will you find out whether the Saudis are really going to place that new big aero engine order? I have to tell the board next week so that we can decide whether we will have to expand our plant.'

The obvious response would be to ask the salesperson in charge of the sale directly. The problem is that many salespeople delude themselves into believing they are going to be successful. How do you come to terms with the fact that you are going to lose an order worth £5 million? Asking the direct question, 'Bill, are we going to win this one?' is likely to get the answer 'Yes, the customer loves us!' What the salesperson really means is that the customer likes the salesperson, not necessarily the product.

Consequently the sales manager needs to probe much more deeply in order to assess the situation more accurately. This involves asking a series of who, when, where, why and how questions. It also means that the sales manager needs to work out what would be considered acceptable (winning) answers, and what would be thought of as unacceptable (losing) responses. Table 16.4 gives an example of the use of this procedure in connection with a £10 million computer sale. The losing answers are thin and unconvincing (e.g. the director of MIS would not have the power to authorise an order of this size).

The salesperson is deluding him or herself and misleading the sales manager. The winning answer is much more assured and provides clear, credible answers to all of the questions (e.g. an executive director is likely to have the power to authorise a purchase of this magnitude).

If the outcome is a losing answer, the sales manager has to decide how important the sale is and how important the salesperson is. If they both have high potential, the sales manager, sales trainer or top salesperson should work with him/her. He or she should be counselled so that they understand why they are being helped and what the sales manager hopes they will learn. In the process, they will also realise that management cares about their development and the success it can bring to both parties.

If the salesperson is viewed as having high potential but the situation has low potential, only a counselling session is needed. Usually it is best done at the end of the day, driving back from a call, using an 'oh, by the way' introduction, and avoiding serious eye contact. By these means the salesperson's ego is not offended.

Table 16.4 Winning and losing orders

Question	Poor (losing answer)	Good (winning answer)
Who will authorise the purchase?	The director of MIS.	The director of MIS but it requires an executive director's authorisation, and we've talked it over with him/her.
When will they buy?	Right away. They love the new model.	Before the peak processing load at the year end.
Where will he/she be when the decision is made – in the office alone, in his/her boss's office, in a meeting?	What difference does that make? I think he/she has already decided.	At a board meeting. But don't worry, the in-supplier has no one on their board and we have two good customers on it.
Why will they buy from us? Why not their usual supplier?	He/she and I go way back. They love our new model.	The next upgrade from the in-supplier is a big price increase, and ours fits right between their models. They are quite unhappy with the in-supplier about that.
How will the purchase be funded?	They've lots of money, haven't they?	The payback period on reduced costs will be about 14 months and we've a leasing company willing to take part of the deal.

When the salesperson does not have high potential but the sale does, the alternatives are a little nastier! Perhaps the salesperson would be a candidate for redeployment to a more suitable post. When neither the salesperson nor the sale has much potential, the basic question is whether the salesperson is redeployed before or after the sale is lost.

16.9 APPRAISAL INTERVIEWING

Appraisal interviewing can provide the opportunity to identify a salesperson's weaknesses and to give praise when it is deserved. One method is to ask the salesperson to write down 5–10 expectations that they hope to achieve during the next year, e.g. to go on a presentation skills course, to go on a time management course, to have monthly sales visits from their sales manager, to meet targets, to move into marketing, etc. The sales manager then sits down with the salesperson and goes through this list breaking it down into quarterly (three-month) sections. At the end of each quarter they have another meeting to see if expectations have been met or shifted in any way. These meetings also provide an opportunity to give or withdraw recognition and acceptance.

16.10 CONCLUSIONS

This chapter has shown the importance of the sales budget in motivating and controlling the salesforce. The sales budget, which itself is determined by the sales forecast, is broken down into sales quotas or targets for individual salespeople and regions. Monetary incentives may be linked to the attainment of quotas and they may be used as one yardstick of achievement.

A more detailed look at the kinds of measures used to evaluate salespeople was then taken. Two broad measures are used – quantitative and qualitative indicators. Such measures can be used to evaluate, control and motivate salespeople towards better performance.

PRACTICAL EXERCISE

Dynasty Ltd

Dynasty Limited is a radio paging service that has operated since the mid-1970s when radio pagers took Hong Kong by storm. Hong Kong still has the world's highest concentration of population carrying radio pagers, currently estimated at around 2 million. When the Hong Kong Government decided to introduce a new telecommunications technology called CT2 (cordless telephone generation two) Dynasty jumped on the bandwagon of contenders in pursuit of a licence. After some negotiation it was awarded one of the four licences to operate a CT2 network in Hong Kong. The company is about to launch this service.

Raymond Chan is Dynasty's sales manager with the task of setting up a salesforce. Whilst CT2 is a sophisticated technology, Chan feels that a deep understanding of the technology is not a prerequisite for his salespeople. Instead, how to deal with customers, who tend to be very time-conscious and results-orientated, is more important. He believes that CT2 is a personal product. The new recruits should have experience in selling products to end-users and must have broad social contacts.

When reviewing his recruitment plan with his superior, John Lee, it became apparent that Lee had different ideas. Lee is a strong advocate that new recruits must be familiar with the product and its technology since that is what they are selling. An inside knowledge of these new products would also impress would-be customers and give the salespeople an edge over the competition. Lee favours recruiting from within the telecommunications industry, since such people are familiar with the developments of the technology. Apart from that, they are likely to talk the same language as people working in engineering, technical support and service.

DISCUSSION QUESTIONS

1 Justify what general factors you consider should be taken into account when recruiting salespeople for the positions described in the exercise. In particular, suggest how the performance of such salespersons could be evaluated.

2 State whether you agree with Chan or Lee, or neither.

3 Suggest and justify the kind of commission structure that you would put into place.

PRACTICAL EXERCISE

MacLaren Tyres Ltd

MacLaren Tyres is a company involved in the import and marketing of car tyres manufactured in the Far East. David MacLaren established the business in 1990 when a friend living in Singapore told him of the supply of tyres from that area which substantially undercut European prices. Although Far Eastern tyres were not as long lasting as European (average 18,000 miles compared with 25,000), they were produced to a high standard which meant that problems like weak spots, cracks and leaks were no more serious than with European tyres.

MacLaren believed that a viable target market existed for the sale of these tyres in the UK. He was of the opinion that a substantial number of people were interested primarily in the purchase price of tyres. This price-sensitive target market could roughly be described as the mid-lower income family who owned a second-hand car which was over three years old.

He decided to buy a consignment of tyres and visited tyre centres to sell them. Initially business was slow but gradually, as distributors began to believe in the quality of the tyres, sales grew.

By 1997 MacLaren had taken on the role of general manager and had recruited five salespeople to handle the sales function. A brief personal profile produced by MacLaren of each of his salespeople is given below.

Profiles of MacLaren salespeople

Peter Killick
Joined the company in 1992. Has an HND (business studies) and previously worked as an insurance salesperson for two years. Aged 27. Handles the Tyneside area. Gregarious and extrovert.

Gary Olford
Joined the company in 1993. No formal qualifications but sound track record as a car salesperson and, later, as a toy sales representative. Aged 35. Handles the Manchester/Liverpool area. Appears to be hard-working but lacks initiative.

Barrie Wilson
Joined the company at the same time as Olford. Has an HNC (mechanical engineering). Was a technical representative for an engineering firm. Aged 28. Handles the London area. Appears to enjoy his work but lacks the necessary 'push' to be really successful in selling.

Ron Haynes
Joined the company in 1994. Has a degree in industrial technology. Previous experience includes selling bathroom suites and textile fabrics. Aged 29. Covers the Birmingham area. Appears to lack enthusiasm but sales record is about average.

Kevin Harris
Joined MacLaren Ltd in 1996. Has a degree in business studies. Only previous experience was as a marketing assistant during the industrial training period of his degree. Aged 25. Handles the Bristol area. Keen but still very raw.

Salesforce data

MacLaren decided that the time had come to look in detail at the sales records of his sales representatives. His plan was to complete a series of statistics which would be useful in evaluating their performance. Basic data for the year 1998/99 relevant to each salesperson are given below.

	Sales (£000s)	Gross margin (£000s)	Live accounts (1998/99)	Calls made	Number of different customers called upon
Killick	298	101	222	1,472	441
Olford	589	191	333	1,463	432
Wilson	391	121	235	1,321	402
Haynes	440	132	181	1,152	211
Harris	240	65	296	1,396	421

Market data

From trade sources, and from knowledge of the working boundaries each salesperson operated in, MacLaren was able to produce estimates of the number of potential accounts and territory potential for each area.

	No. of potential accounts	Territory potential (£000s)
Killick (Tyneside)	503	34,620
Olford (Lancashire)	524	36,360
Wilson (London)	711	62,100
Haynes (Birmingham)	483	43,800
Harris (Bristol)	462	38,620

DISCUSSION QUESTIONS

1 Evaluate the performance of each of MacLaren's salespeople.

2 What further information is needed to produce a more complete appraisal?

3 What action would you take?

EXAMINATION QUESTIONS

1 What is a sales budget? Discuss the importance of the sales budget in the corporate budgetary process.

2 Quantitative measures of the performance of sales representatives are more likely to mislead than guide evaluation. Do you agree?

3 Produce a balanced argument that looks at the differences between qualitative and quantitative measures of sales performance.

4 If a company loses a potential major order what should sales management do to alleviate the risk of this happening again?

APPENDICES

APPENDICES

CASE STUDIES IN SELLING

Case Study 1 SOPHISTO (UK) PLC

Sophisto (UK) manufacture and market a range of minicomputers to business users. The company was established in 1972 as the UK subsidiary of an American electronics giant which produced a range of mainframe computers and business machines. The American parent company had spotted that the 1970s would become the decade of the minicomputer in a market which had previously been marked by the dominance of the central mainframe computer. This development started in the early 1970s, principally in the United States. During the 1950s and 1960s larger companies' data processing was done on central mainframe computers. From the 1970s onwards companies began to search for ways of bringing computing power to a broader range of applications and for systems whereby more departments could gain access to the computer.

The industry responded to this need by developing the minicomputer. Firms devised time-sharing schemes for computer users which marked the beginning of distributed data processing. The next stage of distributed processing was the marketing of terminals through which the individual departments in a company, such as sales or production, could access information from the minicomputer. However, terminals simply acted as a screen for accessing and inputting information from the mini- or mainframe computer. In addition to this ability to access and input information, functional managers were increasingly demanding direct access to computing power which was more specific to their needs. The industry responded to this need by developing the microcomputer.

Microcomputers

Since the early 1980s, one of the growth markets in the computer industry has been that relating to the microcomputer. Two factors spurred this market growth; one technical or technology led, and the other, market or demand led.

As mentioned earlier, computer users in the 1980s and 1990s were increasingly demanding computing power tailored to the needs of individual managers. This market reason for the development of the microcomputer can be compared with the advantages offered by its technology.

The first major advantage of the microcomputer is that it can be readily linked to other computers in a company. However, unlike a terminal, information can be transferred from say a main computer into the memory of the micro. This information can then be utilised by the user without being logged on to the main computer.

The second major advantage of the microcomputer is that the user has, in effect, a personal work station. Micros can be equipped with the user's own software and peripherals, such as plotters and printers, and as such can be tailored to suit the individual user.

The technological reasons for the growth of the microcomputer have resulted from developments in micro-electronics, and in particular from developments in the technology of the silicon chip. Essentially this has made possible the provision of low cost but substantial computing power upon which the microcomputer is based.

The development of the market for microcomputers

Demand and technology combined made the 1990s the decade of the microcomputer. When microcomputers were first introduced the target market was small businesses. This market has continued to expand as the price of these machines has declined in real terms.

More recently companies with mainframe computers have now purchased microcomputers. Forecasts in the industry suggest that this will continue to be a major growth market – potentially every manager in the future, will have a microcomputer in his or her office.

The issue facing Sophisto is that this growth in the micro market poses both an opportunity and a threat.

The threat of the microcomputer is that pundits suggest that over the next 10 to 15 years mainframe and minicomputers will decline in importance. In short, sales of both these products will give way to the ever-increasing penetration of the microcomputer.

The opportunity facing Sophisto, and other companies in the market, is that the wide range of applications for the micro, coupled with decreasing prices have expanded the total market for computers, particularly for business use. In addition, Sophisto, through its American parent company, has access to substantial research and development expertise and resources.

In fact, it was some two years ago that a confidential report from the US parent company of Sophisto (UK) indicated that plans were already in hand to direct research and development towards the design and production of a range of micro-products. Sophisto (UK), along with other European subsidiaries, had provided a preliminary assessment of likely market needs and product requirements for the UK business market. Sophisto has heard very little more about the proposed new micros since then.

Recent developments

David Perkins, Marketing Director of Sophisto (UK), was waiting for his American visitors in the boardroom of the UK headquarters. The Americans were main board directors of the US giant, and included experts in marketing, finance, production and research and development (R&D). Their visit was prompted by the publication of a market research report covering the computer market in both Europe and the United States. The report indicated that the company had made a serious error of judgement about the speed with which the microcomputer would replace minis and mainframe products.

As indicated earlier, the company had spotted the market signs at an early stage, and as we have seen, had commenced the research programme to develop a product range. However, sales and profits world-wide, including the UK, had continued to grow over the intervening period and consequently the product development programme had not been considered to be urgent. The recently completed market research study indicated differently. A simplified overview of what the research showed is illustrated in Figure A1.1.

A similar pattern to that shown above for the market as a whole was repeated throughout the United States and Europe.

The diagram illustrates that although the total market for minicomputers had continued to grow throughout the 1980s, this growth rate had slowed. In contrast, by the early 1990s, the market for micros had already moved past that

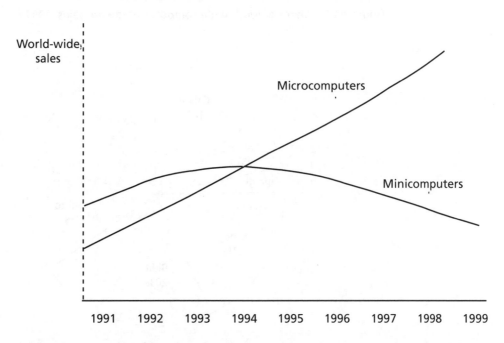

Figure A1.1   Worldwide sales of microcomputers and minicomputers 1991–1999

for the minicomputer. Sophisto's major products appeared to be entering the decline stage of their life-cycle much earlier than had been predicted.

The growth of the microcomputer market, and in particular, the advantage which some competitors had taken of this growth, was reflected in market share. Again, with growing world-wide sales the US parent had failed to recognise that its share of world markets was falling. The market research report illustrated the extent of this fall as shown in Figs A1.2 and A1.3.

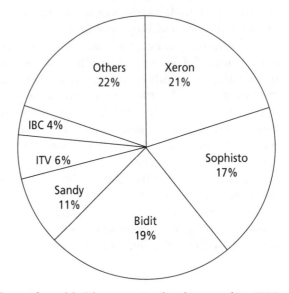

Figure A1.2   Share of worldwide computer hardware sales, 1992

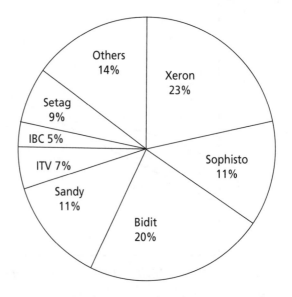

Figure A1.3   Share of worldwide computer hardware sales, 1999

This fall in market share was especially worrying to Sophisto's American planners. Not only did it indicate that market share had fallen dramatically without the company even realising it, but it also placed the company at a distinct disadvantage in the marketplace with respect to their competitors. Sophisto's major competition had already secured a foothold in the new growth market with well-established products and distributor networks. As well as this, one new entrant, Setag, had come from nowhere in 1992 to secure 9 per cent of the market in 1999. In addition, the competition had well-developed software (the programs for computers) as well as the hardware (the computer) itself. Finally, having well-developed market shares in the micro market gave competitors an edge with respect to cost, and therefore price. In short, Sophisto were already lagging well behind.

The meeting

When the American executives finally arrived at Sophisto (UK) they were immediately taken to the boardroom where they were introduced to Perkins and his senior management. It quickly became clear what the meeting was intended to achieve.

The Americans indicated that the development of the new micros was now a priority R&D project. All other development work on improving existing mini-products had been terminated and the staff and resources had been switched to the new project. It transpired that since commencing the development work two years ago, some progress had been made. Specifically, the meeting was intended to achieve a clear focus for the remaining development work.

Sophisto (USA) realised that each national market for micros was likely to differ in some respects. Not only were some markets growing faster than others, but more importantly, certainly as far as product development was concerned, each country differed in terms of likely end-uses and specific user requirements. What they were seeking was for each of the companies operating in different regions and countries throughout the world to provide market information to guide specific hardware and software development.

There was also a second and somewhat more unpleasant reason for the Americans' visit. It quickly became clear that headquarters back in America largely blamed the operating divisions for not spotting what was happening in their individual markets and for not reporting this back to head office. Each operating company of Sophisto in a particular country had its own market research budget. The amount spent on this activity was monitored and approved, or otherwise, by headquarters on an annual basis. However, once the overall annual budget for market research had been approved for a particular company, management were free to spend this money on whatever market research projects they felt were appropriate. Each of the Sophisto divisions was responsible for its own sales and profits, and therefore pricing, distribution and promotion decisions were at each company's discretion according to the particular marketing and competitive environment prevailing in their national market. R&D, product development and major investment decisions, were taken in America.

Perkins and his management team were both worried and aggrieved by this second aspect to the meeting. They pointed out that apart from headquarters informing the divisions that they were developing a micro range some two years ago, they had neither heard anything about how this development was progressing, nor had they been asked, either then or subsequently, to contribute their views, expertise and knowledge of the UK market to the US parent. David Perkins went even further; he pointed out to the American executives that no formal system of reporting currently existed for the national divisions to feed market data back to group headquarters, nor indeed had any such system ever existed.

The meeting was in danger of degenerating into an unfruitful, and potentially dangerous (at least for David Perkins), squabble. At this point, Perkins decided to introduce a more positive approach while at the same time supporting his personal view that Sophisto (UK) had spent its marketing research budget wisely. He asked his personal assistants to bring in a report prepared by his marketing research manager, who was not present at the meeting.

Implications of the report

Each of the individuals present at the meeting was given a copy of this report which focused on the market for microcomputers in the United Kingdom. It had been commenced two years ago when the parent company had announced its development programme. In fact the report constituted an interim report of a continuing survey of the UK market.

The survey had already uncovered some interesting facts about the micro market. For example, the report showed that the UK market at least was, as far as micros were concerned, growing much more rapidly than anyone at headquarters, or indeed many industry pundits, had envisaged. This fact, of course, was reiterated by the US report. It also confirmed that Sophisto (UK)was losing market share in computers to major competitors.

The American executives became annoyed when Perkins pointed to this in his report. After all they knew this to be the case; indeed it had prompted their visit to Europe. They also insisted that, formal reporting arrangements or not, it was part of Perkins and his staff's, job to point out such things to headquarters. Again the discussion was becoming heated.

Perkins continued by drawing the attention of the meeting to the second part of the report. In this, Perkins' researchers had also included a detailed appraisal of developments in the business micro market in their survey. An example of the type of data they had collated is shown in Table A1.1.

Scanning through the report, the American managers were astonished at the amount of relevant data that Sophisto (UK) had collected relating to the market.

Table A1.1   The UK market for microcomputers: principal business applications and frequency of use

Application	Frequency of use (%)*
Word processing	69
Financial analysis	50
Basic accounting	38
Database access	38
Personal record keeping	35
Engineering/scientific	24
Graphics	22
Games	21

(*Frequency = % of respondents citing this as an application.
Number of respondents = 3,000 managers in businesses already using microcomputers.)

They were even more astonished when Perkins told them that the interim report had been completed and submitted direct to the Research and Development headquarters in America. Their astonishment was based not so much on the fact that Perkins had submitted the report, but more because he informed them that it had been returned by R&D within two weeks along with a rather caustic memo suggesting that this type of information was interesting, but essentially irrelevant to their important development activities.

Perkins had retained a copy of the memorandum.

APPLICATION QUESTIONS

Acting as an external marketing consultant to Sophisto (UK) Plc, prepare a report for the senior consultant of *your* company on the following:

1 What management and organisational problems do you perceive in the situation outlined, and what relevance do they have to effective marketing at Sophisto (UK)?

2 How might the application of the product life-cycle concept have helped avert the problems at Sophisto (UK)?

(N.B. The senior consultant of your company is not from a marketing background.)

Case Study 2 SUNDERLAND CERAMICS LIMITED

Early background

Sunderland Ceramics Limited is a limited company, first founded in 1982 as a sole proprietorship by its then owner, Jim Gofton. In 1988 it became a limited company because sales had grown, and Jim felt the need for some 'protection' in terms of limited liability.

Jim formed the company using his own capital, and with the help of his bank, after being made redundant from his previous company, St. Austell Potteries plc of Redruth in Cornwall. Jim was in fact a Cornishman born and bred, but he had heard so many good things about the north-east of England in terms of its willing workforce and industry location packages, that he saw his redundancy as an opportunity, and decided to relocate with his wife and family. Initially, he considered Durham, but quickly realised that this small university city would probably not welcome a manufacturing concern, so he settled upon Sunderland, a coastal town that had been famous for shipbuilding, located about 10 miles to the east of Durham.

He had acquired substantial experience in the design, production and sales of pottery products. When he was made redundant, Jim was responsible for sales and marketing of St. Austell Potteries' 'Birchtree' range of oven-to-table cookware with matching tableware, all made from the finest stoneware.

Sunderland Ceramics was founded on the basis of Jim's view that a gap in the market existed for a well-designed, high-quality, and, most important of all, a continually available, range of glazed tableware. This continuity of supply lay at the heart of Sunderland Ceramics' marketing strategy and, in Jim's view, was the key feature of its so far successful record.

Jim knew, from his experience at St. Austell Potteries, that many purchasers of dinner services had become disillusioned and sometimes angry when designs of the products which they had purchased, or intended to purchase, were removed from the range. For example, many newly wedded couples select a particular range of tableware from which, over a period of years, they intend to build up a complete dinner service. Frequently, the particular design becomes obsolete before the purchasers have been able to complete the set. Other purchasers who had bought complete dinner services found that breakages of individual items, plates, cups, etc., could not be replaced, after only a short period of time.

The unique attraction of Sunderland Ceramics' products was that customers were given a written guarantee at the time of purchase that any particular design would be supplied, irrespective of order size, for a minimum period of ten years from the initial purchase date. In the event of being unable to meet this commitment the company undertook to refund money to the value of the customer's first order, or to provide a complete replacement that satisfied the customer's aesthetic requirements.

Market trends since the early 1980s

This period has witnessed a resurgence of novelty, stylish and well-designed tableware products. The traditional market for china and porcelain has lost share to both stoneware and earthenware which are synonymous with the trend for cheaper tableware.

Socio-economic and lifestyle changes have contributed to greater demands for manufacturers to produce a wider range of consumer goods which can be seen by the emphasis on tableware co-ordinating with interior designs, right down to matching placemats.

What is not in doubt is that the market sector is vibrant and is changing the look of meal times for good. Entertaining is more spontaneous and relaxed than ever before, with meals being taken in the kitchen, lounge or even the garden. This trend is also mirrored in house design which tends to reflect this informality with 'through' lounge/dining areas, rather than the provision of a separate dining room.

The result has been a steady move away from the use of formal and perhaps classic designs of tableware, towards colourful, friendly and even avant-garde styles, better-suited to today's more casual everyday eating habits.

Royal Doulton entered this market in 1990 with their 'Expressions' range which is colourful and aimed at the mid-market. This range is attracting a completely new and much younger buyer.

Johnson Brothers – brand leaders in value for money, stylish, well-designed, all-occasion tableware – introduced three brand new ranges in 1992, all with handpainted designs. Their 'Heritage White' range continues to be an international success.

Royal Wilton's new 'Blueberry' handpainted range has seen increased sales of 100 per cent growing year on year for the past three years. They have extended their range to include kitchenware, cookware and microwave ovenware.

The trend is thus a discernible move away from muted and nondescript designs towards brighter products that are practical and functional. It is also estimated that such designs will actually 'grow' sales of products, demand for which has hitherto been viewed as being inelastic.

Company background – 1982 to date

Sales and marketing were carried out on a mail-order only basis with advertising initially being targeted at north-east of England households through local newspapers, magazines and commercial radio stations. Following the company's incorporation on a limited basis in 1988, it has promoted its products through national newspapers and some of the 'glossy' women's magazines. The company has not yet engaged in television advertising, but is considering doing so in 2000.

The company is now considering using the Royal Mail 'mosaic' system for targeted leaflet drops and direct mail. This system relates locations to each other in terms of 58 different 'home types'. Initially, the postcode system was developed to help mechanise the sorting of mail. It relates any address in the United Kingdom to a street or area, and on average each individual postcode covers 15 households or dwellings.

Altogether, the Royal Mail file holds 25 million addresses which allows them to locate addresses and use them within its geographical analysis system. Mosiac is thus a system that offers an ideal basis on which to build sample frames for a variety of projects from marketing research to direct mail. With the help of mosaic it is possible to measure which neighbourhood characteristics seem to deliver the best mailing response. It is then possible to score different *home types* on a *prospect scoring* model which aims to maximise response for subsequent mailings.

It is current practice within the company that whenever a customer sends in an order, her or his name is logged on a database. The company has, in fact, been approached on a number of occasions by direct mailing organisations with a view to selling its database to them, but it has so far resisted such approaches.

All production was initially carried out in factory space leased from the local authority and comprised of an area of what was previously an engineering fabrication shop (or factory). The local authority had converted this in 1981 into industrial units. In 1982, the initial workforce and organisation of Sunderland Ceramics was as follows:

Jim Gofton (age 43) – sales/production/marketing/accountancy.

Liz Gofton (age 45) (Jim's wife) – design/distribution/packaging plus general clerical and secretarial duties.

Fred and Freda Weekes (ages 58 and 57 respectively) – both potters who were made redundant from St. Austell Potteries at the same time as Jim Gofton. They were very good friends of Jim and Liz and decided to move to Sunderland with them in order to start a new life and a second career in the north east.

'Geordie' Ness (age 44) – general labourer and 'dogsbody' who had been made redundant from a shipyard in Wallsend, and who perceived that a move to Sunderland would also satisfy his almost manic love of being close to his favourite soccer team. Geordie's wage was initially heavily subsidised by a local council grant as part of a job creation initiative.

From these modest beginnings, Sunderland Ceramics has flourished. Turnover has not only increased substantially, but has done so in a market that is typically characterised by relatively slow growth.

Table A1.2 shows the index of market growth for this type of product in the United Kingdom over the period 1986 to 1999.

By late 1987 Jim Gofton had realised that Sunderland Ceramics was at a decision point. Jim had to decide whether to aim for further growth and expansion or to let the company remain as it was. By this time the workforce had expanded to twelve people, with most of this increase having been on the production side. The company by then had nine potters including Fred and Freda Weekes, who had never regretted their move from Cornwall. Jim's son, Lionel, who was 18 had also joined the company as a trainee manager having attained five 'O' Levels (now GCSEs) in Art, History, Geography, Sociology and Economics plus a Grade D 'A' level in Sociology. He felt that he was not too academically inclined, but wanted to 'try his hand' at management.

Table A1.2   Index of sales of tableware product for the UK (1987 =100)

1986	98
1987	100
1988	101.5
1989	102.4
1990	103.8
1991	106.1
1992	107.3
1993	109.0
1994	112.1
1995	109.6
1996	103.9
1997	101.8
1998	102.1
1999	107.7 (9 months data)

Jim's dilemma had, in part, been prompted by the fact that a number of retail buyers had recently expressed an interest in stocking Sunderland Ceramics' products in their stores. Their interest suggested that there might be an opportunity to expand the business substantially as mail-order sales accounted for only a small percentage of UK total sales of this type of product.

United Kingdom sales of ceramics through the various outlets in 1990 and 1998 are shown in Table A1.3.

Table A1.3   UK ceramic sales by outlet 1990 and 1998

Sales in 1990	(%)
Specialist	38
Department stores/chain stores	48
Mail order	7
Other outlets	7
Sales in 1998	(%)
Specialist	24
Department stores/chain stores	46
Mail order	12
Other outlets	18

Jim realised that if he did decide to embark upon this route to expansion, things would have to change. He would have to expand production which would mean finding new premises. As things stood, his part of the factory was fully utilised and the Health and Safety Executive had informed him that it would be illegal to employ any more people in the space that was now being used. The fact was that there was physically no more room for expansion on the present site. Such a programme of expansion required additional finance. To date, growth had been financed using Jim's own capital, bank loans and retained profits. Therefore, in 1988, Jim, in consultation with Durham Associates Limited, a company specialising in advising small businesses, turned his company into a private limited company in order to reduce his personal liability and to take advantage of the opportunities afforded by limited liability.

In the event, the advice from Durham Associates was 'spot on' and by the end of 1998, Sunderland Ceramics Ltd had grown almost 100 per cent compared to 1990. They had moved into a new factory in Sunderland and had doubled the size of their workforce. They still only sold through the medium of direct mail and had not seen the necessity of selling through 'traditional' retail outlets, on the premise that such 'middlemen' would push the price of the products up to an unacceptable level.

Towards the middle of 1999 the company faced another crossroads. Jim was advised by his trusted consultants that he would have to introduce much more formal and sophisticated planning and control procedures, possibly with specialists being brought in to take charge of functions which, up to now, he had managed himself. New machinery would have to be installed incorporating the latest technology. This would probably mean retraining some of his potters and losing some of the craft skills inherent in the trade. His two long-standing friends and employees, Fred and Freda Weekes, although well over the official retirement age, had indicated their desire to finally retire to the nearby seaside resort of Easington. Jim also felt that his basis for competing in the market might have to change and that he would have to consider moving into selling to the retail trade.

He realised that if he was to expand he would have to give some thought to different sources of finance. At least one of Jim's personal friends had expressed an interest in becoming a shareholder in Sunderland Ceramics Limited. It was also possible that the company might seek funding from the Alternative Investment Market.

By late 1999 Jim felt sufficiently confident about his business to consider further the problems posed by expansion. His reservations were concerned less with his own products and his personal management skills than with the general cautiously optimistic economic climate, and the fact that the Government was at its half point term of office. For small, but growing businesses like his he felt that this was of greatest relevance. He was also aware of the large numbers of bankruptcies that were still occurring amongst small companies like his.

His son Lionel is now office manager and Jim has asked him to contact Durham Associates with a view to them preparing a preliminary report about the changes which the possible expansion would involve, particularly in the area of sales and marketing, and as to whether or not the economic climate is right to enable the company to expand at the present time.

Additional information required by Durham Associates in order to supply appropriate advice is supplied in Tables A1.4 and A1.5.

Table A1.4   Sunderland Ceramics' product portfolio 1999

Brakeware	– a complete dinner and tea service with salt/pepper/vinegar sets, tureens, etc., all in five different (non-changing) patterns, utilising the same basic shape.
Software	– A Danish style range in plain white introduced in 1992.

Table A1.5   Index of Sunderland Ceramics' sales (1986 = 100)

1986	100	
1987	165	
1988	174	
1989	185	
1990	192	
1991	201	
1992	220	
1993	225	
1994	240	
1995	255	
1996	261	
1997	265	
1998	268	
1999	273	(9 months data)

Sources: Pinpoint Analysis Limited; Market Intelligence Limited (MINTEL report – Housewares Casual Dining); Dept of Trade and Industry Business Monitors

APPLICATION QUESTIONS

1 Advise the company upon the pros and cons of keeping its current sales channel of distribution, and consider whether it should seek to sell its range through specialist pottery shops and/or department stores.

2 Advise the company upon its proposed use of more 'visible' above-the-line promotion through TV, rather than traditional selling approaches, together with its proposed use of mosaic database selling.

3 Advise the company as to the advantages and drawbacks of selling its database to direct mail organisations.

4 Give the report, with appropriate justifications, as suggested in the last paragraph of the case study.

Case Study 3 GARDNOV LIMITED

Richard Booth is worried. It is the end of his first month as the newly appointed sales manager of Gardnov Ltd and things have not gone as well as expected. He joined the company with considerable enthusiasm and optimism, feeling that his experience and logical, positive approach would stand him in good stead in his new post, even though he had not previously worked for a company dealing with similar types of merchandise. His selling background was based in the more aggressive product fields of double glazing and home security products.

Gardnov Ltd was established ten years ago to supply garden products to the retail trade. Essentially a wholesaler, Gardnov stocks a very comprehensive range of garden products including garden tools, pumps and pond products, barbecues and garden furniture. They carry a Gardnov branded line of garden ornaments and these are made by manufacturers to Gardnov designs and specifications, the most popular being a range of garden gnomes featuring the likenesses of famous political figures. Most of the leading United Kingdom branded products are carried, together with some of the major overseas suppliers' brands. All of these products are included in the company's annual catalogue which is mailed out to garden centres and retail outlets throughout the UK regardless of whether or not they are existing customers.

Although retail customers may order direct from the catalogue (and a number do), some 90 per cent of all sales are obtained through the company salesforce of six salespeople, all male, organised to cover the UK on a regional basis. The salesforce are each paid a straight salary which in 1999 averaged £21,000 each, within a range of £16,500 to £27,300. The position of a salesperson within this range depends upon his age and the length of time he has been with the company. A mid-range company car is provided, together with an expense account that covers fuel costs and a modest entertainment allowance.

Richard Booth has worked in sales for some twenty years and had previously been regional sales manager for a leading manufacturer of double glazing and home security products. On commencing his appointment at Gardnov Ltd (the previous sales manager having retired) Booth decided that he would spend his first four weeks simply observing how the salesforce operated by accompanying them on sales visits and by talking to customers. He felt this would give him a sound basis on which to assess the current situation, and he could then put together a strategic sales plan for the future.

What he has found out during these four weeks now forms the basis of his present worries. Essentially, what he has seen and heard suggests that the company salesforce is generally lethargic and lacking in motivation. Although sales have increased by some 5 per cent on average over each of the past ten years, the total market, as Booth established from secondary marketing research data, has been growing at an annual rate of over 10 per cent.

Some of the more worrying elements that Booth has established in his first four weeks are as follows. Each salesperson is assigned a region to cover. In each region the previous sales manager had divided accounts into three categories –

A, B and C – according to their sales potential. 'A' accounts were major customers and were to be visited weekly. 'B' accounts were to be visited once every two weeks, and 'C' accounts once a month. In addition, Booth established that each salesperson had been allocated a target for opening new accounts in his region.

What Booth has discovered is that over the past two years virtually all of the salesforce had only called regularly on 'A' category customers, while 'B' category customers were being visited about once in six weeks and 'C' category customers were hardly ever visited. In addition, not one new account had been opened during the past four months.

Even worse, Booth had visited a sample of customers in each region and was dismayed to hear that even regular customers felt that they did not relate closely to Gardnov's salesforce. A number of customers commented that recently the salesforce had been more like order-takers rather than order-makers. In addition, a high proportion of the customers visited suggested that Gardnov's salespeople were unable to answer questions about some of the products in the catalogue. They felt that the salespeople showed little interest in their customers, and had little enthusiasm for the products they were selling. Their main aim seemed to be to minimise the time spent with the customer, even when a visit *was* made.

Booth knew that all six of the salesforce were experienced salespeople, and had been with the company for an average of five years falling within a range of two to twelve years, in an industry where the average length of stay for sales representatives was only three years. He was not sure what the problem was, but knew that he would have to take immediate steps to improve sales performance.

His problem is that he does not want to start his career with Gardnov by antagonising the salesforce, but is determined to increase motivation, and ultimately sales. First, he needs to gain their co-operation and confidence, then he hopes to be able to remedy the present situation.

APPLICATION QUESTIONS

1 What steps should Richard Booth take to investigate further the problems highlighted by his initial research, while at the same time, gaining the co-operation of the salesforce? In your answer indicate what information Booth will require.

2 What are the disadvantages of the present salary-only compensation plan? What advice would you give to Booth about devising and implementing a new system of compensation for the salesforce?

Case Study 4   ALLWARM KNITTING LIMITED

Allwarm Knitting Ltd has been producing and selling yarns from their base in Huddersfield for almost 100 years. The soft water of the surrounding Pennine hills made it a perfect place for production because of the scouring and cleansing processes that wool went through before the final yarn was ready. In order to obtain a sliver that could be satisfactorily spun into a woollen thread, the following operations were necessary: willowing, oiling and blending, teasing, carding, condensing and roving. The Pennines were also suitable for the rearing of different breeds of sheep that produced different wool types and ultimately yarns for warmth, softness and breathability.

Many of these wools are still produced to the same formula today, and this fact is emphasised in the company's promotion that emphasises tradition and skill.

It is still a private company and the directors have never seen the need to go to the market to raise additional capital. The company has always sold through specialist shops and through some department stores under the brand name 'Yorkshire wool'. Ten years ago they were approached by a large department store group to produce a range of knitting yarns under the group's brand name. Management rejected the idea as they saw it as the first step towards giving up control of a brand that had been built up over 100 years.

The company's product range has always been extensive and currently includes a wide range of colours and yarn types. It has always been their policy to be a full-range producer which has entailed the holding of stocks of a large variety of qualities and colours at the factory for immediate dispatch to customers. A recent problem has been that financing such a large stock of finished yarns has severely drained working capital, such that the first ever overdraft facility has now been arranged with the bank.

The company's hand-knitting yarns are produced using pure new wool or blends of wool and more exclusive natural fibres such as mohair, angora and cashmere. The company has taken consistent pride in the quality of its products and believes that its brand name is well known and respected throughout the world by customers and the trade alike. For this reason, the company has always withstood moves to produce knitting yarns containing artificial fibres despite price advantages and wear-resistance qualities.

In the 1960s knitting was popular and its main purpose then was to provide cheap garments such as sweaters for utility rather than aesthetic appeal. After a lull in the late 1970s to the mid-1980s when hand knitting became less popular, the years since then have witnessed a return to knitting at home. One reason for this has been that it has become fashionable to wear hand-knitted garments. Younger women in particular like the idea of being able to knit an individual garment using top quality material at a fraction of the cost of a similar shop-bought item. Major fashion houses now make knitwear a prominent feature of their collections. Another reason for the return to home knitting has been the development of knitting machines that are simple to use and have come down dramatically in price since the 1980s.

Changes in fashion are reflected in the consumption statistics for hand-knitting yarns (see Table A1.6). Shown alongside these statistics is the percentage share of the total market held by Allwarm Knitting Limited as well as the volume taken up by artificial fibres.

Table A1.6 Consumption statistics for hand-knitting yarns

Year	UK Sales (kg millions)	% share which is purely artificial fibres	Allwarm % share of UK sales
1979	10.0	not available	7.2
1980	9.8	not available	7.3
1981	9.6	0.9	7.3
1982	10.4	1.4	7.2
1983	11.1	2.0	7.0
1984	12.0	3.1	6.8
1985	14.1	4.2	6.5
1986	14.8	4.8	6.1
1987	15.1	5.3	6.0
1988	15.4	5.9	5.8
1989	15.6	6.2	5.6
1990	15.4	6.4	5.5
1991	15.3	7.0	5.2
1992	15.2	7.4	5.2
1993	15.4	8.1	5.1
1994	15.2	8.3	5.0
1995	15.2	8.5	4.9
1996	15.5	8.6	4.8
1997	15.2	8.6	4.9
1998	15.4	8.7	5.0
1999	15.6	8.8	4.7

Note: Per cent share of mixed fibres in relation to total sales is not known.

Despite a steady market, Allwarm's market share has tended to diminish over recent years and management decided that some action should be taken to arrest this decline in sales. A market research study was commissioned to establish facts and data in relation to consumption patterns. This study was completed at the end of 1999.

The research found that although total hand-knitting yarn consumption was steady between 1988 and 1999, of the total amount sold, yarns incorporating artificial fibres had increased at the expense of natural fibre yarns. The principal reason for this was found to be the price advantage of artificial yarns over natural yarns (approximately 30 per cent cheaper). The study also found that there had been a shift by distributors (especially department stores) from stocking branded yarns to unbranded yarns as they were cheaper. It was also discovered that many of the cheaper hand-knitting yarns were being sold through market outlets as 'manufacturers' seconds'. Such yarns would not pass stringent quality tests carried out by Allwarm and other quality manufacturers. There is no legal requirement to subject yarns to quality testing, and although many such yarns were classed as 'seconds', many were not really 'seconds' in the true sense of the word. They were actually manufactured to less rigorous standards and market traders were using the 'seconds' ploy as a selling technique to allow buyers to think they were getting a bargain.

The survey also pointed out the fact that although quantities of imported hand-knitting yarns was negligible at the moment, there was a strong likelihood that this would increase considerably. Yarns from the former East Germany had made inroads into the UK market, especially those incorporating artificial mixed fibres.

Allwarm does not own any distribution outlets. It does have a 'mill shop' on the factory site for the sale of yarn that is of 'second' quality on a relatively minor basis of colour imperfection or the yarn blend not being quite up to specification. All substandard yarn in terms of its strength and the likelihood of breakage is always disposed of or reprocessed, and never sold to the general public.

A UK salesforce of ten sells direct to specialist knitting yarn shops (accounting for 85 per cent of sales), with department stores accounting for the remainder. This concentration is historic because Allwarm feel that the specialist shop is the most appropriate way to sell their high-quality 'Yorkshire wool' branded yarns. Many customers seek advice from retailers when they purchase hand-knitting yarns and the company has always believed that its reputation in the trade is such that specialist retailers are likely to recommend their product to such customers in preference to cheaper unbranded or mixed-yarn products.

The salesforce is remunerated on a fixed salary, reviewed annually on the basis of sales. All employees share an annual bonus payable before Christmas. This is based on a percentage of the employee's annual salary. The bonus was typically around 10 per cent until 1990 and then around 5 per cent until 1995, since when nobody has received a bonus.

Another market research study has been commissioned using group discussions with groups of ten housewives in categories C1 and C2 who knit at home. As yet the research has to be formally reported, but initial findings suggest that brand name seems to be relatively unimportant when choosing a brand of knitting yarn. In a C1 focus group only 3 out of 10 were able to recall 'Yorkshire wool' spontaneously although they all said they had heard of the brand when prompted. A C2 focus group was worse in that not a single respondent was able to spontaneously recall the 'Yorkshire wool' brand and only half had ever heard of it after prompting. In total, six focus groups will be completed together with a report within four weeks.

DISCUSSION QUESTIONS

1 Allwarm Knitting has decided to attempt, through its distributors, to obtain a database of its end customers in order to be able to target them directly with

promotional material from the company in order to build up the strength of the brand. How do you envisage that such a system should work? Explain the difficulties and the potential expense of setting up and servicing such a system.

2 Do you feel that some kind of direct marketing facility might be appropriate to help the company to arrest its declining share of the market? How might such a facility work in terms of targeting both distribution outlets and end customers?

3 The company has an e-mail facility for business to business purposes. It is now contemplating setting up a website for end customers to encourage a knitting club. Advise them upon the type of information that should be incorporated in this website.

EXAMINATION TECHNIQUE

APPENDIX **2**

INTRODUCTION

Many able and talented students fail to do justice to themselves in examinations. This section of the book is designed to help remedy the problem of under-achievement by providing some guidelines on effective ways of preparing for examinations. However, before dealing with specific points of detail, the importance of positive thinking needs to be emphasised; intending examinees must have confidence in their own potential. Such confidence can be developed by giving yourself adequate time to prepare for examinations and by paying attention to the following points on examination technique.

PLANNING AND SETTING OBJECTIVES

Only the very talented or very lucky candidates can sit down and do all their revision the night before the examination. The vast majority of individuals need to plan their work and set themselves objectives. By doing this, substantial improvements in examination performance can be achieved.

The need to plan and organise work prior to an examination sounds self-evident but in practice substantial numbers of examinees pay insufficient attention to this aspect of their preparation. A first stage in planning is to obtain a good idea of what is expected of you by examining a copy of the relevant syllabus. This will state the general objectives of the course and will detail the topics to be covered. If you are studying for an examination which will be set and marked by the college you are attending, obtaining a syllabus should be a simple matter of requesting it from your tutor, assuming that you have not been given one at the outset of the course. Candidates for examinations set by an external body can obtain a syllabus from the examining authority. Usually this will be quite detailed and will give a precise indication of the relative import-ance of topics. Once you have obtained a syllabus check it carefully against your course notes to ensure that they provide a complete coverage of topics.

The next stage in planning involves finding out about the requirements for the examinations by obtaining copies of past papers and checking that there have not been any changes in the examination regulations since the previous paper. Amongst the most important pieces of information you will derive from the examination papers is the amount of time available to answer each question. As part of your revision programme you should practise completing answers to questions within the time limit. This point cannot be stressed too strongly; to use a sporting analogy, it is clear that many students prepare for an exam as if for a marathon, by practising writing long essays, and during the examination find for the first time that they have to take part in an 800 metres event! The specimen examination answers which are frequently available for professional examinations provide a very useful aid when trying to establish the type and length of answers required.

Finding out the date and time of your examination is obviously important and allows you to draw up a revision timetable. For most people 'little and often' is a more effective and less painful way of revising than intensive and lengthy periods over a short period of time. However, it must be admitted that circumstances and individual preferences do not always permit or require this general rule to be followed. A revision timetable will therefore reflect your own particular needs, but should attempt to be as specific as possible about time allocations and the topics to be covered.

Once you have drawn up a timetable check the topics covered against those indicated on the syllabus to ensure a match between the two. If at all possible set objectives for each topic on the timetable and check progress against these. Few people will be able to work precisely according to every aspect of their timetable, because of unforeseen circumstances, but do attempt to catch up on the schedule as soon as possible, even if it requires extra work. However, do not study very late at night, particularly immediately prior to the examination; this might actually impair your performance and, even worse, your health.

REVISION

It is impossible to give hard and fast rules about when to start revising, but about eight weeks before the examination is a reasonable guideline. It is possible to start earlier than this but most students will not have finished their course of study before this time. Many students leave much less than eight weeks for revision, but this may result in limited or superficial coverage of the syllabus and over-heavy reliance on 'question spotting'.

The importance of active learning cannot be over-emphasised when revising. Innumerable candidates for examinations have spent hours and hours reading as part of their revision programme without actually remembering or understanding anything but a fraction of their work. One very effective way of promoting active learning is to take brief notes on the topic being revised. These brief notes should incorporate all the sources of information relevant to the topic such as lecture notes, textbooks, examples, your own ideas and so on. When making notes try to write down the key points and space the notes out so that you can find topics quickly at a later date. Diagrams and illustrations can be used, as these often serve as useful aids to one's memory.

Some students find it useful to condense their notes with each successive revision session. Thus what start out as reasonably detailed notes on a particular topic are eventually reduced to a few basic statements and key words which provide leads into the main aspects of the problem.

Another useful way to promote active learning is to set tests every few days on the areas you have revised. Many students do not find it easy to set such tests. It may be possible to obtain the co-operation of a tutor to set the tests, but in any event past examination questions and discussion questions from textbooks should provide help when setting these self-evaluation tests. Of course it is important that the time allocated to the test is closely related to the time available during the examination. When the test has been completed, evaluation of performance is important and, although self-evaluation is fundamental, the views of fellow students, tutors or other hopefully knowledgeable third parties can be invaluable.

A revision aid which is much under-utilised is that of studying with groups of other students who are revising for the same examination. This form of group work provides a forum for pooling information, questioning ideas and evaluating performance. The organisation of such groups can take many forms including brainstorming sessions, individual presentations on selected topics, informal discussions of questions and so on. One of the main benefits of this type of approach to revision is that it encourages brevity and a full understanding of subjects which have to be discussed with fellow students. It is, of course, vital that the discussions do concentrate on the work for the examination and are not sidetracked on to other perhaps more immediately pleasant topics.

READING AND REMEMBERING

It has already been pointed out that long hours spent reading do not necessarily result in the effective acquisition of knowledge and that note-taking is one way of improving learning while reading. However, the process of reading about a subject also involves skills which can be improved. The most obvious point about different individuals' reading skills is the speed at which they read. Some people read very much more quickly than others and, if this can be combined with good understanding, it is obviously an advantage when revising. At the same time fast reading speeds for their own sake are not necessarily advantageous; understanding and remembering are the ultimate objectives.

Quick and efficient reading can be developed by paying attention to a number of points. First of all it is helpful to adopt a comfortable, but not soporific, position in good light and to approach the reading in a positive manner rather than viewing it as an unpleasant task. Then it is wise to develop the habit of reading in sections, i.e. looking at the meaning of sentences as a whole rather than concentrating on each word in isolation. This practice of reading in sections is not easy to describe but the more you read with this principle in mind the more your reading skills are likely to improve. A further point to bear in mind when developing an approach to quick and efficient reading is not to read for too long. Although there are individual differences in this respect, approximately thirty to forty minutes at a time is usually the maximum time span before a break of several minutes should be taken.

Finally it is important to re-emphasise the importance of making brief notes on the material being read. These should include details of points not fully understood so that you can pursue them with your tutor or study group.

A valuable spin-off of reading widely is that it can help to improve your vocabulary. A good vocabulary is undoubtedly an invaluable asset when it comes to interpreting and answering examination questions. Unless you are quite clear about what particular words in an examination question mean, you are going to waste time thinking about them and ultimately may completely misinterpret the question. To avoid this pitfall it is good practice to make a list of words encountered in your reading which cause difficulty, along with their dictionary definition. This list should be committed to memory and the words should be used where appropriate in self-evaluation tests.

The role of good note-taking and self-evaluation tests in promoting effective learning have already been stressed. One other way to remember information is by using word association. Perhaps the most common way of using this technique is to take the first letter of each of the words to be remembered and to make them into another word. For example, AIDA can be used to remember the key factors in selling and for advertising, namely, attention, interest, desire and action. Other word association techniques might involve making up simple stories or rhymes. The objective of all of these aids to remembering is to increase your familiarity with, and ease of recall of, the subject matter being revised.

REMEMBERING AND APPLYING KNOWLEDGE

The main objective when revising is to collect together all relevant information and attempt to remember it in context. However, this is not an end in itself since it is necessary to be able to use this information to answer the examination questions. Practice in applying knowledge to questions before the examination is as important as remembering it. Probably the most common cause of students under-achieving in examinations is that they do not answer the question! Instead they just write down an expanded version of their notes on the topic, which are unlikely to address themselves to the particular issues raised in the question.

The problem of applying knowledge is relatively simple if the examination questions are predominantly descriptive. This type of question merely requires you to demonstrate your knowledge about a particular topic without having to demonstrate higher level skills of analysis. Such questions will typically start

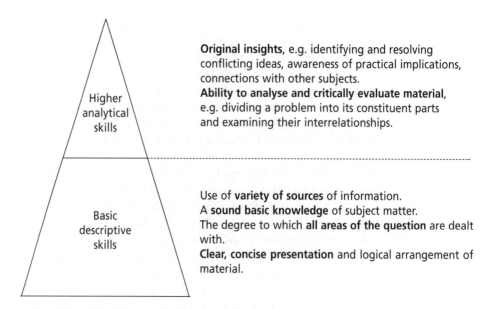

Higher analytical skills

Original insights, e.g. identifying and resolving conflicting ideas, awareness of practical implications, connections with other subjects.
Ability to analyse and critically evaluate material, e.g. dividing a problem into its constituent parts and examining their interrelationships.

Basic descriptive skills

Use of **variety of sources** of information.
A **sound basic knowledge** of subject matter.
The degree to which **all areas of the question** are dealt with.
Clear, concise presentation and logical arrangement of material.

Figure A2.1 Hierarchy of skills

with words such as 'describe', 'state', 'outline', 'explain' and 'define'. When answering descriptive questions include relevant definitions and explanations of all the points required by the question. Good answers will probably also include examples and/or empirical evidence to illustrate the points covered.

Analytical questions pose much greater difficulties in terms of using knowledge to answer a question. The hierarchy of skills illustrated in Figure A2.1 indicates the broad difference between descriptive and analytical questions.

Questions which are analytical in nature will start with words such as 'discuss', 'evaluate', 'assess', 'criticise', and 'analyse'. This type of question requires the examinee to show early in the answer that the question is understood and to set up a framework for the remainder of the answer. It is then important to present the relevant points of view, support them with examples and show awareness of the criticisms which can be levelled at particular points of view. An answer to an analytical question should end with a conclusion which summarises very briefly the key issues and presents the student's own considered judgement on the topic.

Some questions will have a clear descriptive component and an analytical component as in the following example: 'Identify the main elements of the marketing mix and assess their relative importance for marketing consumer durables.' In such cases it is reasonable to assume that the descriptive part will be allocated a lower proportion of the total marks than the analytical component. This should be reflected in the amount of time spent in answering the two parts of the question.

EXAMINATION NERVES

Careful revision and preparation should help to minimise the problem of examination nerves. Last-minute panic could mean not obtaining the mark one's preparation warrants. It is important to keep calm and believe in yourself. Those individuals who are particularly prone to stress should talk about it with friends, family or welfare counsellors, as the very act of discussing the problem may help to reduce anxiety. Everyone finds examinations stressful to some extent, but if the exams are approached in a positive manner and by a candidate in good physical health this stress should not be harmful. Of course if there are health or other medical problems a doctor should be approached well before the examination and the relevant details brought to the attention of the examining authority.

ANSWERING EXAMINATION QUESTIONS

Once under examination conditions, and when the examination questions have been distributed, it is vital that time is taken to read all the instructions and questions carefully. If questions are then rated in terms of whether they can be adequately answered, it should finally be possible to list the required number of questions in the order they will be attempted. As a general rule it is wise to begin with a question where the subject matter is well known. This helps to build up confidence and means the more difficult ones can be left until later.

The next step is to make an essay plan after thinking about the question for a few minutes. This plan will consist of brief notes made on the answer paper in which the main points and structure of the essay will be outlined. Writing an essay plan helps to give direction to an answer and enables the scope of the answer to be gauged. Gauging the scope of an answer is an important prerequisite to deciding how much time can be devoted to its component parts. It is good practice to start your actual answer on a new page and when it is finished to lightly cross out the essay plan. The plan should, however, be handed in at the end of the examination.

When writing an essay under examination conditions students should attempt to make their writing as legible as possible as this will avoid trying the patience of the examiner who ultimately marks the paper. Other simple but important points to remember include numbering the answers correctly, and making sure that any additional papers have your name on and are attached to the answer book in the correct order.

One of the keys to success during an examination is correct pacing, so that an equal amount of time is spent on each answer. This skill should have been developed during revision and cause few difficulties during the real examination. If a question has not been finished during its allocated time it should be brought to a swift conclusion and the next one commenced. The value of completing all of the required number of questions cannot be over-emphasised. It is very difficult to get a good overall mark if the final question is not attempted or only just started when time expires. Allow time for planning before each question.

Answers should be written in a clear and logical manner with as good a style as the conditions permit. As time is at a premium, avoid waffle, do not keep repeating certain words. It is not usually necessary to rewrite the question before starting – this wastes valuable time. Refer to the question on the examination paper and circle key words as appropriate. The length of an answer is obviously dependent on size of handwriting, time available and knowledge of the subject, but as a general rule at least two or three sides of A4 paper are needed to write an adequate answer.

The style in which an examination answer is written depends on the nature of the examination and the particular question asked; some papers require an answer in essay form, others require reports, and in some instances the examinee must present an analysis of a case study. It is important to research the issue of the required style of answers and to practise preparing them before the examination.

Essay-type answers can take many forms but will usually have the following components:

1 an opening paragraph which goes to the heart of the question and gives an indication of how the problem will be approached;
2 the main body of the answer in which the examinee puts forward a reasoned case supported by appropriate facts and empirical evidence;
3 a conclusion which draws together the strands of the argument and relates them back to the question.

There is no doubt that some students find writing essays under examination conditions difficult. In such cases it may be possible to introduce some greater degree of structure by using numbered headings and sub-headings within the answer. However, these should not degenerate into notes; on the whole this style is more appropriate to descriptive rather than analytical answers.

Case studies are an increasingly common feature of many examinations and may require answers to be presented in report form. Any question which does specifically ask for a report will almost certainly involve a proportion of total marks being awarded for the layout and presentation of the answer. In these circumstances examinees must take care over the form of their answer by paying attention to correct report format, although allowances will be made by the examiner for the fact that it has been prepared under examination conditions.

CONCLUSION

Passing examinations is not an end in itself. A course of study should be seen as a vehicle for personal development and improved understanding. It may also help individuals to obtain a new or better job. Those students who select their course of study carefully, apply themselves diligently and revise in a systematic manner should be able to cope with the final hurdle of an examination without too much difficulty. Obviously, things do go wrong on occasion and most people do fail a few examinations during their education but this should not be seen as the end of the world. Opportunities for retaking the examination or other courses of study are usually available if mishaps do occur.

LEADING PROFESSIONAL BODIES IN THE UK AND IRELAND

The Advertising Association, Abford House, 15 Wilton Road, London SW1V 1NJ. Tel: (0207) 828 2771. The professional body for advertising, except agency, personnel.

Association of Exhibition Organisers, 10 Manchester Square, London W1M 5AB. Tel: (0207) 486 1951.

Association of Market Survey Organisations Ltd, c/o Marplan Ltd, 119-127 Marylebone Road, London NW1 5PU. Tel: (0207) 723 7276.

British Export Houses Association, 69 Cannon Street, London EC4N 5AB. Tel: (0207) 248 4444. This is also the address of the London Chamber of Commerce and Industry who provide additional services in terms of education and help to exporters.

British Franchise Association, Thames View, Newton Road, Henley-on-Thames, Oxon RG9 1HG. Tel: (01491) 578050.

Chartered Institute of Marketing, Moor Hall, Cookham, Maidenhead, Berks SL6 9QH. Tel: (016285) 24922. The examining and professional body for marketing profession.

The Communications, Advertising and Marketing Education Foundation (CAM), Abford House, 15 Wilton Road, London SW1V 1NJ. Tel: (0207) 828 2777. The examining and educational body of the advertising industry, excluding advertising agencies.

Institute of Advertising Practitioners in Ireland, 35 Upper Fitzwilliam Street, Dublin 2. Tel: Dublin 785685.

Institute of Direct Marketing, 1 Park Road, Teddington, Middlesex TW110AR. Tel: (0208) 977 5705.

Institute of Export, Export House, 64 Clifton Street, London EC2A 4HB. Tel: (0207) 247 9812. The examining and professional body for export.

Institute of Practitioners in Advertising, 44 Belgrave Square, London SW1X 8QS. Tel: (0207) 235 7020. The examining and professional body for personnel in their member agencies.

Institute of Professional Sales, Moor Hall, Cookham, Maidenhead, Berks SL6 9QH. Tel: (016285) 24922. The examining and professional body for the selling profession.

Institute of Public Relations, 1 Great James Street, London WC1N 3DA. Tel: (0207) 405 5505. The professional body for public relations practitioners.

Institute of Sales Promotion, Arena House, 66/8 Pentonville Road, London N1 9HS. Tel: (0207) 837 5340.

Irish Exporters Association, 17 Merchants' Quay, Dublin 8. Tel: Dublin 770285.

Irish Commercial Travellers' Federation, Gillabbey House, Connaught Avenue, Cork. Tel: Cork 23319.

The Market Research Society, 15 Belgrave Square, London SW1X 8PF. Tel: (0207) 235 4709. The examining and professional body for marketing research.

Marketing Institute of Ireland, South County Business Park, Leopardstown, Dublin 18. Tel: Dublin 2952355.

Public Relations Institute of Ireland, 50 Waterloo Road, Dublin 4. Tel: Dublin 689169.

BIBLIOGRAPHICAL REFERENCES

Ackoff R.L. and Emsott, J.R. (1975) 'Advertising at Anheuser-Busch, Inc.', *Sloan Management Review*, Spring, pp. 1–15.

Adams, J.S. (1965) 'Inequity in social exchange', in Berkowitz, L. (ed.), *Advances in Experimental Social Psychology*, 2, Academic Press, New York.

Anderson, R.E. (1996) 'Personal selling and sales management in the new millennium', *Journal of Personal Selling and Sales Management*, 16(4) pp. 17–52.

Anderson, R.E. and Rosenbloom, B. (1992) 'The world class sales manager: adapting to global megatrends', *Journal of Global Marketing*, 5(4) pp. 11–22.

Anderson, R.E., Mehta, R. and Strong, J. (1997) 'An empirical investigation of sales management training programs for sales managers', *Journal of Personal Selling and Sales Management*, 17(3), pp. 53–66.

Avolonitis, G., Manolis, C. and Boyle, K. (1985) 'Sales management practices in the UK manufacturing industry', *Journal of Sales Management*, 2(2), pp. 6–16.

Baker, K., Germingham, J. and MacDonald, C. (1979) 'The utility to market research of the classification of residential neighbourhoods', *Market Research Society Conference*.

Barnet, H., Hibbert, R., Curtiss, J. and Sculthorpe-Pike, M. (1995) 'The Japanese system of subcontracting', *Purchasing and Supply Management*, December, pp. 22–6.

Bickerton, P., Bickerton, M. and Pardesi, U. (1996) *Cybermarketing*, Butterworth-Heinemann, Oxford.

Biss, A. (1985) 'The narrowcasting naturals', *Campaign*, 31 May.

Blenkhorn, D. and Banting, P.M. (1991) 'How reverse marketing changes buyer-seller relationships', *Industrial Marketing Management*, 20, pp. 185–91.

Bonoma, T.V. (1982) 'Major sales: who really does the buying', *Harvard Business Review*, May-June, pp. 111–19.

Bowman, P. and Ellis, E. (1982) *Manual of Public Relations*, Heinemann, Oxford.

Boyacigiller, N. (1990) 'The role of expatriates in the management of interdependence, complexity and risk in multinational corporations', *Journal of International Business Studies*, 21(3), pp. 357–81.

Bradley, F. (1998) *International Marketing Strategy*, Prentice Hall, London.

Brooks, R. and Wragg, T. (1992) 'Channelling customer loyalty', *Total Quality Management*, December, pp. 361–3.

Bruderev, W. (1993) 'Bridging the divide', *Financial Times*, 3 June.

Bureau of Business Practice (1986) 'National Accounts: Trends for the Eighties and Beyond', *Special Report*, 30 August, USA.

Burnett, K. (1992) *Strategic Customer Alliances*, Financial Times/Pitman Publishing, London.

Business Week (1996) 'Revolution in the showroom', *Business Week*, 19 February, pp. 70–6.

Buzzotta, V.R., Lefton, R.E. and Sherberg, M. (1982) *Effective Selling Through Psychology: Dimensional Sales and Sales Management*, Wiley, New York.

Cateora, P.R. and Graham, J.L. (1998) *International Marketing*, Irwin/McGraw-Hill, Maidenhead.

Cardozo, R.N. (1980) 'Situational segmentation of industrial markets', *European Journal of Marketing*, 14, pp. 5–6.

Cardozo, R.N., Shipp, S.H. and Roering, K.J. (1987) 'Implementing new business-to-business selling methods', *Journal of Personal Selling and Sales Management*, 7(2), pp. 17-26.

Cateora, P.R. (1998) *International Marketing*, Irwin, Boston.

Christopher, M., Payne, A. and Ballantyne, D. (1991) *Relationship Marketing*, Butterworth-Heinemann, Oxford.

Churchill, D. (1986) 'Cracks appear in the image', *Financial Times*, 27 February.

Churchill Jr, G.A., Ford, N.M. and Walker, Jr, O.C. (1992) *Sales Force Management: Planning, Implementation and Control*, 2nd edition, Irwin, Homewood, Ill.

Clark, K.B. and Fujimoto, T. (1990) 'The power of product integrity', *Harvard Business Review*, November/December, p. 107.

Cline, C.E. and Shapiro, B.P., (1978) *Cumberland Metal Industries (A)*, case study, Harvard Business School.

Collin, S. (1997) *Doing Business on the Internet*, Kogan Page, London.

Corey, E.R. (1991) *Industrial Marketing: Cases and Concepts*, 4th edition, Prentice Hall, Englewood Cliffs, New Jersey.

Coulaux, C. and Jobber, D. (1989) *Motivation of Consumer Salespeople*, University of Bradford Management Centre Working Paper.

Cox, A., Hughes, J. and Ralf, M. (1995) 'Influencing the strategic agenda: the challenge for purchasing leadership', *Purchasing and Supply Management*, pp. 36–41.

Cundiff, E. and Hilger, M.T. (1988) *Marketing in the International Environment*, Prentice Hall, Englewood Cliffs, New Jersey.

Darmon, R.Y. (1974) 'Salesmen's Response to Financial Initiatives: An Empirical Study', *Journal of Marketing Research*, November, pp. 418–26.

Deans, K. and Rajagopal, S. (1991) 'Effective purchasing management', *Purchasing and Supply Management*, March, p. 15.

Decormier, R. and Jobber, D. (1993) 'The counsellor selling method: concepts, constructs and effectiveness', *Journal of Personal Selling and Sales Management*, 13(4), pp. 39–60.

Department of Trade and Industry (1989) *The Single Market – An Action Checklist for Business*, HMSO, London, May

Department of Trade and Industry (1993) *Best Practice Benchmarking*, DTI Publications, London.

Dessler, G. (1979) *Human Behaviour: Improving Performance at Work*, Prentice-Hall, Englewood Cliffs, New Jersey.

Doyle, P. and Hutchinson, J. (1973) 'Individual differences in family decision-making', *Journal of the Market Research Society*, 15, p. 4.

Drucker, P. (1973) *Management:Tasks, Responsibilities, Practices*, Harper & Row, New York, p. 132.

Egan, C. and McKiernan, P. (1994) *Inside Fortress Europe: Strategies for the Single Market*, Addison-Wesley, Wokingham.

Engel, J.F., Blackwell, R.D. and Miniard, P.W. (1993) *Consumer Behaviour*, Dryden Press, San Diego.

Festinger, L. (1957) *A Theory of Cognitive Dissonance*, Row & Peterson, New York.

Financial Times Survey (1999) *International Technology*, Financial Times, 7 April, p. 1.

Fisher, L. (1976) *Industrial Marketing*, 2nd edition, Business Books, London.

Fisher, R. and Ury, W. (1991) *Getting to Yes: Negotiating Agreement Without Giving In*, Business Books, London.

Forden, J. (1988) 'Doing business with the Germans', *Director*, July p. 102.

Galbraith, A., Kiely, J. and Watkins, T. (1991) 'Sales force management – issues for the 1990s', *Proceedings of the Marketing Education Group Conference*, Cardiff Business School, July, pp. 425–45.

Greenberg, G. and Greenberg, H.M. (1976) 'Predicting sales success – myths and reality', *Personnel Journal*, December, p. 61.

Gronroos, C. (1990) 'Marketing redesigned', *Management Decision*, 28(8), pp. 5–9.

Gronroos, C. (1994) 'Quo vadis marketing? Towards a relationship marketing paradigm', *Journal of Marketing Management*, 10, pp. 347–60.

Guide 2B (1993) 'International direct marketing', *Marketing*, 22 April, pp. 23–6.

Gummesson, E. (1991) 'Marketing orientation revisited: the crucial role of the part-time marketer', *European Journal of Marketing*, 25, pp. 60–75.

Herzberg, F., Mausner, B. and Bloch Snyderman, B. (1959) *The Motivation to Work*, 2nd edition, Wiley, New York.

Hill, J.S., Still, R.R. and Boya, U.O. (1991) 'Managing the multinational sales force', *International Marketing Review*, 8(1), pp. 19–31.

Hise, R.T. and Reid, E.L. (1994) 'Improving the performance of the industrial sales force in the 1990s', *Industrial Marketing Management*, 23, pp. 273–94.

Hogarth, R. (1975) 'Cognitive processes and the assessment of subjective probability distributions', *Journal of the American Statistical Association*, 70(350), pp. 271–89.

Honeycutt Jr, E.D. and Ford, J.B. (1995) 'Guidelines for managing an international sales force', *Industrial Marketing Management*, 24, pp. 135–44.

Howard, J.A. and Sheth, J.N. (1969) *The Theory of Buyer Behaviour*, Wiley, New York.

Japanese External Trade Organisation (1976) 'Selling to Japan: know the business customs', *International Trade Forum*, 12.

Jeannet, J.P. and Hennessey, H.D. (1995) *Global Marketing Strategies*, Houghton Mifflin, Boston.

Jefkins, F. (1989) *Jefkins School of Public Relations - A Broadsheet*.

Jobber, D. (ed.) (1997) *The CIM Handbook of Selling and Sales Strategy*, Butterworth-Heinemann, Oxford.

Jobber, D. and Lee, R. (1994) 'A comparison of the perceptions of sales management and salespeople towards sales force motivation and demotivation', *Journal of Marketing Management*, 10(2).

Jobber, D. and Millar, S. (1984) 'The use of psychological tests in the selection of salesmen: a UK survey', *Journal of Sales Management*, 1, p. 1.

Jobber, D., Hooley, G. and Shipley, D. (1993) 'Organisational size and salesforce evaluation practices', *Journal of Personal Selling and Sales Management*, 13(2), pp. 37–48.

Kearney, A.T., Consultants (1994) *Partnership of Power Play*.

Kennedy, G., Benson, J. and Macmillan, J. (1980) *Managing Negotiations*, Business Books, London.

Kent, C. (1985) 'Outgunning the Sloane Ranger', *C & E International*, July.

Kinniard, R.W. (1993) *How Europe Sells – Measuring the Effectiveness of the Field Sales Force*, R. W. Kinniard & Co. Ltd., 97 Ayr Road, Newton Mearns, Glasgow, G77 6RA.

Kotler, P. (1999) *Marketing Management: Analysis, Planning and Control*, 5th edition, Prentice-Hall, Englewood Cliffs, New Jersey.

Lancaster, G.A. and Baron, H. (1977) 'Exhibiting for profit', *Industrial Management*, November.

Lancaster, G.A. and Reynolds, P. (1998) *Marketing*, Butterworth-Heinemann, Oxford, pp. 229–30.

Lancaster, G.A. and Wright, G. (1983) 'Forecasting the future of video using a diffusion model', *European Journal of Marketing*, 17, p. 2.

Learning International Organization (1988) 'Selling Strategies for the 1990s', *Training and Development Journal*, March.

Lee, A. (1984) 'Sizing up the buyers', *Marketing*, 29 March.

Leenders, M.R. and Blenhorn, D.L. (1988) *Reverse Marketing: the New Buyer-Seller Relationship*, The Free Press, New York.

Levitt, T. (1962) *The Marketing Mode*, McGraw-Hill, New York.

Likert, R. (1961) *New Patterns of Sales Management*, McGraw-Hill, New York.

Lodish, L.M. (1974) 'Vaguely right approach to sales force allocations', *Harvard Business Review*, 52, January–Febuary.

Luthans, F. (1981) *Organisational Behaviour*, McGraw-Hill, New York.

Lynch, J. (1992) 'A new approach to salesperson evaluation', *Proceedings of the European Marketing Academy Conference*, Aahus, July.

McCarthy, E.J. (1960) *Basic Marketing: A Managerial Approach*, 1st edition, Irwin, Homewood, Ill.

McDonald, M. (1988) *How to Sell a Service*, Heinemann, London.

McDonald, M. and Rogers, B. (1998) *Key Account Management*, Butterworth-Heinemann, London.

McHatton, R.J. (1988) *Total Telemarketing*, Wiley, New York.

Magrath, A.J. (1989) 'To specialise or not to specialise?', *Sales and Marketing Management*, 141(7), June, pp. 62–8.

Magrath, A.J. (1997) 'A comment on "personal selling and sales management in the new millennium"' *Journal of Personal Selling and Sales Management*, 17(1), pp. 45–47.

Maher, P. (1984) 'National account marketing: an essential strategy, or prima donna selling?' *Business Marketing*, December, pp. 34–45.

Maslow, A.H. (1943) 'A theory of human motivation', *Psychological Review*, July.

Mayer, M. and Greenberg, G. (1964) 'What makes a good salesman', *Harvard Business Review*, 42, July–August.

Millman, T. and Wilson, K. (1995) 'From key account selling to key account management', *Journal of Marketing Practice*, 1(1), pp. 9–21.

Montcrieff, W.C. (1986) 'Selling activity and sales position taxonomies for industrial sales forces', *Journal of Marketing Research*, 23(2), pp. 261–70.

Montcrieff, W.C., Shipp, S.H., Lamb, C.W. and Cravens, D.W. (1989) 'Examining the roles of telemarketing in selling strategy', *Journal of Personal Selling and Sales Management*, 9 (3), pp. 1–20.

Moss, C.D. (1979) 'Industrial salesmen as a source of marketing intelligence', *European Journal of Marketing*, 13, p. 3.

North, B. (1993) 'Consumer goods companies take direct stance', *Marketing*, 20 May, pp. 24–5.

O'Connor, J. and Galvin, E. (1997) *Information Technology in Marketing*, Pitman, London.

O'Connor, J. and Galvin, E. (1998) 'Creating value through e-commerce', Financial Times Management, London.

PA Consultants (1979) *Sales Force Practice Today: A Basis for Improving Performance*, Institute of Marketing.

Paul, W.J., Robertson, K.G. and Herzberg, F. (1969) 'Job enrichment pays off', *Harvard Business Review*, March–April.

Payne, A.F.T. (ed.) (1995) *Advances in Relationship Marketing*, Kogan Page, London.

Rackham, N. (1987) *Making Major Sales*, Gower, Aldershot.

Randall, G. (1975) 'The use of tests and scored questionnaires in salesmen selection', in Millar, K.M. (ed.), *Psychological Testing in Personnel Assessment*, Gower, Aldershot.

Reed, J. (1983) 'How Perkins changed gear', *Marketing*, 27 October.

Richer, J. (1995) *The Richer Way*, WMAP Business Communications.

Robinson, P.J., Faris, C.W. and Wind, Y. (1967) *Industrial Buying and Creative Marketing*, Allyn & Bacon and the Marketing Science Institute, New York.

Rosenburg, L.J. and Campbell, D.P. (1985) 'Just-in-time inventory control: a subset of channels', *Journal of the Academy of Marketing*, 13, pp. 124–33.

Sasaki, T. (1991) 'How the Japanese accelerated new car development', *Long Range Planning*, 24, p. 17.

Saunders, J.A. and Hon-Chung, T. (1984) 'Selling to Japan', *Journal of Sales Management*, 1, p. 1.

Schill, R.L. and McArthur, D.N. (1992) 'Redefining the strategic competitive unit: towards a new global marketing paradigm', *International Marketing Review*, 9(3), pp. 5–23.

Schuster, C.P. and Danes, J.E. (1986) 'Asking questions: some characteristics of success-ful sales encounters', *Journal of Personal Selling and Sales Management*, May, pp. 17–27.

Semlow, J. (1959) 'How many salesmen do you need?', *Harvard Business Review*, May–June, 37, 3.

Shipley, D. and Kiely, J. (1988) 'Motivation and dissatisfaction of industrial salespeople – how relevant is Herzberg's theory?' *European Journal of Marketing*, 22, 1.

Shipley, D. and Jobber, D. (1991) 'Sales force motivation, compensation and evaluation', *The Service Industries Journal*, 11 (2), pp. 154–70.

Smith, P.R. (1993) *Marketing Communications: An Integrated Approach*, Kogan Page, London, pp. 240–3.

Stalk, G., Evans, P. and Schulman, L.E. (1992) 'Competing capabilities: the new rules of corporate strategy', *Harvard Business Review*, March–April, pp. 57–69.

Stamford-Bewley, C. and Jobber, D. (1989) *A Study of the Training of Salespeople in the UK*, University of Bradford Management Centre Working Paper.

Strakle, W. and Spiro, R.L. (1986) 'Linking market share strategies to salesforce objec-tives, activities and compensation policies', *Journal of Personal Selling and Sales Management*, August, pp. 11–18.

Swenson, J. and Herche, J. (1994) 'Social values and salesperson performance: an empir-ical examination', *Journal of the Academy of Marketing Science*, 22(3), pp. 283–9.

Taeger, D. (1992) '3Ms got it taped', *Total Quality Management*, December, pp. 353–5.

Talley, W.J. (1961) 'How to design sales territories', *Journal of Marketing*, January 25, 3.

Turnbull, P. and Cunningham, M. (1981) *International Marketing and Purchasing*, Macmillan, London.

Tyagi, P.K. (1990) 'Inequities in organisations, salesperson motivation and job satisfac-tion', *International Journal of Research in Marketing*, 7, pp. 135–48.

Vroom, V.H. (1964) *Work and Motivation*, Wiley, New York.

Webster, F.E. (1995) *Industrial Marketing Strategy*, Roland, New York.

Weitz, B.A. (1981) 'Effectiveness in sales interactions: a contingency framework', *Journal of Marketing*, 45, pp. 85-103.

Welford, R. and Prescott, K. (1996) *European Business*, Pitman Publishing, London, p. 208.

Wells, W.D. and Tigert, T.J. (1971) 'Activities, interests and opinions', *Journal of Advertising Research*, 11 November, p. 35.

Wendell, A. and Hempeck, D. (1987) 'Sales force automation – here and now', *Journal of Personal Selling and Sales Management*, 7 August, pp. 11–16.

Wilson, M. (1999) *Managing a Sales Force*, Gower, Aldershot.

Winkler, J. (1996) *Bargaining for Results*, Heinemann, Oxford.

Wolfe, A. (1991) 'The Eurobuyer: how European businesses buy', *Marketing Intelligence and Planning*, 9(5), pp. 9–15.

Wood, W. (1994) 'Reinventing the sales force', *Across the Board*, April, p. 24.

Worcester, R. M. and English, P. (1985) 'Time for PR to Mature?' *PR Week*, 1 November.

Wotruba, T.R. and Castleberry, S.B. (1993) 'Job analysis and hiring practices for national account marketing positions', *Journal of Personal Selling and Sales Management*, 13(3), pp. 49–65.

Zeira, Y. and Harari, E. (1977) 'Managing third country nationals in multinational corporations', *Business Horizons*, October, pp. 83–8.

FURTHER READING

The titles are listed under a number of logical sub-headings. This is a comprehensive review of textual literature in the field of selling and related areas over 20 years. Note that a number of these titles will now be out of print. Some of the titles cited are not the latest editions, so if you place an order for any title, ensure that you specify that you require the latest edition.

Sales functions/techniques

Adams, T. (1985) *The Secrets of Successful Selling*, Heinemann, London.

Barber, M. (1997) *How Champions Sell*, McGraw-Hill, Maidenhead.

Bird, D. (1998) *How to Write Sales Letters that Sell*, Kogan Page, London.

Claybaugh, M.G. and Forbes, J.L. (1992) *Professional Selling – A Relationship Approach*, West Publishing, New York.

Denny, R. (1996) *Selling to Win*, Kogan Page, London.

Fisher, R. and Ury, W. (1989) *Getting to Yes: Negotiating Agreement Without Giving In*, Business Books, London.

Futrell, C.M. (1984) *Fundamentals of Selling*, Irwin, Homewood, Illinois.

Gabay, J. (1996) *Teach Yourself Copywriting*, Hodder and Stoughton, London.

Gillam, A. (1982) *The Principles and Practice of Selling*, Heinemann, Oxford.

Hafer, J.C. (1993) *The Professional Selling Process*, West Publishing, St Pauls, Minnesota.

Jackson, D.W. Jr., Cunningham, W.H. and Cunningham, I.C.B. (1988) *Selling: The Personal Force in Marketing*, Wiley, New York.

Kennedy, G., Benson, J. and MacMillan, P. (1980) *Managing Negotiations*, Business Books, London.

Kossen, S. (1982) *Creative Selling Today*, Harper & Row, New York.

Lancaster, G.A., Seekings, D., Wills, G. and Kozubska, J. (1985) *Maximising Industrial Sales*, MCB University Press, Bradford.

Lawrence, J. (1977) *If You're Not Selling, You're Being Outsold*, Wiley, New York.

Lidstone, J.B.J. (1991) *Manual of Sales Negotiation*, Gower, Aldershot.

Lidstone, J.B.J. (1992) *Beyond the Pay Packet*, McGraw-Hill, New York.

Manchester Open Learning (1998) *Making Effective Presentations*, Kogan Page, London.

Manning, G.L. and Reece, B.L. (1984) *Selling Today: A Personal Approach*, Brown, New York.

March, R.M. (1990) *The Honourable Customer: Marketing and Selling to the Japanese in the 1990s*, Longman Professional, Melbourne.

McDonald Morris (1996) *The Pocket Guide to Selling Services and Products*, Butterworth-Heinemann, Oxford.

Mercer, D. (1988) *The Sales Professional*, Kogan Page, London.

Miller, R.B., Heiman, S.E. and Tuleja, T. (1988) *Strategic Selling*, Kogan Page, London.

Murdock and Scott (1998) *Personal Effectiveness*, Butterworth-Heinemann, Oxford.

Oberhaus, M.A., Ratcliffe, S. and Stauble, V. (1993) *Professional Selling: A Relationship Process*, The Dryden Press, Fort Worth, Texas.

Pederson, C.A., Wright, M.D. and Weitz, B.A. (1986) *Selling – Principles and Practice*, 4th edition, Irwin, Homewood, Illinois.
Rackham, N. (1994) *Spin Selling*, Gower, London.
Schiffman, S. (1997) *25 Top Sales Techniques*, Kogan Page, London.
Schiffman, S. (1997) *High Efficiency Selling*, Wiley, New York.
Seltz, D.D. (1982) *Handbook of Effective Sales Prospecting Techniques*, Addison-Wesley, New York.
Tack, A. (1989) *Increase Your Sales the Tack Way*, Gower, Aldershot.
Weymes, P. (1990) *Handbook of Sales Training and Development*, Kogan Page, London.
Winkler, J. (1989) *Winning Sales and Marketing Tactics*, Heinemann, London.

Sales management

Allen, P. (1993) *Selling: Management and Practice*, 4th edition, M & E Handbooks, Pitman, London.
Anderson, R.E., Hair, J.E. and Bush, A.J. (1992) *Professional Sales Management*, McGraw-Hill, New York.
Bolt, G.J. (1987) *Practical Sales Management*, Pitman, London.
Churchill Jr. G.A., Ford, N.M. and Walker Jr. O.C. (1992) *Sales Force Management: Planning, Implementation and Control*, 2nd edition, Irwin, Homewood, Illinois.
Coner, J.M. and Dubinsky, A.J. (1985) *Managing the Successful Sales Force*, Lexington Books, Massachusetts.
Dalrymple, D.J. (1988) *Sales Management: Concepts and Cases*, Wiley, New York.
Donaldson, B. (1997) *Sales Management, Theory and Practice*, Macmillan, Basingstoke.
Elsby, F.H. (1969) *Marketing and the Sales Manager*, Pergamon, Oxford.
Futrell, C.M. (1994) *Sales Management*, Dryden Press, Fort Worth, Texas.
Holmes, G. and Smith, N. (1987) *Salesforce Incentives*, Heinemann, London.
Jobber, D. (ed.) (1997) *CIM Handbook of Selling and Sales Strategy*, Butterworth-Heinemann, Oxford.
Likert, R. (1961) *New Patterns of Sales Management*, McGraw-Hill, London.
Noonan, C. (1986) *Sales Management: The Complete Marketer's Guide*, Allen & Unwin, London.
Noonan, C. (1997) *Sales Management*, Butterworth-Heinemann, Oxford.
Rogers, L. (1987) *Handbook of Sales and Marketing Management*, Kogan Page, London.
Senton, D. and Kirkby, P. (1985) *Organising for Improved Sales and Materials Management*, Macmillan, Basingstoke.
Stafford, J. and Grant, C. (1986) *Effective Sales Management*, Butterworth-Heinemann, Oxford.
Stanton, W.J., Buskirk, R.H. and Spiro, R.L. (1991) *Management of the Sales Force*, 8th edition, Irwin, Illinois.
Still, R.R., Cundiff, E.W. and Govoni, N.A.P. (1981) *Sales Management: Decisions, Strategies and Cases*, Prentice-Hall, New York.
Wilson, M.T. (1983) *Managing a Sales Force*, 2nd edition, Gower, Aldershot.

Promotion/communications/brands/consumer behaviour

Aaker, D.A. (1991) *Managing Brand Equity*, Free Press, New York.
Aaker, D.A. and Myers, J.G. (1982) *Advertising Management*, Prentice-Hall, Englewood Cliffs, New Jersey.
Assael, H. (1994) *Consumer Behavior and Marketing Action*, South-Western, Cincinnati, Ohio.

Bednall, S. and Kanuk, W. (1997) *Consumer Behaviour*, Prentice Hall, Englewood Cliffs, New Jersey.

Bovee, C.L. and Arens, W.F. (1992) *Contemporary Advertising*, Irwin, Illinois.

Brannan, T. (1998) *A Practical Guide to Integrated Marketing Communications*, Kogan Page, London.

Butterfield, E. (1995) *Excellence in Advertising*, Butterworth-Heinemann, Oxford.

Coulson-Thomas, C.J. (1983) *Marketing Communications*, Heinemann, London.

Cowley (1998) *Understanding Brands*, Kogan Page, London.

Cumins, J. (1989) *Sales Promotion: How to Create and Implement Campaigns that Really Work*, Kogan Page, London.

Cummins, A. (1995) *Sales Promotions*, Kogan Page, London.

DeChernatony, L. and McDonald, M. (1997) *Creating Powerful Brands*, Butterworth-Heinemann, Oxford.

Dolphin (1994) *The Fundamentals of Corporate Communications*, Butterworth-Heinemann, Oxford.

Engel, J.F., Blackwell, R.D. and Miniard, P.W. (1990) *Consumer Behaviour*, 6th edition, The Dryden Press, Chicago.

Engel, J.F., Warshaw, M.R. and Kinnear, T.C. (1991) *Promotional Strategy: Managing the Marketing Communications Process*, 7th edition, Irwin, Homewood, Illinois.

Farbey, S. (1997) *How to Produce Successful Advertising*, 2nd edition, Kogan Page, London.

Fill, C. (1997) *Marketing Communications*, 2nd edition, Butterworth-Heinemann, Oxford.

Foxall, G.R. (1990) *Consumer Psychology in Behavioural Perspective*, Routledge, London.

Gabbott, M. and Hogg, G. (1998) *Consumers and Services*, Wiley, Chichester.

Griffin, T. (1993) *International Marketing Communications*, Butterworth-Heinemann, Oxford.

Hart, N. and O'Connor, J. (1983) *The Practice of Advertising*, Heinemann, London.

Hirschman, E. and Holbrook, M. (1992) *Postmodern Consumer Research*, Sage, London.

Ludlow, R. and Panton, F. (1997) *The Essence of Effective Communications*, Prentice-Hall, London.

McCorkell (1998) *Advertising that Pulls Response*, McGraw-Hill, Maidenhead.

McDonald, C. (1992) *How Advertising Works: A Review of Current Thinking*, Advertising Association, London.

McGann, A.F. and Russell, J.T. (1983) *Advertising Media*, Irwin, Homewood, Illinois.

MacRae, C. (1997) *The Brand Chartering Handbook*, Addison Wesley, London.

Nicosia, J.M. (1966) *Consumer Decision Processes*, Prentice Hall, Englewood Cliffs, New Jersey.

Quelch, J.A. (1989) *Sales Promotion Management*, Prentice Hall, Englewood Cliffs, New Jersey.

Randall, G. (1997) *Brands*, Kogan Page, London.

Rice, K. (1997) *Understanding Customers*, 2nd edition, Butterworth-Heinemann, Oxford.

Robinson, W.A. and Schultz, D.E. (1982) *Sales Promotion Handbook*, Crain Books, Chicago.

Rossiter, J.R. and Percy, L. (1987) *Advertising and Promotion Management*, McGraw-Hill, New York.

Schiffman, L.G. and Kanuk, L.L. (1998) *Consumer Behaviour*, 6th edition, Prentice Hall, New York.

Schultz, D.E., Tannenbaum, S.I. and Lauterborn, R.E. (1993) *Integrated Marketing Communications*, NTC Business Books, Chicago, Illinois.

Shimp, T. (1997) *Advertising, Promotion and Integrated Marketing Communications*, 4th edition, Dryden, New York.

Smith, P. (1998) *Marketing Communications*, 2nd edition, Kogan Page, London.

Smith, P., Berry and Pulford, A. (1997) *Strategic Marketing Communications*, Kogan Page, London.

Stobart, E. (1998) *Brand Power*, Macmillan, Basingstoke.

Sutherland, M. (1993) *Advertising and the Mind of the Consumer*, Allen & Unwin, Sydney.

Toop, A. (1992) *European Sales Promotion: Great Campaigns in Action*, Kogan Page, London.

White, P. (1996) *Advertising – What It Is and How to Do It*, 3rd edition, McGraw-Hill, Maidenhead.

Wilkie, W.L. (1986) *Consumer Behaviour*, Wiley, New York.

Wilmshurst, J. (1993) *Below-the-Line Promotion*, Butterworth-Heinemann, Oxford.

Yadin, D. (1997) *Creative Marketing Communications*, Kogan Page, London.

Service marketing

Albrecht, K. and Bradford, L. (1990) *The Service Advantage*, Irwin, Homewood, Illinois.

Bateson, J.E.G. (1992) *Managing Services Marketing – Text and Readings*, 2nd edition, The Dryden Press, New York.

Berry, L.L. and Parasuraman, A. (1991) *Marketing Services: Competing through Quality*, The Free Press, New York.

Berry, L.L., Futrell, C.M. and Bowers, M.R. (1985) *Bankers who Sell: Improving Selling Effectiveness in Banking*, Irwin, Homewood, Illinois.

Brown, S.W., Gummesson, E., Edvardsson, B. and Gustavsson, B. (1991) *Quality Service*, Lexington Books, Lexington, Massachusetts.

Christopher, M. (1992) *The Customer Service Planner*, Butterworth-Heinemann, Oxford.

Cowell, D.W. (1994) *The Marketing of Services*, 2nd edition, Butterworth-Heinemann, Oxford.

Ennew, C., Watkins, T. and Wright, G. (1994) *Marketing Financial Services*, Butterworth-Heinemann, Oxford.

Gronroos, C. (1990) *Service Management and Marketing: Managing Moments of Truth in Service Competition*, Lexington Books, Lexington, Massachusetts.

Harris, N.D. (1989) *Service Operations Management*, Cassell, London.

Heskett, J.L.A., Sasser, W.E. and Hart, C.W.L. (1990) *Services Breakthroughs: Changing the Rules of the Game*, The Free Press, New York.

Irons, K. (1997) *The Marketing of Services*, McGraw-Hill, Maidenhead.

Lovelock, C.H. (1992) *Managing Services*, 3rd edition, Prentice Hall, Englewood Cliffs, New Jersey.

Murdick, R.G., Render, B. and Russell, R.S. (1990) *Service Operations Management*, Allyn and Bacon, New York.

Payne, A. (1993) *The Essence of Services Marketing*, Prentice Hall, Hemel Hempstead.

Roe (1996) *Marketing Professional Services*, Butterworth-Heinemann, Oxford.

International selling/marketing

Cateora, P.R. (1998) *International Marketing*, Irwin, Homewood, Illinois.

Dahringer, L.D. and Muhlbacher, H. (1992) *A Global Perspective*, Addison Wesley, Reading, Massachusetts.

Doole, I. and Lowe, R. (1999) *International Marketing Strategy, Analysis, Development and Implementation*, International Thompson Business Press, London.

Hakansson, H. (ed.) (1991) *International Marketing and Purchasing of Industrial Goods: An Interaction Approach*, Wiley, Chichester.

Hawkinson, G. and Cowking, P. (1997) *The Reality of Global Brands*, McGraw-Hill, Maidenhead.

Jain, S.C. (1990) *International Marketing Management*, PWS Kent Publishing, Boston.

Keegan, W.J. (1989) *Global Marketing Management*, Prentice Hall, Englewood Cliffs, New Jersey.

Kochan, E. (1997) *The World's Greatest Brands*, Macmillan, Basingstoke.

Landor Associates (1991) *The World's Leading Brands: A Survey*, Landor Associates, London.

Noonan, C. (1997) *CIM Handbook of Export Marketing*, Butterworth-Heinemann, Oxford.

Ohmae Kenichi (1985) *Triad Power: The Coming Shape of Global Competition*, Free Press, New York.

Palowoda, S.J. (1993) *New Perspectives in International Marketing*, Routledge, London.

Paliwoda, S. and Thomas, M. (1997) *International Marketing*, 3rd edition, Butterworth-Heinemann, Oxford.

Porter, M.E. (1986) *Competition in Global Industries*, Harvard Press, Cambridge, Massachusetts.

Root, F.R. (1987) *Entry Strategies for International Markets*, Lexington Books, Lexington, Massachusetts.

Turnbull, P.W. and Paliwoda, S.J. (1986) *Research in International Marketing*, Croom Helm, London.

Usunier, J.C. (1997) *Marketing Across Cultures*, 2nd edition, Prentice-Hall, London.

Retailing/wholesaling/logistics/direct marketing

Berry, L.L. (1996) *Direct Selling*, Butterworth-Heinemann, Oxford.

Bird, D. (1998) *Commonsense Direct Marketing*, 3rd edition, Kogan Page, London.

Christopher, M. (1992) *Logistics and Supply Chain Management*, Pitman, London.

Christopher, M. (1995) *Marketing Logistics*, Butterworth-Heinemann, Oxford.

Cook, D. and Walters, D. (1991) *Retail Marketing*, Prentice Hall, London.

Cooper, J., Browne, M. and Peter, M. (1991) *European Logistics*, Blackwell, Oxford.

Corstjens, M. and Corstens, J. (1997) *Store Wars*, Wiley, London.

Cox, R. and Brittain, P. (1994) *Retail Management*, 3rd edition, Pitman, London.

Fernie, J. (ed.) (1990) *Retail Distribution Management: Strategic Guide to Developments and Trends*, Kogan Page, London.

Fraser-Robinson, J. (1997) *The Essential Secrets of Effective Direct Mail*, McGraw-Hill, Maidenhead.

Hutchinson, N.E. (1987) *An Integrated Approach to Logistics Management*, Prentice-Hall, Englewood Cliffs, New Jersey.

Linton, I. (1997) *Database Marketing*, Pitman, London.

Reitman, J. (ed.) (1996) *Beyond 2000 – The Future of Direct Marketing*, Business Books, London.

Stern, L.W. and El Ansary, A.I. (1988) *Marketing Channels*, 3rd edition, Prentice Hall, Englewood Cliffs, New Jersey.

Thomas, T. (1998) *Royal Mail Guide to Direct Marketing for Small Businesses*, Butterworth-Heinemann, Oxford.

Walters, D. (1994) *Retail Management – Analysis, Planning and Control*, Macmillan, Basingstoke.

Walters, D. and White, D. (1989) *Retail Marketing Management*, Macmillan, Basingstoke.

Marketing strategy

Aaker, D.A. (1992) *Strategic Marketing Management*, Wiley, New York.

Baker, M. (1997) *The Marketing Manual*, Butterworth-Heinemann, Oxford.

Bradmore, D., Joy, S., Kimberley, C. and Walker, I. (1997) *Marketing Visions*, 2nd edition, Prentice-Hall, New Jersey.

Cravens, D.W. (1987) *Strategic Marketing*, 2nd edition, Irwin, Homewood, Illinois.

Day, G.S. (1984) *Strategic Marketing Planning*, West Publishing Co, St Paul.

Dibb, S., Simkin, L. and Bradley, D. (1996) *The Marketing Planning Workbook*, Routledge, London.

Dibb, S., Simkin, L., Pride, W.M. and Ferrell, O.C. (1997) *Marketing Concepts and Strategies*, 3rd edition, Houghton Mifflin, London.

Doyle, P. (1997) *Marketing Management and Strategy*, 2nd edition, Prentice Hall, London.

Egan, P. and Thomas, M. (eds) (1998) *CIM Handbook of Strategic Marketing*, Butterworth-Heinemann, Oxford.

Fifield, P. (1997) *Marketing Strategy*, 2nd edition, Butterworth-Heinemann, Oxford.

Hooley, G.J. and Saunders, J. (1993) *Competitive Positioning*, Prentice Hall, Hemel Hempstead.

Hooley, G., Saunders, J. and Piercy, N. (1998) *Marketing Strategy and Competitive Positioning*, 2nd edition, Prentice Hall, London.

Jain, S.C. (1985) *Marketing Strategy and Planning*, South-West Publishing, Cincinnatti.

Jobber, D. (1998) *Principles and Practice of Marketing*, McGraw-Hill, Maidenhead.

Kotler, P., Armstrong, K., Saunders, J. and Wong, V. (1998) *Principles of Marketing*, Prentice-Hall, New York.

Lancaster, G.A. and Massingham, L.C. (1998) *Marketing Management*, 2nd edition, McGraw-Hill, Maidenhead.

McDonald, M. (1998) *Marketing Plans*, 3rd edition, Butterworth-Heinemann, Oxford.

Mintzberg, H. (1997) *The Rise and Fall of Strategic Planning*, Prentice Hall, New York.

O'Shaughnessy, J. (1988) *Competitive Marketing*, 2nd edition, Allen & Unwin, London.

Ohmae Kenichi (1990) *The Borderless World*, Harper Collins, New York.

Palmer, B. and Hartley, R. (1997) *The Business and Marketing Environment*, 2nd edition, McGraw-Hill, Maidenhead.

Peters, T. (1988) *Thriving on Chaos*, Macmillan, New York.

Piercy, N. (1994) *Market Led Strategic Change*, Butterworth-Heinemann, Oxford.

Porter, M. (1985) *Competitive Advantage – Creating and Sustaining Superior Performance*, The Free Press, New York.

Procter, T. (1996) *Marketing Management: Integrating Theory and Practice*, International Thomson Business Press, London.

Quinn, J.B., Mintzberg, H. and James, R.M. (eds) (1988) *The Strategy Process*, Prentice-Hall, Hemel Hempstead.

Ries, A. and Trout, J. (1997) *Marketing Warfare*, McGraw-Hill, New York.

Saunders, J. (ed.) (1994) *The Marketing Initiative*, Prentice Hall, Hemel Hempstead.

Thomas, M.J. (ed.) (1994) *Gower Handbook of Marketing*, 4th edition, Gower, Aldershot.

Trout, J. with Rivkin, S. (1995) *The New Positioning*, McGraw-Hill, Maidenhead.

Webster, F.E. (1997) *Industrial Marketing Strategy*, 3rd edition, Wiley, New York.

Weitz, B.A. and Wensley, R. (eds) (1988) *Readings in Strategic Marketing: Analysis, Planning and Implementation*, Dryden, Hinsdale, Illinois.

Wilson, R.M.S. and Gilligan, C. (1998) *Strategic Marketing Management*, 2nd edition, Butterworth-Heinemann, Oxford.

Marketing – general

Davidson, H. (1998) *Even More Offensive Marketing*, Penguin, London.

Gabay, J. (1996) *Teach Yourself Imaginative Marketing*, Hodder & Stoughton, New York.

Lancaster, G.A. and Massingham, L.C. (1999) *Essentials of Marketing*, 3rd edition, McGraw-Hill, Maidenhead.

Lancaster, G.A. and Reynolds, P. (1995) *Marketing*, Butterworth-Heinemann, Oxford.

Lancaster, G.A. and Reynolds, P. (1998) *Marketing*, Macmillan, Basingstoke.

Lancaster, G.A. and Reynolds, P. (1999) *Introduction to Marketing*, Kogan Page, London.

Lancaster, G.A. and Withey, F. (1999) *Marketing Fundamentals Workbook*, Butterworth-Heinemann, Oxford.

Patten, T. (1997) *Successful Marketing for the Small Business*, Kogan Page, London.

Rapp, S. and Collins, T. (1990) *The Great Marketing Turnaround*, Prentice Hall, Englewood Cliffs, New Jersey.

Relationship marketing/service quality/customer care

Christopher, M., Payne, A. and Ballantyne, M. (1996) *Relationship Marketing*, Butterworth-Heinemann, oxford.

Fisher, R. and Brown, S. (1988) *Getting Together: Building a Relationship that gets to Yes*, Houghton Mifflin, Boston.

Fraser-Robinson, J. (1997) *Customer Driven Marketing*, Kogan Page, London.

Hallberg (1996) *Not all Customers are Created Equal*, Wiley, London.

Leenders, M.R. and Blenkhorn, M.R. (1988) *Reverse Marketing*, The Free Press, New York.

McDonald, M. and Rogers, L. (1998) *Key Account Management*, Butterworth-Heinemann, Oxford.

McKenna, R. (1998) *Real Time*, McGraw-Hill, Maidenhead.

McKenna, R. (1992) *Relationship Marketing*, Century Business, London.

Payne, A., Christopher, M., Clark, E. and Peck, S. (1998) *Relationship Marketing for Competitive Advantage*, Butterworth-Heinemann, Oxford.

Peppers, D. and Rogers, M. (1996) The *One-to-One Future*, Piatkus, London.

Peppers, D. and Rogers, M. (1997) *Enterprise One-to-One*, Piatkus, London.

Ranjaniemi, P. (1994) *Consumer Involvement*, Routledge, London.

Reichheld, F.F. and Teal, T. (1996) *The Loyalty Effect*, Harvard Business School Press.

Rust, R.T. and Oliver, R.L. (1994) *Service Quality: New Directions in Theory and Practice*, Sage, London.

Schonberger, R. (1990) *Building a Chain of Customers*, Free Press, New York.

Steward, A. (1997) *Managing Major Accounts*, McGraw-Hill, Maidenhead.

Steward, M. (1997) *Keep the Right Customers*, McGraw-Hill, Maidenhead.

Vavra, T.G. (1992) *Aftermarketing: How to Keep Customers for Life through Relationship Marketing*, Irwin, Homewood, Illinois.

Zeithaml, V.A., Parasuraman, A. and Berry, L.L. (1990) *Delivering Service Quality: Balancing Customer Perceptions and Expectations*, Free Press, New York.

Marketing research

Chisnall, P. (1997) *Marketing Research*, 5th edition, McGraw-Hill, Maidenhead.

Crouch, S. (1995) *Marketing Research for Managers*, 2nd edition, Butterworth-Heinemann, Oxford.

Crouch, S. and Housden, M. (1996) *Marketing Research for Managers*, 2nd edition, Butterworth-Heinemann, Oxford.

Public relations

Black, S. (ed.) (1996) *The Practice of Public Relations*, Buterworth-Heinemann, Oxford.

Cutlip, S.M., Center, A.H. and Broom, G.L. (1985) *Effective Public Relations*, Prentice-Hall, Englewood Cliffs, New Jersey.

Haywood, R. (1984) *All About PR*, McGraw-Hill, Maidenhead.

Haywood, R. (1996) *Public Relations for Marketing Professionals*, Butterworth-Heinemann, Oxford.
Jefkins, F. (1988) *Public Relations*, 3rd edition, Pitman, London.

Not-for-profit/public sector marketing

Batsleer, J., Rornforth, C. and Paton, R. (eds) (1991) *Issues in Voluntary and Non-profit Management*, Addison-Wesley, Wokingham.
Chapman, D. and Cowdell, T. (1997) *New Public Sector Marketing*, Pitman, London.
Coddington, W. (1993) *Environmental Marketing*, McGraw-Hill, New York.
Kinnell, M. and McDougall, J. (1997) *Marketing in the Not-for-Profit Sector*, Butterworth-Heinemann, Oxford.
Kotler, P. and Andreasen, A.R. (1987) *Strategic Marketing for Non-profit Organizations*, 3rd edition, Prentice-Hall, Englewood Cliffs, New Jersey.
Lovelock, Ch. and Weinberg, C.B. (1984) *Marketing for Public Nonprofit Managers*, John Wiley, New York.
Peattie, K. (1992) *Green Marketing*, Pitman, London.
Wilson, A. (1984) *Practice Development for Professional Firms*, McGraw-Hill, Maidenhead.

Sales forecasting

Bowerman, B.L. and O'Connell, R.T. (1987) *Forecasting and Time Series*, 3rd edition, Duxbury Press, London.
Clifton, P., Nguyer, H. and Nutt, S. (1985) *Marketing Analysis and Forecasting*, Heinemann, London.
Lancaster, G.A. and Lomas, R.A. (1985) *Forecasting for Sales and Materials Management*, Macmillan, Basingstoke.
Makridakis, S., Wheelwright, S.C. and McGee, V.E. (1983) *Forecasting – Methods and Applications*, Wiley, New York.
Makridakis, S. and Wheelwright, S.C. (1989) *Forecasting Methods for Management*, Wiley, New York.

Market segmentation

Bonoma, T.V. and Shapiro, B.P. (1983) *Segmenting the Industrial Market*, Lexington Books, Lexington, Massachusetts.
McDonald, M. and Dunbar, J (1997) *Marketing Segmentation*, 2nd edition, Macmillan, Basingstoke.

Product/brand management

Crawford, M. (1991) *New Products Management*, Irwin, Homewood, Illinois.
Doyle, P. and Bridgewater, S. (1998) *Innovation in Marketing*, Butterworth-Heinemann, Oxford.
Kapferer, J-N. (1997) *Strategic Brand Management*, 2nd edition, Kogan Page, London.
Morse, S. (1998) *Successful Product Management*, 2nd edition, Kogan Page, London.

INDEX